SEVENS

A Chronology of
End Time Bible Prophecy

REBECCA L. BERNDT

Paperback ISBN 978-1-945169-70-0
eBook ISBN 978-1-945169-71-7

Publishing Services Rendered by
Orison Publishers, Inc.
PO Box 188, Grantham, PA 17027
www.OrisonPublishers.com

Unless otherwise indicated, all Scripture quotations are taken from the New King James Version. Copyright © 1982 by Thomas Nelson, Inc. Used by permission. All rights reserved.

Scripture quotations marked ESV are from The Holy Bible, English Standard Version®, copyright © 2001 by Crossway Bibles, a publishing ministry of Good News Publishers. Used by permission. All rights reserved.

Scripture quotations marked TEV are taken from TODAY'S ENGLISH VERSION first edition copyright© 1976 by American Bible Society. Used by permission.

Scripture quotations marked AMP are taken from the Amplified® Bible Classic, Copyright © 1962 ,1958 ,1954, 1964, 1965, 1987 by The Lockman Foundation. Used by permission.

Scripture quotations marked NASU are taken from the NEW AMERICAN STANDARD BIBLE (update), © Copyright the Lockman Foundation 1960, 1962, 1963, 1968, 1971, 1972, 1973, 1975, 1977, 1995. Used by permission.

Scripture quotations marked WEB are from the World English Bible, a public domain modern English translation of the Holy Bible.

Scripture quotations marked YLT are taken from The Young's Literal Translation Bible: public domain.

Scriptures marked KJV are taken from the KING JAMES VERSION: public domain.

NOTE: Superscript numbers found in passages of Scripture are linked to definitions found directly below that passage.

We have used a system of single letters to document Greek or Hebrew definitions given under various Bible quotations; for example, the definition of the Greek word for 'love' would be noted in this way:
agape G26T – brotherly love, affection, good will, love
the G refers to Greek, 26 is the reference number for the word, and T indicates Thayer's definition

S following the number refers to Strong's definition:
Biblesoft's New Exhaustive Strong's Numbers and Concordance with Expanded Greek-Hebrew Dictionary. Copyright © 1994, 2003, 2006 Biblesoft, Inc. and International Bible Translators, Inc.

T following the number refers to Thayer's definition:
Thayer's Greek Lexicon, Electronic Database. Copyright © 2000, 2003, 2006 by Biblesoft, Inc. All rights reserved.

B following the number refers to Brown Driver & Briggs' Hebrew definition:
The Online Bible Brown Driver & Briggs Hebrew Lexicon, Copyright © 1993, Woodside Bible Fellowship, Ontario, Canada. Licensed from the Institute for Creation Research.

V following the number refers to Vine's definition:
Vine's Expository Dictionary of Biblical Words, Copyright © 1985, Thomas Nelson Publishers.

J refers to a definition given by Jamieson, Fausset, and Brown Commentary on that specific verse:
Jamieson, Fausset, and Brown Commentary, Electronic Database. Copyright © 1997, 2003, 2005, 2006 by Biblesoft, Inc. All rights reserved.

To my husband,
who over many years
has been my sounding board,
my companion in discovery,
and my greatest encourager.

Thank you! I love you!

TABLE OF CONTENTS

TABLE OF CONTENTS

Preface

Considering events of the last seventy years regarding Israel and its restoration as a nation, and considering also the strong worldwide impetus toward globalism, the topic of Biblical prophecy is one of the most important facing the church today. The Bible has much to say about events that will occur at the return of Christ and the close of the age; and yet for the church in general, awareness of what Scripture teaches on the subject is woefully meager. It seems most often to be up to individuals to grab what they can find here or there that seems right to them (or seems to suit them), with the result that there is little unity within many congregations, as well as within the church as a whole.

There has been enough confusion and disharmony among those who do study and teach it -- men of honor and credibility within the church -- that discouragement sets in. With so many contradictory voices, pastors and other leaders in the church, whose place it would be to bring Biblical teaching to their people, lack the confidence that an accurate understanding of the subject is even possible. Their lives are already filled with other very important issues, and the amount of time and study that would be required of them just to arrive at their own personal understanding of it seems overwhelming – and, I might add, probably has a feel of futility to it.

And yet God has given us this body of prophetic Scriptures, which, when all added together, makes up a very extensive portion of the Word. Surely, He has given it because He considered it important – even vital -- for His people to understand. Surely, it is for us to understand and receive light from, and thereby become equipped and prepared for what is coming. And surely, there is no generation for whom *understanding it is more important, than for ours*. Even if it is not the baby boomers who will see Jesus' return, this topic is for us and for our children to grapple with and in turn, be teaching to the next generation. We dare not plead a lack of time or of motivation when it comes to the effort and diligence required to address God's Word on this topic. If we will seek God for time and grace to do this, God will supply and will grant light, that the church might be **knowledgeable and prepared** for what is coming in the years, months, and weeks leading up to Christ's return.

Even as I prepare this manuscript for publication, the weight of the hour rises up repeatedly in my mind. We are near the end of the 'Day of Man,' the 6 days/6,000 years God has allotted to man to be in charge of the earth. Daily we are seeing the emptiness and failure of all man's attempts – apart from God – to manage his own affairs, much less the affairs of the earth. I see so clearly the enemy's increasing pressures upon men to follow delusions and to seize and hold control, with no thought for God or His ways. We are facing dark days that will only increase in their intensity and tribulation as this age is brought to a close. It is not a time to be ignorant of the season we are in. If Jesus could rebuke the religious leaders of His day for being able to read the sky to predict the weather but not able to discern the signs of the times, how much more wouldn't He stress today the importance for His own people to be *aware* of the times we are in. This is a topic of supreme importance for the church.

This book is the product of many years of study – on and off – of this topic. I have probably included more detail than the average believer is interested in, but sometimes it's in looking at the details that legitimate questions and objections are answered. I have shared answers to my own questions with the hope that the answers I found will help someone else who is seriously seeking truth. It is my desire to write with enough clarity to assist leaders in the church in coming to their own understanding of end-time prophecy, and in turn, be at least somewhat equipped to teach it to their people. It seems to be God's best way – that leadership has His mind, and they then bring it to the people over whom God has made them shepherds.

I have attempted to bring together a large, cohesive view of the Scriptures which pertain to end-time events. It is not an easy task, because Old Testament prophecies come to us as seemingly random insights, separate from an orderly context of time. The New Testament has more chronology and order to it, especially Jesus' primary teaching on the end -- the Olivet Discourse -- and the book of Revelation, which is very chronological. But even in the New Testament, chronology has eluded many.

This is especially true when it comes to the issue of the timing of the rapture, which for most Christians – understandably -- is the most important question. The verses which seem to add to the confusion are sprinkled throughout the New Testament. For example, there is Jesus' promise in Revelation 3:10, "Because you have kept the word of my patience, I also will keep you from the hour of testing which is to come on the whole world to test those who dwell upon the earth." The "hour of testing" being most logically "the Great Tribulation," this would seem to indicate that the church is taken before the Great Tribulation begins at the midpoint. But both of the chronological accounts put the rapture of the church at Jesus' second coming, right after the amazing events in the heavens of the sun being darkened, the moon turned to blood, etc. (Matt. 24:29-31, Rev. 6:12ff & 7:9-14). But when we study Revelation 12, we read of those who "keep the commandments of God and have the testimony of Jesus Christ" who are here for the duration of the reign of the beast *and* the wrath of God, i.e., three and a half years. This is indisputable, and yet doesn't fit with 1 Thess. 5:9, which tells us that as the people of God, we are not "appointed to wrath, but to obtain salvation by our Lord Jesus Christ." Then to add to the confusion, Paul tells us that the dead shall be raised and we shall be changed *at the last trump* (1 Cor. 15:52). With bewilderment, we see that the last trump of Revelation doesn't sound until *the middle of the wrath of God*, which again, doesn't fit with 1 Thess. 5:9.

Too many, seeing these varying messages, have avoided the topic completely, taking the 'pan' view – that everything will pan out in the end. Others have picked and chosen which view they personally prefer, and then, when serious about it, have worked to pull the rest of the Scriptures into harmony with their view. This invariably leads to "wrenching and twisting" the Word, which Peter saw happening already in his day in regard to some of Paul's writings on the end:

> **. . . in which are some things hard to understand, which untaught and unstable people twist to their own destruction, as they do also the rest of the Scriptures. 2 Peter 3:16**

Such twisting is neither necessary nor right, as Scriptures do *not contain* contradictions, nor require twisting in order to arrive at an understanding of them. The key thing is to have a heart to receive instruction and knowledge, whatever the direction it takes us, and *whatever it may mean for us personally*. When we have a heart like this, the Holy Spirit will be our Instructor; He will cause the truth to become evident and the words to be plain and straightforward, not torturous and knotted. (See Prov. 8:5-9). We must love the truth, even if it means facing and dealing with our own fears, preconceived ideas, or pet beliefs. All of these can affect our heart's ability to *hear* the words of the Lord, and that is always *the crucial issue*. Jesus said repeatedly, "He that has ears to hear, let him hear." The ability to hear is related to our hearts, and our hearts must be kept clean from fear or bias or indifference – from any issue which would interfere with our passion and love for the truth of God and His Word. It is the failure to cultivate that love that will, in the end, open up the multitudes of the earth to the deceptions that will destroy them.

I cannot emphasize this enough – each of us must yield our hearts and minds to the truth of God as we approach His Word. We must do this in the study of any topic in the Word, but we must do it particularly when it comes to studying end-time Scriptures. We must face our fears and yield them to Him. End-time events can be scary, and we must know the *sufficiency of the Lord* and that He will *always be with us*, navigating us, if necessary, through troubled and dangerous waters so that we *need not fear*. If we are commanded repeatedly in the Word to "FEAR NOT," then to allow fear in our lives is a sin. Fear will steer us off course. God is always greater than the thing we fear. This is something we need to establish for ourselves, our loved ones, and for our whole future – WE WILL NOT FEAR but will trust God at all times!

When all the events of the end take place, they will take place *only one way* – the way that Scripture says they will. Our fondest wishes and most skillful torquing of the Word will blow away like ashes in the wind, and we will be the ones who will lose if our beliefs are not grounded securely in the truth of the Word. Therefore, wisdom says, *seek truth now.* This book is an attempt to do that, and to assist the reader in his own quest for truth. It isn't that I claim to *have* all the truth, but I desire to share what I do see, and perhaps in doing so, to enable the reader to be better equipped to pursue his own deeper study of the Word. I believe God will continue to unfold further light as we move closer to the end. But we do want a solid foundation to begin with, and it is my hope that in this book, we can see truth together that will help lay that foundation. It is a marvelous topic. The seeming contradictions simply add to the challenge, but knowing that they only *appear* as contradictions makes one even more determined in the quest for truth. There is a way to reconcile all the Scriptures and fit them into *one whole, harmonious picture.*

I have not written this with a goal of simply addressing contradictions. Rather, I have attempted, as I said, to *lay a foundation.* There may be questions which arise which go unanswered at the time, because the explanation of them involves another extensive section of foundation which it isn't feasible to go into at that point. Therefore, I encourage patience. There is no question that I seek to avoid, but if you can bear with me, the answer will come in time. To answer a question without giving full information is to run the risk that the answer is not satisfactory, and that is worse than not answering it at all. So, I would rather wait, continue to lay the foundation, and progress with patience through the whole process.

It is a complex unfolding of events that will take place at the end – events that deal with all the inhabitants of the earth: the various different groups associated with the church, as well as the Jews, and then, of course, unbelievers. The amazing thing is that God has given us so much information and so many details about these events. He has nuances of dealings with and counsel for different groups and sorting it out is no small task. In fact, it's a virtual impossibility to accomplish in one book, but we can let the Holy Spirit lead us to bring forth for *this* book what should be in it.

May that Holy Spirit be with you as you read, and minister light and grace directly to you. John told us that as Christians, we have received an anointing which teaches us all things and we don't need "any man to teach us" (1 John 2:20, 27). That is not to say that we don't need teachers or listen to them, as God *has* placed them in the Body to assist us. What it does mean, is that we don't ever need to accept what a teacher says as *the* truth without the Holy Spirit ministering it to *us* as truth. HE is the real Teacher, and even while listening to someone teach, we are listening to the Holy Spirit and are checking things out in the Word. There is no replacement for you opening your Bible and getting into the Word for yourself to see if what I (or anyone else) am saying *is* true. You will learn things on a cognitive level just by reading this book. But God desires you to know His truth at a *deeper* level than the mind; He desires us to be *established* and *grounded* in truth. This requires that you are searching out truth for yourself – that is, to satisfy your own heart; that you have (or want) a relationship with the Holy Spirit *in the Word;* and that you are submitting to Him the things you hear and read. You are letting Him teach you and reach you at that level that is deeper than your mental understanding. *This* is the goal of each of us as God's children. So, take your time with this. Open the Word for yourself, and check things out for yourself. Pray over what is said, asking the Holy Spirit to show you if something is right or not. Many times, you will need to withhold judgment and just remain in a 'receiving information mode.' But as you continue to receive, God will begin to synthesize things for you. Certain things will begin to settle down inside you as truth, and as you continue to learn, they will continue to be confirmed as truth. This is you letting the Holy Spirit teach you, and in the process, you are becoming established in truth for yourself. This is important and is pleasing to the Lord!

PART 1
A CHRONOLOGY
OF
EVENTS

CHAPTER 1

The Basis
of Prophetic Chronology

Although this book is based primarily on John's *Revelation*, we will not cover everything in Revelation, but rather use it as a *resource for the sequence of events*. For this, we rely on the "series of sevens" found in Scripture, and particularly in the book of Revelation. The number "seven" can hardly be over-stated in its importance to end-time study. As we will see, when pertaining to prophecy, it actually signifies *chronology* – that is, the arrangement of events in the order of their occurrence. It is as though God has given it to us specifically to help us navigate accurately through events that are coming.

Seven is the biblical number of perfection and completeness, and as God works upon the earth throughout the years and centuries of time, **the use of "seven" indicates the completion – to God's satisfaction – of one season and the beginning of the next season in the accomplishing of *His redemptive work* on the earth.** When this is recognized, it becomes the most obvious of themes with which to approach the study of end-times, and to gather successive events together into a somewhat orderly and cohesive whole.

In writing a book that is based primarily on Revelation, we encounter the same problem that Revelation itself has; that is, that events are often so complex that the format of a simple chronology alone is not possible – more information must be given for full understanding. The Holy Spirit handled this problem by inserting explanatory sections at various places within the book. Since that seems the best possible way to go about it, this book takes the same approach. As mentioned above, the events given in the *sevens* provide sequence and order, but we will be pausing to take a more in-depth look at various topics as we proceed.

The Rapture

We will cover the rapture more fully when we get to it in the chronology. For us as Christians, it is the highpoint of our study of end-times. Unfortunately, the *timing* of it is one of the greatest points of disagreement among Christians. Connected to the timing question is the question of *who* will see Jesus when He comes for the church? Matthew tells us that when the sign of the Son of Man appears in heaven, "all the tribes of the earth will mourn and they will see the Son of Man coming on the clouds of heaven with power and great glory" (24:30). Revelation 1:7 agrees with this, saying, "Behold, He is coming with clouds, and every eye will see Him, even they who pierced Him. And all the tribes of the earth will mourn because of Him." Clearly, both these passages indicate that *all people of the earth* will see Jesus when He appears. Additionally, it is made very clear in Matthew that this appearance of Jesus coincides with the great gathering of His elect in the rapture (v. 31).

We are presented here with two questions. John tells us that when we see Him, we shall "be *like Him, for we shall see Him as He is*" (1 John 3:2). The first question is, if all see Him, how is it that only some who see Him will be changed to be like Him, and not *all* who see Him? Because obviously, *not all are taken to be with Him!* This is a question we will answer later. The second question is, how do we *know* that this is the rapture and not some later gathering of "tribulation saints"? I want to answer this very simply, and directly from Scripture. To answer it let's consider several verses that all speak of the same thing:

> **For as in Adam all die, even so in Christ shall all be made alive.**
> **But each one in his own order: Christ the first fruits, afterward those who are Christ's *at his coming*. 1 Corinthians 15:22-23**
>
> **For this we say to you by the word of the Lord, that we who are alive and remain *until the coming* of the Lord will by no means precede those who are asleep. 1 Thessalonians 4:15**
>
> **I pray God your whole spirit and soul and body be preserved blameless *unto the coming* of our Lord Jesus Christ. 1 Thessalonians 5:23 KJV**
>
> **Therefore be patient, brethren, *until the coming* of the Lord. See how the farmer waits for the precious fruit of the earth, waiting patiently for it until it receives the early and latter rain. You also be patient. Establish your hearts, for *the coming* of the Lord is at hand. James 5:7-8**
> (emphasis added to all)

Do you see how each of these Scriptures makes it clear that we, the church, will *be here* until *the coming* of the Lord? Now we consider the question the disciples asked which caused Jesus to give the prophetic teaching of Matthew 24. They asked, "What will be the sign of Your coming and of the end of the age?" (v. 3). In response, Jesus laid out a whole series of events which would *precede* <u>His coming</u>. Those events culminated in the magnificent sign of His own appearance in the skies *to gather His elect*, even as we see in v. 30 quoted above, when "all the tribes of the earth will mourn." **This** is **His coming** and this is when He gathers His church unto Himself. We will look at this again more fully, and as we do, will see *where this event fits into the chronology.*

Daniel's Seventy Weeks

Although the book of Revelation will be the springboard for almost all of our study, we are actually going to begin our chronology with an important Old Testament prophecy. Given to Daniel over five hundred years before Christ, it provides us with a glimpse down future centuries and millennia all the way to the close of the age. It may seem cryptic at first glance, but as we take a closer look, we will see that it provides a few key markers for understanding the body of prophecy that we are given in the New Testament.

Throughout our study, we will see over and over that Israel plays a very central role in God's plans all the way to the end. For the Christian who reads the prophetic Scriptures with a simple and unbiased approach, there is no question but that God *is not done* with His ancient people Israel. Though after Christ's first coming, He "goes away...and returns to [His] place, till they acknowledge their offense,"[1] it is never an issue of *permanent abandonment*, but of timing; timing that involves both God's grace to the Gentiles, and His wise and strategic dealings with His precious, though erring, Israel. The church has *not* replaced Israel in God's plans, but after He has restored Israel to rightness with Him, the multiplied promises to Israel that have not yet been fulfilled will come to pass! The Messiah will indeed one day sit upon the throne in Jerusalem and rule all the earth, surrounded by His people Israel, who for the many years of the Millennium will finally walk with Him in covenantal faithfulness.

In this Daniel scripture, we will see the 'sevens' showing up right away. The scope of the prophecy is a period of time which is called 'seventy sevens.' In 'seventy' we see ten times seven; ten indicating testing and trials and

---

1 Hosea 5:14-15

seven indicating a purpose of God fully accomplished, so together indicating the completion of God's purposes through chastisement. This is a prophecy completely focused on Israel. Though she has been in a deep and persistent state of rebellion, there is a work that God is doing in her through many centuries of national homelessness and trials. At the close of the age, God's *testing and disciplinary* work will intensify to a degree not previously known.[2] In "seven and ten and seven," we hear God saying that His work with her is perfect, and that His gracious and strategic disciplines will result, by the end of this age, in the perfect completion of His purposes. She will be brought to the place of wholeness and righteousness before Him. The prophecies related to her will all be fulfilled, indicating His work completed.

It is not only His dealings with Israel that will be perfectly wrapped up and completed within those seventy sevens, but His dealings also with the church and with the unbelieving world. Included also will be the *completion of His plan to recover the earth from Satan and restore it to the redeemed sons of Adam.* That is what He speaks of in the prophecy we are about to look at, when He says that seventy periods of seven are required "to seal up the vision and prophecy." All that is prophesied as part of the plan of redemption will be accomplished.

The reaching of God's purposes in all of it is *sure.* At the end will be His judgment unto destruction, as well as His mercy unto salvation. On display for all to see, will be God's unparalleled wisdom, foreknowledge, and grace! As we head into our study, taking the hand of the Holy Spirit as our guide, it will be our privilege to see these things prophetically *before they take place* and to give glory to God for the perfectness of His plan as it unfolds by faith before our eyes.

---

2 Jer. 30:5-7; Dan. 12:1; Matt. 24:21-22

A BIRD'S EYE VIEW – FROM THEN TO THE END

CHAPTER 2

Daniel's Prophecy
of the Seventy Weeks

Wbegin our study with a Scripture that may actually be the most difficult to understand of all that we will look at. This Old Testament prophecy from the book of Daniel gives us a bird's-eye view of end-time events, and therefore a framework of sorts into which we will fit the rest of the events of the end. First a little background into this Scripture.

Background of Daniel 9

The persistent idolatry and rebellion of His chosen people had broken God's heart and had brought His judgment upon them in the form of destruction, death, and exile -- first the Northern Kingdom of Israel in 722 BC at the hands of the Assyrians, and then the Southern Kingdom of Judah and its capitol Jerusalem in 583 BC at the hands of the Babylonians. When commissioning the prophet Isaiah, God had warned him that He was sending him to a people with deaf ears, blind eyes, and hardened hearts; that is, they would not hear or receive from him the words God would give him for them. Their hearts were rebellious, turned *away from God*. When Isaiah questioned God as to how long this national spiritual condition would persist, God informed him, in a rather cryptic response, that it would last right up until the end of the age (Is. 6:8-13). We might not be confident that God *was* speaking there of the end of the age, except for so many other prophetic words that indicate the same thing in clearer language. The resistance of the nation of Israel to God will persist until the close of the age.

For this prophecy in Daniel, we go back in time to around 538 BC. Now an old man, Daniel had been among the first group taken into captivity in 606 BC, almost seventy years prior to this. He was aware of the prophecy of Jeremiah which predicted that after seventy years in captivity, there would be a return of Jews to their own land of Israel.[1] The seventy-year mark was approaching, and Daniel had set himself to seek the Lord with fasting and repentance regarding this promise of return to the land. While in prayer, he was visited by Gabriel with an answer from God. It is this message from Gabriel which sets the stage for this book, because while Daniel was praying about something in the *immediate* future (something fulfilled a few years later), we will see that God was looking past the present, far down into the *distant* future. God was looking all the way to the END of His work with His covenant people Israel, when His heart would finally be fully satisfied in regard to them.

---

1 Jeremiah 29:10

In this word to Daniel, God gave a "clock" of sorts – a time frame – in which He promised to accomplish six things in the Jewish people over a time period of 490 years. These six things *are associated with the national repentance of Israel and their return to the God of their fathers.* This time frame will take us right up to the close of the present age, giving us a few key markers as reference points for events which are unfolded in much more detail in the New Testament. This, then, is the background for this prophetic word.

Daniel 9:24-27

This is not a simple Scripture to understand, so let's read the whole thing, and then go through it verse by verse.

> 24 Seventy weeks are decreed on your people and on your holy city, to finish disobedience, and to make an end of sins, and to make reconciliation for iniquity, and to bring in everlasting righteousness, and to seal up vision and prophecy, and to anoint the most holy.
>
> 25 Know therefore and discern, that from the going forth of the commandment to restore and to build Jerusalem to the Anointed One, the prince, shall be seven weeks, and sixty-two weeks: it shall be built again, with street and moat, even in troubled times.
>
> 26 After the sixty-two weeks the Anointed One shall be cut off and shall have nothing: and the people of the prince who shall come shall destroy the city and the sanctuary; and the end of it shall be with a flood, and even to the end shall be war; desolations are determined.
>
> 27 He shall make a firm covenant with many for one week: and in the midst of the week he shall cause the sacrifice and the offering to cease; and on the wing of abominations shall come one who makes desolate; and even to the full end, and that determined, shall wrath be poured out on the desolate. Daniel 9:24-27 WEB

Verse 24

Seventy "weeks" or sevens – the word here translated "weeks" is *shabua* in the Hebrew. It refers to a seven-year period of time. Every seventh year in Israel was a Sabbatic year, that is, a year of rest. The Hebrews were to plant no crops that year, but to let the land rest. This was part of the Jewish calendar by command of God,[2] so this term denoting a seven-year period of time was very familiar to the Jews.

The entire time frame of the prophecy encompasses seventy of these *shabua,* or 490 years. Gabriel explains that God has marked out this 490-year period of time in which He is going to accomplish six things in relation to Daniel's people, the Jews, and their holy city, Jerusalem:

1. **Finish the disobedience –**
   "finish" – *kala* H3607B - to restrict, restrain, keep back (their rebellious rejection of God)
2. **Make an end of sins** - "end" is both words:
   a. *tamam* H8552B – to be completed, finished, at an end;
   b. *chatham* H2856B - to stop, fasten, or lock with a seal
3. **Make reconciliation for iniquity –**
   "reconciliation" – *kaphar* H3722B - to cover, atone for sin
4. **Bring in everlasting righteousness** – rightly related to God, and righteousness throughout their lives, conduct, and relationships that they would not depart from again.
5. **Seal up the vision and prophecy –**
   "seal up" – *chatham* (see above); that is, to complete and fulfill all prophecy
6. **To anoint the most holy** – both the Most Holy Place (in the temple) and the Most Holy One (Jesus, the Messiah): the two brought together finally!

---

2   The instruction regarding Sabbatic years was given in Leviticus 25:3-4. The Jews had neglected to follow this command of God, and in 2 Chronicles 36:21 we see that God removed them from their land in order that the land might enjoy 70 years' rest. This tells us that for 490 years (7 x 70) the Jews had dwelled in the land and failed to observe the 7th-year Sabbatic rest. So, their exile in Babylon looked *back* 490 years, while we will see that this prophecy looks *forward* 490 years. (Interesting how the number seven shows up over and over in God's dealing with His people.)

The fulfilling of these six things will bring restoration in Israel's relationship to God and will situate them in the New Covenant, under His Lordship, prepared for His Millennial reign in their midst.

As given, this 490-year period of time is not attached to any specific dates. The task of the student of the Word is to find the corresponding dates in history, based on the information given. This is what we will proceed now to do.

NOTE: The key for the numbers and letters after the Hebrew/Greek words is found on the copyright page at the front.

Verse 25

In verse 25 Gabriel identifies the *starting point* of this 490-year period. He reveals it as beginning when an authorization is given for the rebuilding of the city of Jerusalem. History indicates that this occurred when the Persian King Artaxerxes I allowed Nehemiah to lead a group of Jewish exiles in a return to Jerusalem to restore the city.[3] The biblical account of it is found in Nehemiah 2:1-8. This date is well-known in history as the 1st of Nisan, 445 BC; in our calendar, March 14, 445 BC. This gives us a clear starting point for this 490-year time period.

Gabriel went on to break down the first 69 of these weeks into two parts -- 7 sevens and 62 sevens. In 7 sevens (49 years), the street and wall (i.e., the city) would be rebuilt. It would be an additional 62 sevens (434 years), until Messiah would arrive.

> 7 sevens (49 years)
> + <u>62</u> sevens (<u>434</u> years)

Total - 69 sevens (483 years) until the Messiah would be presented to Israel.

Where does 483 years from March, 445 BC take us? This mathematical and calendrical puzzle was carefully re-searched and calculated by Sir Robert Anderson around 1892, as is set forth in greater detail in Appendix 1 in the back of this book. Using the resources at his disposal, Sir Robert concluded that the 69 weeks of years -- to the *day* -- were concluded on Palm Sunday, the year Jesus was crucified. Since the calculations are in the Appendix, our focus here is to see if there's a time of *presentation* in Jesus' life and ministry; is it simply a matter of any date of His first coming, or is there a sense of fulfillment and *appropriateness* to that date for Israel and the Messiah? Let's take a closer look and see why this date makes sense, not just according to the calendar calculations, but spiritually also.

The End of the Sixty-Ninth Week and the Presentation of Messiah

You will remember that consistently throughout His ministry, Jesus discouraged people from proclaiming Him as the Messiah. Matthew tells us that Jesus charged the multitudes that they "should not make Him known" (Matt. 12:16). Jesus wasn't out to gain a following – to present Himself publicly as the Messiah in order to attract people. I suspect that is because He wanted people to come into the recognition of who He was *on their own*, based on the godly realities that they saw in Him – the presence of the anointing, the truths He taught, and the works He did. He wanted them to be convinced in their own hearts, not convinced from someone else's words. He didn't want to come with a big hoorah and hullaballoo – with parades and fanfare, aiming for an earthly kingdom. He came quietly, coming underneath people and meeting them at the point of their need, providing the opportunity for them to see for themselves who He was.

But there *was* to come a time when He *would* be officially presented to Israel as Messiah. Zechariah prophesied of that day:

> **Rejoice greatly, daughter of Zion!**
> **Shout, daughter of Jerusalem!**

---

3   This is not the first return from exile, which Daniel was praying about in chapter 9. His prayer was answered around 536 BC when King Cyrus of Persia gave authorization for a group to return to rebuild *the temple*. See Ezra 1:1-2.

Behold, your king comes to you!
He is righteous, and having salvation;
Lowly, and riding on a donkey,
Even on a colt, the foal of a donkey.
                                    Zechariah 9:9 WEB

We see lowliness here – humility; not coming with regal ceremony and an army following, but *riding on a donkey,* bringing righteousness and salvation to Israel. Arriving in this fashion was to help to identify Him *as Messiah;* when He came this way – with lowliness – it was to signal a time of recognition. They were to BEHOLD their King! Here is *presentation* of Messiah as King of Israel, and a command not just to recognize, but to receive Him and celebrate Him publicly! Here, on *this* day, there *is* to be acclaim by all of Israel – shouting and rejoicing! Did such a day and time occur in Jesus' life?

We know this Scripture was fulfilled on Palm Sunday, so let's take a closer look at Palm Sunday, not only answering that question, but searching for a link with Daniel's prophecy.

35 They brought [the colt] to Jesus. They threw their cloaks on the colt and set Jesus on them.
36 As he went, they spread their cloaks in the way.
37 As he was now getting near, at the descent of the Mount of Olives, the whole multitude of the disciples began to rejoice and praise God with a loud voice for all the mighty works which they had seen,
38 saying, "Blessed is the King who comes in the name of the Lord! Peace in heaven, and glory in the highest!"
39 Some of the Pharisees from the multitude said to him, "Teacher, rebuke your disciples!"
40 He answered them, "I tell you that if these were silent, the stones would cry out."
                                    Luke 19:35-40 WEB

On Palm Sunday, Jesus arrived in Jerusalem in exactly the manner prophesied, on a young donkey. We see a great crowd of Jesus' disciples also acting *exactly in line with Zechariah's prophecy.* The Spirit of God was moving on them to give great public honor and praise to Jesus. Jesus *received* the acclaim that day; there was no rebuke from Him. Why? Because He knew both these Old Testament prophecies – both Daniel 9, that the Messiah would come at the close of the 69th week, *and* Zechariah's prophecy that it was on a donkey that He would be *officially presented to Israel as their King and Messiah.* Mark's account says that the crowd cried, **"Blessed is He who comes in the name of the Lord! Blessed be the kingdom of our father David, that comes in the name of the Lord!"[4]** They knew He was the Messiah, the Son of David and heir to David's throne, and the day had come for the public proclamation of this in *His* city -- the 'city of the great King.'[5]

The Pharisees and religious leaders heard and knew, obviously, that it was *Messianic* acclaim. And it drove them nuts. They appealed to Jesus to silence the crowd. But Jesus knew that on this very significant day – the Father's chosen day for His presentation -- SOMEONE had to cry out the fantastic truth: that the Messiah of Israel, the very Son of God, was present in Jerusalem with salvation, righteousness, and deliverance. Even if it had to be stones crying it out, it must be proclaimed! They had had the three and a half years to see who He really was -- to see how He knew the Father, how He shared the Father's heart with them and cared for them with the Father's compassion. It was time for the verdict. Would His own people receive Him? Sadly, the religious leaders, representing the nation as a whole, rejected Him with a hatred that was deep and unrelenting. Jesus knew this and knew that His suffering and death were just around the corner.

But how wonderful that there *was* a crowd of disciples there to shout forth His praises on this His day – the day *that concluded the 69th week of Daniel's prophecy.* And this was the day, remarkably, that was

---

4   Mark 11:1-10
5   Ps. 48:2

identified by the calculations of Sir Robert Anderson as the very end of the 69th week. 483 years after 1st of Nisan, 445 BC, *to the exact day,* was **April 6, AD 32 – Palm Sunday,** the day of Jesus' triumphal entry into Jerusalem!

Messiah Cut Off and the City Destroyed

Verse 26

Let's continue now with verse 26:

> **After the sixty-two weeks the Anointed One shall be cut off and shall have nothing: and the people of the prince who shall come shall destroy the city and the sanctuary; and the end of it shall be with a flood, and even to the end shall be war; desolations are determined.**

Remember, these 62 weeks are in addition to the 7 weeks it took to rebuild the city, so they take us to the end of the 69th week. We see that *after* the 69th week, the Anointed One (the Messiah) would be cut off and killed and left with nothing. There is no throne, no crown, no physical kingdom -- all of which pertained to the throne and kingdom of David which the Messiah was to inherit. His death, of course, took place the very week of Palm Sunday.

Gabriel goes on to speak of "the people of the prince that shall come"; notice the future tense, as if to say that the *people* will come before the prince. These people will destroy the city and the temple. The end of the city will be with overflowing destruction, and even to the end (of the age), there will be battles over the city; rather than being established and prosperous, Jerusalem will continue under a decree of desolation, which, we might add, has proven true over the last two thousand odd years. Looking back now, we understand that this prophecy of destruction was fulfilled in AD 70 when the Roman general Titus came and set a prolonged siege against Jerusalem; finally breaching the walls, he killed over one million people and took almost 100,000 captives to sell in the slave markets of Rome.[6] The temple was utterly destroyed, and what was left of the Jewish nation was scattered again among the nations in a revisiting of captivity for them.

Jesus saw all this coming and it broke His heart. He knew Daniel's prophecy -- what was coming for Him following the end of the 69th week, *and* what was coming for the city and the nation. Look at the sorrow in Him at that same Palm Sunday event:

> **41 When he drew near, he saw the city and wept over it,**
> **42 saying, "If you, even you, had known today the things which belong to your peace! But now, they are hidden from your eyes.**
> **43 For the days will come on you, when your enemies will throw up a barricade against you, surround you, hem you in on every side,**
> **44 and will dash you and your children within you to the ground. They will not leave in you one stone on another, because you didn't know the time of your visitation."**
>
> **Luke 19:41-44 WEB**

How closely this coincides with Daniel 9:26! Jesus knew exactly what was coming. The door of opportunity closed for Israel as a nation that day (not for Jews as individuals); the clock stopped, God's dealings with the nation of Israel were suspended, and His covering over them removed. These events were prophesied (and fulfilled) with no mention yet of the 70th week.

Before we continue, we should note that, as is clearly evident from history, it was the Roman people – the army of the Roman empire, that destroyed Jerusalem. This tells us that the prince that will come in the future is somehow linked to the Roman empire.

---

6   Josephus, *The Works of Josephus, The Wars of the Jews* (Hendrickson Pub., 1987), Chapter 9.

The Seventieth Week

Verse 27

We now go on to the concluding verse, where we find the final week:

> **He shall make a firm covenant with many for one week: and in the midst of the week he shall cause the sacrifice and the offering to cease; and on the wing[1] of abominations shall come one who makes desolate; and even to the full end, and that determined, shall wrath be poured out on the desolate. WEB**

[1]*kanaph* H3671S – wing, extremity, edge, pinnacle

"He" refers to the person last mentioned, the prince that would come, associated with a presumably *revived* Roman Empire (as it has now passed away). The 'clock' of 70 weeks will begin ticking again when that future leader will make a covenant with the nation of Israel for a seven-year period -- the 70th week. Whenever this treaty is made, it will finally bring to an end the pause that has existed ever since the Sunday before Jesus' death.

We will see that this leader who makes the treaty is the antichrist, the one who will head up the global empire at the end. At the beginning of the 70th week, he is rising in power and world influence, capable of making and enforcing such a covenant. Given how troubled Israel's position is in the world today, we can see how desirable such a treaty would be for them. It will certainly take pressure off them, affirm their covenantal relationship with God via their temple worship, and ensure peace with their neighbors.

Either the temple has been rebuilt before this treaty is made, or it will certainly be allowed by the treaty itself to be rebuilt. Given how contested just the temple mount itself is, it is likely that the treaty gives Israel rights of access and of building on that location. Either way, we know their Old Covenant worship system will be reinstituted, as we see it *interrupted* in the middle of that seven-year period.

This same prince who makes the treaty with Israel will break it in the middle of the seven-year period, causing the sacrifices and offerings to cease. He will bring in "the height of abomination," that is, the pinnacle, the *most extreme sacrilege* possible -- one that desecrates the Holy of Holies in the temple and unavoidably leads to desolation, incurring the wrathful judgment of God. This abomination will continue until both it and the prince who perpetrates it are brought under judgment – judgment decreed by God and therefore inevitable and absolute.

Key Markers

These two events mentioned in v. 27 are *key markers:* The treaty is the one clear event given by scripture to mark the beginning of the last seven-year period. When that treaty is made, we will know we have entered the 70th week. And as we go forward in our study, we will see that the desecration at the midpoint of those years will serve, more than once, to orient us time-wise with other events of the end that will take place.

In Conclusion

In this remarkable prophecy we see glimpses of both the first and second comings of the Messiah. In fulfillment of many Old Covenant promises, God sent His Son 2,000 years ago, knowing *ahead of time* that Israel would not receive Him and would instead turn Him over to the Romans to be executed on a cross. With astonishing precision, God spoke of dates and times when certain things would be accomplished. The ending of the 69th week happened exactly on time, followed by the two events prophesied. We can be confident that the events of the 70th week will occur with the same precision. What we *don't* know is the exact length of the gap between these two 'weeks.' We do know we are still in that gap because the temple has never been reconstructed, allowing for temple worship to be carried on. We also know, on the basis of this remarkable passage, that seven years from when the treaty begins, all six things listed in v. 24 will be accomplished!

As we go on now with more details of end-time events, we will find that most of them will take place within that last seven-year period. It is a time packed with momentous events, particularly the last half of it. It is a period of *transition* from the old age to the new, and is filled with extreme pressures, deep testing, and magnificent conflict between two clashing kingdoms – the kingdom of God and that of Satan. We will pursue our study by continuing to follow the pathway of sevens.

Before we proceed to actual end-time events, we will look in the next couple of chapters at the general indicator provided in the Word as to the length of time of the gap; that is, the length of time between Christ's first and second comings.

Keeping the Dates Straight

606 BC – The first Babylonian exile occurs under Nebuchadnezzar – Daniel and his friends are taken from Judah to exile in Babylon.

586 BC – Jerusalem is taken and destroyed, along with the temple.

538 BC – Daniel seeks God regarding the prophesied return after 70 years of exile (Daniel 9).

536 BC – The first return to Israel – to rebuild the temple - takes place under Ezra's leadership.

445 BC – The 70-week period, prophesied by Gabriel, begins with a return from exile to rebuild the city.

SECTION 2
CHRONOLOGY OF THE PRESENT AGE

CHAPTER 3

Transition to the Book of Revelation

As we have seen, with the closing of the 69th week, God's dealings with Israel paused for an undisclosed length of time. With the execution and resurrection of Messiah, salvation became available to all, and God's attention was turned toward the ministry of salvation to the Gentile world. There were numerous prophecies in the Old Testament regarding God's planned mercy to the Gentiles (non-Jews).[1] But the exact nature of their fulfillment, including the key part which the spiritual alienation of the Jews would play, had been hidden. As Paul explained in his letter to the Romans:

> **For I do not desire, brethren, that you should be ignorant of this mystery, . . . that blindness in part has happened to Israel until the fullness of the Gentiles has come in. And so all Israel will be saved. Romans 11:25-26**

There are numerous times in Scripture where the term "mystery" is used. It refers to a truth present all along, but deliberately hidden from man's understanding until such time as God chooses to reveal it. A mystery requires *revelation* – unveiling – to understand it! There is a hint of this mystery in Isaiah 49. Seeing ahead of time the "failure" of Jesus' ministry to the Jews, the Father shared His greater plan with Him years before it came about:[2]

> **"It is too small a thing that You should be My Servant to raise up the tribes of Jacob, and to restore the preserved ones of Israel; I will also give You as a light to the Gentiles, that You should be My salvation to the ends of the earth." Isaiah 49:6**

In the outworking of God's redemptive work in the earth, the season which followed the close of the 69th week has been the *gathering of a Gentile bride.*

The Gap – the Church Age

We see therefore, that it is the church that occupies God's attention and fills the gap between the 69th and 70th weeks of

---

1 Gen. 22:18; Ps. 22:27; Ps. 67:2; Is. 9:2; Is. 42:1, 6-7; Is. 54:3; Is. 60:3-5
2 See this whole remarkable conversation in Isaiah 49.

Daniel. It has already been almost 2,000 years since the birth of the church at Pentecost, and this season of the church will last until Christ returns to take her unto Himself. Around that same time, we will arrive at what we commonly call 'the end-times,' when the 'clock' of the 70 weeks will resume and God will again turn His focus upon Israel.

The question for us now is whether there is any clue in Scripture as to the length of the church age, as that would give us an idea of the length of the gap between the 69th and 70th weeks of Daniel. For this we move into the book of Revelation.

Introduction to Revelation

The Apostle John, now very elderly, had been exiled to the island of Patmos for his faith. The first chapter of Revelation introduces us to the rest of the book. It tells us that the Father showed Christ how the *wrap-up* of events on the earth would take place; Christ then proceeded to send an angel to show these same things to John so that *John could communicate them to the seven churches.* That is to say, as we shall see, it was communicated *to the church* – to all the people of God.

Notice that there is a blessing pronounced on those who read, hear, and keep what is written in the book (v. 3). Revelation was *not to be sealed* when it was given to John: "Do not seal the words of the prophecy of this book, for the time is at hand" (Rev. 22:10). It was given to be read, studied, and *understood,* although understanding has eluded many who have read it. It seems a little paradoxical that though we are assured that the truths given in Revelation are not to be sealed, but to be understood, yet they are not always readily apparent. The volumes written over the centuries about the book of Revelation are so filled with varying and contradictory viewpoints, from the sublime to the ridiculous, that they leave no question that the truths contained there require more than *mental* activity to be understood; and that consequently, many scholars have stumbled around in the dark in a vain attempt to understand what is written.

If there is one phrase that is repeated many times throughout the book, it is the admonition Jesus often gave in His teachings: "He that has ears to hear, let him hear." These are not physical ears, but the inner ears of the heart – ears that are able to hear the voice of the Holy Spirit, leading to a response of obedience and faith. Before His death, Jesus had promised the disciples to send the Holy Spirit, Who, He said, will "teach you all things" (John 14:26). The same Holy Spirit who inspired all the Scriptures now dwells in those who love Jesus and receive His Spirit. If we approach the Word with teachable and humble hearts, we will be able to hear the Holy Spirit in His teaching ministry to us. He is the One who reveals – unveils – to us the words of Jesus and of the Scriptures. Having the help of the Holy Spirit is <u>absolutely required</u> to begin to understand Revelation and other prophetic Scriptures. In addition, there is the responsibility to <u>search out the Word diligently</u>. This requires effort and time. I love the words of Solomon:

> **My son, if you . . . incline your ear to wisdom, and apply your heart to understanding;**
> **Yes, if you cry out for discernment, and lift up your voice for understanding,**
> **If you seek her as silver, and search for her as for hidden treasures;**
> **Then you will understand the fear of the Lord and find the knowledge of God.**
> **For the Lord gives wisdom; from His mouth come knowledge and understanding;**
> **He [stores up]**[1] **[sound wisdom]**[2] **for the upright. Proverbs 2:2-7**

[1]*tsaphan* H6845S - to hide (by covering over); to reserve, protect
[2]*tushiyah* - JFB - lit., essence, real being; that which is solid, substantial, having permanence and
stability (as opposed to what is fleeting, worldly, temporary)

We are commanded to search out the Word for the wisdom – the light – that is there. We search for it as an earthly man would hunt for gold or silver. The searching and hunting are necessary, because the Lord has *hidden* the realities and substances that *pertain to eternity* – those that give us *entrance to and understanding of His eternal kingdom.* These substances are exceedingly precious and are not for the casual or uncommitted seeker. They are for one who has rightly esteemed their value and considered that the investment of time and energy and focus are *well worth* the effort required. The payback for *you* of time and effort given to the Word of God is something that will become clearer to you only after the investment has been made. One payback can be known up front – it is the delight the Father will find in someone who values His Words and seeks them out! What a blessing – to know you are a delight to Him!

Another point that needs to be made before we launch into Revelation, is that all the prophetic Scriptures together are like a giant jigsaw puzzle. This is why so much work is required to come to a full and accurate picture of future events. Every prophetic tidbit must fit in its proper place of understanding. And it *does* all fit together. This means we must be patient, rather than hasty. If we are too hasty in coming to conclusions, then we may think we have the whole picture, when we actually don't have all the pieces yet; and there will be error somewhere. This means we must hold our conclusions a bit loosely, and not get dogmatically or emotionally attached to them. We may think we have the big picture, but then we run into something that doesn't fit with that picture, and we must be willing to make adjustments to see where that bit fits in. Besides that, there may be some aspects that don't come to light until we get closer to the actual time of fulfillment.

It is all going to happen *only one way* – the way that Scripture sets forth. God is not going to accommodate our personal preferences. It will be exactly as He has said. Therefore, wisdom says, "Find out what the Word is actually *saying*, so that you are not disappointed or taken by surprise!" It is our desire in this study to be honest in looking at the Word, and in looking at *all* the Word. That's not to say we have full understanding, but that we desire to be on the pathway toward that, and not on a path that leads to straying.

All that being said, we want to come back around to the fact that it is the Father's desire that we understand what He has given us in His Word, and more specifically, in the book of Revelation. Revelation was given to us in the church *so that we might understand it* – it *is* possible! Why understand it? Why is it important? *So that we may be* **prepared and equipped** *for overcoming all challenges and for moving into the close of the age with great confidence and fearlessness.* If you have fear regarding end-time events, and you avoid the book of Revelation because of fear, then you need to turn around and face that fear and draw near to God for Him to teach and strengthen you. He does *not want His people fearing what is coming!* Instead, He wants us alert, aware, prayerful, and prepared! I pray that this study will help you to change from fear to faith, from apprehension to joyous anticipation, and from ignorance to wise preparedness!

In fact, the vision given John of Christ in this very first chapter should help with that! Please do read it. It begins the *apocalypses* – the *revealing* of Jesus Christ. In His first coming, His divinity was veiled in human flesh; He was brought forth vulnerable to pain and suffering and death -- to be the Lamb the Father was providing for the atonement of the whole world. But in the vision John was given, we see Jesus in great power, glory, and invincibility in the midst of seven golden lampstands. It isn't possible to capture with human words what John really saw. We can only attempt to describe it. His eyes are as flames of fire – seeing through every barrier and every façade with utter holiness; his feet glowing like pure, burning brass. Out of His mouth comes a sharp, two-edged sword and His face shines like the sun. He is "Alpha and Omega," the first and the last, Lord of all; unveiled not only as the central Person in all of history, but in all the wrap-up events that will take place as God closes out this age. He will be moving and directing all and holding all within His hand and within His power; for by His death and resurrection He became Lord over all – past, present, future, the living and the dead, all things seen and unseen. And He is working all things toward the great end of getting a spotless Bride for Himself from the earth. As He stands there in glory, He tells John that He has a message to give him that he is to pass on to the seven churches of Asia that He stands in the midst of, and which He names in v. 11: Ephesus, Smyrna, Pergamos, Thyatira, Sardis, Philadelphia, and Laodicea.

Three Major Divisions of the Book
Please notice v. 19:

> **Write the things which you have seen, and the things which are, and the things which shall be hereafter.**

In this verse we see the three-fold division of Revelation, given by Jesus Himself:

1. <u>The things you have seen</u> - This is the vision of Christ and the lampstands, Jesus in His place and ministry now, unveiled in power and glory – chapter 1.
2. <u>The things which are</u> - The letters to the seven churches, representing the present age – chapters 2-3.
3. <u>The things which shall be hereafter</u> (or 'after this') - The Lord Himself identifies to John where in Revelation this third stage begins:

After these things I looked and saw a door opened in heaven, and the first voice that I heard, like a trumpet speaking with me, was one saying, "Come up here, and I will show you the things which must happen after this." Revelation 4:1 WEB

Notice this verse begins with, "After these things."[3] To what things is He referring? We see that chapters 2 and 3 consist of Jesus' messages to each of the seven churches. If we look at chapter 4 and the following chapters, we see that they are dealing with events at the end of the age. This bears out the approach we will take to the seven letters of chapters 2 and 3, that these seven letters *fill up the present age* and take us chronologically to the end of the age. This is not the only approach to these seven letters; in fact, there are three different ways to understand them:

1. They are individual messages to each of those seven local churches, all located in Asia Minor (present day Turkey) and in existence in John's Day. The messages fit each local church at that time and place.
2. Each message contains truths that are applicable and relevant to all Christians of all time and need to be received in that way by each of us.
3. Each letter was given in a specific chronological order and is a prophetic/historic message to a specific *time period* making up the church, all the way from the letter to Ephesus -- which was directed to the general church at the time of the apostles, to the letter to Laodicea -- directed to the church of the final period before the return of Jesus.

A study of this third approach reveals an amazing correlation between the contents of each letter and the time period of the church with which it corresponds. This is mainly history for us now, as we are looking at them from the vantage point of the final age; we can look back in time and see the correlation. Seeing them as messages to these consecutive periods of time in the church means that all together, they fill up the time between the 69th and 70th weeks of Daniel, and therefore provide a rough time table for the length of the gap. If they were *only* messages to the contemporary churches of John's time, it wouldn't make sense for chapter 4 to begin with the words "Come up here, and I will show you what must take place after this," because as soon as that generation of believers was gone, there would still be the remaining centuries of time before the end-time events spoken of from chapter 4 onward.

We are going to take the third approach and look at how each letter corresponds with a specific period of time that the church has been through since its beginning. We are not going to look at the cities as they were contemporary with John. Nor are we going to look in detail at each historic time period. Our main focus will be to look in general terms at the history of each age for the purpose of correlating those events with the contents of that letter. This will give us what we are looking for, the approximate length of the gap of time between the 69th and 70th weeks of Daniel.

Keep in mind the vision of Jesus in such purity and power, standing in the midst of the seven lampstands – i.e., *the church*. These seven are seen there *from the perspective of heaven:* That is, as burning lamps, as recreated spirits joined unto Christ and seen purely in that "new man" identity; created "after God in righteousness and true holiness" (Eph. 4:24). Though we tend to lose sight of this easily, this is always as God sees us – *"in* Christ Jesus"

---

3   We will take a closer look at this phrase later at the beginning of chapter 7; suffice to say here that a more accurate and literal translation of this phrase (*meta tauta*) would be "alongside, although *beginning* later, than, these things." I.e., a time overlap is indicated.

– holy and spotless. Although He sees us this way, in the reality of our beautiful, perfect, re-created spirits, He is, of course, not oblivious to our weakness and failings as we live amid the struggles and tests of life down here.

And *that* is the view we will get of the church as we move into the second and third chapters of Revelation. We will see her as she is facing challenges and moving through conflicts, losses, and victories in real time here in the world. We are going to see amazing things as we look at these church ages -- things that wouldn't have been imagined at the inception of the church on Pentecost. As we see these things, we will understand better the fiery perceptiveness and the invincible holiness seen in the vision of Jesus, for there is much in these churches that will *come under His judgment.* In this vision is the warning for the church of all ages, that all things are "naked and open to the eyes of Him to whom we must give account" (Heb. 4:13), and that "our God is a *consuming fire.*" For though He sees us as perfect *in Christ,* issues of sin, error, and consecration must still be dealt with faithfully on our part. "Let us therefore have grace, with which we may serve God acceptably, with reverence and godly fear" (Heb. 12:28-29, emphasis added).

CHAPTER 4

The First
Three Church Ages

We begin now to look at these letters and the correlation of each letter with the events and conditions that correspond with that period of time in the church. As we do so, we will see that Jesus addresses certain challenges present in each period – tests that could bring defeat to the church and to the saints individually; He also sends forth a call in each age for them *to overcome*. At the end of each letter, He holds out specific promises to those who do overcome. For many years I didn't really understand these "overcomers." I saw them almost as super-Christians who rise above not only the challenges, but also above the 'average Christian,' and therefore come close to being superheroes. These overcomers will clearly participate in Christ's Millennial rule. That left me wondering as to the end state of the 'average Joe' Christian: What happens to these others who are less successful in overcoming?

The Overcomers

Not only have I failed to find the answer to that question, but I have come to realize the question itself is not legitimate because it is based on a faulty understanding of the overcomers. The church, operating always in hostile, enemy territory, faces many assaults and challenges which threaten *to pull her out of her normal mode and biblical way of operating!* Some of the tests are church-wide and are named specifically in these letters; others, common to every believer, are more personal and are elements of the maturation process in our lives. The Lord, anticipating these challenges, has issued the warnings and instructions found in these letters so the saints will be equipped to overcome the assaults; and, in overcoming, *will successfully maintain the pattern and instructions of the New Testament for the church!* Therefore, we see in these letters the call of God to keep our eyes on Him in difficult times, to take hold of His grace, and, holding onto Him and His Word, maintain the steadfastness of a true and faithful walk with Him. *Overcomers are not superheroes, but simply normal, New Testament saints who, going through tests and assaults, remain faithful to the Lord Jesus and come out victorious.* As Watchman Nee, a brother of deep understanding in the Word, has said, the overcomers are those who "are not abnormal during the time of abnormality." Being those who maintain what is normal for disciples and for church life, they end up standing out in times of decline, thus giving leadership to others (whether intentionally or not). They rise up in times of challenge, danger, deception, and apostasy to "walk according to the normal pattern in the beginning. The will of God never changes; it is just like a straight line. Today men fall, fail, and continually go downward; but the overcomers are recovered anew into the will of God."[1] They "stand out" for the simple reason that they don't fall into error and decline along with others. (Or, if they do, they repent and recover themselves.) Keep this in mind as we go through these letters: As God forewarns of assaults, both personal and church-wide, He calls the saints to *maintain a faithful, overcoming walk with Him.*

The First Church Age - Ephesus

The Church	Praised For:	Rebuked For:
Ephesus APOSTOLIC AGE (ca. AD 32-98) Rev.2:1	- Their faithful service and labor, patience and endurance - Their detecting and testing of false leaders in the church - Hating the deeds of Nicolaitans: *nico-* to conquer *laity* – people	- Leaving their first love Jesus warned them to repent or their lampstand would be removed from its place.

Each of these churches was a *lamp* – it was to give light! The light came from the presence of the Holy Spirit in their midst. This is what makes the church unique in all the earth – it bears the life and presence of God Himself. This is also what makes the church the unique target of Satan's wiles and attacks. He is always seeking to bring in either 1) unconfessed sin and/or 2) error, because either of these will grieve and quench the Holy Spirit, eventually forcing *His withdrawal* from His people! The Lord will try continually to show the problem to the people for it to be dealt with. If they won't deal with it, those issues will not only damage God's work among them, but the Holy Spirit will finally withdraw and will be replaced by *a religious spirit* which will deceive God's people into thinking all is fine. They will carry on as usual, only without the presence of the Lord Himself in their midst.

This wily and strategic work of the devil was beginning already in this first church age. Hence the many warnings in the epistles to God's people to be watchful, to test the spirits, to be on the lookout for "another Jesus, another gospel, or another spirit than the one you've received."[2] The apostles saw the dangers clearly and worked to equip the saints to do the testing themselves so they would be protected once the apostles were gone. Here we see Jesus Himself giving the same warning: "If you don't deal with sin and problems in your midst, *your light will be removed!*" It is US – GOD'S PEOPLE – who must stand guard and protect the presence of the Holy Spirit in the church. Unfortunately, in spite of the willingness of God to help us with this responsibility, the history of the church has been a succession of times of light and victory giving way to sin and error, bringing in darkness.

The Ephesian church was in the first stage of error. They were serving God diligently, 'laboring' with patience and endurance, and yet they had moved from what must always be our heart's motivation – our deep love for Jesus. Their service had become fixed and habitual and was no longer lit by the passion of love for Him. *What keeps the flame of the Spirit burning brightly in our lives and our churches?* It is keeping Him first and doing all out of honor and love for Him! This *beginning of a problem* was a heart issue with the Ephesian saints.

But there was another problem arising in their midst as something from outside them. And that was the problem of the "Nicolaitans." Now there may have been an obscure group in that early church that was actually called by that name, but we are helped most today by the name itself, which means literally, "to overcome and conquer the laity, the people."[3] And that is exactly what was creeping into the church while the apostles were still alive. Here we draw a connection with warnings given over and over in the gospels and epistles. Jesus had warned more than once:

"Beware of the leaven of the Pharisees, which is hypocrisy." Luke 12:1

1   Watchman Nee, *The Orthodoxy of the Church* (Anaheim, CA: Living Stream Ministry, 1970), p. 12.
2   2 Cor. 11:4
3   Rev. 2:6 - *Nikolaites* G3531, from *Nikolaos* G3532S – victorious over the people: from *nikos* G3529T – victory, to utterly vanquish; and *laos* G2992T – a people, people group

Leaven, or yeast, is hidden and disappears in a lump of dough, but while "the baker" is busy with other things, the leaven works throughout the dough, quietly expanding its life and influence. Jesus alerts us here, that just as the hypocritical Pharisees arose in Judaism and dominated the people (see Matt. 23), there would be men who would arise in the church who are not genuine, who bring in compromise and corruption and end up oppressing the saints.

Paul saw the danger of preachers who would subtly bring in a counterfeit Jesus, a counterfeit Holy Spirit, and a similar-but-false gospel:

> **For if he who comes preaches another Jesus whom we have not preached, or if you receive a different spirit which you have not received, or a different gospel which you have not accepted — you may well put up with it! 2 Corinthians 11:4**

None of the vocabulary would change – only the *reality behind the words*. And John taught:

> **Beloved, do not believe every spirit, but test the spirits, whether they are of God; because many false prophets have gone out into the world. 1 John 4:1**

All these warnings were for the purpose of alerting the people of God to *the necessity* of constant watchfulness and discernment on their part!

We must see the connection between these warnings and the issue of the Nicolaitans. Notice again the literal meaning of the word. These were men who arose as *leaders* who made a distinction between the ministers in the church and the ordinary people. They claimed superior knowledge, superior gifting, superior calling and credentials, and did that in order to take control of the people, even while introducing error. Jesus had instructed the disciples in the way authority works in His kingdom:

> **25 You know that the rulers of the Gentiles lord it over them, and those who are great exercise authority over them.**
> **26 Yet it shall not be so among you; but whoever desires to become great among you, let him be your servant.**
> **27 And whoever desires to be first among you, let him be your slave —**
> **28 just as the Son of Man did not come to be served, but to serve, and to give His life a ransom for many. Matthew 20:25-28**

Contrary to His instruction, the Nicolaitan error sought to infiltrate the church with the world's (and Satan's) kind of authority. This error eventually took strong hold in the church, as we will see going forward, causing the whole Body of Christ to suffer deep loss. Instead of equipping the saints by ensuring they were filled with the Holy Spirit and then releasing them into their giftings, they inserted themselves between the Lord and His people, took a position *over* them, and brought them into subservience to their own authority. They repressed the Holy Spirit in the people, thereby robbing them of their freedom in the Lord and of their Spirit-led ministry to one another (see 1 Peter 4:10). Fortunately, under the watchful care of the apostles, the Ephesian saints *tested* these "leaders," as well as other attempts of the enemy to infiltrate the church; they found them to be speaking lies and did not tolerate it.

Notice also that God says He hates these deeds – HE DOES NOT WANT ANYTHING THAT SUBJUGATES HIS PEOPLE! But God was not going to come down and expose and judge this problem! He has committed the care of the church to us His people and equipped us to do it. We simply have to hate what God hates and remain faithful and diligent. When we are not diligent, false pastors, apostles, prophets, etc., *leaders* in the church (as well as non-leaders) can arise, bringing in subtle lies and problems. This causes a mingling with the world and joins the church to the world. It defiles God's people, and without testing, will cause their light to go out. It's because of all this that before they departed this life, the voices of the apostles all rose in urgent warnings that were sprinkled throughout their epistles!

During this first church age, under the watchful care of the apostles, the gospel was preached far and wide and the church flourished. Many were converted, and the apostles worked to ground believers in the truth, teaching them to live in the Spirit and to judge sin in their lives. They taught them to be on guard against error and to discern works of the enemy. They could *see* the dangers that would come when they were gone, and they were urgent about warning and equipping the saints. The New Testament was written during this time and became the enduring bedrock for the church.

Summary
Jesus identified three main issues in the Ephesian church:

1. They were faithfully testing workers in the church and thereby identifying false workers. This kept the church relatively pure from error and defilement.
2. While continuing to be busy and faithfully laboring for the Lord, they were departing from their first love and thereby running the risk of losing the Holy Spirit in their midst.
3. They hated, called out, and resisted the work of Nicolaitanism in their midst, thereby keeping the intrinsic unity of the Body of Christ.

We will see that all three of these issues remained very real threats that led to further problems for the churches of the future.

The Second Church Age - Smyrna

The Church	Praised For:	Rebuked:	Notable Characteristics
Smyrna PERSECUTION AGE AD 64 – 313* Revelation 2:8	- Their works, tribulation, poverty, and spiritual wealth	No rebuke	Warned of tribulation "10 days," there were ten Roman emperors under whom the suffering was most intense; the suffering climaxed for 10 years under Diocletian: Nero 64-68 (Paul killed) Domitian 95-96 (John exiled) Decius 250-253 Trajan 104-117 (Ignatius martyred) Maximin 235-237 Valerian 257-260 Marcus Aurelius 161-180 Aurelian 270-275 Severus 200-211 Diocletian 303-313
	*Although the Apostle John lived into the 90's AD, we put the beginning of this age around the time of Paul's death, as that's when the first great period of persecution took place under Emperor Nero.		
"Smyrna" *smurna* G4667T – myrrh, a bitter gum and costly perfume; representative of suffering in Scripture			

As the church spread farther and farther in the first age, the ire of Satan was aroused, leading to the particular challenge of this church, periods of intense persecution. Most of the persecution came from the authority of the Roman Empire and was instigated by Satan in an attempt to destroy the church by force from without. Many saints laid down their lives for the gospel during this time period, including Polycarp, a disciple of the Apostle John and elder of the church in Smyrna. The deaths of these saints gave glorious testimony of the power of God to keep His own in victory under the most severe of tests.

This church was also troubled by attack from a different front – those who claimed to be Jews – i.e., "God's authentic people." The Jews, scattered throughout the Roman Empire, were often violently opposed to the young church. They launched vicious lies and verbal attacks and were often instigators of physical persecution against believers. God let this church know that He saw and understood the trials caused by these who were actually of the "assembly of Satan."

The faithfulness of the saints during this period is an example to us. If times come when following Christ brings danger, may we draw on the Lord's great grace, and following their example, always remain true to Him, regardless of the cost!

Although seeds of error were present in this period, they were overshadowed and even held at bay by the persecution. Persecution always serves to cleanse and refine the church – false believers disappear like fog in the sunshine. Finding that persecution only strengthened the church, Satan decided to change his strategy, bringing this age of persecution from civil authorities to what it seemed would be a close, and beginning the third age with a new, more wily strategy against the church.

The Third Church Age - Pergamos

The Church	Praised For:	Rebuked For:	Notable Characteristics
Pergamos The STATE CHURCH (AD 315 – 590) Revelation 2:12	Faithfulness to Jesus' Name and His faith despite where they were living – at Satan's throne! The faithful martyr, Antipas, is commended: *anti* – against *pas* – everything, all	- Permitting the doctrine of Balaam - Permitting the doctrine* of the Nicolaitans *The fact that this had progressed from *deeds* to *doctrin* shows how entrenched and accepted it had become.	This church is found to be dwelling *where Satan's throne is!*
"Pergamos" – from *purgos* G4444S – tower; and *gamos* G1062T – a wedding, marriage Hence, the joining in marriage of the church and the "tower," that is, the tower of earthly, worldly protection and power; *or* possibly a marriage that results in the church *as* a tower of earthly defenses.			

Balaam and Nicolaitanism

Something extremely tragic occurred in the church in this third age. Jesus Himself here states – and He states it twice, as though once is insufficient for such an appalling thing – that the church is now to be found *where Satan's throne is.* This is the *church* -- the temple of the living God, "the pillar and ground of the truth,"[4] the one He poured out His precious blood for, that is now to be found in the den of His great enemy. What has happened!? We look to the letter itself for clues and find that the reasons for such a statement are clearly given. The church is charged with having within it those who <u>hold</u> both "the doctrine of Balaam" and the "doctrine of the Nicolaitans" (vv. 14-15). Before we look closer at these two doctrines, we should note that the Greek for "hold" is *krateo*, which means "to seize hold of and thus gain control and power."[5] We will see that those men about whom the apostles repeatedly warned, have arisen and *grabbed power* along the lines of these two false teachings, working great damage within the church. We have already seen that Nicolaitanism is the elevating of the clergy within the church as a special class that dominates and controls the people of God. We shall see in this church age the joining of Nicolaitanism *with* the doctrine of Balaam, to bring about a consolidation of power in the hands of a strong, worldly clergy – a clergy which then, like Balaam, is able to lead the church straight into union with the god of this world! Let's take a look at the Old Testament incident to which Jesus refers here, and which gives us insight into what took place back then.

---

4   1 Timothy 3:15
5   *krateo* G2902T

Balaam and Balak

Numbers 22-25; 31:8,15,16

Israel's forty years of wandering in the wilderness were over, and they had already won several decisive victories over strong enemies when their encounter with Balaam and Balak took place. Balak, king of Moab, had seen the invincible power of Israel's army and was terrified. With "the rewards of divination" in their hands, a delegation from him came to Balaam to hire him to curse Israel. In other words, Balak sought spiritual power with which to neutralize Israel as an enemy. And Balaam, a "prophet for hire," was mightily tempted. He wanted the great honor, power, and wealth which Balak offered him. Though the story makes clear that he had a communicating relationship with God, it became evident that his desire for Balak's rewards was stronger than his integrity before God.

When God absolutely forbade him to curse Israel, Balaam, still coveting the worldly rewards, devised a craftier strategy. He knew they would lose God's blessing and protection if they could be *seduced into sin*. His advice to Balak was: use your young women to tempt the Israelites to participate in your Moabite idolatry! This involved:

1. Eating food offered to their idols
2. Sacred fornication (a part of their worship ritual)

In response to the seduction, thousands of Israelite men ended up breaking two of the covenantal commandments of the Lord: "Thou shalt worship no other god besides Me," and "Thou shalt not commit fornication." As Balaam had anticipated, God had to judge them for this, and 24,000 Israelite graves were left in Moab.

Balaam – not of the people, foreigner[6]   *Balak* – waster[7]

Notice that though Balaam had a spiritual connection of sorts to God, he was not a godly man – he was not of the people of God, but a 'foreigner.' And in getting involved with the people of God, he opened the door to "the waster" – the devil -- with tragic results for the people of God. We must see the whole incident as correlating with the church. Just as Balak found himself powerless to curse Israel from without and so came up with a more subtle strategy, so also the enemy found persecution to be ineffective against the church, and now came up with a craftier strategy of seduction from within.

What Happened in Pergamos?

The mighty Roman Empire had been weakening. It was no longer as powerful and cohesive as in the past. All great empires of the world have used religion as a unifying element within their kingdoms. Religious unity eliminates restlessness and division from among the people. Rome had used emperor-worship, along with the mystery religions, but was finding it could no longer control the cohesiveness of the empire via religion; at the same time, Christianity had proven to be unstoppable within the empire. Rome had come against the church in one brutal onslaught after another and had not been able to stamp it out. In fact, it just grew faster and stronger under persecution. In the Lord it was invincible, just as Israel was when she walked with God (and therefore could not be cursed by Balaam).

In fact, the empire reached the point where it became more beneficial for them to *embrace* Christianity than to *fight* it. As Pergamos began, there were rival claims to the throne. On the eve of a great battle, Constantine, son of the last emperor, had his significant vision. Although there are variations in the account, the general idea is that he saw a vision of the cross and received the directions, "In this sign conquer!" Proceeding into battle the next day under the sign of the cross, he went on to win a decisive victory that placed the western half of the empire in his hands.

---

6   Balaam *(bilam* H1109S)
7   Balak *(balaq* H1111S)

NOTE: The key for the numbers and letters after the Hebrew/Greek words is found on the copyright page at the front.

On the other hand, the *church also* was in a weakened state due to the planting of false believers – Balaams -- within it, as well as seeds of error that had not been effectively weeded out. Satan had been working strategically, both through the divisions within the empire, as well as through his own agents planted within the church. By the early 4th century, the time was ripe for the union that Satan had been planning. Having been unsuccessful at destroying the church by force, it was time for him *to join the church!* His plan was to make Christianity the new state-sponsored religion. And with his victory under the "sign of the cross," Constantine was softened and primed to go with Satan's plan. In AD 313 Constantine *legalized* Christianity throughout the Roman Empire. If legalizing had simply meant "freedom of religion," it would've been fine. But such freedom was unknown back at that time, and when Emperor Theodosius declared it to be the official religion of the Roman empire several decades later, in AD 380, it meant that the empire's version of Christianity would now be *mandated,* enforced by the military might of Rome.

Like Balaam, ungodly men within the church assented to this union, selling out the safety and purity of the church and leading it into spiritual union with the world. Now everyone in the empire was a "Christian" – not because they had received Christ in believing response to the gospel, but by the rite of baptism – forcible baptism, if necessary. Because of its new link with the state, this church achieved great wealth, power, and position, even as Balaam acquired from Balak. These compromised church leaders were now able to use the power of the sword – the authority of the state – to enforce their will upon all peoples, as all the people were now under the jurisdiction of the state church of Rome.

Nicolaitanism

This is how "the Nicolaitans" honed and developed their power – in bed with a ruthless earthly empire. Over time, including throughout the next church age, the church developed into a rigid, hierarchical system of worldly authority. Levels of authority ranged from priests and nuns at the bottom, through bishops, arch-bishops, and cardinals to what finally developed into the position of the pope, the "vicar of Christ,"[8] at the top. Those who submitted to these powerful leaders were subjugated, exploited financially, and frequently corrupted spiritually by them.

In exchange for the power, wealth, and prestige that accompanied these positions, the church gave "spiritual authorization" to the emperor. He now ruled "by divine right," and beware anyone who questioned or rose up against him. This was the church in bed with the state, and both of them under Satan's thumb -- a church compromised, disempowered, and, in fact, an instrument for Satan's use; even as Jesus said to Pergamos: "I know where you dwell – where Satan's throne is." This then is the terrible tragedy that began first with the legalizing, and later the mandating of Christianity as the new state religion of Rome.

Now the church was gradually led into greater and greater error; the old pagan system of idolatry was subtly merged with the church's doctrines and practices, superimposed, of course, with Christian terms and names. No longer did the church consist only of born-again believers, but of *everyone within the Roman Empire.* Hence the name she took, the Catholic (universal) Church. Now every region under the banner of Rome was considered Christian, whether they wanted to be or not. The church had taken over the known world – it had become universal, and that whole domain was given the name "Christendom." The kingdom of Christ *had come* – by fiat of the Emperor! This is *Pergamos* – the age of the marriage of the Church of Jesus Christ with the great empire of Rome! The church, now married to the tower, has *become* the tower. No more persecution from the persecutor! He would now be the *protector!* (Or so one might suppose.) The bad seeds sown in the Ephesus age, long working 'underground,' had now come to open fruition in this wholistic manifestation of error.

But it was a false and grievous system and had brought idolatry into the heart of "the church." It actually took the old gods and goddesses of paganism, "sainted" them with Bible names, inserted the worship of them into the church calendar, and in a hidden way, allowed the demons behind them to continue to be worshipped. Nothing had really changed spiritually in the Roman Empire. The worship of false gods had simply been covered over with the veneer of a pseudo-Christianity. All the *heart dealings* with God, required to be a part of the true church, would now be done away with and replaced with rites and rituals.

---

8   Vicar means "instead of; a person who acts in the place of another." Hence, the "Vicar of Christ" denotes the pope as the representative of Christ on the earth, claiming the same power and authority as Christ. See 1 Timothy 2:5 and John 14:16-18.

Over time there was a progressive selling out of the pure gospel. The proclamation of the Word, by which people hear the good news and come to faith in Christ, was replaced by ritual. Baptism was turned into the ritual by which someone who did not have heart faith, could still enter the church and become "a Christian." Salvation through simple faith in the gospel was replaced by the doctrines of works, purgatory, and penance. To the intercessory work of Christ was added the intercession of Mary and the saints. Confession to and absolution by a priest became mandatory for forgiveness instead of every believer able to approach the throne of grace by the blood of Jesus. The Word was taken from the people – after all, they were not qualified to read and understand it – only the clergy could do that. Rather than using the language of the people, services were conducted in Latin to hide further the Word from the people, and the clergy claimed the authority to hold people's spiritual destinies in their own hands.

The Lord's Contention with Pergamos

Because of all the corruption, the Holy Spirit was forced to withdraw, and Jesus identified Himself to this age as "the One who has the sharp double-edged sword." He warned that if they didn't repent, He would "come to them quickly and fight against them with the sword of My mouth" (Rev. 2:12, 16). And indeed, as soon as this union of church and state took place, there were those saints who withdrew from it; they knew that the persecution would not cease, it would just come now from *within* the church.[9] Through the centuries of the state church – from Pergamos and (as we shall see), on through Thyatira and even Sardis, there were always those groups of faithful saints who resisted the state church; they took their stand on the Word of God, spoke out boldly against the lies, error, and abuse, and often paid the price with their own lives. Because what the state church couldn't tolerate above all, was disunity. They couldn't handle the "heretics." *Heresy* meant simply "one who dissents, a group that divides off away from the whole." This was the same disruption to the cohesive, unified religious/political system that the empire had fought against before it embraced Christianity.

We don't know as much as we would like to know about these small groups that continuously sprang up throughout the centuries of the state church. They didn't have the chance to become well-organized; they were defamed and vilified by the organized church, and there were continual efforts to silence their voice through persecution and banishment. But they were, for the most part, voices of the true church, faithfully raised in proclamation and defense of the faith once delivered to the saints. Along with faithful believers *within* the church system, they were the ones to whom Jesus said, "I know your works, and where you dwell. . . and you hold fast my name, and have not denied my faith, even in those days wherein Antipas (who was "*against ALL*"[10]) was my faithful martyr, who was slain among you, where Satan dwells" (Rev. 2:13). It is said that Antipas lived during the reign of Domitian and died a martyr, but we can see him also representing all the faithful of the Lord who, surrounded by deep darkness and iniquity in the church, were forced, by their faith, to the place of being *against everything* that surrounded them in the church. We owe much to those faithful and courageous saints who kept the light burning into the dark night of the medieval world when the state church held sway in Christendom.

Although the Lord includes this state church in His address to Pergamos, looking back, it is the faithful ones within, and those small persecuted groups *outside*, that we empathize with, and indeed, feel honored to identify with. They had their struggles, certainly, including possible struggles with error; but they could see through the state church and knew it was not the dwelling place of the Lord, but rather of His great enemy, Satan. And we feel that John could have been speaking of them when he wrote, "I have no greater joy than to hear that my children walk in truth" (3 John 4). Truth that is walked in, even at great price, is truth to rejoice in. May each of us walk always in truth that brings the joy and commendation of the Lord, even though a price be paid for it, and we might find ourselves "outside the camp, bearing His reproach"![11]

---

9   Leonard Verduin, *The Reformers and their Stepchildren* (Grand Rapids: Eerdmans Publishing Co., 1964), p. 32.
10   Rev. 2:13 – *Antipas* G493; some say this is another name for 'Antipater.' However, we are more inclined to take the name literally from its two parts: *anti* G473T - opposite to, against; and *pas* G3956T – each, every, any, all, the whole, everyone, all things, everything; therefore, "against all."
11   Heb. 13:13

CHAPTER 5

The Fourth and Fifth Church Ages

The Fourth Church Age - Thyatira

The Church	Praised For:	Rebuked For:	Notable Characteristics
<u>Thyatira</u> THE PAPAL CHURCH Roman Catholic ("universal") (ca. 590 – the End) Revelation 2:18	Works, self-giving love, service, faith, patience There were many godly men and women within the Roman system that truly loved God and led lives of piety and service.	- Tolerated *(instead of testing)* the self-pro-claimed prophetess Jezebel, who drew God's people into fornication and idolatry.	This church age is a continuation of the Pergamos age, with the two problems associated with Balaam even more deeply rooted with Jezebel. In it is found "the depths of Satan."
"Thyatira" *thuateira* G2363S – uncertain derivation. Wikipedia traces the word back to the Greek *thugatera* – "daughter," a plausible meaning, seeing how this church age has been born directly out of the union which took place during Pergamos.			

The Lord begins this message with sincere praise for the service, self-giving love, patience, and works of the saints of Thyatira. And indeed, this age had its saints – both within and without the organized church -- who were character-ized by their deep consecration, piety, and service to the Lord. But Jesus identified Himself to this age as the One who has "eyes like a flame of fire, and feet like fine brass" (v. 18). We see the reason for this in the rest of the message: It's a scathing indictment and warning against a portion of this church which is associated with the "depths of Satan" (v. 24). What we saw in an introductory fashion in Pergamos, we see now as an entrenched system in "that woman Jezebel." As with the mention of Balaam, we also gain great insight with a look at the Old Testament reference to Jezebel.

Jezebel
1 Kings 16:29 – 19:21, 2 Kings 9:22-37

Jezebel, a witch and priestess of the gods Baal and Astarte, was the daughter of the evil King Ethbaal of Sidon, a priest of the same gods. She seduced weak King Ahab of Israel (the Northern Kingdom) into marriage, and then used the civil power of his kingship to impose the idolatrous worship of Baal upon Israel. Using force, intimidation, and seduction, Jezebel brought Baal worship, its abominable practices, its image (idol), and its priests and prophets into the heart of Israel. She suppressed the worship and the laws of the true God, killed the prophets of the Lord, and oppressed godly Israelites with her wickedness.

With Balaam in Pergamos, we saw the initial stages of a corrupt church. We see now in Thyatira an **established religious system** which claims to be *the* church, represented as "that woman Jezebel." She claims prophetic status – that is, the ability and authority to speak for God – and as such, continues the two practices begun in Pergamos:

1. She teaches and seduces God's servants to commit fornication and
2. To eat things sacrificed unto idols.

Let us take a closer look at this church age. With time, the state church which began under Constantine became more and more entrenched in error and false teaching. The church was still in bed with the kings of the earth, and, like Jezebel of old, used the authority of the king to suppress the truth of God's Word, as well as to hound, persecute, and kill countless numbers of those who refused to submit to its idolatry. We notice that this Jezebel system involved things *taught* (doctrines) and things *practiced*. Here are some examples of these:

Papal (Jezebel) Doctrines:

1. One is not saved purely by trusting in Christ's atonement:
   • Good works are necessary for salvation.
   • If one doesn't quite measure up, a temporary time of suffering in Purgatory may be expected before achieving entrance to heaven.
   • Forgiveness can be achieved through the purchasing (yes, with money!) of indulgences.
2. There was no longer the preaching of the gospel and calling people to faith in Christ, based on that gospel. It was the rite of baptism that now saves a person. If, as an adult, you came to personal faith in Christ, and chose to be rebaptized as a believer, you became a target of the church for persecution and even death.
3. The exaltation of Mary
   • Mary was ascribed sinlessness (the "immaculate conception").
   • She ascended bodily to heaven ("the assumption").
   • She carries out the role of mediatrix (intercessor) in heaven.
   • She was given the name "Mary, Mother of God," and "Queen of Heaven."[1]
4. The traditions and practices of the church carry the same authority as Scripture (and sometimes greater, as when the church teachings contradict and supersede Scripture; e.g., 1 Tim. 4:3 – forbidding to marry.)
5. Only the clergy are fit to read, interpret, and teach Scripture – lay people are not allowed to read it. This was a strong manifestation of Nicolaitanism, which had now moved from merely being practiced (the *deeds* of the Nicolaitans, Rev. 2:6), to being established and taught within the church (the *doctrine* of the Nicolaitans, Rev. 2:15).
6. The Roman Catholic Church is the only way to salvation. If you leave it, you are damned.

---

1 Ultimately, this title "Queen of Heaven" reveals the truth about this transformed "Mary." Astarte, worshipped by Jezebel, was the Phoenician counterpart of the Babylonian "Queen of Heaven." It was this goddess (who went by different names in different countries) who was given the name of "Virgin Mary, Mother of God" under Roman Catholicism. Thus, the pagan system being superimposed on the church here was *the same one* that Jezebel brought into the heart of Israel in 890 BC! This has been seen, known, and written about by many devout men in the church. As Alexander Hislop stated so succinctly in his landmark work, *The Two Babylons*, "It has been known all along that Popery was baptized Paganism; but God is now making it manifest, that the Paganism which Rome has baptized is, in all its essential elements, *the very Paganism* which prevailed in the ancient literal Babylon" (p. 2, Introduction).

Papal (Jezebel) Practices:

1. There were forced conversions at sword point - those who refused were killed.
2. Rites and ritual replaced the preaching of the Word.
3. Only the ordained clergy could perform the rites and rituals; lay people were not fit to serve in that way.
4. Images and relics were venerated, the liturgy replaced Spirit-led worship, and an altar (for sacrifice) replaced the "table of the Lord."
5. Christ was sacrificed over and over at the "altar" every time "mass" was celebrated. The bread and wine were believed to change in actual substance to become the body and blood of Christ, re-offered again in sacrifice at each service, and worshipped and adored by the people as it was held up by the "priest," the one who did the "slaying." This was blatant denial of the once-for-all offering of Christ, the Lamb of God.
6. The man who fills the office of the pope is considered "the vicar of Christ." That is, he stands in the place of Christ, with the same authority, when he officially speaks in his office. His words then are considered "infallible," carrying the same authority as Scripture.
7. Celibacy was mandatory for the clergy – nuns and priests, etc.
8. Confession to a priest was mandatory, with absolution following from the priest.
9. Self-flagellation (beating) and the selling of indulgences were practiced to obtain forgiveness.
10. There was ruthless intolerance and persecution of other faiths.
11. A wealthy and powerful hierarchy of ecclesiastical offices developed where corruption, bribery, nepotism, and gross sexual abuse and immorality were common.

What a sorry state! Because in this age the evil is *entrenched*, Jesus calls it not "the throne of Satan," but "the *depths of Satan*." There is a freedom that comes with absolute power – freedom to carry out deep wickedness with impunity. But nothing escapes the One with eyes like flames of fire; He sees all, and there will come a day of reckoning.

Vatican II

It might be worth noting that in our day, especially with Vatican II (a series of large policy meetings called by the pope and held in Rome between 1962 and 1965), a few changes were made, such as allowing the Mass to be in the language of the people rather than in Latin. These changes were made primarily to accommodate a more contemporary age and open the church up to a greater variety of people and ideas. It was not done in repentance for the multitude of their iniquities against the Lord, His Word, and His people, nor did the changes correct the fundamental false doctrines at the core of Catholicism. Instead, Vatican II confirmed repeatedly the teaching that Christ's atoning work in death and resurrection was not sufficient for the remission of sins.[2] It upheld the Council of Trent, which said emphatically that anyone who claims they are saved by faith alone in Christ's atoning work, and that they are assured, by faith, of entrance into heaven upon death *is anathema* – that is, they are under an ecclesiastical curse pronounced on them by the church. Instead, Vatican II reaffirmed the necessity of *works* added to the atonement of Christ – works such as participating in Catholic baptism and the Mass (primarily the Eucharist); penance; the purchasing (by various means) of indulgences as a way to remove the guilt of sin; and others. Priests and nuns still today initiate their own works of suffering, such as putting stones in their shoes, wearing haircloth shirts, and whipping themselves. Even after these are done, *assurance* of salvation and acceptance in heaven at death is *not possible,* and it's most likely that the sinner will enter the fires of Purgatory upon death, where he will suffer for a certain length of time to finish paying for his sins, before he is allowed into heaven. Besides all that, the key (idolatrous) role that Mary plays in the salvation of people remains the central focus. Mary, as the "mistress of heaven" and "co-redemptrix" with Christ, is the one who dispenses the graces of salvation and eternal life; it is *through her* that access to Christ is achieved. She is continually exalted, prayed to, and served by adherents of Roman Catholicism.

---

2 Dave Hunt, *A Woman Rides the Beast* (Harvest House Publishers, 1994), pp. 351-359.

All of these clearly indicate that despite any perceptions of softening at Vatican II, Jezebel -- with her idolatries and deceptions -- retains a firm grip on the Roman Catholic system of doctrines and practices. All of these are components of a *false gospel* which denies the all-sufficient power of Christ's blood to impart full righteousness and salvation simply through faith in Him. Such error and corruption are never to be tolerated by Christ's true followers. As the apostle Paul said, the *curse* is on those who teach and endorse any such violation of the true gospel:

> **. . . there are some who trouble you and want to pervert the gospel of Christ.
> But even if we, or an angel from heaven, preach any other gospel to you than what we have
> preached to you, *let him be accursed.* Galatians 1:7-8** (emphasis added)

The endorsement of Vatican II of this continuing false gospel must be kept in mind when any future moves are made by the pope and Vatican to claim and reclaim leadership in the worldwide religious community.

Thyatira Will Continue Until Jesus' Return

This church is the first one which will continue until Jesus' return. Jesus warned that her failure to repent, when called by God to do so, meant that she – as well as those with whom she committed fornication – would be cast into *great tribulation* (a term which refers exclusively to a period of time within the 70th week), and her children would be killed with death. And indeed, as is plain to see, the Roman Catholic Church continues up until this day and will remain until the end.

Even within such a corrupt system, the Lord sees those who hold saving faith in Jesus and walk faithfully with Him. They are to hold fast what they have until He comes. Like all the other churches, this one produced those who arose to overcome the danger and deception. Jesus promised He will one day "give them power over the nations," which they shall rule "with a rod of iron. . . even as I received of my Father" (Revelation 2:26-27). At that time, the true and righteous rule over the nations which proceeds from the throne of heaven will be experienced in the earth.

The Faithful Within Thyatira

As we mentioned before, throughout the centuries of Pergamos and Thyatira, we find faithful bands of men and women who sprang up wherever the Catholic church held sway. They persistently and laboriously translated and hand copied portions of the Scripture into their own language. They preached and taught the Word, understanding that it alone is the basis of our saving faith. They baptized *believers* and sought to lead separated lives of obedience to Christ. They knew the true church would always be a smaller group within the larger civic community – that it was not comprised of the whole community. They often met in woods or cellars or other secret places, as their gatherings were forbidden by the state church. They practiced nonviolence and faithfully cared for the poor among them. They were hounded and banished, arrested, tortured, burned at the stake, drowned. They were labelled "heretics" and maligned with lies and false accusations, as a guilty Catholic church worked to criminalize them and justify its own wickedness against them. Because of the police power that backed Catholicism, they rarely had the chance to become established, and we don't hear much about them. But it's important to know that they were faithfully there, a testimony to the Lord and His truth. They will shine with the glory of the Lord in the ages to come.

The Fifth Age – Sardis

The Church	Praised For:	Rebuked For:	Notable Characteristics
Sardis REFORMATION CHURCH (1517 - End) Rev. 3:1	A few individuals with undefiled garments who will walk with Jesus	- A name that they live, but are dead - Works that are not complete - Forgetting how they'd received and heard	This church seems that it should have life, but in fact, does not.
"Sardis" – etymology unknown			

After the long dark night of Thyatira, there was a fresh stirring in the church as strong new leaders came forth. Men such as Martin Luther (Germany), Ulrich Zwingli (Switzerland), and John Calvin (France/Switzerland) arose, seeking assurance of salvation which they had not been able to find within Catholicism. Luther especially sought to reform abuses and errors within the Roman Catholic Church. With the failure of those attempts, these men became leaders outside the church, Luther eventually founding the Lutheran Church in Germany and Calvin founding Presbyterianism. These reformers, and others like them, restored the pre-eminence of Scripture as the sole authority for the church. There was also restoration of salvation by grace alone through faith, which in itself eliminated many of the worst errors of Catholicism.

What Was the Problem with Sardis?

This all sounds very good, so we must ask ourselves, what was the Lord referring to in His rebukes of this church? What did He mean when He said, "I know your works, that you have a name that you live, but you are dead"? Or when He said, "I have not found your works perfect before God"? Or, "Remember how you have received and heard, and repent. If you do not watch, I will come upon you as a thief and you will not be ready"? The key for understanding the deficiencies of Sardis is found in the letter to Thyatira, where Jesus warned Jezebel that if she didn't repent, He would "kill her children with death" (Rev. 2:23). Children come out of *union*; remember with whom Thyatira was in spiritual union. The strategic error of the Sardis age was that these reformed churches followed the fornicating behavior of their mother, the Roman Catholic Church, and became STATE CHURCHES. The initial union of the church with the world plummeted Pergamos to the very place where Satan dwells. **The same union, entered into by Thyatira's daughters, brought them into spiritual death.**

This affected them in multiple ways, perhaps the primary one being that now a system of doctrine and practices was required that would accommodate the presence of unbelievers within the church as the usual thing. We see the doctrine of re-generational (infant) baptism, present in Roman Catholicism, also present in these state churches. Infants were "born again" in water baptism, thus providing a way that all in a given locality could become "believers" without a heart decision being required. In reality, all in these churches were *not* born again, and the call of the Spirit is for them to remember how they had initially *received* and *heard*, and to hold fast to what they had received. What had they initially received? Luther *initially* believed that the church was comprised only of those who, through repentance and personal choice, had come to saving faith in Christ. Later, he reneged, moving in the direction of a state-sponsored and state-protected church. This cast him back onto the need for re-generational baptism as the entry point into the church. The Lord calls them to repent, lest they end up losing what they had with Him, and therefore losing out at His return, being unprepared.

This religious system of the state church also meant that the active presence of the Holy Spirit had to be quenched, as He would have immediately *exposed* the unbelief and sin, calling people to repentance and faith. In response, some would have rejected true faith while others would have come into a vibrant living faith, and this would have caused a split in this system – unthinkable in the case of a state church! (See 1 John 4:1-5, especially v. 5.) Maintaining the *system* is the priority. To allow the division that Jesus had said would inevitably come with the preaching of the gospel, was *unacceptable* (Matt. 10:34-39).

Without the freedom of the Spirit, true spiritual growth is hindered, and Jesus says He had found their works incomplete before God (v. 2) – something had stopped their growth, and they had not continued on to spiritual maturity. These had begun aright, but then fallen aside into sin and error. Their garments were now defiled (v. 4) -- they were no longer receiving cleansing. They were not walking in a personal relationship with Jesus whereby they were confessing His name before men, which means He would not confess their names before the Father; instead, their names, *once written in the Book of Life,* were going to be blotted out! This is a very precarious position for this church – we get the impression that they are tottering between life and death, and there are, in fact, many who will not make it into life. They have turned from the course they were once on and are pursuing a different direction – one *away* from eternal life.

Yet, as with Thyatira, there is *mixture* here - not all are lost. There are those who are not walking cleanly with God, and yet there are those who "have not defiled their garments"; meaning that they had truly and personally received *and continued in* the cleansing that comes through faith in the blood of Christ. Jesus promised that they would "walk with me in white, for they are worthy," and, "I will not blot out his name from the book of life but will confess his name before my Father and before his angels" (vv. 4-5).

On a personal level, the letter warns each of us to continue in the Word and in humility before God, and to heed the words, "Therefore let him who thinks he stands take heed lest he fall" (1 Cor. 10:12).

The Restoration of the Word of God

Before leaving Sardis, we need to highlight the restoration of the Scriptures which took place at this time. As we've said, the Jezebel system suppressed the Scriptures, keeping them from the people. As early as the 1380's, John Wycliffe translated the Latin Vulgate into English. Though outlawed by England's Catholic Church, it triggered a hunger in the people for the Scriptures. William Tyndale translated the New Testament from Greek manuscripts in 1526. Encountering fierce resistance in England during the translation process, Tyndale fled to Germany, where he completed the manuscript and smuggled it back to England in cotton bales. The printing press, having been invented in the mid 1400's, made mass production of Bibles now possible. Tyndale's translation was taken to be a direct attack on the authority of the Catholic Church of England as well as upon the laws of England (which backed the church), and rightly so. Leaders in the Church of England gathered and burned as many copies as they could find. Tyndale was arrested and executed. After his death the Tyndale Bible became the foremost translation to find its way into the hands of English-speaking people, contributing enormously to the enlightenment of people and to progression into the next church age. Meanwhile, translations had also been made into the languages of Europe, and everywhere, people were learning the Word of God for themselves. This was probably the single greatest factor that served to weaken Roman Catholic domination throughout Europe.

For Further Reading:
A Woman Rides the Beast, Dave Hunt
The Two Babylons, Alexander Hislop
The Reformers and Their Stepchildren, Leonard Verduin
The Riches of Revelation – Vol. 1, Edward F. Vallowe
The Seven Letters to the Seven Churches, Chuck Missler
The Orthodoxy of the Church, Watchman Nee
Revelation – An Expository Commentary, Donald G. Barnhouse
Pagan Christianity? Exploring the Roots of our Church Practices, Frank Viola
The Meek and the Mighty – The Emergence of the Evangelical Movement in Russia, Hans Brandenburg

On the link of Roman Catholicism with the Letter to Thyatira and Jezebel:
Vallowe, Chapter 5
Missler, pp. 745-753, 818-825 (Kindle)
Nee, Chapter 5
Barnhouse, pp. 57-64

On the Persecution of the Saints by the Roman Catholic Church and the "Reformation" State Churches:
Hunt, pp. 254-262
Barnhouse, p. 61
Verduin
Brandenburg

CHAPTER 6

The Sixth and Seventh Church Ages

The Sixth Age - Philadelphia

The Church	Praised For:	Rebuked For:	Notable Characteristics
Philadelphia MISSIONARY CHURCH (1730 – the End) Revelation 3:7	- A little strength - Had kept His Word and not denied His name - Had kept the 'word of His patience'	No rebuke	This church was characterized by great evangelistic fervor and saw much cooperation (brotherly love) between groups as they carried the gospel far and wide.
"Philadelphia," *Philadelpheia* G5359, from *philadelphos* G5361, from *philos* G5384S – dear, a friend; and *adelphos* G80S – a brother; hence, "love of brethren"			

The wonderful restoration of the Word of God into the hands of the people was probably the single greatest reason for the swelling of new spiritual life that took place throughout the western world beginning in the 1700's. With the recovery of the Word came a restored vision of the church: understanding was restored of the New Testament church where all were brothers, as opposed to the division of clergy and laity. An "ordained leader" wasn't necessary to administer the Lord's supper -- brothers could do this in simple gatherings around the Lord's name, for these gatherings constituted the church (Matt. 18:20). Brothers could minister the Word as the Spirit led, and provide other ministries as the Spirit gave gifts for the work, for the Spirit fell on all, and all had received gifts for the benefit of the whole. There was no longer "father" or "reverend," but simply brothers and sisters in the Lord. This was a necessary recovery from the centuries of the state churches that had been so deeply affected by Nicolaitanism. This recovery of the "priesthood of all believers" -- that all had equal access to the throne of God via the blood of Christ -- is reflected in the name of the church, Philadelphia, meaning 'brotherly love.' This simple name spoke volumes of the profound restoration of the way members of Christ's body were interrelated; it also perhaps explains why there is no further mention (as in the letter to Laodicea) of the *restoration of the church* from the religious, man made systems that dominated under the errors of Pergamos, Thyatira, and Sardis.

The mission of the church was also clarified and renewed, bringing a tremendous upsurge in evangelism. Behind this upsurge are the words of the One "who has the key of David, who opens and no man shuts," Who says, ". . . I have set before you an open door, and no man can shut it" (vv. 7-8). Around 1740 George Whitfield began conducting evangelism crusades, soon followed by Charles and John Wesley. In the 1800's as a revival of the Holy Spirit, known as the Great Awakening, swept through Great Britain and the United States, Finney, Moody, Spurgeon, and others continued the great preaching crusades. On the foreign front, William Carey went to India, followed by Adoniram Judson and others. Hudson Taylor founded the great China Inland Mission, followed by others. C.T. Studd, a famous British cricket player in his youth, went with his wife to India; they also joined Hudson Taylor in China for a while. Later, leaving his invalid wife in England, he left for the Sudan to begin mission work in what was considered the largest unreached area in the world at that time. Studd was known to have said that he had tasted all the pleasures of the world, but none brought him so much pleasure as leading his first convert to faith in Christ.[1] He lived all his adult life with the burden of unsaved souls on his heart, a passion shared by many of this age.

But it wasn't just leaders who went forth. Mission agencies and Bible training schools for lay people – such as Moody Bible Institute -- arose in many of the denominations, including the Presbyterians, Congregationalists, Baptists, and the newly formed Methodists, as well as the Christian and Missionary Alliance. Great missionary outreaches were undertaken in China, India, South America, and Africa. In the spirit of 'brotherly love,' there was cooperation among many of these groups to see souls saved and the gospel go forth to the unreached. There was great openness to women ministers, and they also were accepted and trained in lay Bible Schools and sent forth.

This great move for world evangelization has continued unabated till this day and continues to increase. The twentieth century knew its Smith Wigglesworth, Billy Graham, Watchman Nee, Richard Wurmbrand, Norman Grubb, Pat Robertson, Reinhard Bonnke, and the list goes on and on – heroes of the faith behind the Iron and Bamboo Curtains, as well as in the free world; countless other men and woman who have and do labor tirelessly, whose names are better known in heaven than on earth. And now we add the great ministries of our day such as Trans World Radio, which blankets great sections of the earth with the gospel via radio; or SAT-7, who does the same thing with satellite TV; or Every Home for Christ, whose great army of foot soldiers faithfully carries the printed page of the gospel on foot door to door in countless nations around the world. And these names are only a few of the great array of saints who, in the spirit of brotherly love and self-sacrifice, have labored, and still do labor, to fulfill Jesus' mandate. To be counted among them -- among those for whom the Lord had "opened a door which no man can shut" -- and then to be faithful to that call, would be among the greatest honors possible in God's great kingdom.

This lovely church, Philadelphia, will continue to the end, as we note in His words, "Behold, I come quickly" (v. 11); she *will complete* the Great Commission, thus ushering in the Lord's return. What a great company that will be, when all are gathered together in the air! What a day to look for and hasten toward!

Along with a renewed emphasis on world evangelization, the Philadelphia Age also saw a renewed interest in the study of end-time Scriptures. This had all but passed away during the ages of the state churches, as they saw themselves as the fulfillment of the kingdom of God on the earth. After all, the church was now linked with civil authority, and had "come into the kingdom," fulfilling the promise of rule upon the earth. There was no need to look for a future kingdom on the earth; Jesus would one day return, all would be resurrected, there would be judgment, and then eternal heaven for believers. The prophetic Scriptures were spiritualized and allegorized, making an accurate understanding of them virtually impossible; and indeed, they were largely neglected. For others, when a literal fulfillment of them was sought, it was looked for in past or present events on the earth. But now, with the Scriptures restored and with churches again dis-attached from the state, there was a renewed interest in prophecy, with the expectation of its literal fulfillment at the end of the age.

In Summary

Jesus gives no rebuke to Philadelphia. Though having little strength, they have responded faithfully to the

---

1 Norman P. Grubb, *C. T. Studd - Cricketer and Pioneer* (Chicago: Moody Press, 1962), p. 33.

door opened before them, and the Lord tells them to "hold fast what you have, that no one may take your crown." It pleases Him that in this age, things that were askew are righted, and the momentum for world evangelism is restored. The church as a whole has benefited from the errors and darkness of the past. Coming now out of Philadelphia, it has a richness of understanding gained through centuries of accumulated wisdom; great men and women have walked with God, searched the Word, learned lessons, and recorded their experiences for the benefit of all who came after them. If we will but be consecrated and look to the Lord, He will lead us on to the end in victory, whatever challenges may lie ahead. He walks faithfully with us and will see us through as we hold tightly to His hand. Though we shall see Laodicea languishing sadly, Philadelphia will continue on to the end, victorious.

The Seventh Church Age - Laodicea

The Church	Praised For:	Rebuked For:	Notable Characteristics
Laodicea LUKEWARM CHURCH (1900 – the End) Revelation 3:14	There is *no praise* for this church!	lukewarmness, spiritual dullness, blindness, poverty, and nakedness	This letter is almost entirely given over to an obvious and grievous problem: This church is in terrible spiritual condition and doesn't know it! Steeped in spiritual misery and self-deception, its *self-assessment* is completely opposite of Christ's assessment of it!
"Laodicea" *Laodikeia* G2993S – from *laos* G2992T – people; a people, tribe, nation; and *dike* G1349T – a right, justice; a suit at law. Hence, literally, "people's rights"			

We have now arrived at the final church age. This is *our* age – the church of today. This letter is primarily a stunning indictment against this church, beginning with Jesus' statement that she is "neither hot nor cold," but lukewarm. This condition of complacency and self-satisfaction is so distasteful to Jesus that He warns that He will "spit them out of His mouth"! He goes on to describe their spiritual condition: *they* think they are "rich, have become wealthy, and have need of nothing," and yet they don't know that in reality, they are "wretched, miserable, poor, blind, and naked"! He proceeds to hold out to them the remedy for their condition:

> **"I counsel you to buy from Me gold refined in the fire, that you may be rich; and white garments, that you may be clothed, that the shame of your nakedness may not be revealed; and anoint your eyes with eye salve, that you may see." Revelation 3:17-18**

The Lord's call to this church – if they have ears to hear it – is to repent! If anyone will hear His voice and open the door as He knocks, He will come in to them and establish intimacy with them. This is His church, and yet He is standing *outside* of it, seeking entrance! His invitation is to the individual. He is no longer expecting the church as a whole to repent. What is going on here? The fullness of the church ages has come upon this church, and yet they are in a state of deception so profound that there is no longer a place for Jesus among them!

It is significant that this church is found in Laodicea, which means literally, "people's rights." We understand this simply by looking around the culture we are living in. This is the Entitlement Age. The mindset that pervades our society is that each person *deserves* good things. There has been a decreasing emphasis on personal responsibility, on humility, service, integrity -- on *sin* and on our accountability to God. Each one is most aware of himself and what should be coming to him – what should be handed to him. This has invaded the church also. We speak in churchy terms and do churchy things, but there is a lack of depth, reality, and power.

Laodicea's deep deception means that she no longer sees with the inner eye of the spirit. Something has happened to cause the inner light to go into darkness, bringing her into deception:

The lamp of the body is the eye. If therefore your eye is good, your whole body will be full of light.

But if your eye is bad, your whole body will be full of darkness. *If therefore the light that is in you is darkness, how great is that darkness!* Matthew 6:22-23 (emphasis added)

Jesus explained how that condition occurs. He said it's caused by a divided heart – an evil heart that doesn't put Him first anymore but has allowed another love to come in alongside Him. Of course, it doesn't look evil, because so many "good" things are going on! The "love" that Jesus specifically warns of here is the love of money -- ironically, Laodicea's very issue. Inadvertently, materialism has stepped into first place, while we are thinking Jesus is still in first place. Jesus said that this darkens the inner eyes of the heart, causing the kind of spiritual blindness -- deception -- found in Laodicea (Matt. 6:19-24). The deception is made all the more profound by us *not realizing our inner eyes have gone into darkness!* We think we still see! This is Laodicea's condition.

Beyond her blindness is her wretchedness and nakedness. This is not something to be seen in the natural. This is her *spiritual condition* and must be discerned. Scripture depicts nakedness as the condition of the person *whose sins are not removed.* Adam and Eve saw their nakedness once they had sinned, and God made clothing to cover them. Isaiah spoke of confusion and shame being removed as he joyfully declared that God "has clothed me with the garments of salvation and covered me with the robe of righteousness" (Is. 61:10). The fact that Laodicea is naked indicates that she is no longer repenting as she needs to, and that the blood of Christ is no longer being received for cleansing. Instead, she is remaining in her sins – without being aware of it – and that causes her miserable condition before the Lord.

God wants His people to be led by the Spirit, but self (the lifted-up soul), not spirit, is in the lead in Laodicea. There needs to be a return to the cross of Christ. The cross tells us that, in truth, all we deserve *is* the cross! *We* should have been the ones hanging there, not Jesus! Once we see that, then we see that anything better than the cross is God's grace – which we will *not demand* but will receive with deep humility and gratitude. We will no longer clamor for "our rights" and for what we "deserve." The cross calls us to total consecration to Christ, teaching us to forsake everything that is of the old life and of the earth; not only what is sinful, but what is *good.* Because there is *good* in the Tree of the Knowledge of Good and Evil! But it is a good that pertains to death rather than life. And God looks at Laodicea and for all their "good," sees *death.* The antidote is that they repent deeply and humbly, make a fresh and full surrender to Christ, and allow Him to restore their spiritual eyes and to clothe them with His own righteousness.

It is God's love that He speaks with such severity to Laodicea. His words are a veritable *shredding* of the image they have of themselves. He knows that they need the truth spoken strongly if they are going to be able to recognize their condition and turn from it. If they can hear His voice and repent as He says, they will avoid the great apostasy and deception which Jesus and Paul prophesied for the church in the season before His return (Matt. 24: 4-5, 10-12; 2 Thess. 2:3). If they don't repent, and many won't, they will be caught up and swept away in the dangers, deceptions, and finally, the catastrophic judgment of that end-time. How *vital* it is that we continue, all our life, to hear His voice and obey it! We tend too much to blindness and ignorance to expect to make it without listening regularly to His words!

Conclusion of the Seven Letters to the Churches

Though this 'bird's eye' view of the church can be distressing – to see its departure from the Lord and the depths of iniquity that it sank to, yet God *used* all of it. The dark times were a test and worked like a sieve, separating; choices had to be made in the face of failure and sin and offense, and choices clarify things. They either draw us closer to the Lord or move us farther away; but either way, they clarify the direction we're going. Through it all, God was at work, calling and sanctifying His own people, forming them to be overcomers who on the last day will shine with His glory.

These seven lampstands were all shining brightly. Each age had those who were maintaining the life light of Christ. There is an indictment of errors, of wicked men, and of the *systems* which Satan managed to install under the banner of Christ. Yet Christ saw the light of true saints in each age, even those who were to be found dwelling where Satan's throne was, and those in the "depths of Satan," or those within the state church of Sardis. Some of those saints were found within those evil systems and some were outside the systems. But no matter how profound the problems were, there were always those on the earth who were true representatives of Christ – men and women whom Christ commended for their faithfulness and steadfastness.

It is such a gift to us from the Lord to have His perspective on the things that have taken place in the church – including His perspective on the church of our own day! Even as God's people, we tend to see things from a natural perspective, which is faulty and defective. How can we correct an error if we don't perceive it as error? We can get so accustomed to something being a certain way within the church that it just seems normal. How we need God's eyesight to know what is pleasing and not pleasing to Him! What a loving gift these seven letters are – to the churches of every age! How seriously we ought to study them and take them to heart, that we might gain and *walk in* the things that God values!

What a succinct insight to see the church as *in essence*, a bearer of God's life, giving light; to see that no matter what else we might have going for us, if we lack the Lord's life – His Presence – in our midst, we have lost our identity as a church! We have lost our testimony in the world and before the Lord! And with that loss, the priority is to seek Him for what is needed in order *to regain* that testimony. This is the primary thing we are to value as His people – His presence in our midst. Thank you, Jesus, for clarifying that and holding it before us, Your people, forever!

As we conclude this look at the church age, we see again the significance of *seven* – signifying the completion of God's work with His called-out ones, *the church*. All is brought to perfection – both in the sense of the full *number* who are saved, and also in the sense of spiritual maturity. And at the close of the age, this beauteous "new creation" of God, the Bride, will have made herself ready, and, "dressed in fine linen, clean and white," will be presented "faultless before the presence of His glory with exceeding joy"![2]

Although with Laodicea we are taken to the conclusion of the church age, we do not see in this letter any mention of the return of Jesus and the catching up of the saints. **We have seen in these two chapters of Revelation the chronology of the seven church ages, and we will pick up the chronology again in chapter 8 with the seven seals of Revelation chapter 6.** Because there has been no mention as yet of the return of Christ, we will be *looking* for that *most significant and highly awaited* event as we continue our study.

Israel Toward the Close of the Church Age

Before we leave Laodicea, we need to comment on an important development for Israel that has taken place during this final church age. It is tremendously significant that after 2,000 years with no homeland, Israel is now back in their own land of Israel, with self-rule. God had prophesied through Hosea *His departure* from Israel ("Ephraim") and Judah:

> **I will return again to My place till they acknowledge their offense. Then they will seek My face; In their affliction they will earnestly seek Me." Hosea 5:15**

For almost 2,000 years, since the closing of the 69th week on Palm Sunday, the Jewish nation – as a nation -- has been forsaken by God. God prophesied that in a coming time of *tribulation* they would seek Him early and earnestly.[3] Hosea goes on, giving voice to the seeking that will take place:

> **Come and let us return to the Lord; For He has torn, but He will heal us; He has stricken, but He will bind us up.**
> **After two days He will revive us; on the third day He will raise us up, that we may live in His sight.**
> **Hosea 6:1-2**

---

2   Jude 1:24; Rev. 19:7-8
3   Deut. 4:30, Jer. 23:20

Remember that Peter taught us very explicitly and *in the context of end-time events,* that "with the Lord, one day is as a thousand years, and a thousand years as one day" (2 Peter 3:8). Here we are now, seeing -- after approximately 2,000 years -- *Israel's return to her land.* Here are the 'two days' prophesied by Hosea. Her return to the land is indeed as the tiny green shoots appearing on the trees after a long winter (see Matt. 24:32-33). End-time events will bring enormous pressures against them, and in that affliction, as they seek Him, *He will be found;* and at the end of the 70th week, they will find national restoration, and in the 3rd millennium (since His first coming), Israel will indeed *live in His sight,* occupying the land of Israel under His Kingship.

The Balfour Declaration in Great Britain in 1917 opened the door to the establishment of a national home for the Jews in their ancient land of Israel. This was followed in 1948 with the granting of independent statehood to Israel. Since then, Jews from around the globe have streamed home to Israel. Through much adversity and many challenges, the fledgling nation has grown in strength and independence. This, of course, is not the fulfillment of the O.T. Scriptures which predict a return *accompanied by national repentance and great resulting blessing under their Messiah.* Those Old Testament Scriptures are yet future. But this 20th century return to their land is a significant prophetic development which positions them for the events of the 70th week and God's dealings with them during that period of time.

Summary of Sevens So Far

70 sevens for God's complete work with Israel, from 445 BC to the End.
**The gap between the 69th and 70th sevens is filled with the seven periods
of the Church Age.**

SECTION 3

TRANSITIONING TO THE CLOSE OF THE AGE

CHAPTER 7

Scenes in
the Throne Room

We have completed the first series of sevens in Revelation – the **letters to the seven churches**, which constitute **the present age**. We move on to Revelation 4 and 5, which provide a heavenly behind-the-scenes introduction to the events of the end and to the scroll (which continues our chronology). Immediately in chapter 4, verse 1, we are told that we are entering the third division of the book of Revelation, "the things which shall be hereafter."

> **After[1] these things I looked and saw a door opened in heaven, and the first voice that I heard, like a trumpet speaking with me, was one saying, "Come up here, and I will show you the things which must happen after[1] this." Revelation 4:1 WEB**

[1]*meta* G3326T - in the midst of, amid, denoting association, union, accompaniment

Before this, John has been seeing things taking place on the earth. Now, as God prepares to reveal things that will take place at the end of the age, the perspective changes, and John is invited to view things from heaven itself. We should note that twice in this verse, at the beginning and the end, the Holy Spirit uses the little word *meta*. Most versions translate this "after," but the word means "at the same time as," although the thing mentioned second (in this case, the events of chapter 4 and following), may *begin* later than the first thing (the church ages). In other words, these scenes from heaven were seen *alongside* the messages to the church (probably alongside Laodicea, the 7th), not *after* the church age was over. Therefore, we see these scenes as *preparatory*, leading up to the rapture and all the other events that will bring this age to a close.[1]

John now finds himself 'in the spirit' and being given a vision of the throne room of heaven. He sees the throne and perceives One sitting on the throne. Around the throne are twenty-four other thrones with elders seated on them. Dressed in white and wearing crowns, we would think these to be twelve representatives of Old Testament saints and twelve representatives of New Covenant saints.[2] In front of the throne are seven flaming lamps; intimately associated with the throne, he saw four living beings, which we know from other references to

---

1   NOTE: We will comment on *meta* in more detail in chapter 15 when we look at Matt. 24:29 in relation to the timing of the rapture.
2   This glimpse of saints seated with Him in heaven reminds us of the many references to the ruling and judging role they will have in the future: Ps. 122:5, 132:12, Dan. 7:22-27, Matt. 19:28, 1 Cor. 6:2, 2 Tim. 2:11-12, Rev. 2:26-27.

be seraphim.[3] We see a responsive kind of worship taking place between the seraphim and the elders; it is worship which honors God as the Creator of all things. This sets the stage for all that follows, because as Creator of all, He is also the supreme Ruler over all. He is *the One* authorized to set forth and bring about all that follows in the book of Revelation, including what follows immediately in chapter 5.

We are still in the throne room in chapter 5, but now a very significant event takes place, initiated by the Supreme One on the throne. He is holding a scroll,[4] rolled up and sealed with seven seals, with writing on both sides. But He is not the one to open it. In fact, *a man* must open it; but when one is sought who is qualified to open it, no one is found – in heaven (among the saints), or on the earth (living at the time), or under the earth (among the dead in hell).

It always intrigues me that John obviously had a sense of how *vital* this scroll was, because as the search continues and no one is found, he becomes intensely distressed, weeping much! He must have sensed that *everything* hinged upon this scroll being opened! But one of the elders had inside information, and he reassured John, "Look! The Lion of the tribe of Judah, the Root of David, has overcome to open the scroll and its seals." And then John saw Him – a Lamb, standing in the very heart of the scene, looking as though it had been slain. The Lamb stepped forward and took the scroll out of the Father's hand. We then see following in the rest of the chapter what I think must be the most remarkable praise event found anywhere in Scripture.[5] It is just simply, well, *out of this world!* It includes not only the living ones and the elders, but uncounted myriads of angels, as well as *every creature in heaven, on the earth, under the earth, and in the sea!* It appears that all living beings in the whole creation see and celebrate this event! What tremendous thing does the scroll signify? Whatever it is, it is so great that it merits a closer look as to what is really going on!

The Scroll of Completed Redemption

One thing that I have come to realize and appreciate about the book of Revelation, is that although it was written in Greek and in a location completely outside of Israel, it is a *very Jewish book!* It was written by a Jew as He received it from the Jewish Messiah, and it is the description of how events will take place that will fulfill *Jewish* prophecies written centuries earlier by and for Jews. It's probably not being *read* by very many Jews – except those who know their Messiah – but nonetheless, the Old Testament Scriptures are referenced again and again, and along with the Holy Spirit, provide the single most valuable resource for understanding the book. And this is what we find now in regard to the scroll which Jesus takes.

The Law of the Kinsman-Redeemer

To understand the scroll and what it signifies, we go back to an Old Testament practice which God instituted for the Jews centuries earlier. Every Israelite family received an allotment of land when they entered Canaan under Joshua, and it was God's will for that allotment to remain within that family down through the generations. God's instructions stipulated that if an Israelite came on hard times and lost land or went into servitude (or sold a child into servitude), they were not to be oppressed, but to be paid fair wages and then released at a stipulated time.[6] The Israelites were to have respect for one another and for a brother's well-being.

However, if an Israelite fell on hard times and found himself in the possession of *a foreigner* in the land, then a kinsman (specifically, an uncle or a cousin) could redeem him. This is called the "Law of the Kinsman-Redeemer," set forth in Leviticus 25:47-50. If an Israelite had to sell himself (or a family member) to a stranger, lost his land to a stranger, or an Israelite died, leaving a widow, then a near relative (the nearest one who was willing and who could pay the required redemption price) had the option of purchasing back the land or the family member or marrying the widow to provide a son to carry on the dead man's line. Release in the

---

3 Seraphim (lit. *burning ones* - see Ps. 104:4) have six wings (Is. 6:2); cherubim (lit. the plural for *blessing*), similar beings, have four (Ezek. 1:6, 10:1-20; Ex. 25:18-20). Seeming to be a unique and very sentient class of God's servants in heaven, both seraphim and cherubim are intimate associates of the Lord and are very involved in our worship of Him.
4 Though sometimes translated "book," the Greek word is *biblion*, which means a small scroll with writing on it.
5 It's somewhat of a puzzle when we see the four living beings participating in the worship of the redeemed (Rev. 5:8-10). Many of the original manuscripts use the pronoun "us" in v. 9, and the pronoun "them" in v. 10. This inconsistency would usually be a problem grammatically, but here it may provide the solution to the problem. Perhaps it was an antiphonal song, with the elders singing v. 9, speaking of themselves as being redeemed; and the living beings singing v. 10, using "they" when referring to the redeemed.
6 Lev. 25:39-40 stipulates release in the Year of Jubilee; Ex. 21:2 and Deut. 15:12 in the seventh year.

Year of Jubilee applied even with a non-Israelite, and the terms of the redemption were to be negotiated fairly based on how close or far away the next Year of Jubilee was at that time. God realized things wouldn't always go smoothly for His people, but He didn't want oppression taking place, and so He made this provision for them.

The primary Old Testament example of this is in the story of Ruth, widowed daughter-in-law to Naomi. With no man to work her dead husband's land, Naomi desired to sell it to a near kinsman who would also marry Ruth and raise up children on behalf of the dead husband. A relative, Boaz, agreed to do both, thus becoming a "kinsman-redeemer." He married the widowed Ruth and paid the price needed to *redeem the inheritance* of that family.

We get further insight into the scroll aspect of it from Jeremiah when he purchased a family plot of land from his cousin. A deed with the purchase agreement was written on a scroll, apparently with open (public) information on the outside of the scroll and sealed (private) stipulations on the inside. The public writing probably included the signatures of the witnesses. When finished, the scroll was sealed. Invasion from Babylon was imminent, and the possession of the land would not take place immediately. Instead, the terms and conditions of redeeming that property would now remain hidden indefinitely into the future; but because of the document, the legal ground of the purchase was established.

Our Great Kinsman-Redeemer

The Jewish practice of the kinsman-redeemer is another way in which God has chosen to unveil the mighty redemption which He planned long ago would be carried out by our kinsman, the Son of David, son of Adam. The Father had to accede to the loss of His precious creation in the Fall. And the loss was devastating – the Father lost intimacy with us, and we went into bondage to the stranger, Satan, whose oppression and enslavement of man has known no bounds. But the Father had a buy-back plan set in place even before the Fall. As the plan unfolded, Jesus was brought forth – Son of Man, Son of God – to pay the awful redemption price for lost humanity. He paid the price, opening the way for righteousness and new life – eternal life – to be given as a gift to all who believe. We surrender our lives to Him and become reinstated now as *adopted sons and daughters of God* – with His very nature becoming our new nature! All that Jesus inherits as the beloved Son now likewise comes to those who share by faith in His death and resurrection – and to them is given the Holy Spirit as the pledge and Guarantor of their *full redemption and inheritance*, which is yet coming (Eph. 1:13-14).

The Scroll Contains the Plan for the Completion of the Purchased Redemption

When the sealed scroll appears in Revelation, we consider the complete picture in which it is presented: John's initial sorrow, the astonishing outbreak of praise as the Lamb steps forth and takes it, all the events which come forth from the opening of the seals leading up to, finally, the opening of the scroll itself. With the opening comes the amazing series of judgments released upon Satan and his kingdom, leading finally to the glorification of the Lord Jesus and the transition of the kingdom of the earth into His hands. **We are left in little doubt that this is *the great document of purchased redemption* which represents the captivity and not-yet-completed restoration of fallen man and his lost inheritance; and which contains the stipulations and conditions under which the great Kinsman-Redeemer will complete the full redemption of that which He purchased 2,000 years ago.** *This* is why so much hinges upon this scroll, and why all that comes after in Revelation issues forth from what is written in it.[7]

Restoration of the Original Plan

Regarding this great redemption, we must understand that from the beginning, God has had more in mind than the rescuing of individuals from hell. His purpose is the restoration of the *original plan:*

- Redeemed men, having taken of the Tree of Life (Christ), would be sealed in sinlessness and would *live out the life of God* through their own lives.

---

7   I am greatly indebted to J. A. Seiss and his comprehensive study of the book of Revelation, *The Apocalypse*, for these insights into the scroll. (Grand Rapids: Zondervan), pp. 111-114.

- The mortal bodies of the saints, damaged by sin and death, should be replaced by *immortal bodies.*
- Man, under God's headship, should rule on the earth.
- Nature and the earth itself, taken back out of Satan's grasp, would be restored to their original beauty under God's righteous rule.
- Redeemed man would share, with Christ, unimagined glories in the countless ages to come.

God's plan for how all of this is to take place is contained in the scroll, and the plan will play out in the events of Revelation, beginning with the seals on the scroll. We see from this that though the foundation of our redemption has been accomplished in our rebirth, the *fullness* of it is more future than present. That is why, with the unfolding of events which Jesus taught would precede His coming, He exclaimed,

> **"When these things begin to come to pass, . . . lift up your heads, for your *redemption* draws near!" Luke 21:28** (emphasis added)

Clearly, our *full (personal) redemption* will be accomplished *at the rapture,* when we receive new bodies; equally clearly, this redemption is associated with *the scroll.* Therefore, we would understand that whenever the rapture *does* take place, there will be an *association with the scroll* in some way!

A Few Thoughts on Christ's Return

Before we continue with Revelation 6, we must note that there has been no mention yet of *Jesus' return* – His second coming. Scripture is very clear that our catching up to be with Him takes place at His coming:

> **. . . in Christ all shall be made alive. But each one in his own order: Christ the first fruits, afterward those who are Christ's *at His coming.* 1 Corinthians 15:22-23**
> **Therefore be patient, brethren, until *the coming* of the Lord. James 5:7**
> **. . . so that He may establish your hearts blameless in holiness before our God and Father *at the coming* of our Lord Jesus Christ. . . 1 Thessalonians 3:13** (emphasis added to all)

In the pattern of Christ, we will receive immortal bodies, which we are told will take place at *Christ's coming;* we are encouraged to wait patiently for *His coming;* and our hearts will be established in holiness at *His coming.* We see clearly from these three witnesses that the rapture of the saints will take place at Jesus' coming. And, in fact, as we have just seen, the completion of our redemption is associated with the scroll, and the Lamb has only now taken the scroll in hand. Therefore, we look for His coming and our completed redemption to be drawing near in our chronology.

The Transition Chapters – Revelation 4 & 5

Revelation 4:1 has informed us that we are moving into the things that follow and conclude the present (church) age. There is nothing in the events of Rev. 4 and 5 to tie them into the chronology of the "sevens." Instead, they serve simply as *a vital introduction* to the next series of seven, the seals. It has been suggested by some that Rev. 4:1, the call for John to "come up here" into heaven's realms, is actually the rapture taking place. Interpreting this as the rapture of the church is quite a stretch. Revelation is a book where God is speaking *in detail* about events which concern the end of this age and *concern, above all, the church,* as well as the Jews. How is it possible that He would obscure *so significant and momentous an event* as His coming for His Bride, in a verse that doesn't even mention the church or any specifics of the rapture?! It is difficult to believe that an event *so looked for and longed for* by both Christ and the church, should get such a cursory and superficial mention in the Father's own revelation of Jesus Christ in His great end-time exploits to take His people and retake the kingdom of the earth! No -- in fact, as we proceed, we will find that much more is said about the rapture, and it is said openly and directly when it takes place.

Keep in mind the overview of Daniel's 70 weeks and that we are on the lookout for the beginning of the 70th week, which, as you remember, will begin with a treaty between a prince of the "revived Roman Empire" and

Israel. Since the fall of Jerusalem in AD 70, the Jews have not been in possession of their homeland. They were scattered in a repeat exile at that time and remained -- by and large -- as often-persecuted pilgrims in countries across the globe -- from China, India, and Russia, to western Europe and the Americas. That is, until 1948, when their homeland was restored to them. Clearly, the possession of their own land is a pre-requisite for the treaty which will be made with them. As we move further now into "the things which shall be hereafter," we will be looking in New Testament scriptures for an indication of the treaty which will be made and which signifies the beginning of the 70th week. That, of course, is when these *very significant and essential* end-time events will take place which will wrap up the present age and usher in the kingdom age of Christ.

CHAPTER 8

The First Four Seals – the 70th Week Begins

We are moving now into events which pertain to the end of the age. And yet we won't immediately see anything that indicates – in the chronological progression – that the church has been removed from the earth. Instead, with no mention of the church leaving, we will see that the seals indicate the beginning of the 70th week of Daniel. Some may have objections to this, and we will take a close look at what Scripture says about that timing issue as we progress through the seals. At this point in our study, we would give two general reasons in support of this viewpoint (that the church is present into the 70th week):

1. To have a transition time from the church back to the Jews at the *end* of the church age is consistent with the transition from Jew to Gentile at the *beginning* of the church age. There was overlap when the Old Covenant was transitioning to the New – it was at least three and a half years from the end of the Old Covenant – that is, when John began to proclaim the kingdom -- until the kingdom was inaugurated at Pentecost. Then there was an additional period in this same transition: Jesus initially "signed off" on the Jews a few days before His death (at the close of the 69th week), and yet the door of the kingdom wasn't opened to Gentiles for several more years until Peter preached to Cornelius at Joppa.[1] In addition, the temple, with its whole system of Old Covenant worship, continued for several decades after the formation of the church. In short, the transition from the old dispensation of law to the new one of grace did not happen abruptly but involved a variety of transitions and overlaps.

2. The overlap of the church age into the next series of seven (the seals on the scroll) is entirely consistent with the pattern of all the sevens of Revelation: *the last in each series contains within it the next series* – they unfold in a kind of telescopic manner. So rather than a clean ending and a subsequent new beginning with the next series, each new series is linked with the previous by being *contained in* the conclusion, the seventh, of the previous series. This indicates the continuity of the sevens. We may not be given the total length of time of each of the series, but we know at least that there is not a time gap *between* them: the **series of sevens** in Revelation, when put together, give us a view of the complete time period *from*

---

1 Matt. 23:38-39 and Acts 10 (It is thought that Acts 10 takes place at least five years after Pentecost.)

the beginning of the first church age at Pentecost, all the way to the seventh bowl judgment at the end of the 70th week. Consistent with this pattern, **the seventh church age contains within it the first six seals, as we see in the following chart:**

THE SEVENS IN REVELATION

The seventh in each series releases the next series.

SEVEN CHURCH AGES:

1. Ephesus
2. Smyrna
3. Pergamos
4. Thyatira
5. Sardis
6. Philadelphia
7. Laodicea

This first series, lasting ca. 2000 years, links the 69th and 70th weeks of Daniel, straddling the gap between them.

It is not explicitly stated that Laodicea contains the seals.

Nevertheless, in the chronology of Revelation, we don't see the church *leaving* until the 6th seal, showing that the pattern of the 7th *containing the next six* applies also to the seventh age.

-------------------------------- **The 70th week of Daniel: The Seals, Trumpets & Bowls** ------------------------

SEVEN SEALS ON THE SCROLL:

1st Seal - The 70th week begins with the treaty.
2nd Seal
3rd Seal
4th Seal
5th Seal - The midpoint of the 70th week — the Great Tribulation begins.
6th Seal - The saints are raptured (Rev. 6:12–14; 7:9).
7th Seal - The scroll is opened — GOD'S WRATH BEGINS (Rev. 8:1):

SEVEN TRUMPET JUDGMENTS:

1st Trumpet
2nd Trumpet
3rd Trumpet
4th Trumpet
5th Trumpet
6th Trumpet - the 144,000 appear in heaven (Rev. 14) — God's work with them
7th Trumpet   is completed.

SEVEN BOWL JUDGMENTS:

1st Bowl
2nd Bowl
3rd Bowl
4th Bowl
5th Bowl
6th Bowl
7th Bowl - The Jewish remnant completes its return to God.

These three series — the seals, trumpets, and bowls — comprise the **70th week of Daniel**

These two series, the trumpets and bowls, are contained within the scroll and comprise the **Day of the Lord's Wrath**

Although the *beginning* of each of these listed events is chronological and sequential, when each is finished can vary. For example, the 5th trumpet judgment ends at or before the 6th begins, and the 6th ends before the 7th begins. On the other hand, though Thyatira, Sardis, Philadelphia, and Laodicea begin sequentially, each *continues* up to the close of Laodicea. Similarly, the event which begins at the 5th seal, the Great Tribulation, continues on until the conclusion of the bowl judgments.

The remainder of our chronological study will *pertain to the scroll.* As can be seen from the chart, the last three groups of seven which mark out the sequential order of events are all SCROLL EVENTS. Therefore, we would understand all three groups as pertaining to the final execution of Christ's full redemptive work! Having seen in Revelation 5 that the Lamb has taken the scroll into His hands, we proceed now to Revelation 6, where we see the Lamb begin to remove the seals. Keep in mind that this is a scroll, with the contents hidden inside the roll, so <u>all the seals must be removed before it can be opened and the contents revealed</u>. <u>We will see certain events unfold with each seal -- events that are preparatory for what is contained within the scroll</u>. As we go through each seal in Revelation 6, we will look at Matthew 24 at the same time.

The Seals and the Olivet Discourse

Introduction to Matthew 24

Matthew 24, also known as the Olivet Discourse, contains Jesus' foremost teaching on the events which will precede His return. The timing of the teaching is just days after Palm Sunday and a day or so before His betrayal and death. The 69th week having just been completed, we see Jesus formally ending this three and a half-year season of opportunity for Israel:

> 37 "O Jerusalem, Jerusalem, the one who kills the prophets and stones those who are sent
>   to her! How often I wanted to gather your children together, as a hen gathers her chicks
>   under her wings, but you were not willing!
> 38 See! Your house is left to you desolate;
> 39 for I say to you, you shall see Me no more till you say, 'Blessed is He who comes in the
>   name of the Lord!'" Matthew 23:37-39

Having just left the temple for the last time, the suffering that lay ahead for the Jewish people was weighing heavily on His heart. As the disciples savored the beauty of the temple, oblivious to what was so clear to Jesus, Jesus responded with the forecast of its utter destruction. Desiring more information, the disciples asked of Him,

> "Tell us, when shall these things be? And what shall be *the sign of your coming*, even of the
> *end of the age*?" Matthew 24:3 (emphasis added)

In a remarkable fast-forward, Jesus proceeded with this teaching in Matthew 24, which takes us from the (presumed) beginning of the 70th week, through events leading up to the desolation of the temple at the midpoint, and then all the way *up to the catching up of the church* (vv. 30-31).[2] That is, these are the events leading up to *His coming*. The disciples' question gives us clear understanding as to what Jesus was speaking of. They were asking what they could look for in order to be aware *ahead of* His actual return.[3] The events Jesus spoke of and the order in which they occur correspond with the seals on the scroll. Therefore, looked at side by side, they provide a strong *chronology* for events which precede Jesus' return.

---

2   In this amazing chapter, neither Matthew nor Jesus states explicitly that the Olivet Discourse deals with the 70th week. However, Jesus' reference in verse 15 to "the abomination of desolation spoken of by Daniel the prophet" undoubtedly refers to the desecrating event of Daniel 9:27, therefore linking this future period of time with those final seven years. Knowing that the 69th week has just been concluded, Jesus skips over the gap between the 69th and 70th weeks and resumes with the narrative of the 70th week. Most remarkable.
3   The other two accounts of the Olivet Discourse (Luke 21 and Mark 13) omit this question and state only the question regarding the destruction of the temple. Although those two accounts are valuable for study, we will use Matthew's account here, as it is more comprehensive than the other two.

Let us take a look now for ourselves:

The First Seal

Revelation 6	Matthew 24
White horse rider Has a bow (no arrows) Crown given to him Goes forth conquering and to conquer v. 2	"Take heed that no one deceives you. For many will come in My Name saying, 'I am Christ' and will deceive many." vv. 4-5

As Jesus removes each of the first four seals, John hears one of the living beings call out, "Come!" This is a command to the rider on the horse to be released and come forth. As we will see, it is evil that is coming forth with each seal, evil carried out by the kingdom of Satan. And yet, because Jesus is releasing each seal, we know that it is all taking place with the full permission and *timing authorization* of the Lord Himself.

With the first seal, the rider that is beckoned goes forth on a white horse, carrying a bow, but having no arrows. He is given a crown. As with each of the seals associated with a horse and rider, the horse signifies power in motion. This rider is going forth with power and activity, in the act of conquering, in order to overcome and prevail. In other words, he is after domain and dominion in the earth. The very important thing for us to note is the part that correlates especially with Jesus' warning in Matthew 24 of deception; that is, he goes forth on a *white* horse. White signifies purity, and we know that when Jesus will appear on earth for the last great battle in Revelation 19, He will come on a white horse. But the description of Him there *is very different* from this rider. This rider carries a bow, but no arrows, perhaps hinting that there will be bullying and intimidation, but that in reality he has no real power, just empty threats. Unlike the white-horse rider of Rev. 19, this one is *unnamed* – there is an anonymity to him which is significant; and there is no sense of the great glory, majesty, and power that will accompany Jesus' return at the later time. Rather, coupled with Jesus' warning of *counterfeit christs*, we can see that the white horse signifies exactly that: This is a false christ being carried forward by deceit as he seeks dominion in the earth. Here is insight from the early church father Hippolytus on the *imitation* strategy this man will employ:

> Now, as our Lord Jesus Christ, who is also God, was prophesied of under the figure of a lion, on account of His royalty and glory, in the same way have the Scriptures also aforetime spoken of Antichrist as a lion, on account of his tyranny and violence. For the deceiver seeks to liken himself in all things to the Son of God. Christ is a lion, so Antichrist is also a lion; Christ is a king, so Antichrist is also a king. The Saviour was manifested as a lamb; so he too, in like manner, will appear as a lamb, though within he is a wolf. The Saviour came into the World in the circumcision, and he will come in the same manner. The Lord sent apostles among all the nations, and he in like manner will send false apostles. The Saviour gathered together the sheep that were scattered abroad, and he in like manner will bring together a people that is scattered abroad. The Lord gave a seal to those who believed on Him, and he will give one like manner. The Saviour appeared in the form of man, and he too will come in the form of a man. The Saviour raised up and showed His holy flesh like a temple, and he will raise a temple of stone in Jerusalem.[4]

> *Hippolytus, ca 170 – 235 A.D., was a disciple of Irenaeus, who was a disciple of Polycarp, who was discipled by the Apostle John.*

There will be *many* coming in Jesus' name with a false anointing, but this one is *the* counterfeit christ, who, in a unique way, is on the focused path to global domination. As we will see, he will gain the dominion he seeks, and that dominion will continue until the end of the seven-year period.

---

4   Hippolytus of Rome, "Treatise on Christ and Antichrist, #6" *The Ante-Nicene Fathers.* (Online - http://www.earlychristianwritings.com/text/hippolytus-christ.html.)

The Seventieth Week – the Jews

Prophecy students understand, although it is not explicitly stated by Scripture itself, that the first seal, as well as the beginning of the Olivet Discourse, is when the treaty is made between the 'Roman prince' who is to come (the 'white horse rider'), and 'the many'[5] in Israel (Dan. 9:27). This, of course, is the treaty that marks the beginning of the 70th week and the resumption of the 490-year 'clock' of God's work with Israel. It has particular significance in that it will apparently provide for the return of the temple mount to Israel and the rebuilding of the temple there, a remarkable political and religious achievement. We would expect that whatever the status of this man prior to the 70th week, this accomplishment, previously unattainable by any world leader, will contribute considerably to building his prestige, visibility, and authority on the world stage, and will serve as a key component of his strategy as he goes forth 'conquering and to conquer.'

We understand, therefore, that in the approximate time frame of this first seal, the temple is rebuilt and Jewish worship resumes -- the first time since the temple was destroyed in AD 70 that all this is possible. It is most probable that the treaty also will establish peace between Israel and the nations of the earth, particularly Israel's neighbors. This is a thrilling time for the Jews and would certainly cause them to look with gratitude to the 'prince' who has made this possible.

We must be keenly aware, however, that the resumption of their temple worship does not mean a change of heart on their part toward God. They have received this man as someone to lean upon and trust, in fulfillment of Jesus' words,

> **I have come in My Father's name, and you do not receive Me; if another comes in his own name, him you will receive. John 5:43**

In other words, this treaty occurs in the midst of their ongoing alienation from the God of Israel, despite the fact that it facilitates resumed temple worship. The fact is, that as the 70 weeks resume, their *hearts* are in the same place they were centuries before when the temple was destroyed. What Jesus had said of their forefathers is still true of them now:

> **You hypocrites! Well did Isaiah prophesy of you, saying, 'These people draw near to me with their mouth, and honor me with their lips; but their heart is far from me.' Matt. 15:7-8 WEB**

God's indictment of their worship is devastating:

> **"He who kills a bull is as if he slays a man; he who sacrifices a lamb, as if he breaks a dog's neck; he who offers a grain offering, as if he offers swine's blood; he who burns incense, as if he blesses an idol. Just as they have chosen their own ways, and their soul delights in their abominations, so will I choose their delusions and bring their fears on them. Because when I called, no one answered, when I spoke, they did not hear. But they did evil before My eyes and chose that in which I do not delight." Isaiah 66:3-4**

Though centuries have passed, they are still walking in their own ways, delighting in that which God hates. Despite their ritual worship, they scoff at God in their hearts; in their disdain of Him they make this treaty, a **"covenant with death,"** and in doing so, come into **"agreement with hell"** (Is. 28:14-15). They choose this covenant as their safety from the storm to come; but it is constructed of *lies*. To their own great hurt do they choose God's enemy rather than God Himself. This treacherous covenant will utterly fail them:

> **The hail will sweep away the refuge of lies, and the waters will overflow the hiding place. Your covenant with death will be annulled, and your agreement with Sheol (hell) will not stand; when the overflowing scourge passes through, then you will be trampled down by it.**
> **Isaiah 28:17-18**

Dire things lie ahead for Israel. But let us continue to the second seal.

---

5   So it is in the Hebrew, indicating that a minority – perhaps faithful to God - do not consent to the treaty.

The Second Seal

Revelation 6	Matthew 24
- Red horse rider - Has great sword - Removes peace from earth – people killed v. 4	"There will be wars and rumors of wars; nation rising against nation, kingdom against kingdom." vv. 6-7a

This seal is fairly self-explanatory, telling us that as "the prince" is on the move, there will be an increase, not decrease, in wars. (Not that he is directly or overtly causing them.) Red often signifies conflict and bloodshed, and the rider is likely a powerful principality of strife and war. The mention of "kingdom against kingdom" brings to mind not just earthly kingdoms in opposition, but the kingdom of darkness in increasingly intense conflict with the kingdom of light.

The Third Seal

Revelation 6	Matthew 24
- Black horse rider - Has a set of balances: "A measure[1] of wheat for a denarius[2] and three measures[1] of barley for a denarius;[2] see thou hurt not the oil and the wine." [1]choenix – wheat for one day [2]denarion – about a day's wage vv.5-6	"There will be famines." v. 7b

Here is a black rider, signifying death -- death by starvation. It's long been humanity's goal (at least on the surface) to eliminate hunger on the earth, but we will find ourselves *less* successful with this as we approach the end of the age. Many on the earth will find themselves in the situation of earning daily just enough for food for that day. A day's work will purchase a day's amount of wheat, and a bit extra of barley, being a cheaper food. The warning not to hurt the oil and wine leads us to think that there will remain a wealthy upper class that is not affected by what's going on in the earth. This would seem to indicate the loss of the middle class and the division of society into the very poor and the very rich. It appears that more and more of the world's wealth will become concentrated in the hands of a very few, leaving many so poor that they will scarcely be able to sustain life.

The Fourth Seal

Revelation 6	Matthew 24
- The pale[1] horse - Riders are Death and Hell – they are given power over ¼ of the earth to kill with sword, hunger, death, and wild beasts [1]chloros G5515T – yellowish pale, green vv. 7-8	There will be pestilences and earthquakes in various places." v. 7c

The color of the horse brings to mind the sallow color of death. It's easy to visualize this horse as pale and cadaverous, going forth with its ghastly riders to carry out its mission on the earth.

In Scripture the term "wild beasts" can symbolize principalities and powers of darkness, even as the beast kingdoms are under the control of fallen angels.[6] 'Wild beasts' is possibly a reference to *people* who have become so complicit with the devil as to take on demonic personalities, losing even normal human sympathy and affection. Paul warned:

---

6   Is. 13:21-22, Lev. 26:22, Ezek. 34:5, Mark 1:13.

But know this, that in the last days, grievous times will come.
For men will be lovers of self, lovers of money, boastful, arrogant, blasphemers, disobedient
to parents, unthankful, unholy, without natural affection, unforgiving, slanderers, without
self-control, *fierce,*[1] no lovers of good, traitors, headstrong, conceited, lovers of pleasure
rather than lovers of God; holding a form of godliness, but having denied the power thereof.
Turn away from these, also. 2 Timothy 3:1-5 WEB (emphasis added)

[1]*anemeros* G434T – not tame, savage, fierce

The effect of the seals is cumulative and downward to hell. In this seal we simply see that the results of the previous seals – war and famine, coupled with additional causes of death mentioned in both our sources -- have led to *Death* with *Hell* following. Like the previous riders, these two are persons – fallen angels: Death,[7] moving about and killing people as he sees opportunity (i.e., legal ground), with Hades[8] following. Since those dying proceed to hell, we understand them not to be saints, but to be unsaved. The "fourth part of the earth" referred to here is possibly one fourth of the geographical area rather than one fourth of the population. Either way, it certainly will involve *many* people, indicating catastrophic events and great distress. In the Olivet Discourse, Jesus summed up events at this point, saying,

"All these are the *beginning of sorrows,*"[1] Matthew 24:8 KJV (emphasis added)

[1]*odin* G5604T –the pangs of childbirth

A new world order – one under Christ's rule – is being birthed during these last seven years. Jesus depicted these first four seals as the beginning of labor pains; that is, relatively mild compared to the intense contractions the world is headed for. We will find that the fifth seal marks the midpoint of that seven years, and things will continue to intensify until the final series of seven, the bowl judgments, sees the old order brought down to make way for the new.

The Link Between the 1st and 4th Seals

We have already noted that God called Antichrist's treaty with Israel "a covenant with death . . . and with hell." We have noted as well the *cumulative* nature of the seal events: From this treaty which initiates the seals, events have proceeded, which, by the time of the fourth seal, are culminating in death and hell for one quarter of the earth! Although the treaty seems GOOD for Israel initially, we cannot miss *God's* assessment of it and the fruit it is bearing in the earth by the midpoint. Israel was always called to play a strategic role as a leader nation in the earth – strategic in representing the true God to the nations.[9] Still alienated from God, she has unfortunately fallen prey to deception and made a treaty that, in her God-given position of spiritual influence, has served as an activator for the Destroyer in the earth. Within a few short years, this "covenant with Death and Hell" has opened the door to an unprecedented level of suffering and death globally: Death, with Hell following, is prevailing over one fourth of the earth. Satan is the power behind Antichrist, but remember that at this point, Antichrist himself does not yet *appear* as anything other than a good man!

Some Final Comments on the First Four Seals

- We know that wars, famine, disease – leading to death -- have been working for millennia. None of these are new, but there will be a particular focus and intensity to these events as they are used at this time to drive the people of the earth toward one world government.

---

7   When all the firstborn offspring of Egypt were killed in the final plague, the Lord referred to Himself as the one bringing the judgment (e.g., Exod. 12:12-13). Yet, in actuality, he used an angel of darkness for that judgment, as we see when He referred to the one doing the killing as "the Destroyer" (Exod. 12:23; see John 10:10 and James 1:17). It is very likely that the angel He was referring to was the Spirit of Death. This angel, though not of God, has a legal right to function because of man's transgression, and God uses the angel at times for His own purposes.

8   The Greek name for the place of the dead, located under the earth: 'Sheol' is the Hebrew name for this place. This is simply a holding place for the unrighteous dead, not the lake of fire (Gehenna) into which Hades itself will one day be cast.

9   Abraham's seed would be a blessing to all the earth (Gen. 22:18, Deut. 26:18-19, 1 Chron. 16:8-36), but what has the greater power to bring blessing also has the greater power to bring the curse. Here we see Israel's great potential for good being wrongly used to bring great harm to the earth.

- It's important for us to note that though God is *overseeing* and authorizing the release of these events, they do not come from Him, but through the cooperation of evil men partnering with powerful princes of darkness. God is lifting certain restraints and allowing the rise of evil *at this time.*
- These events, which produce such chaos and suffering, are an essential part of Satan's plan to *facilitate his rise to power* through the antichrist, a rise which is part of God's plan for the close of the age. We will look more at this later.
- The seals, including Antichrist's rise to power, *bring the earth into the place of final readiness for the return of Christ* – they are a necessary transitional phase. Jesus explained, **"All these things must come to pass. . . "** (Matt. 24:6).
- Then He added, **". . . but the end is not yet."** Jesus is instructing the disciples on events that will *lead up to* the end and His return. The church is still present on the earth, and here we see the overlap between the seventh church age and the seals. The seal events are *preparatory* for His return and the end of the age.
- Although lawlessness has been working in a hidden way for centuries, both among God's people [10] as well as in the world, we can see already at this time that it has increased greatly, manifesting in greater power, openness, and flagrant arrogance in the earth. It will continue to manifest and increase until it reaches its full development, releasing the greater powers of darkness and bringing Satan's purposes to a climax of fulfillment. (Or what he hopes will be a fulfillment.) God will allow this *for His own purposes* in the earth, as we will see more fully in the coming chapters.
- During this period of the seals, the global kingdom over which Antichrist will preside is coming into the final stages of readiness. In the next chapter we will look at what Scripture tells us of that kingdom.

We are going to pause now between the 4ᵗʰ and 5ᵗʰ seals. As we do keep in mind that Jesus is giving this information *to His disciples* so that they can be *forewarned* and instructed as to what the conditions will be prior to His return. **With the 5ᵗʰ seal we will find ourselves at the midpoint of the last seven years, where the kingdom and the power of Antichrist reach their fullness. Before continuing to that, we're going to take a look at the kingdom and the man.**

As we think about these seal events, we could be very daunted by what lies ahead. But Jesus has comfortingly commanded us, "See that you be not troubled!" (Matt. 24:6). We will obey that as we hide in Him, rest in Him, and take encouragement from the Scriptures:

He shall deliver you in six troubles, yes, in seven no evil shall touch you. In famine He shall redeem you from death, and in war from the power of the sword. You shall be hidden from the scourge of the tongue, and you shall not be afraid of destruction when it comes. You shall laugh at destruction and famine, and you shall not be afraid of the beasts of the earth. Job 5:18-22

And Peter assures us:

The Lord knows how to deliver the godly out of temptations and to reserve the unjust under punishment for the day of judgment. 2 Peter 2:9

---

10   The "mystery of iniquity" – 2 Thess. 2:7

CHAPTER 9

The End-time Kingdom - Visions of Daniel and Revelation

We are paused here between the 4th and 5th seals. Antichrist comes to full power at the 5th seal, so we are taking the time to look at the kingdom and the man before we continue our chronology.

This kingdom – the one the antichrist presides over -- and its 'spiritual predecessors' are all called beast kingdoms in the Scriptures. That is, they are earthly, human displays of the kingdom of darkness, and as such, many (if not all) of their leaders, as well as their policies, are characterized by demonic brutality and *inhumanity*.

Before we take a look at them, we reflect briefly on some of the empires that rose during the twentieth century. When communism prevailed in Russia, it transformed that government into a beast-like monster that had no regard for human life or for justice. The Nazi regime under Hitler was the same. Along with other communist regimes, these were characterized by godlessness, ruthlessness, brutality, and injustice; in them we have examples of beast kingdoms, and they help us understand the kingdom that is yet to come.

We take a step backward in time to understand what is coming. God's desire had been that Israel would be the head of the nations as they obeyed Him; as such, they would be a light and a testimony to the world as to the nature of God and how to walk with Him. Israel failed at this, however, as we saw in chapter 1: after much long-suffering on God's part, both the Northern and Southern Kingdoms were taken into exile. The land was virtually emptied, the temple destroyed, and their national autonomy completely lost. The deep sin of Israel and the judgment it incurred meant that God's desire to use Israel in this way would be delayed. Furthermore, this was not a temporary loss for Israel, but one that would remain until the end of the age, because God knew their spiritual blindness and hardness of heart would continue until the end.

Through Nebuchadnezzar, king of Babylon, God revealed to Daniel *the alignment of kingdoms that would successively be in power in the earth, right up to the end of the age.* It would *not* be Israel that would have the pre-eminence, but rather, a succession of pagan kingdoms would dominate in the earth and be used at various times to bring judgment on Israel. In spite of these kingdoms, God would continue to work His purposes in the earth until the end of the age, when His kingdom would rise, bring down Satan's rule, and become established as head in all the earth.

Daniel's Kingdom Visions

These visions of Daniel, plus the visions of the kingdom in Revelation, are our sources for understanding the end-time kingdom. We are going to take a brief overview of them just to get the big picture.

Nebuchadnezzar's Dream of the Great Image - Daniel 2:31-45

1. **Babylon** – gold head – 626-539 BC
2. **Medo-Persia** – silver chest & arms – 539-330 BC
3. **Greece** – brass belly & thighs – 330-146 BC
4. **Rome** – iron legs -- 146 BC-AD 476 -- A time gap separates this empire from the final kingdom.
   Rome – feet & toes – iron/clay – the ten-toed restored Roman kingdom of the end.

The Roman kingdom, in the form of ten divisions/kings, will be the world empire in power when Christ returns at the end. "In the days of these ten kings shall the God of heaven set up a kingdom which shall never be destroyed or left to other people" (vv. 34, 44).

NOTE: Daniel is talking of the kingdom of God as a manifest world power, not the spiritual "mystery" kingdom (the church), which was unknown in the Old Testament.

Comments:

- The head of gold was in power when Nebuchadnezzar received this dream. Behind him was the principality which first found expression at the Tower of Babel, was still present in Babylon, and remains the *head* of all the succeeding kingdoms.
- The two legs represent the separating of the Roman Empire into the East and West divisions; this took place around AD 285, when the empire became so large that it was difficult to administer from one location.
- There is a time gap between the legs and the ten toes. This gap coincides roughly with the gap between the 69th and 70th weeks of Daniel. The toes represent what has often been called "the revived Roman Empire" – the kingdom at the end. (It is interesting to speculate on the Roman Catholic Church being the entity that links the legs with the toes during this time gap.)
- Notice how in this dream, God was spanning the centuries, going from the present (ca 600 BC), all the way to the end of these earthly pagan kingdoms.
- This dream agrees with Gabriel's information (Dan. 9:26) that the prince – i.e., the antichrist – that makes the 7-year treaty with Israel presides over the *Roman* empire (the empire that destroyed Jerusalem in AD 70).

In the next vision, notice that these are the very same kingdoms, just depicted differently.

Daniel's Vision of Four Great Beast Kingdoms - Daniel 7:2-27

These beasts arose out of the sea as the four winds strove upon the sea:

1. **Babylon** - lion with eagle's wings
2. **Medo-Persia** - bear on its side with three ribs in mouth
3. **Greece** - leopard with four wings and four heads
4. **Rome** – extremely strong and terrible and different from the others; devouring the whole earth
   - iron teeth
   - claws of brass
   - ten horns
     Another "little horn" came up among the ten. He is apparently the instigator of three of the ten being plucked up by the roots. He has eyes like a man and a mouth speaking great things.

Comments:
Worldwide turbulence – both in the spiritual and natural – causes the bursting forth of these heathen kingdoms as one struggles against and achieves dominance over another.

- The four winds strove upon the sea.
  - Four is the number of the earth.
  - Winds, the same as *spirits* in Hebrew, can refer to either good or evil angels; in this case, probably ruling spirits of darkness striving with each other and causing the rise and fall of these different kingdoms.
  - The sea represents the mass of humanity – vast, unstable, susceptible to tossing by the wind (Rev. 17:15).
- Like the lion in the jungle, Babylon was virtually invincible in the earth; as an eagle, she sought her prey from a distance and swooped in to seize it. The lion was as royalty among beasts, and the eagle among birds, signaling the supremacy of Babylon as the head of gold. (In the ancient world, a lion with eagle's wings, known as a griffin, was widely used as a symbol of divine power, and the lion itself symbolized the king of Babylon.)
- Of the Medo-Persian empire, the Mede was the weaker and the Persian more dominant. The bear, an animal of great strength and aggression, is raised on one side, probably signifying the dominance of the Persian leadership. The three ribs may signify the three main conquests of this empire - Babylon, Lydia, and Egypt.
- Like the leopard, Alexander the Great of Greece moved with great swiftness to subdue great portions of the earth and bring them under his control. He died when still young, and his vast kingdom was divided four ways among his four generals. Out of the largest division, the Syrian/ Seleucid kingdom, came Antiochus Epiphanes, prototype of the antichrist.
- Here, the fourth empire, the Roman, is depicted *in its end-time form*, as seen by the ten toes. Devouring the whole earth, it will be a worldwide kingdom. A horn represents power. Consistent with the ten toes of the previous image, there will be ten divisions to the kingdom.
- A "little horn" will arise:
  - *Little,* perhaps indicating that he will not come on the scene with great suddenness, power, and drama, but will arise in a less conspicuous way.
  - He will completely uproot three of the ten horns – these are the ten kings who receive power 'one hour' with the beast: "These have one mind and shall give their power and strength unto the beast" (Rev. 17:12-13). Most likely, three of the kings will resist his global take-over and he will simply remove and replace them. Nothing will be allowed, at that time, to stop his rise to complete control in the earth.
  - He will have eyes like a man – the eyes are the window into the soul. That is, he will not seem to have the savage and beastly qualities of a godless pagan, but the heart and empathy of a man.
  - But he will have a mouth that speaks great, exalted, and presumptuous things.
- Under this little horn, war will be waged against God and the saints for a 'time, times, and half a time' – that is, for three and a half years, until the kingdom comes to the saints of the Most High!

This vision informs us that the ten-region confederacy of this global kingdom will already be in place when Antichrist makes his appearance. **The division of the earth into ten sections with leader/kings over them will be one of the first indicators that the earth is moving into end-time events.**

The domain of all four of these empires included, in turn, the geographic area to which Israel and Judah were taken captive (roughly corresponding to present-day Iraq). Each of them successively ruled the Jews, particularly those in exile – including the places of their original captivity and then also in the lands to which they were eventually scattered. The Roman Empire, of course, was the one which ruled Israel during Jesus' time, and which carried out His execution by crucifixion.

The Kingdom Visions of Revelation

We now proceed to the descriptions of the last kingdom as they are found in the book of Revelation. Here also, this kingdom is called a beast kingdom. When man turns away from the truth of God and gives himself over to rebellion and wickedness, he gradually loses the natural human qualities of justice and compassion, and progressively takes on the wickedness of the spirits to which he is yielding. Paul tells us that Antichrist and those who promote his kingdom will use every conceivable strategy of deception in order to promote and protect their wickedness (2 Thess. 2:10). This will make them as beasts, feral in their wickedness. They will become agents and *manifestations* of the kingdom of darkness, indwelt and controlled by spirits of evil.

God has wanted His people to understand this succession of kingdoms and the pre-eminence that they would have in the earth. He wants us to understand the *unity and continuity* of the kingdoms, particularly in their agenda and their nature. They are all backed and enforced by powerful spirits from Satan's kingdom, and tend to be hostile to God and His people and purposes in the earth. God wants us to be wise and know what we are up against, not to cause us fear, but to assure us that He is in control and is greater than any power of that kingdom. His plan leading to ultimate victory was formed long ago and will be surely and inevitably *carried out* -- He *is* the Alpha and the Omega, supreme from beginning to end.

The following are two references from Revelation that speak either of the end-time kingdom or of its king, the antichrist. The kingdom and the king are so closely linked, and Revelation can be so fluid in how it uses the term "beast," that sometimes it's difficult to tell which is being referred to - the kingdom or the head of the kingdom. It needs to be surmised from the context.

These references are found in *parenthetical* portions of Revelation – that is, portions that are outside the sequences of sevens. Whenever a portion is parenthetical, we must determine when it occurs based on the content of the passage.

The Beast (Antichrist) and his Empire - Revelation 13:1-2
1. A beast rose up from the sea having:
   a. seven heads with the name of blasphemy
   b. ten horns with crowns
2. The beast was like a leopard and had:
   a. feet like a bear
   b. mouth like a lion
3. The Dragon gave him his *power, his throne,* and *great authority.*

The Beast Which Carries Mystery Babylon - Revelation 17:3, 9-12
1. The beast has
   a. seven heads
   b. ten horns
2. The angel's explanation of the beast:
   The seven **heads** are **seven mountains,** which are **seven kings/kingdoms.**
   Five of these are in the past.
   One is in the present.
   One is future.
   The **ten horns** are **ten kings** which rule briefly during the reign of Antichrist.

Comments:

- Both visions depict a beast with seven heads:

These heads are *kings/kingdoms*; of the seven, five are *past*. One, the sixth, is present, and since the vision was given to John during the time of the **Roman Empire** (contemporary with the New Testament), that is the one spoken of as being in the present. The seventh is depicted as future, and we understand it to be **the end-time kingdom**. Each head had rulership over the beast at a specific point in time, but the beast is *of one nature and character*.

The identity of the heads:

We know four of them from Daniel: **Babylon, Medo-Persia, Greece, and Rome**. Here, where *seven* are listed, we see the fourth kingdom (Rome) being the *sixth* kingdom. Therefore, we look backward in time for the first two kingdoms, and we find *Egypt* and *Assyria*. Both of these kingdoms were patterned after Babel, and both were tools in Satan's hands to oppose God's people in the earth: Egypt oppressed Israel before their deliverance under Moses, and Assyria took Israel into captivity with excessive and notorious brutality. These were not mentioned in Daniel, presumably because they were already past, and God was directing Daniel's understanding from the present (the kingdom of Babylon) toward the future. But here in Revelation, we stand at the perspective of the end of the age, looking backward; in that backward look we see all these kingdoms, and understand from them what to expect in the final kingdom. So then, here are the seven heads named:

1. Egypt
2. Assyria
3. Babylon
4. Medo-Persia
5. Greece
6. Rome
7. Revived Rome

The beast finally being *complete with seven heads* (well, almost complete, as we shall see), shows us that these Scriptures are presenting the time period of that seventh head, the end-time kingdom. The beast in both visions has <u>ten horns</u>: We already know that these represent ten divisions of the global empire. In Revelation 13 there are crowns on the horns, showing that the *kingdom* -- under its head, the beast, has risen to full power on the earth; that is, the chapter depicts conditions during the Great Tribulation.

Notice the characteristics of the end-time beast:

> **Now the beast which I saw was like a leopard, his feet were like the feet of a bear, and his mouth like the mouth of a lion. Revelation 13:2**

The features of the previous kingdoms (Dan. 7) are consolidated in this final, fierce king/kingdom: the speed and stalking ability of the leopard, the great ravaging power of the bear, and the intimidating roar of the lion, raging with threats and blasphemy. We are told clearly that the dragon, i.e., the devil,[1] is the power behind the man and the kingdom! This is God, finally allowing Satan the thing he has lusted after since the Garden of Eden! We will look later at why God does this.

A Few Bad Men

God created man to be his designated, legal ruler of the earth. He put all things under his dominion: Man was to "fill the earth and subdue it and have dominion over every living thing on the earth" (Gen. 1:28). In yielding

---

1 Rev. 12:9

to Satan's seduction, Adam and Eve's position of dominion was surrendered to Satan. Although he obtained this position by disobedience to God -- by lies, craftiness, and usurpation, he became, nevertheless, the prince of this world.[2] Under his evil rulership lies a dark kingdom with a hierarchy of fallen angels and demons, spoken of in the New Testament as "principalities, powers, the rulers of the darkness of this age, and spiritual hosts of wickedness in the heavenly places" (Eph. 6:12). These dark, rebel spirits occupy the atmosphere around the earth, constantly inciting to evil and seeking and maintaining power and influence over the people of the earth. Paul called Satan the "prince of the power of the air, the spirit who now works in the sons of disobedience" (Eph. 2:2). These kingdoms we see in Daniel and Revelation are (along with others) *earthly and visible manifestations* of this unseen – but extremely real -- kingdom of evil.

The Serpent's Seed

Although all who are not a part of the kingdom of God lie under the influence of Satan, there are some in the earth who have a more deliberate cooperation with him. We recall God's words to Adam and Eve following their disobedience:

> **I will put enmity between you and the woman, and between your seed and her Seed; He shall bruise your head, and you shall bruise His heel." Genesis 3:15**

Down through the millennia since the fall, there has been the relatively small group of the woman's seed, i.e., those who sought and followed God.[3] And there has been the relatively small group of those who followed Satan – that is, followed him knowingly and by choice. Those constituting these two groups have been, by and large, the primary history-makers in the earth, and it is those two groups who will be in pitched combat at the end.

In the temptation of Jesus by the devil, we see Satan's attempt to *strike a bargain with Him*, exchanging servitude to him for the wealth and power that he can bestow. This, indeed, has been Satan's customary *mode of operation*. **As the prince of this world, he has been fully positioned to offer men such rewards of iniquity.** A great many have responded to that invitation, yielding obedience and even worship to Satan, becoming 'movers and shakers' in the earth, accumulating great, great wealth and power, and manipulating people and events for their own selfish purposes; then passing this heritage on to their children and to the generations that followed them. These are "Satan's seed" – those who are in conscious, deliberate alignment with his evil purposes in the earth.

We are told in Revelation 18:23 that the *merchants*, the "tradesmen," of Babylon are the "great men" – the kings, the lords, the nobles and chiefs, the generals and 'grandees,' the power-brokers of the earth. Throughout time, these men and women, the seed of Satan, have *traded* in all the commodities of earth: luxury, wealth, power, slaves, and even the "souls of men" (v.13). Satan's manifest kingdom on the earth has become an increasingly vast and powerful network of men and women with no scruples, who have worked continually, both behind the scenes and on center stage, to promote their own selfish ends, and in doing so, to promote the purposes of Satan in the earth. Though they work behind an endless variety of fronts and masks that appear good, their works are *always* evil. These are the leaders, in nation after nation and century after century, which constitute Babylon, the seed of the serpent.

The average person, even many of God's people, have been largely unaware of this vast network of evil operating in the earth. But God, of course, has seen all along; the iniquity has been accumulating – it has been "treasured up,"[4] and will, as we shall see later in the book, reach a tipping point, bringing down upon these evildoers fiery vengeance at the hands of God. Furthermore, God will, now at the end, *purposefully* bring this wicked cabal of Satan's seed into climactic conflict with the seed of Christ, the saints. Though the battle will be fierce, *the outcome is assured*.

---

2   John 12:31; 14:30; 16:11; 1 Cor. 2:6
3   We understand this to be not all of Eve's offspring, but the specific "seed" whose line would defeat the serpent's seed. "And Adam knew his wife again, and she bore a son and named him Seth, 'For God has appointed another seed for me instead of Abel, whom Cain killed'" (Gen. 4:25). This, of course, is the line that led to Jesus, the Seed, who is the true life of all who are godly.
4   Romans 2:5

Conclusion of the Kingdom of Antichrist

Before leaving this subject, let's take a brief look at where things are today in the development of this kingdom. This is primarily a study of the Scriptures themselves and what they teach us, but as developments in the earth coincide with Scripture's predictions, we can hardly overlook them. Israel is already back in its land, which, of course, is a pre-requisite to the events of the end. For now, we will just add that there is a very strong and dominant surge of globalism around the earth. This surge is what is undoubtedly leading to the full development of that end-time kingdom. It operates both behind the scenes clandestinely, as well as in more obvious ways in the governments of many (if not most) nations, all of which co-operate with the United Nations/European Union (and many other front organizations whose baseline agenda is globalism) in promoting the decline of independent nationalism and the increase of interdependency among nations. The primary stated goal of globalists is a "New World Order" in which both resources and population are managed from centralized leadership, presumably for the good of all. The operation of globalism within our own federal government, as well as in other nations of the earth, has become increasingly clear, open, and unapologetic. If this increasingly arrogant and brazen surge toward globalism takes hits and seems to be diminished, we can be sure that it will re-emerge, only with a craftier and more subtle strategy! Not until Jesus returns will the danger pass.

The stated agenda -- global health, peace, and prosperity -- will **undoubtedly continue to appear beneficial for all.** This agenda will be the *velvet glove covering the iron fist of ultimate control* of all the earth. The deceptive strategies of the velvet glove include playing up fears of overpopulation, with the accompanying fears of inadequate resources and of climate change affecting those resources, resulting in famine; fears of continued war, including nuclear war; fears of inequitable allocation of earth's resources; and similar themes. These fears will, in fact, flow together with *the seal events*, which, being precipitated by man in cooperation with evil spirits, will all work together to impress upon the peoples of the world the *dire necessity* of a unified global government; a government which will ultimately consolidate all power in the hands of one world leader – a compassionate one, of course – who can enforce peace and can *manage* all these resources, nations, and needs *for the benefit of all.* As God's people, we keep in mind God's own description of this global government once it finally rises to power: the description found in Revelation 13.

Although the true agenda is barely veiled, many will fall for it, being easily duped by deceit, because, as Paul states, "they did not receive *the love of the truth*" (2 Thess. 2:10). A world that has rejected truth will continually be susceptible to false fears, fears which will project them into ineffective and self-destructive pseudo-remedies; this world will miss the reality that the only thing they *truly have to fear* is falling into the hands of the living God, who is *a consuming fire* (Heb. 12:29). Man straying from God will *ever and always* miss the mark and, in missing the mark, will fall into the hands of the enemy. This the enemy knows well and is totally banking on; it is the heart of his strategy against man and God. All of this deception is necessary, of course, because as we've mentioned, Satan must have the cooperation of man to enact his plans upon the earth.

At the time of this writing, the *Club of Rome* has already divided the earth into ten regions, ostensibly for economic and eventually political cooperation within each region.[5] (Although we do not yet see a leader over each region.) Key to the implementation of this global plan is the diminishing of any nation(s) which stand out as exceptional and independent; all must be brought to the place of subservient equality and *dependency on* global solutions to problems. More information on all this is readily available online. This is relevant for us to be aware of, as we have seen that the ten-region dividing of the earth will be a very early indicator of last day events, preceding even the appearance of the antichrist. (Whether the present divisions remain in place or are restructured is uncertain.)

Those of us alive in the early part of this 21st century know not only from our history lessons the destructive nature of absolute power in the hands of a few, but we are also not far removed time-wise from seeing for ourselves the ravaging dictatorships of the last century, notably Communism and Nazism. We are also familiar with the scourge that Islam can be. We ourselves may have suffered from these or have personal knowledge of

---

5   Mihajlo Mesarovic, Eduard Pestel, "Regionalized and Adaptive Model of the Global World System," a report prepared as part of the "Strategy for Survival Project," September 17, 1973. This report can be found online.

others who have. In considering the general knowledge that the peoples of the world have regarding these kinds of government – including some that are still under them – we have to ask ourselves, **how it is that some of these same people will consent to the reviving of a kingdom with that very same brutal and implacable nature?** As we move on now to the man who will head up this kingdom at the end, understanding the *strategy he takes* in his rise to power will help us answer this question.

Closing Comments

The Lord has declared many times and in many ways His remarkable purpose for this earth:

> **All nations whom You have made shall come and worship before You, O Lord, and shall glorify Your name. Psalm 86:9**

> **For the earth shall be full of the knowledge of the Lord as the waters cover the sea. Isaiah 11:9**

> **All the ends of the world shall remember and turn to the Lord, and all the families of the nations shall worship before You. For the kingdom is the Lord's, and He rules over the nations Psalm 22:27-28**

> **And the Lord will be king over all the earth. On that day the Lord will be one and his name one. Zechariah 14:9 ESV**

> **For the earth will be filled with the knowledge of the glory of the Lord, as the waters cover the sea. Habakkuk 2:14**

> **In His days the righteous shall flourish; and abundance of peace until the moon is no more. He shall have dominion also from sea to sea, and from the river to the ends of the earth. Yes, all kings shall fall down before Him; all nations shall serve Him. Psalm 72:7-8, 11**

Under God's blessing, this *legal* and *righteous* 'global government' will thrive, for *this* Ruler has purchased the rights to it by His own pure blood. But first (as always), the enemy will seek to install his counterfeit, persuading an erring and gullible mankind that his plan will work. But we are getting ahead of ourselves. Let us go on, now, to see how his plan to "get ahead of the Lord" will play out in other ways also.

THE RISE AND REIGN OF THE COUNTERFEIT CHRIST

CHAPTER 10

The Antichrist –
Going Forth to Conquer

We arrive now at our discussion of this well-known end-time figure who will sit for a brief time as sole ruler of the earth. We tend to think of him as a man with horns, a wicked, iron-fisted tyrant who will top the list of history's tyrants. And indeed, he is all that. But along with that, the Scriptures also depict a whole different side to him, which is very important for us to understand. We know him best by the name **Antichrist**, although he is called that only once in Scripture. That one reference, however, contains much insight regarding this man. We will look at that; and we will look at his **pathway to power**. What is his *strategy* as he goes forth conquering? We know that he reaches the point of **full power** at the midpoint of the 70th week. That key point is what Paul called "the revealing of the Man of Sin," and it separates the man *before* the midpoint from the man *after* the midpoint; that is, it shows us that there are *two distinct phases* to this man's career, and understanding both of them – but especially *the first phase* – is essential for God's people. We will look in this chapter at the *components that make up his strategy for achieving world power and control.*

"Antichrist"

We have already mentioned that the backdrop for the 70th week is the white horse rider going forth to conquer. More directly, he's out to "take over the earth." We coupled the fact that he is going forth on a *white* horse, with Jesus' warning of deception, "Many will come in My name, saying 'I am Christ,' and <u>shall deceive many</u>" (Matt. 24:5). That is, they – and specifically, this one - will come in Jesus' name claiming His *christos* - His anointing,[1] His *authorization*. We get more insight on this from the place in Scripture that gives us the name "Antichrist" for this end-time ruler:

> **Little children, these are the end-times, and as you heard that the Antichrist is coming, even now many antichrists have arisen. By this we know that it is the final hour.**
> **They went out from us, but they didn't belong to us; for if they had belonged to us, they would have continued with us. But they left, that they might be revealed that none of them belong to us. 1 John 2:18-19 WEB**

---

1 *Christ,* from the Greek *christos* G5547 -- "the anointed one" or "the anointing." Some may have come claiming literally *to be Christ,* but the craftier strategy, and one seen much more commonly, is the person who comes simply "in His Name," claiming His anointing and His authorization.

John first makes it clear that there is *one* person coming in the future whom he calls "the Antichrist." He then states that already at that time, *many antichrists* had arisen. Whoever these people were, they had arisen *from within* the church, and then proceeded to leave the church, making it clear that they never had truly been the Lord's. He continues in 1 John 4, urging God's people to test the spirits of those who mingled with and ministered among them. These people were not saying or doing things outwardly which disqualified them. It was the *spirit* in which they ministered that needed to be tested, not necessarily the things about them that were easily observed. I.e., these people *appeared* to be fine. They were among God's people. They were saying and doing "the right things" (for the most part). But their spirits needed to be tested, because John knew that there were many *false prophets* already active in the church. He went on to connect these false teachers/preachers with the *spirit of antichrist* and stated that these spirits were *of the world;* that is, they were *not* from the kingdom of God. What can we deduce from all this?

1. These people had arisen within the church, many in *leadership* roles.
2. They operated not *in the anointing,* but in a *religious spirit* from the kingdom of darkness. That is, they carried a *counterfeit, deceptive* anointing.
3. These spirits were (are) *anti-christos:*

   anti – against and in place of   *christos* – the anointing or the anointed one
4. That is, they <u>war against</u> the anointing, <u>seeking a way to remove the Holy Spirit</u> from among God's people <u>and to replace Him with themselves</u>. These spirits seek *legal ground* in a church or individual, primarily through sin and/or error, and once they've gained that ground, will exert a control that, even with the best of intentions, the person(s) involved will have a *very difficult time overcoming.* (That is, of course, without discernment and resisting in Jesus' name.)
5. It's crucial to understand that these spirits are not anti-*Jesus.* In fact, they are religious and love to talk about religion – including Jesus -- and to do religious things. Everything *appears* to be correct and the same as always – the status quo is not disturbed. But the *life* of Christ becomes subtly replaced by these religious spirits.
6. Because it is the *life* of the Lord that is being attacked, it is Jesus in His *now, present-moment activity and reality* -- **which always comes via the Holy Spirit** -- that they war against. The gifts of the Spirit will cease; the ministry of the Word will become more academic and mental, less anointed, less life-giving. There will be fewer and fewer people who become born again, baptized in the Spirit, healed, or delivered. Things will become very 'proper' and 'under control.'
7. When crossed or challenged, these spirits manifest with great viciousness. When manifesting through a person to protect their territory, they will change a usually benign person into an 'attacker' who does not move based on the Word, but moves, even with lies and unrighteousness, to *protect the sphere of influence of the spirit,* whether that sphere is an individual, a congregation, or even a whole denomination. Most frequently, it is someone *with the anointing, bringing an anointed message or ministry,* who will come under attack. (Consider the centuries of persecution perpetrated by the Roman Catholic Church against small bands of true believers who warred against the RCC with the Word of God.)
8. Incidentally, I (the author) have observed that spirits of infirmity seem to operate freely under this religious spirit: all manner of physical diseases and afflictions, including premature death, are seen in the domain of these spirits.
9. These spirits CANNOT BE SEEN IN AN OUTWARD WAY – they *must* be tested for! It is precisely because of the *subtlety* of their activity that John warns so strongly and teaches so thoroughly about them, and commands that they be discerned and tested for. The Holy Spirit Himself is required in order to detect them, as John warned. John went on – *very importantly* – to give the church the way to test for these spirits (1 John 4:1-3).

In fact, the church has largely missed these warnings and instructions from John – it is very rare for a spirit operating *within the church* to be identified as an "antichrist spirit." They are likely to be called a spirit of control, or a religious spirit (both of which may be correct), or even "Jezebel" or some other spirit. But the name given by John, "antichrist spirit," captures the essence of the *damage* done by this spirit and also captures *the way* in which he does the damage – by assaulting, surreptitiously and insidiously, the very presence of the Holy Spirit among God's people, and then replacing the anointing with itself. He does this by gaining legal entrance and ground via error and sin that are not identified, acknowledged, and repented of.

The Pathway to Power

Now the reason I have gone into such detail regarding antichrist spirits is because John is very clearly *giving us the pattern and the mode which Antichrist will follow as he "goes forth conquering."* The connection between present evil spirits within the church and this coming world ruler is *undeniable.* In fact, I believe **the reason that we have failed to identify and therefore deal effectively with this spirit in the church is because we've associated the Antichrist Spirit with the *second phase* of the antichrist's career -- the great anti-God person of terrible wickedness -- *rather than the deceiver of the first phase.*** But John was teaching us how the antichrist will be in the deceptive first phase! He was not only teaching us about spirits that were a problem back then and which are RAMPANT in our churches yet today; he was also giving us valuable insight into how the antichrist will first arise and then go forth "conquering and to conquer"! That is, he will do this primarily *from within the church.*

Components of His Ascent to Power
1. In Jesus' Name as a Pretender
    The predominant means of acquiring power is deception! From Jesus:

    > **4 Take heed that no one deceives you.**
    > **5 For *many* shall come in My Name. . . and shall deceive*many.***
    > **11 Then many false prophets shall rise up and deceive *many*.** (These are the very ones John warned against.)
    > **24 For false christs (*anointed ones*) and false prophets will rise and show great signs and wonders to deceive, if possible, even the elect. Matthew 24:4-5, 11, 24** (emphasis added)

    We note how this picture expands: first, many come *in Jesus' name,* deceiving; next, they act as prophets, meaning they claim to *speak for Him,* and deceive further. Then these false christs and false prophets will rise up and begin to operate in *great signs and wonders,* and the deception at that point has become so finely tuned that God's very elect are endangered by it. These three statements are made progressively – the first, at the beginning of the 70th week, the second, around the midpoint, and the last, in the midst of the Great Tribulation, the time of *greatest testing.* We will be looking at Revelation 13, the chapter on the antichrist, and will find that he and his assistant, the false prophet, will "do great wonders" and will "deceive them that dwell on the earth by means of those miracles which he had power to do . . ." (Rev. 13-14 KJV). This fits with what we have already seen: one with a false anointing who is actually *against* Christ – His *enemy* -- will come forth, claiming His anointing, claiming to speak for Him, and *doing many great signs and wonders in His name!* This man operates *as if he is a Christian* – from *within* the church! Jesus makes absolutely clear the outcome of all this: *MANY are deceived* and end up *following* this false leader!

2. Feigning Godly Character
    The early apostles understood the subtlety this man would operate in, and they passed that knowledge on to their disciples. This is how Hippolytus described him:

    > Let all of you, then, of necessity, open the eyes of your hearts and the ears of your soul, and
    > receive the word which we are about to speak. For I shall unfold to you today a narration full of

horror and fear, to wit, the account of the consummation, and in particular, of the seduction of the whole world by the enemy and devil; and after these things, the Second Coming of our Lord Jesus Christ…. For these things must first be; and thus the son of perdition — that is to say, the devil — must be seen….

Above all, moreover, he will love the nation of the Jews. And with all these he will work signs and terrible wonders, false wonders and not true, in order to deceive his impious equals. For if it were possible, he would seduce even the elect from the love of Christ. **But in his first steps he will be gentle, lovable, quiet, pious, pacific,[2] hating injustice, detesting gifts, not allowing idolatry; loving, says he, the Scriptures, reverencing priests, honoring his elders, repudiating fornication, detesting adultery, giving no heed to slanders, not admitting oaths, kind to strangers, kind to the poor, compassionate.** And then he will work wonders, cleansing lepers, raising paralytics, expelling demons, proclaiming things remote just as things present, raising the dead, **helping widows, defending orphans, loving all, reconciling in love men who contend, and saying to such, "Let not the sun go down upon your wrath;" and he will not acquire gold, nor love silver, nor seek riches. 24 And all this he will do corruptly and deceitfully, and with the purpose of deluding all to make him king.** For when the peoples and tribes see so great virtues and so great powers in him, they will all with one mind meet together to make him king. And above all others shall the nation of the Hebrews be dear to the tyrant himself, while they say one to another, Is there found indeed in our generation such a man, so good and just? That shall be the way with the race of the Jews pre-eminently, as I said before, who, thinking, as they do, that they shall behold the king himself in such power, will approach him to say, "We all confide in thee, and acknowledge thee to be just upon the whole earth; we all hope to be saved by thee; and by thy mouth we have received just and incorruptible judgment."[3] (emphasis added)

We are hard put to find someone with such sterling character among God's *true* people! This man will be *remarkable!* Reminding us of the 1st seal, THIS then – *imitating Christ* -- is the pathway of Antichrist as he pursues power and builds a following in both *the church* and the world! Can you see how *in all outward characteristics* this man will conform to godliness? Because the *consent* and backing of the peoples of the earth are necessary for his rise, he must cover his actual agenda behind an appearance of godliness and with this astonishingly winning persona. It is this impeccable character of godliness that will make discerning him *so difficult.* Most Christians are aware that the one who makes the treaty with Israel *will be* the antichrist, but because they will be looking for a wicked, godless man, his identity will elude some of them even when he makes this treaty.

3. Acquiring and Consolidating Political Power

As he comes forth, a worthy and pious leader, he will also be rising rapidly from relative obscurity to a place of **political influence and power**. This rise will take place amid the great traumas and tragedies of the first four seals – wars, great inequity in wealth and resources, plagues and disease, and death resulting from all of them: Issues, we might add, that are triggered by the kingdom of darkness for the very purpose of creating and demonstrating the dire necessity of a competent and compassionate world leader who can lead and manage the whole earth for the protection and benefit of all people! The world will be *crying out* for someone who is essentially GOOD, who demonstrates great leadership skills, and who is willing to step up and *take charge!* This man will be the perfect, 21st century 'Renaissance Man,' **the man of the hour** – hand-designed for the need!

We see clear hints of this political adeptness in Daniel. This man is the one who will make the binding treaty with Israel -- one that will allow Israel a temple and worship on the unwinnable, disputed temple mount! This

---

2 "peace-loving"
3 Hippolytus of Rome, "Discourse on the End of the World, the Antichrist, and the Second Coming of Christ, Sections 23 & 24" *The Ante-Nicene Fathers.* (Online - https://www. biblestudytools.com/history/early-church-fathers/ante-nicene/vol-5-third-century/hippolytus/appendix-works-of-hippolytus.html.)

will be a remarkable demonstration of political skill and authority already at the beginning of the 70th week; an authority obviously respected by all other nations, as they allow and honor the treaty. No wonder an undiscerning Israel receives him as a messiah! Furthermore, in his rise to power, he will have the political clout to remove (and presumably replace) three of the world's ten regional leaders.[4] These are a couple glimpses we get from the Word before seeing him at the fullness of his power.

Speaking and acting as Christ, he will go forth to extend the beneficent influence and kingdom *of Christ* politically in the earth! It's important to note that here in America, we are accustomed to spiritual leaders and political leaders, but we don't generally see a merging of the two; a person is either one or the other. But with this man, we will see a return to the pattern that was the norm for the largest part of human history – the union of the religious with the political *for the maximum consolidation of power and control of the people.* **This man will bring a return to the merging of the political with the religious.** And this, of course, is part of his imitation of Christ; because Christ's kingdom in the Millennium *will be a political* kingdom. He will "shepherd with a rod of iron" and also be worshipped as *King and Lord of all the earth!* Antichrist will be presenting himself AS the Christ – the one qualified to be followed and worshipped by all of humanity. Of course, we know that this political kingdom of righteousness will be instated in the earth only after the return of the true Christ.[5]

As we've mentioned elsewhere, his rise to power will be seen on the world stage, when, flexing the muscles of his political power and influence, he is able to remove three of the ten kings:

> . . . the ten horns that were on its head, and the other horn which came up, before which three fell, namely, that horn which had eyes and a mouth which spoke pompous words, whose appearance was greater than his fellows.
> 24 The ten horns are ten kings who shall arise from this kingdom. And another shall rise after them; he shall be different from the first ones and shall subdue three kings.
>
> Daniel 7:20,24

We note particularly that the ten are *already in place* as he ascends to power. This act of removal, as well as making the treaty with Israel, not only empowers him, but will enable us to identify him.

All of this, then, is a picture of Antichrist *in the first phase* of his career – rising within the church and from there, going into the world as a marvelous deceiver and skilled political operator, inspired and instructed by the master deceiver, Satan himself. All three of these aspects belong to our true Christ, encompassing both His first and second comings. Doesn't it make sense that in coming as an *alternate, counterfeit Christ,* the antichrist would seek to imitate the true Christ in the fullest and most convincing way possible? How else would even the elect be susceptible to deception from this man? Why would Jesus find it necessary to warn His disciples repeatedly about deception, if the ones seeking to deceive came in the name of Buddha, Allah, or some other obviously false god? He will appear to be all that Christ is – he will just do it *on his own,* carrying *a different spirit* than the Holy Spirit, and that will make *all the difference in the world!*

Ringleader in the Apostasy

The New Testament warns us of a great apostasy that will occur alongside Antichrist's rise to power. Mentioned in the following verse, we see what "apostasy" means:

> Let no one deceive you by any means; for that Day will not come unless the [falling away][1] comes first, and the man of sin is revealed, . . .   2 Thessalonians 2:3

[1] *apostasia* G646T – a falling away, defection, apostasy

---

4   Daniel 7:8
5   The similarity of his rise to power with those in the church whose stated goal is to gain dominion over the key aspects of human life and culture *(before Christ's return)* is concerning and worth watching with discernment. We know Christ's kingdom in the Millennium will be *a political kingdom,* but He will inaugurate it *after His return;* He alone can purge the earth of wickedness and send Satan's minions to prison for the duration (Is. 24:21-23).

This verse is from Paul's primary teaching on the antichrist at the midpoint. We will take a look at that shortly, but first, notice the Greek definition: Apostasy is 'a falling away from the faith, a defection from truth.' Only someone who has known the truth – that is, a Christian or Jew – can commit apostasy, forsaking that truth. Although apostasy is not unusual in the church in terms of various individuals or groups departing from the truth from time to time, this verse seems to indicate an apostasy that is out of the ordinary. The use of the definite article ('the'), indicates Paul is speaking here of a very specific and presumably *massive* falling away; as, a large portion of the professing church will depart from the faith at this time in the future. This would coincide with the repeated use of "many" in the teaching of Jesus that we looked at above. Those "many" that are deceived *follow* their deceiving leader, departing with him from the faith.

In the part of the Olivet Discourse that correlates with the 5th seal, Jesus warned:

And then many will be offended,[1] will betray one another, and will hate one another.
Matthew 24:10

[1]*scandalizo* G4624S – to be snared, to stumble, trip up; figuratively, to be enticed to sin or apostasy

You will be betrayed even by parents and brothers, relatives and friends; and they will put some of you to death. Luke 21:16

As this oppressive, global kingdom comes to power, it is characterized by suspicion, fear, coercion, and betrayal. There will be pressures against the church and such subtle seductions of the enemy operating among and against God's people, that Jesus warns many will stumble and turn away from the faith. Filled with suspicion and fear – amidst disagreement over who is *truly of God* -- some will betray loved ones, thinking to do what's 'right' (and perhaps to ensure their own survival). The faithful insistence that "Jesus is *the only* way," will alienate many and bring the accusation of intolerance and narrow-mindedness.

And because lawlessness[1] will abound, the love[2] of many will grow cold. Matthew 24:12

[1]*anomia* G458T – the condition of without law; contempt and violation of law, wickedness
[2]*agape* G26T – love, good-will, affection

Agape denotes the selfless love of God - the love which led Christ to give up His life for us all. That it is used here lets us know that it is not just natural, human love which will grow cold, but the love of God which is found within the community of believers. This is Jesus explaining what is behind the apostasy at the heart level. This cooling of selfless love will take place as lawlessness increases in the earth, as well as in the church. Paul spoke of the hidden work *of lawlessness* (Gk. *anomia*) (2 Thess. 2:7). This iniquity is not the blatant rebellion found in the world, but a *hidden* work of self-will – operating behind the veil of piety -- as opposed to submission to *God's* will. This is the religious flesh dominating instead of the spirit: "Because the carnal mind is enmity against God; for it is not subject to the law of God, nor indeed can be" (Rom. 8:7).[6] When not recognized and repented of over time, it can -- and for many, *will* -- lead to falling away from the faith. <u>Self-will is the root cause of apostasy, as well as of believers being deceived</u>. This is at work in a progressive way in the church: rejection of truth in hidden places of the heart will lead to delusion and then, given the right circumstances, to the betrayal, persecution, and even killing of the righteous, though one may *think* he's still walking with God. Jesus taught,

"If any man *wills (chooses) to do His will*, he shall know concerning the doctrine, whether it is from God or whether I speak on My own authority." John 7:17 (emphasis added)

---

6   It's the *good* of the Tree of the Knowledge of Good and Evil, as opposed to the evil; but it's still the Tree of Death.

Again, we must see that this largely-hidden issue of self-will is *the root* of the deception and the apostasy that will occur. Because they are not submitted to God, deceivers come on their own authority. But even when covered by good deeds and smooth words, their *self-will* shall be detected by those who *love God's will.*

Looking again at the verse above (2 Thess. 2:3), we **see a close association between this apostasy and the revealing of the man of sin**. As the Great Commission is moving toward completion under the great outpouring of the Holy Spirit, great multitudes of new believers are entering the kingdom. So also, events in the world are moving toward the midpoint: Antichrist is building and consolidating his political power and also has a band of loyal followers from the church, many of which are new converts that have just recently been saved and who will, unfortunately, "ride the wave" of this great outpouring right into apostasy with him. The apostasy will reach full-ness *in association with* the unveiling of the Man of Sin, even as Paul points out here. As their false christ openly departs from the faith at that time, so too, the many following him will likewise openly depart from the faith. This is fully consistent with the pattern given us by John that characterizes these spirits.[7]

Further Thoughts on the Apostasy

There are mainline denominations that are departing increasingly from the Scriptures with such unbiblical practices as same-sex marriage, abortion, and the condoning of homosexuality. Some have embraced secular humanism and even abandoned Jesus as "the Savior of the world." There is another section of the church which emphasizes feelings and experiences over faithfulness to the Scripture and is introducing great compromise into the fold of "Christianity": There are no longer absolutes, such as sin, hell, repentance, or the divinity of Christ, but truth is adaptable to the moment and the need. This is essentially the New Age Movement being adapted into the church, with much variation and diversity within this movement itself. All these are fairly overt examples of apostasy.

But probably the segment of the church that is vulnerable to the most subtle attack of deception is the charismatic portion. These Spirit-filled believers are (rightly) receptive to and desiring great outpouring from the Holy Spirit. This outpouring will include tremendous signs and wonders, healings and supernatural manifestations of the Holy Spirit. Signs and wonders are a tremendous gift from the Lord, and a mighty tool of God for evangelization, but as we have seen, *counterfeit signs* will also be a primary instrument of the *deception* that's coming. We see in Matthew 7:13-23 that one may do great signs and wonders in Jesus' name, and yet be doing *their own will* rather than the Father's will. In fact, Jesus warns us (again!) in this passage that *many* will be found in this condition of doing their own will, even while walking in great supernatural works. This failure to submit deeply to Christ's Lordship will end up disqualifying them.

These paragraphs present only a small part of the deviations possible that are pathways to apostasy. There are many more possibilities which will undoubtedly play out; as Jesus said, "The way is narrow that leads to life, and few there be that find it," but "wide is the gate and broad is the way that leads to destruction" (Matt. 7:13-14). And, of course, this broad path includes multitudes of people who are not even associated with the church, who will be taken in by those who speak falsely at this time. For all of the variations of delusion that will be seen at this time, whether in or out of the church, the essential issue is a rejection or a neglect of the truths of Scripture which would lead to repentance, faith, and justification before the Lord. Not being strongly established in truth will leave one vulnerable to lies, and both those who depart from the faith, as well as those who never claim the faith, will have no defense against the deceptions provided by the enemy. On the other hand, loving truth, hating sin, walking in humility and the fear of the Lord, and being filled with the Holy Spirit and abiding in Him all serve to provide strong protection for those who are the Lord's![8]

Diverging Paths Within the Church

This departure from the faith will mean two diverging paths for those who call themselves Christians. Though that divergence may not be apparent until the midpoint, the underlying issues will be present long before then. Moving toward the midpoint and climaxing then, the way will become increasingly narrow; the pressures caused

---

7   John made it clear that those under the influence of these spirits "go out from among us, that it might be *revealed* that they were not of us" (1 John 2:19, emphasis added). In our day of sadly deluded Laodicea, it is more typical that these have risen to unchallenged leadership and therefore remain *(unrevealed)* in the church, damaging it.

    On another note, the seven kingdom parables of Matthew 13 correspond with the seven church ages. The last is the Parable of the Dragnet, where many "of every kind" were gathered in the net and taken to shore to be sorted out, the good from the bad. Not all who seem to enter the kingdom in the final, great outpouring, will pass the tests, but these 'wicked' will be separated out before the end.

8   2 Thess. 2:10

by persecution and deception will cause the bottom-line choices of people's hearts to come forth, clarifying their position before the Lord. This is a necessary time of *fruit bearing*. It is by our *fruit* that our true nature is known. Leaves and stems (words and actions) on different plants can appear the same. But when the fruit comes forth, the plant's true nature is revealed. Once the fruit is displayed and fully ripened, the church will be ready for the *dual* harvest which the angels will carry out:

> **. . . at the end of this age. . . the Son of Man will send out his angels, and they will gather *out of his Kingdom* all things that cause stumbling and those who do iniquity,[1] and will cast them into the furnace of fire. There will be weeping and the gnashing of teeth.**
> **Then the righteous will shine forth like the sun in the Kingdom of their Father. He who has ears to hear, let him hear. Matthew 13:40-43 WEB (emphasis added)**

[1] *anomia* G458T – lawlessness, contempt for and violation of law

There will be a judgment later of those outside the church, but the judgment Matthew speaks of here is for those *within* the church who have not submitted to the Lord from the heart. (Numerous passages show this 'weeping and gnashing of teeth' to be characteristic of hypocrites when they are judged, as in Matt. 24:51.) The separation within the church prior to the harvest will bring a *necessary distinguishing* of the two groups leading into the harvest.

A Time of Great Outpouring

As we think of apostasy and betrayal at this time, we are reminded of lukewarm Laodicea. Her dismal spiritual condition will make the slide into apostasy both widespread and easy. But we are reminded also of *Philadelphia* – that as Jesus predicted, she will at this time finally *complete the Great Commission!*

> **But he who endures to the end shall be saved. And this gospel of the kingdom will be preached in all the world as a witness to all the nations, and then the end will come. Matthew 24:9-14**

This fulfilling of the Great Commission will take place amid tremendous anointing of the Lord in and upon His people. It hasn't come out much in the Scriptures we've been looking at. But even as the spiritual environment found in the world during this period will contribute to the ripening of the tares, so also will the tremendous outpouring of the Spirit of God upon the church empower her to complete her task:

> **Therefore, be patient, brethren, until the coming of the Lord... the farmer waits patiently for the precious fruit of the earth, ...until it receives the early and latter rain. James 5:7**

Already we see the Father beginning to release His "latter rain."[9] This outpouring on the church will not only empower the entrance of a great multitude of believers into the kingdom, but will also bring that final generation of believers to maturity and *readiness* for the gathering of the saints unto Him. How tremendous both those things will be! As believers, we celebrate that this season is coming! The Father has His eyes upon this, and as we can see from this verse, it is something He has been focused on for a long time with great anticipation. *We share His anticipation of this climactic time for the church!*

Once the midpoint arrives, these things will take place amidst the darkness and adversity of a world going madly after a spiritual imposter. Betrayed, scorned, and persecuted, the true Bride will be disdained by the world, but *how lovely she is in the eyes of her Lord*, and *how His longing for her* is intensifying during this very strategic time! But we are getting ahead of our story! It's time to continue our chronology now with the 5th seal.

---

9 See Appendix 2 - the vision of Tommy Hicks.

CHAPTER 11

The Fifth Seal – the Midpoint

Resuming our chronology, we have now arrived at the 5th seal, the **midpoint** of the last seven years. This will mark a great shift in the earth as Antichrist enters *the second phase* of his career.

The Second Phase of Antichrist's Career
Continuing in the path of imitating Christ, Scripture tells us that at this time, this man will receive a deadly wound, followed by a supernatural "resurrection." A creature from the bottomless pit will be allowed to enter his body, bringing him back to life![1] The transformation of spirit and behavior in this man will be immediately obvious to the whole world, as his *act of desecration*, so clearly prophesied in Scripture, will follow closely on the heels of this resurrection. We first heard of it in the familiar verse of Daniel 9:

> . . . **But in the middle of the week**
> **He shall bring an end to sacrifice and offering.**
> **And on the wing[1] of abominations shall be one who makes desolate,**
> **Even until the consummation, which is determined,**
> **Is poured out on the desolate. Daniel 9:27**

[1]*kanaph* H3671S – edge, extremity, wing; pinnacle (of a building)

This event, the "Abomination of Desolation," is a key marker and is associated with the persecution and apostasy in Matthew 24, and is, of course, the next event in both accounts that we've been following chronologically:

---

1   Rev. 13:3; 17:8-11 We will look at this more carefully in *Part 2* of this book.

The Fifth Seal – The Great Tribulation

Revelation 6	Matthew 24
Souls appear under the altar – those slain for the Word of God and for the testimony they held. V. 9	9 Then they will deliver you up to tribulation and kill you, and you will be hated by all nations for My name's sake. 10 And then many will be offended, will betray one another, and will hate one another. 11 Then many false prophets will rise up and deceive many. 12 And because lawlessness will abound, the love of many will grow cold. 13 But he who endures to the end shall be saved. 14 And this gospel of the kingdom will be preached in all the world as a witness to all the nations, and then the end will come. 15 When, therefore, you see the abomination of desolation, which was spoken of through Daniel the prophet, standing in the holy place (let the reader understand) … 21 For then shall be great[1] tribulation[2] such as has not been since the beginning of the world until this time, no, nor ever shall be. vv. 9-15, 21 [1]*megas* G3173T – big, great [2]*thlipsis* G2347T – pressure; translated variously 'affliction, squeezing, trouble'

Jesus speaks here of a number of different aspects of the Great Tribulation and how it will affect believers. We covered some of them in the previous chapter. Paul speaks of this midpoint event, calling it "the revealing of the man of sin":

> **Let no one deceive you by any means; for that Day will not come unless the falling away comes first, and the man of sin is revealed,[1] the son of perdition, . . . 2 Thessalonians 2:3**

[1]*apokalupto* G601T – to uncover, unveil; to make known what was previously hidden

He calls it this because at this point, the veil of piety that cloaked the man in the first phase of his career will be removed. In this act of desecration and in the reign of terror which follows, his true character and agenda will now be on display for all the world to see. The second phase of his career-- absolute, ruthless world domination, his goal all along -- has begun. Paul goes on to describe more fully the nature of this abomination:

> **. . . who opposes and exalts himself above all that is called God or that is worshiped, so that he sits as God in the temple of God, showing himself that he is God. v. 4**

This man will go into the *Holy of Holies in the temple* and declare himself to be God! He will usurp the place that belongs to Christ alone – the "King of kings, and Lord of lords." In doing this, he will reach the fullness of *anti*–*christos*: He **opposes** and **exalts himself above** all that is called God and known as God. That is, he not only seeks to be equal with God, but to take His place, the place which Christ alone has the full right and authority to occupy.[2] This is the clearest description we have in Scripture of what exactly will take place at this time. *This is the wing – the height - of abomination that Daniel and Jesus spoke of.*[3] For godly people, Jews and Christians alike, the horror and sacrilege of this event will leave no doubt as to the wicked and idolatrous nature of this

---

2   When I first studied these verses in 2 Thessalonians years ago, I instinctively felt the issue of apostasy would have a dual fulfillment: That this desecration would occur in the temple in Jerusalem; but that there would also be a fulfillment of it in the spiritual temple, the church. I felt that this man would arise also among the born-again people of God, claiming to be Christ and committing sacrilege within the church, thus leading many astray. Jesus' words in Matthew 24:23-26 – which take place during this time - seem to confirm that, as also do these verses. This claiming to be Christ could be the culmination of the apostasy which Paul speaks of here, for both Christians and Jews.

3   The occurrence of this sacrilege causes us to ponder the final goal of the 70 weeks, the anointing of "the Most Holy" (Dan. 9:24). Whether this verse in Daniel refers to Christ OR the Holy Place isn't clear; perhaps it's both, as the Most Holy One takes His rightful seat in the Most Holy Place. At any rate, the duration of the Man of Sin's time in that holy place will be very short, as it will soon bring down upon his head the dreadful and desolating wrath of God.

man who previously appeared so pious.

Besides being a terrible sacrilege, this act is an egregious violation of Antichrist's treaty with the Jews, and it will inaugurate a time of terror for them which will be all the worse for being so utterly unexpected. The terror will immediately take over Jerusalem and the areas surrounding it in Judea. Jesus' advice, given so many centuries earlier, is, "Flee for your lives!"

From Jerusalem and Judea, the terror will spread to the whole earth, to any who will not bow the knee to this man. Because of that, **the fifth seal marks this event by the appearance of believers in Jesus who will lay down their lives for their faith.** With the apex of evil comes the apex of testing, and martyrdom for some who stand steadfastly against the evil.

As we have mentioned, when Antichrist reaches this height of apostasy and comes out in the open with his agenda, he will *bring with him* into open apostasy the many who are deceived by him, and this includes *Jews.* Like Paul in v. 3 above, Daniel also points out the correlation of apostasy with the coming forth of the Antichrist:

> **In the latter time of their kingdom, when the transgressors[1]** *are come to the full***, a king of fierce face, and understanding dark sentences, shall stand up. Daniel 8:23 WEB** (emphasis added)
>
> [1]*pasha* H6586B – to rebel, transgress, revolt; and *Strong's* - apostatize

We would understand the phrase "are come to the full" as meaning that there will be the *complete development* and ripeness of the apostasy among the Jews, both in terms of the number of them and also in terms of their full, inner commitment to the error and rebellion that it involves. This group will be loyal to Antichrist right through the Abomination and following it. This departure from the faith will undoubtedly be distressing for the faithful in each group, and will contribute to the testing aspect of this time for them!

Jesus Speaks to the Jews

It is interesting that Jesus speaks first (in vv. 9-14) to *believers* about this 5th seal. As with the previous portions of Matt. 24, the correlation with the seals *is assumed,* not specified. However, in v. 15 (see above), Jesus suddenly becomes much more specific, linking this time with Daniel's prophecy. He then goes on:

> **Then let those who are in Judea flee to the mountains.**
> **Let him who is on the housetop not go down to take out things that are in his house.**
> **Let him who is in the field not return back to get his clothes.**
> **But woe to those who are with child and to nursing mothers in those days!**
> **Pray that your flight will not be in the winter, nor on a Sabbath,**
> **for then there will be great oppression, such as has not been from the beginning of the world**
> **until now, no, nor ever will be. Matthew 24:16-21 WEB**

This prophecy of Daniel's is one which *the Jews* would know about! Furthermore, the instructions which follow are directed to those who 'live in Judea,' i.e., to the *Jews.* As I pondered this, I thought, "How extraordinary! It is very unusual for Jesus to be speaking to His followers, and in the middle, to insert a clear word of warning that is specifically for the Jews -- Jews who are probably not even following Him!" After all, with this being in the New Testament, the Jews are not even *reading* this! Trying to process it, I had this thought, which I will just put out here for consideration: Jesus wants His people, the saints, to *be aware* of the great and immediate danger to the Jews at this time in the future. Being aware, I think He wants us to be prepared to assist them in any way possible, because *they* will be taken *completely off guard* by this! I believe this is instruction for the saints!

Revelation 13 – The Antichrist and His Kingdom

Let's continue now and look at specifics of the Great Tribulation as seen in Revelation 13, a chapter which shows the antichrist in the second phase; that is, from the midpoint through the remainder of the 70th week.

    a. A beast arises with 7 heads and 10 horns. His power, throne, and authority come from the dragon, the devil. He experiences a death and "resurrection."

    b. He's given power to continue 42 months (3½ years or "time, times, and half a time"). This period of time is well-established in Scripture (Dan. 12:7; Rev. 11:2-3; Rev. 12:6, 14; Rev. 13:5) and encompasses the whole second half of the 70th week.

    c. He speaks with great arrogance and blasphemy, especially against God and the saints. (See Rev. 12:15.)

    d. It is given to him to make war with the saints and to overcome them. (See Rev. 12:17, Dan. 12:7.)

    e. Power is given him over the whole earth.

    f. All people are required to receive a mark upon the forehead or right hand in order to buy or sell. This mark (Gk., *charagma)*, signifies a stamp, an imprinted mark, an etching.[4] This is a large part of the *test* for all people. Some will have independent means of supply, others will have to rely fully upon the Lord, with a willingness to go without in order to be faithful to Him. If they trust Him in that situation, they will discover new dimensions of His faithfulness!

    g. A false prophet arises, who becomes the validator and enforcer of the authority of the beast.[5] This false prophet seems to become the spiritual powerhouse of Antichrist's administration, having the power to do great supernatural works, including the ability to make an image of the beast and to impart the power of speech to the image, as well as to enforce worship of the beast and the receiving of the mark. The Abomination of Desolation will begin with the *man* in the Holy of Holies, and will continue with this great, enforcing *image* representing him.

    h. The number of the beast is 666 – man's number (6) times God's number (3). Although this number probably has a variety of significant and profound interpretations, we will simply say that six, the number of incompleteness, always falls short of the perfection of the number seven. Man's (as well as Satan's) efforts to seek divinity are ALWAYS futile, regardless of the appearance of being successful.

It is interesting to note the repetition of the phrase, "it was given to him …" All power and authority belong to God and to the Lamb, but God will release the reins on Satan, finally allowing him to go after what he has been itching for from the time he fell. He will be allowed to channel enormous power through this end-time ruler. But all of Satan's *best efforts* will still fall short, and in the end, all that he has labored for will come under judgment and be utterly and thoroughly destroyed.

We refer again to Daniel, as he mentions the great arrogance and blasphemy of this man's speech:

> **Then the king shall do according to his own will: he shall exalt and magnify himself above every god, shall speak blasphemies against the God of gods, and shall prosper till the wrath has been accomplished; for what has been determined shall be done.**
> **He shall regard neither the God of his fathers nor the desire of women, nor regard any god; for he shall exalt himself above them all. Daniel 11:36-37**

Becoming the head ruler of all the earth means that he will have incredible military power at his disposal. Isaiah prophetically shows him bragging on his wisdom and strength and doing as he pleases as he confiscates and gathers the wealth of the earth for himself.:

---

4   Rev. 13:16 – charagma (G5480T S)
5   Here we see the completion of the counterfeit trinity: The Dragon representing the Father, the Antichrist the Son, and the false prophet the Holy Spirit.

"I have removed the boundaries. . . I have robbed the treasuries; I have put down the inhabitants like a mighty man. My hand has found like a nest the riches of the people, and as one gathers eggs that are left, I have gathered all the earth. And there was no one who moved his wing, nor opened his mouth with even a peep." Isaiah 10:13-14

Persecution

Whoever has not been won over through deception will be strong-armed, so that none seem to be left who can resist him. The people of the earth will exclaim, "Who is able to make war with him?" (Rev. 13: 4). Though he confiscates enormous wealth, his greater agenda will be to command worship. Possessing the power to require worship from all on the earth, and furthermore, to execute all who *refuse* his mark and refuse to worship, means great persecution for Jews who are faithful to their (Old) Covenant with God. Many Jews will be killed.

Christians, of course, will also refuse his mark and his worship, becoming special targets, which explains the martyrs we see "under the altar" in the fifth seal.[6] "It was given unto him to make war with the saints, and to overcome them" (Rev. 13:7). This is the persecution which spreads from Jerusalem outward, as we mentioned earlier. Although there were many deaths with the previous seals, these die specifically because of <u>the word of God and the testimony that they hold</u>. It's impossible to assess how many souls John saw there, but we are assured by the conversation that follows that each one is specifically known and cared for by the Lord, including the way in which they die.

The Great Supernatural Activity of Antichrist

The supernatural signs and wonders done by this man and the false prophet will continue into the second half of the 70th week.[7] This, of course, will take place even as those who will not bow the knee to him are being persecuted. This will be a period abounding with supernatural occurrences, some of them of God (through the church), but many of them from the enemy, designed to lead astray anyone who *can* be led astray. Apparently, the enemy, knowing that the true Messiah could appear at any time, will attempt to get ahead of Christ and seduce people into believing He is already "here" or "there." And he will be very successful in this with people who don't love the truth; there will be deceived groups who gather here or there around a specific person or revelation, and vultures (demons) will feed on them, lost as they are in spiritual death and deception (see Matthew 24:23-28).

Daniel speaks also of this man's supernatural powers to deceive and bind people:

> **And in the latter time of their kingdom, when the rebels (apostatizers) have reached their fullness, a king shall arise, having fierce features, who understands dark workings.**
> **He will have great supernatural power *to bind and to blind*; it will not be his own human power; He shall destroy fearfully and shall prosper and thrive; He shall corrupt vast numbers of people, bringing them to destruction, and also the holy people.**
> **Through his understanding of craftiness, he will cause deceit and treachery to push forward in the earth. He will exalt himself in his heart, and through ease and prosperity, he shall corrupt and destroy many. Daniel 8:23-25[8] (emphasis added)**

This man will be instructed by the devil himself and will be *enormously wise* in his implementation of *craft and deception*, his key strategy as he seeks dominion. *As many as he can lull into a sense of security, trusting him, he will be able to destroy in the end, leading them as sheep to the slaughter.*

Paul explained to us how this man can be the source of the downfall of so many people:

> **9 The coming of the lawless one is by the activity of Satan with all power and false signs and wonders,**

---

6 Rev. 6:9-11. Regarding this rather odd phrase "souls under the altar," see Appendix 3.
7 See Matt. 24:23-25; 2 Thess. 2:9-10; Rev. 13:13-15
8 Worded by the author from the Hebrew definitions, S & B (Strong's and Brown Driver Briggs).

10 and with all wicked deception for those who are perishing, *because they refused to love the truth and so be saved.*

11 Therefore, God sends them a strong delusion, so that they may believe what is false,

12 in order that all may be condemned who did not believe the truth but had pleasure in unrighteousness. 2 Thessalonians 2:9-12 ESV (emphasis added)

Only truth can protect from lies, and rejection of truth will bring this terrible deception and consequent destruction upon them. All of this is in preparation for *the coming harvest,* which we will look at later. On the other hand, faithfulness to Christ and abiding continually in Him will be the protection of God's people. If *not* receiving the love of the truth opens one up to lies, then living *in the love of the truth* provides protection from every lie. The fullness of the Holy Spirit is given to every yielded believer, and He is the One who sees all, discerns all, and guides us in the paths of truth where there is safety and protection. Let us be fully yielded and fully dependent upon Him!

Antichrist Previewed in Jewish History

We should also mention that there was a preview of this event, prophesied by Daniel,[9] which took place around the middle of the 2nd century BC under the pagan king, Antiochus IV Epiphanes. Antiochus was a ruler who eventually came out of one of the four divisions of the Greek Empire which arose after Alexander the Great died, leaving no heirs.[10] Antiochus ruled from about 175 – 164 BC as king of the Seleucid division of the empire, which Israel was a part of. He was a vainglorious, cruel tyrant. He made alliance with certain ungodly Jews and in 168 BC, entered Jerusalem and, attempting a forcible Hellenization of Israel, began a reign of terror and extermination of the Jews:

1. He went into the Temple and plundered the treasury and the gold furniture and utensils.
2. His army entered Jerusalem, plundering, murdering, and burning.
3. Men were butchered, women and children sold into slavery.
4. He then began to destroy systematically the Jewish religion, forbidding all practice of it:
   a. No burnt offerings or sacrifices.
   b. No observing of Sabbaths and feasts.
   c. Sacred books were to be surrendered.
   d. No circumcising of babies – mothers and babies were killed if they disobeyed.
   e. Altars and shrines were built for idols, swine were sacrificed, and the Jews forced to participate.
   f. Any Jew not complying was killed.
   g. Late in 168 BC, "the abomination of desolation," an image of Zeus/Jupiter, was set up in the Temple, and the Jews were required to make obeisance to it.

Besides erecting this image in the Holy of Holies, Antiochus offered a swine on the altar of the temple; both were profound desecrations. Deliverance finally came when the Maccabee brothers rose up and led an army, fighting Antiochus, defeating him, and finally removing his presence from Israel.

Daniel prophesied this event in Daniel 11, where his prophecy of this man merged, around v. 31, into a foretelling of *the man whom Antiochus prefigured, the end-time Antichrist.* This tragic and traumatic chapter in Jewish history was burned upon the Jewish psyche, so Jesus' reference in Matt. 24:15 to Daniel's prophecy is potent in giving understanding – both to Christians and to Jews -- of this event that is yet to come. Since it also was an "abomination that makes desolate," the full history of this event is very helpful for insight into events during the Great Tribulation.[11]

---

9   Dan. 8:9-12; 11:21-31.
10   Dan.7:6, 8:8, 11:4
11   Marv Rosenthal, in his *Pre-Wrath Rapture of the Church* (pp. 76-79), does an excellent job teaching on this very difficult time in Jewish history, and showing how it is a fore-shadowing of events under the Antichrist. The historical account of this period in Jewish history is found in *The Books of the Maccabees.*

The Identity of Antichrist

Do we have any clues as to the identity of this man? I cannot speak authoritatively on this but will put forth a few thoughts. Jesus said,

> **I have come in My Father's name, and you do not receive Me; if another comes in his own name, him you will receive.** John 5:43-44

Jesus warned the Jews that another would come – one *not sent by the Father* – and they would receive that one as they *should* have received Jesus. They obviously know the prophecies as to the lineage of the Messiah – He would be from the tribe of Judah, descended from King David.[12] And yet, they may not be in tune with Scripture enough to make this a requirement, as Jesus' statement seems to indicate. They will be open to someone coming with their own qualifications.

Early church fathers believed that this man would come from the tribe of Dan.[13] Dan is not listed among the twelve tribes who come early to faith in their Messiah (Rev. 7:5-8). That, along with the following Scriptures, seems to hold out the possibility of a deceiver coming from this tribe at the end:

> **Dan shall be a serpent by the way,**
> **A viper by the path,**
> **That bites the horse's heels**
> **So that its rider shall fall backward. Genesis 49:17**

This depicts an unexpected assault - and from a serpent (associated with deception) - bringing down a rider that's in full forward motion. The *whole nation* is completely upset when Antichrist turns on them at the midpoint!

> **Dan is a lion's whelp;**
> **He shall leap from Bashan. Deuteronomy 33:22**

Here we see the lion in its stalking and predatory behavior. Bashan today is known commonly as the Golan Heights, a region perpetually contested because of its strategic elevation and location -- strategic both for Israel as well as her enemies.[14] This would be a likely place from which military forces, under Antichrist's control, could launch a sudden invasion.

> **The snorting of his horses was heard from Dan.**
> **The whole land trembled at the sound of the neighing of his strong ones;**
> **For they have come and devoured the land and all that is in it,**
> **The city and those who dwell in it."**
> **For behold, I will send serpents among you,**
> **Vipers which cannot be charmed,**
> **And they shall bite you, says the Lord. Jeremiah 8:16-17 (See also Jer. 4:3-31.)**

The tribe of Dan was located in the mid-section in the western part of Israel; they also had a smaller location in the middle of the northernmost part of Israel, bordering on Lebanon. This northern location may provide a clue as to Dan's possible collaboration with enemies of Israel. Through this smaller location, along with the Golan Heights, a land invasion could be made. The mention of implacable deadly serpents, along with military might, fits the scenario of the end – the blending of deception with the military force of Antichrist. V. 16, along with the

---

12   Gen. 49:10, Jer. 23:5

13   Irenaeus, *Ante-Nicene Fathers, Vol. 1*, pp. 559, 560; Hippolytus, Treatise on Christ and Antichrist, #14&15, *Ante-Nicene Fathers, Vol. 5*, p. 207. (Online, http://www.earlychristian-writings.com/text/hippolytus-christ.html.)

14   Interestingly, a careful study of Ps. 68 shows Bashan and the Golan Heights in Israel to represent the fullness of the Holy Spirit and His gifts in the church. Both are the heights, allowing full view of what the enemy is doing, and therefore providing strategic defense against him. Like this "lion" depiction of Dan, the antichrist will spring forth as an unexpected predator from his piety and supernatural activity.

previous verse in Deuteronomy, may explain the implication of the immediate *enforcing* ability that Antichrist has as Jesus warned in Matt. 24 – when the Abomination of Desolation occurs, *flee immediately* for your lives!

We know already that the antichrist will be associated with the revived Roman Empire of the end (Dan. 9:26-27). That doesn't necessarily indicate whether he will be Jewish or not.[15] In Revelation 13, the beast man is seen rising out of the sea – the masses of humanity. Later in the chapter, the false prophet is seen arising out of the land, a term often used for Israel; so, the connection to Dan could be through the false prophet. In the end, whether the antichrist is Jewish or not, we will see the Jewish people receiving him and being taken in by him.

As we've already mentioned (Matt. 24 and 1 John 2:18), it appears that he will come *as a Christian*. Considering the great friendship of evangelical Christians toward Israel, and then making a suggested link with the tenets of *Dominion Theology*,[16] we would seem to have a plausible pathway for this man's rise within the church, especially in his initial appearing as a deceiver.

It has also been suggested that the antichrist will come as a Muslim – being one and the same as the Muslim Mahdi – the messianic figure of Islam. This suggestion is understandable. The two figures share the same goal – world domination. They seek to gain that position via the same means – by force, if necessary, and promoting chaos in the earth and then grabbing power as the chaos is exploited. Similar to the strategies of the antichrist, Islam also justifies deception when it is used to promote its goals. However, we are forced to ask the questions, "Would a Muslim go to the extent of placing himself in the church, pretending to be a Christian and embracing Christian values and teaching, to achieve this goal? Wouldn't he lose many Muslim followers in the process? Would a Muslim be able to perpetuate, in the name of Jesus, a deception so great, that if possible, the very elect of God might be deceived?" Unless we see that as feasible, I don't know how we can see this man as a Muslim. Satan knows the truth – Jesus Christ is the true Messiah. It is *the truth* that he will seek to counterfeit and imitate, not *another counterfeit*. I personally think it highly unlikely that it is Islam that we will face at the end. Islam does keep pushing forward in the earth; perhaps it will be the Ezekiel War that, before the end, will deal a decisive blow to the power of Islam.

---

15   The early church father Hippolytus appears to think this man will be Jewish, referring to him as, like Christ, being circumcised. See the quote from him in chapter 8 under 'the first seal.'

16   Without going into great detail, we note simply that Dominion Theology teaches that the church will rise progressively to take dominion in the earth over the "seven mountains" of family, religion, education, media, entertainment, business, and government. Only when the church has achieved supremacy in the earth, will Jesus return. Most of the Scriptures we are considering here as end-time, Dominion Theology sees as already fulfilled. Additionally, Dominionists place great emphasis on the supernatural works of the Holy Spirit. NOTE: This is not a personal reflection on anyone who endorses this theology, but simply an observation regarding the teaching itself.

CHAPTER 12

Why the Great Tribulation?

Before we proceed into this chapter, we need to point out that throughout these seven years, God is dealing with three primary groups:

1. The unbelieving world,
2. The church, and
3. The Jews

As we look at the reasons for the Great Tribulation, we will look at each of these and see how God's purposes differ for each group.

We have just taken a somewhat skeletal look at Antichrist and of the events that take place under his leadership. Knowing that God is not only allowing all this, but *directing it,* we ask ourselves "Why?" Why will He allow such tremendous evil and all the pain to humanity that will come from it?

We may not be able to know the full answer to that question, but there are some insights we gain from Scripture. First, and in a very primary way, it is described as a *time of testing*:

> **Because you have kept my word about patient endurance, I will keep you from the hour of trial[1] that is coming on the whole world, to try[1] those who dwell on the earth. Revelation 3:10 ESV**

> [1]*peirasmos* G3986T – trial, proving, temptation; adversity or affliction that serves to test or prove one's character, faith, holiness

The Great Tribulation is the season for the finalizing of people's choices. The testing will be very intense and it is for the purpose of causing all people to *make choices* – true choices from the heart, that will, in turn, *manifest* the bottom line of their hearts. This is the fruit that must come forth and come to full ripeness, because *the time of the earth's <u>harvest</u> is just around the corner.*[1] This harvest involves the wicked as well as the righteous. Therefore, **this time of fruit-bearing means that we will see wicked deeds manifesting in people's lives like never before**; likewise, we will see great righteousness manifesting among the people of God! Let us take a look at what this means for our three groups:

---

1 See Matt. 13:30, 39; James 5:7-8; Rev. 14:14-20

Testing for Unbelievers

Great pressures under the early seals, culminating with the fifth seal, will force people "off the fence" over issues of right and wrong and truth. Paul tells us that all who do not walk in *a love for the truth* will *not have protection* against deception but will fall prey to *"the lie"* (2 Thess. 2:11). I am of the opinion that "the lie" referred to here is the original lie from the Garden – that God can't be trusted, He doesn't have your best interests in mind, you are better off making your own truth and choosing your own path. Don't bother with Him or with trying to please Him. This is the "winner lie" as far as Satan is concerned, because anyone who falls for it removes himself from the protection of God and makes himself vulnerable to the traps and enticements of the devil. This essential issue is always the test for mankind – what to do with God and His Son and His truth – but there will be an *intensification* of this test under the challenges and pressures brought about by the antichrist. Indifference will no longer be possible.

Scripture repeatedly uses the word *anomia* – lawlessness -- to describe this period of time.[2] It is this very culture of lawlessness - a refusal to submit to authority, whether God's or man's - which will take over humankind and will consequently *allow the full manifestation of what is in people's hearts.* When cultural mores and requirements are strong, people usually conform to these requirements – at least outwardly -- in order to be accepted in society; behavior that violates these cultural "laws" must be done in secret. But when these moral and societal requirements grow lax, then uniformity also goes, and what is really in the hearts of people can come forth. **This is the maturing of the fruit of wickedness in preparation for the harvest. It is *God's will* that the fruit of each heart and life come into visible manifestation in the earth as we head into the time of harvest.** It is distressing for the righteous to live among and witness this level of evil, but we are encouraged to know that this is the reason why God is allowing it. He must be fully righteous and justified in the tremendous judgment of destruction that He is going to pour out upon the wicked before the kingdom of this world comes crashing down.

Testing for the Church

There are, as we all well know, many in the church today asserting that the church will not be present for this time of testing. We are not going to deal with that issue in this section, but will leave it for our progression through the *chronology,* which, we will see, does not support the full church leaving before this time. With the Lord's grace, we must face this time and embrace God's purposes in it for the church. As we do, we remember that down through the centuries of church history, during the times of intense pressure and persecution, God's supply of overcoming grace has always carried His people through victoriously. What do we perceive then to be God's purposes for the church during this time?

There will be an unprecedented marginalizing of true believers as all nations turn against them at this time.

> **Then they will deliver you up to tribulation and kill you, and you will be hated *by all nations* for My name's sake. Matthew 24:9** (emphasis added)

Luke's account amplifies this:

> **12 . . . They will lay their hands on you and persecute you, delivering you up to the synagogues and prisons. You will be brought before kings and rulers for My name's sake.**
> **13 But it will turn out for you as an occasion for testimony.**
> **14 Therefore settle it in your hearts not to meditate beforehand on what you will answer;**
> **15 for I will give you a mouth and wisdom which all your adversaries will not be able to contradict or resist. Luke 21:12-15**

---

2   Because of lawlessness, the *agape* of many will grow cold (Matt. 24:21); the antichrist is called "the Man of Lawlessness" (2 Thess. 2:3); this hidden work of lawlessness, the power behind the Man of Lawlessness, was already at work in the early church (2 Thess. 2:7) – it is the power behind the Antichrist Spirit; and finally, all those who "do lawlessness" will be expunged from the kingdom at the end (Matt. 7:23, 13:41).

These are the trials of Jesus Himself that we face – they come on account of Him, and we face them for His sake. He said to the disciples, and says to His disciples of all time,

> **You are those who have continued with me in my trials. I confer on you a kingdom, even as my Father conferred on me. . . Luke 22:28-29 WEB**

As we share in His trials, we share also in His victory over them, even as we share in the authority of the kingdom that will follow.

The Nature of the Trial

Here God identifies the nature of their trial under 'the Assyrian'[3] and reassures His people:

> **Therefore, thus says the Lord God of hosts: "O My people, who dwell in Zion, do not be afraid of the Assyrian. He shall strike you with a rod and lift up his staff against you, in the manner of Egypt.**
> **For yet a very little while and the indignation will cease. . ." Isaiah 10:24-25[4]**

Notice that after urging us *not to fear*, God lets us know that the Assyrian will oppose the saints by "striking with a rod," and "lifting up a staff in the manner of Egypt." These speak of the two primary tests for the church:

1. The rod speaks of persecution. There is a great test brought about by the inability to buy or sell without the mark of the beast. The mark must be refused: Anyone who worships the beast and his image or receives the mark in his forehead or hand will not be saved but will undergo the wrath and judgment of God. And yet to refuse it will mean difficulty in meeting needs, even basic ones, and will also mean the threat of execution and martyrdom. This itself will test the people of God – they will need to rely deeply on the Lord for His care, provision, and protection for them, with a willingness to lay down their lives for Him if called upon to do so. Neither of these tests are something new for the church. They will simply affect the whole church worldwide in a way not before experienced. *The living Christ within us is more than sufficient for the challenge!*

2. The lifting up of the staff after the manner of Egypt brings to mind the challenge Moses encountered from the Egyptian magicians when he displayed the power of God to the court of Pharoah. We have talked about the great supernatural works the enemy will display, even as the Holy Spirit is being poured out upon the church right before the final harvest. This will be *very finely tuned* deception produced by the enemy – his counterfeits both of supernatural *works* as well as of revelatory *teaching* of God and His truth. These counterfeits will be so close to the real thing, that complete reliance on the Holy Spirit will be needed to detect the true from the false. Of the two tests, this one may prove to be the more challenging.

Both of these will test our surrender to the Lord and reliance upon Him, rather than upon ourselves and our own abilities and resources. We will be drawn *into* Him, the more we rely upon Him. We will find Him to be *more than enough,* and ourselves to be *more than conquerors!* In refusing fear and choosing trust, we shall overcome! We will find direction from Jesus as He faced the cross, expressed prophetically through David:

> **I have set the Lord always before me: because he is at my right hand, I shall not be moved.**
> **Psalm 16:8**

---

3   Or "Asshur" - His term here – and in various places in the Old Testament -- for the antichrist.
4   There are elect Jews to whom these words apply, even as they apply to the spiritual 'Zion' which is the church; see 1 Peter 2:5-6 and Heb. 12:22.

As Christ did, and as the saints do whenever they face difficulties, we will set our hearts in such a way that they will hold steadfast, empower us to give testimony, and bring glory to the Lord. With our hearts so set, we will find mighty grace from the Lord to carry us through, *more than overcomers.*[5] We will look later at God's work with the church at this time, but suffice to say at this point, that there will be great power and glory upon His people, even in the midst of persecution.

We must remember also, that with the completion of the Great Commission and the great multitudes that have entered the kingdom, there will be many new believers. There will not be much *time* for the Lord to take them through the usual processes of trials and growth. The trials of the Great Tribulation are a 'crash course' in maturation for many of them.

God's Purpose in this Trial

In the midst of this suffering and testing, the Bride is undergoing an intense time of purification and growth under the outpouring of the Holy Spirit coming to her directly, as well as through the two witnesses (which we will touch on later.) There is a diminishing of the flesh and at the same time, great building up in the Spirit of God's people. The Father's purpose for her is that she come into the perfection of Christ Himself, growing up "in every way into Him who is the Head," that she might be presented to Him a glorious Bride, not having spot or wrinkle or any such flaw.[6] The Jewish maid Esther, a picture of the church, was taken through very careful preparation before going in to King Ahasuerus: Under the guidance of Hegai (a type of the Holy Spirit), she was purified with six months of oil of myrrh (suffering) and six months of 'sweet odors' (Esther 2:12). So also, God's precious people will go through deep and final purifying through suffering and through great anointing in preparation for their heavenly Bridegroom.

At this time the beautiful fruit of holiness will be brought forth upon the whole Bride. This is an *outworking* of the inner righteousness imputed to the saints as a gift.[7] **Because of this work of God in His people, to see this simply as a dark and fearful time is to miss seeing it as God does, an exceedingly precious time which will bear fruit for eternity.**

This is also the time when many are turning away from the faith, and like the world, are not receiving the love of the truth. Like those in the world, they are then left open to deception, even while they may remain professing Christians.

We have not yet dealt with the timing of the rapture, but will simply say here that it appears that this time of tribulation for the church is fairly brief.

Testing for the Jews

This will be a particularly difficult time for Israel. It was this nation specifically which, following centuries of national homelessness and persecution and hostility from the nations, had a covenant – a pledge of friendship – with this man. The shocking act of sacrilege that reveals him for who he really is takes place in their land, their capitol city, and their most holy site, the Holy of Holies. From the moment he commits that act, the people of Israel, especially of Jerusalem and Judea, are his immediate targets. Jesus particularly warned the people of Judea to flee (Matt. 24:16). The shock and horror of this betrayal can hardly be overstated. This was a man they *trusted.* As Jesus prophesied, they had *received* him. For all that Israel has been through as a nation, this now begins what Scripture calls *the worst trial Israel has ever known:*

> **At that time Michael shall stand up, the great prince who stands watch over the sons of your people; and there shall be a time of trouble, such as never was since there was a nation, even to that time. Daniel 12:1**

> **Alas! For that day is great, so that none is like it; it is even the time of Jacob's trouble, but he shall be saved out of it. Jeremiah 30:7 KJV**

---

5   Romans 8:37
6   Eph. 4:13-15, 5:25-27
7   Phil. 2:12-13; 2 Cor. 7:1; Heb. 12:14; 1 John 3:2-3

We are told by other Scriptures that there will be fire, war, captivity, and of course, death.[8] As Daniel prophesies:

. . . for many days they shall fall by sword and flame, by captivity and plundering. Daniel 11:33

In making the covenant with Antichrist, Israel will lean upon and look to him, rather than to their God. The depth of their trust in him will go as deep as their rebellion and blindness toward God. As we pointed out previously, in making this covenant and making it from a place of spiritual blindness, they will unwittingly make a covenant with *death and hell!* Over 2,000 years before they will make this covenant, God had warned them:

**Therefore, hear the word of the Lord, you scornful men who rule this people who are
in Jerusalem.
You have said, "We have made a covenant with death,
And with Sheol we are in agreement.
When the overflowing scourge passes through,
It will not come to us,
For we have made lies our refuge,
And under falsehood we have hidden ourselves." Isaiah 28:15**

At the time the treaty is made, the leaders of Israel are proud scoffers, still deeply resistant to God. God warns that the treaty will devastate them; embracing a false messiah while still rejecting their true Messiah will bring them low. The one they trusted will turn against them, unleashing on them a tremendous storm of evil that, in its rushing devastation, will sweep away the refuge of lies and will utterly smash this covenant. Israel will be ravaged. Daniel was told:

**. . . it shall be for a time, times, and half a time; and when *the power of the holy people has
been completely shattered*, all these things shall be finished. Daniel 12:7** (emphasis added)

It will look like a terrible enemy is doing this. Satan is *finally* positioned to crush these people he has hated so long! But look what the Lord says about all this:

**Oh Assyrian, the rod of my anger, in whose hand is the club of My wrath.
I will send him against a hypocritical nation, and against the people of My wrath will I
give him a charge, to take the spoil, and to take the prey, and to tread them down like the
mire of the streets. Isaiah 10:5-6**

God calls Antichrist's power to devastate His people "the club of My wrath," making clear that *He* is shattering His own people, working among them as though He is out to destroy them![9] Why?

When God looks at Israel at this time, with their rebuilt temple and all the offerings and ritual taking place, what He sees is *continued rebellion against Him* and rejection of their Messiah. It might look all pious outwardly, but God, who looks upon the heart, sees *hypocrisy*. They are essentially in the *same place spiritually* as they were 2000 years earlier when they crucified Christ. He sees the same willful blindness and refusal to repent and turn to Him from the heart. All of this has aroused His wrath. They are not "My people," but "the people of My wrath." The rebellion and spiritual blindness are so deeply embedded in their national psyche, that it is only through the depth and extent of their suffering during this period that they will finally break and turn back to Him. No one understands this as well as God, who has allowed and, in a sense, *constructed*, this whole scenario to accomplish *His* purposes.

---

8 See Joel 3:1-6, Zech. 14:1-2, Amos 9:9, Is. 6:11-13. The restoration spoken of gives an idea of the devastation: Jer. 30:8-21, 31:1-14, Zeph. 3:8-20.
9 This is His people Israel, not the church. Again, we will look more carefully at this later.

This mighty "Assyrian" will completely miss that he is merely a tool in God's hands, and in his arrogance will see himself as the great one, the invincible one, amassing a great kingdom. But God says that when His full work in Zion and Jerusalem is completed, then He will turn and punish the insolent heart of the king of Assyria (see Is. 10:12, 15ff). He will toss aside the tool He has used and rejoice in the completed work!

God's Mercy Throughout the Terror

The last half of this seven-year period is showdown time between God and Israel. It's now or never, and God's purpose is that in the extremity of the trial there will be those who turn to Him.

> **32 Those who do wickedly against the covenant shall he [antichrist] corrupt with flattery; but the people who know their God shall be strong,[1] and carry out great exploits.**
> **33 And those of the people who understand[2] shall instruct[3] many, yet for [certain] days they shall fall[4] by sword and flame, by captivity,[10] and plundering.**
> **34 Now when they fall,[4] they shall be aided with a little help; but many shall join with them by intrigue.[5]**
> **35 And some of those of understanding[2] shall fall,[4] to refine them, purify them, and make them white, until the time of the end; because it is still for the appointed time. Daniel 11:32-35**

[1]*chazaq* H2388B - to strengthen, to prevail, to harden, to be strong, firm, courageous
[2]*sakal* H7919B - to act with wisdom and understanding; to have insight and comprehension
[3]*biyn* H995B – to have or to teach wisdom, discernment, understanding
[4]*kashal* H3782B – stumble, stagger, totter
[5]*chalaqlaqqah* H2519B - flattery, slipperiness, fine promises, smoothness

This is very instructive of God's careful and complex dealings with His people at this time. Notice the separating going on in v. 32. Those who are not loyal to the covenant (the Old Covenant) in their hearts will be exposed and will be vulnerable to deceit and seduction, as we see hints of again in v. 34b. The need for others to join with will make them susceptible to dangerous and deceptive alliances. But those who know God will stand, growing even stronger in the midst of it, and will be used in great ways by God.

In vv. 33-34a, there will be light and wisdom and *help* available, although it will not be enough to stop what is happening. We see in v. 35 that God's work here with the Jews does not have the same finality as with the world and the church. There is opportunity to make mistakes, to learn, to turn around and change direction. Even those of understanding will fall, but repentance is still available - it is all for their *refining and purifying*. God declares again later this separating and purifying of Israel as His goal:

> **Many shall be purified, made white, and refined, but the wicked shall do wickedly; and none of the wicked shall understand, but the wise shall understand. Daniel 12:10**

In this separating, some of them will turn early, with true hearts. Others will hold out longer and will begin to turn only under God's direct wrath when it comes. It will be difficult to see Israel go through this. Many will be killed and go through great suffering – young and old, children and families. The devastation of the Holocaust under Hitler has caused Israel to vow, "Never again!" But tragically, even that vow has been uttered out of self-sufficiency, not out of humble reliance upon God. Only repentance and faith in the blood of Jesus can spare anyone from the fruit of their rebellion. This vow will dissipate like ashes in the wind when they go through this terrible time that is yet future.

Isaiah speaks of the strangeness of God acting in such a way against Israel - of God working his *strange work* and bringing to pass His *strange act,* "strange" here meaning "alien, foreign." In chapter 28 he goes on to say that

---

10   NOTE: Joel agrees with this reference to captivity, saying that in the day when God settles all the scores, He will recompense the nations around Israel for selling the children of Judah and Jerusalem out of the country into slavery, Joel 3:1-7. See also Zech. 14:2.

God, who created the multiplicity of plants and crops, and who has perfect knowledge of how to grow and harvest each plant effectively without destroying it in the process (vv. 23-29), also *knows exactly* what kind of rough treatment is needed in His final harvest of Israel. <u>Not a grain or kernel will be damaged or crushed, but that it will be a redemptive hurt</u>. We can be comforted by this – that God sees and knows every individual; He is weighing every aspect of this trial and knows the ones who are His elect. His eyes will be on them and His protection over them, even when they do not yet know Him.

The Remnant

A wonderful promise regarding this difficult time is found in Daniel 12:

> **And at that time your people shall be delivered, everyone who is found written in the book. v.1**

God knows perfectly each one who will eventually come to Him, and His protection is over them. A remnant will come through all of it and be the Lord's, as the Word prophesies:

> **And so all Israel will be saved, as it is written: "The Deliverer will come out of Zion, and He will turn away ungodliness from Jacob…" Romans 11:26**

What will His completed work with this remnant look like?

> **It will come to pass in that day that the remnant of Israel, and those who have escaped from the house of Jacob *will no more again lean on him who struck them, but shall lean on Yahweh, the Holy One of Israel, in truth.***
> **A remnant will return, even the remnant of Jacob, to the mighty God.**
>
> **Isaiah 10:20-21 WEB** (emphasis added)

And from Zephaniah:

> **I will leave in your midst a meek and humble people,**
> **And they shall trust in the name of the Lord.**
> **The remnant of Israel shall do no unrighteousness and speak no lies,**
> **Nor shall a deceitful tongue be found in their mouth. Zephaniah 3:12-13**

Here is strategic, amazing wisdom from "the Lord of hosts, wonderful in counsel and excellent in working."[11] Even as He promised in Daniel 9, He knows just how to bring His work with Israel to completion by the end of the 70th week. Although it will be such a difficult time from a human standpoint, from God's standpoint, it is a necessary and glorious time, issuing forth in the beauty of holiness for His people Israel.

A Fourth Group

Although we are not focusing on them here, it might be good to mention a fourth group also going through this period of time. Probably a much smaller group, these are those who have not professed faith in Christ and who therefore do not go in the rapture, but who also do not take the mark of the beast. They survive, remarkably, both the Great Tribulation as well as the Day of the Lord judgments and stand before Jesus at the end of the 70th week, and are judged by Him as either 'sheep' or 'goats.' The righteous 'sheep' (Matt. 25:31ff) will enter the Millennium as believers, and, still having mortal bodies, will, along with the Jews, repopulate the earth during that 1,000-year period. We will take a closer look at them later.

---

11   Isaiah 28:29

Summary of the First Five Seals

We have spent extra time on some of this explanatory material relating to the Great Tribulation, so before we continue, let's review the chronology of the seals we've covered. Toward the end of **the seventh church age**, Laodicea, we see the **first four seal** events begin to unfold: Antichrist is coming forth as a good man and a great leader, gaining authority and power in the earth, unperceived (except by discerning saints, as well as others who are complicit with him) as to what his malevolent intentions really are. As he rises, the ten regional divisions of the earth are probably already in place, with a leader over each of them taking his position, although individual nations may still have their autonomy. Wars, famine, and disease are occurring around the world, along with great economic disparity – a few are wealthy, most are in great poverty. There is widespread death. True believers are being increasingly marginalized by an unbelieving world, even as they move – amidst both persecution and great anointing -- to complete the Great Commission.

Finally, with the **fifth seal**, the antichrist comes to full power, resulting in great persecution, particularly of Jews and Christians. Jerusalem is occupied by Antichrist; Jews are in flight, being persecuted and killed, with some being sent, again, into exile and slavery. As we know, this "man of sin" remains in power for the appointed duration – the final 3½ years -- although as we shall see, something happens that diminishes the effectiveness of his power. Great supernatural signs and miracles are occurring, some from God through the saints, and others from Satan in a confusing counterfeit strategy to lead people astray.

We state again - *we have not yet seen the catching up of the church* as we have progressed chronologically. We are now on the **cusp of the sixth seal**, and everything is about to change.

But before we proceed with the chronology, there is one more important issue we need to deal with, and that is the care of the Heavenly Father for His people under the rule of Antichrist.

CHAPTER 13

God's Care for His People During the Great Tribulation

By late spring of 1991, after studying end-time Scriptures rather intensively for about nine months, I had come to the belief that the church will be here for part of the Great Tribulation. This was troubling for me, and I went to the Lord about it, asking Him how He was going to take care of His people during that time if they couldn't buy or sell (because they would refuse the mark of the beast). I asked Him specifically whether they needed to stockpile food and provisions ahead of time, or whether He was going to provide for them supernaturally. Within a day or two of my question, I was out on our deck with my Bible early one Sunday morning. It was a lovely morning and quiet, as the rest of the family were all still in bed. I opened the Bible and found myself reading in Mark 8.

As you will see if you go there, it is the account of the feeding of the 4,000. Jesus multiplied seven loaves and a few small fish, fed everyone, and afterward the disciples gathered seven baskets of fragments left over. I then proceeded to read what followed the feeding, in vv. 9-21. This is a bit lengthy, but it is so important, that I'm going to put it out here before we discuss it.

> **9 Now those who had eaten were about four thousand. And He sent them away,**
>
> **10 and immediately got into the boat with His disciples, and came to the region of Dalmanutha.**
>
> **11 Then the Pharisees came out and began to dispute with Him, seeking from Him a sign from heaven, testing Him.**
>
> **12 But He sighed deeply in His spirit, and said, "Why does this generation seek a sign? Assuredly, I say to you, no sign shall be given to this generation."**
>
> **13 And He left them, and getting into the boat again, departed to the other side.**
>
> **14 Now the disciples had forgotten to take bread, and they did not have more than one loaf with them in the boat.**
>
> **15 Then He charged them, saying, "Take heed, beware of the leaven of the Pharisees and the leaven of Herod."**
>
> **16 And they reasoned among themselves, saying, "It is because we have no bread."**
>
> **17 But Jesus, being aware of it, said to them, "Why do you reason because you have no bread? Do you not yet perceive nor understand? Is your heart still hardened?**

18 Having eyes, do you not see? And having ears, do you not hear? And do you not remember?

19 When I broke the five loaves for the five thousand, how many baskets full of fragments did you take up?" They said to Him, "Twelve."

20 "Also, when I broke the seven for the four thousand, how many large baskets full of fragments did you take up?" And they said, "Seven."

21 So He said to them, "How is it you do not understand?" Mark 8:9-21

This is a remarkable incident with which I was already familiar, and which had blessed me in the past when I realized what Jesus was saying. Along with the feeding incident, it contains part of God's answer to my question. In Dalmanutha some Pharisees, faithfully consistent with their usual hostility toward Him, came testing Him. I would guess that this incident, as unremarkably typical as it was, barely registered with the disciples. And so, a short time later, when He charged them to "beware of the leaven of the Pharisees and the leaven of Herod," they did not connect it with the encounter that had just happened.

It was probably getting on toward mealtime again, and their stomachs were growling, and Jesus' comment coincided with their realization that they had *forgotten those seven baskets of leftovers!* There they were on the ship, and no food! I can just feel their frustration with themselves: "What dufuses we are!! There was all that food, and we forgot – *again!*" (I'm sure this wasn't the first time they'd forgotten to plan ahead for provisions.) They proceeded to assume that Jesus, in a very kind way, was rebuking them for their irresponsibility and forgetfulness.

But Jesus was in a *whole different place* than they were, and He rebuked them for their blindness and *slowness* in understanding. This was the second supernatural feeding in just a short time, and by now, they should have been connecting the two amazing miracles with *God's heart and character and ability* toward them! His supernatural provision had been lavished freely both times, and with much left over. Yet here they were, such a short time later, seeing it all as depending on them, and beating themselves up internally for failing to be on top of things. This is the typical mentality of *independence from God* -- causing guilt over our failure to perform up to our own and others' expectations -- that we find in 'natural' man; that is, man who hasn't learned dependence upon and implicit trust in God's care for us.

What God had very emphatically spoken to me in the past, through this incident, was, "You must understand, that when your heart is tender and open to Me and trusting Me, there is nothing you can do or fail to do, that is truly a problem. I can *always* come through for you, meet whatever need you have, and fix whatever problem you have. *I have the resources, the ability, and the willingness to come through for you always!* Do not kick yourself over your lack of perfection – the times when you *forget* something, or when you fail at something, or when you don't come through in the way you – or others – think you should. None of that is a problem for Me when you are looking to Me. *I can and will fix anything* for you. *The problem for Me* arises when a person's heart is hard and resistant and hostile to me. That's when My hands are tied and I can do nothing to help! My concern in the situation was not over where the next meal was coming from. I knew the Father's heart, and His ability and willingness to provide. What I was concerned with was the rebellious hearts of the religious leaders, rebellion that was *veiled over* with religiosity and piety and assumed superiority. I knew the disciples did not discern these issues, and could be hoodwinked by them, and that's where My true concern was. But they were still caught up in issues of guilt, self-reproach, inadequacy, irresponsibility, and so on; and because of that, could not come to where *I* was and understand what I was wanting to teach them."

I realized that day on my deck, that God was taking the lessons of that incident and applying them to His people at the end-time. That when that time comes, a time of seeming lack and impossibility over the *basic necessities* for food and other provision, God's provision will be *more than enough* if we are looking to Him and seeing Him correctly; that is, seeing His great love, ability, and willingness to provide for us in ways we couldn't imagine, even if we tried. *He will be faithful.* I was sitting there, pondering that, when a tiny whiff of a breeze came along. It lifted a page of my Bible and turned it over so that now I was at Mark 6 and the feeding of the 5,000! (Incidentally, it was 5,000 men, so with women and children, it was likely a crowd as large as 15,000, and that's probably a conservative estimate.) I proceeded to read *that*, and the incident that followed that feeding. Here it is:

> **45** Immediately He made His disciples get into the boat and go before Him to the other side, to Bethsaida, while He sent the multitude away.
>
> **46** And when He had sent them away, He departed to the mountain to pray.
>
> **47** Now when evening came, the boat was in the middle of the sea; and He was alone on the land.
>
> **48** Then He saw them straining at rowing, for the wind was against them. Now about the fourth watch of the night He came to them, walking on the sea, and would have passed them by.
>
> **49** And when they saw Him walking on the sea, they supposed it was a ghost, and cried out;
>
> **50** for they all saw Him and were troubled. But immediately He talked with them and said to them, "Be of good cheer! It is I; do not be afraid."
>
> **51** Then He went up into the boat to them, and the wind ceased. And they were greatly amazed in themselves beyond measure, and marveled.
>
> **52** For they had not understood about the loaves, because their heart was hardened.

Mark 6:45-52

Now when I read this, the Holy Spirit began immediately to speak to me, drawing this out as a picture of things in the end-time. This is what I heard Him saying:

> As in the incident back then, I am no longer with My disciples physically, but have left them in order to be with My Father in heaven. I have given them instructions to launch out and go to the other side. That is, the church, represented by the boat, is out on the sea of the world, with instructions to be faithful until they arrive at the other side – which is the end, My return. The fourth watch, between 3 am and 6 am, is the darkest part of the night. It represents the period at the end of the age, when the wind – the blowing of the enemy – will be strong against them. He will be stirring up great waves of turmoil in the world, seeking to bring fear and to push them off course. This will be a difficult time. But I will walk near them; I will be there supernaturally. But I will never impose Myself on anyone, even on My people, and I will wait to be *invited* to be in their midst and to help them. The *key issue,* again, is that My people have *tender hearts toward Me;* that they keep their hearts open and trusting and let Me into every situation so that I am *able* to help them. As in this story, My Presence is the needed thing; with it, every need is met.

This was for me such a sweet and instructive word. We have talked about the *test* aspects of this period of time, and surely, this will be a key test for God's people. **Whenever there is a breakdown in the systems of human society, particularly the usual means of protection (e.g., a strong and just military/police force) or of provision, it becomes necessary for *individuals* to establish God Himself as their Protector and Provider.** There are so many promises in God's Word that assure us of His willingness to do just this for His people – to provide for and protect them in every type of situation. Will we have this kind of heart to receive all that He is willing to do for us in this time of need? *Knowing* that He will be there – surely and infallibly – will make us fearless overcomers, no matter what the challenge. Even in the face of death, we will fear *no evil,* for He is with us!

So, in these two supernatural feedings, along with the incidents that followed, I heard the Lord's answer to my question. It was yes to both parts of my question: He will provide through those who have set food aside ahead of time, *and* He will provide supernaturally. And as with these feedings, when the ones with provision, no matter how inadequate it seems, are willing to share it, holding it up to Him for His blessing, He will *multiply it* and make that provision *supernatural* so that there is more than enough to meet the need! The key is that hearts be open, tender, trusting, yielded to Him, and determined to be faithful to Him, *no matter the cost*. What a lovely God we serve, with all that we need to be *more than overcomers!*

Although there is more that could be said about this period of time, we are going to move on now to the very remarkable sixth seal. The events of this seal are unveiled in Scripture as utterly amazing – thrilling for some, and terrifying for others, but one way or the other, impacting every person on the earth.

---

18 The Lord knows the days of the upright and blameless, and their heritage will abide forever.

19 They shall not be put to shame in the time of evil; and in the days of famine, they shall be satisfied.

39 But the salvation of the [consistently] righteous is of the Lord; He is their Refuge and secure Stronghold in the time of trouble.

40 And the Lord helps them and delivers them; He delivers them from the wicked and saves them, because they trust and take refuge in Him. Psalm 37 AMP

* * *

18 The Lord watches over those who obey him, those who trust in his constant love.

19 He saves them from death; he keeps them alive in times of famine. Psalm 33 TEV

* * *

7 The angel of the Lord encamps around those who fear him, and delivers them. ESV

16 The face of the Lord is against those who do evil, to cut off the memory of them from the earth.

17 When the righteous cry for help, the Lord hears and delivers them out of all their troubles. ESV

21 Evil shall slay the wicked: and they that hate the righteous shall be desolate.

22 The Lord redeems the soul of his servants: and none of them that trust in him shall be desolate. KJV

Psalm 34

GOD STEPS ONSTAGE

CHAPTER 14

The Sixth Seal

We summarized conditions on the earth leading up to and including the Great Tribulation at the end of chapter 12. So, we know the earth is gripped in the rule of Antichrist when the next prophesied event, the sixth seal, takes place. Let's look now, comparing it with Jesus' teaching in the Olivet Discourse.

The Sixth Seal

There are actually several events associated with this seal and we will look at them separately, so our discussion of it will be quite extensive. These three events are as follows:

1. Cosmic and Seismic Phenomena

Revelation 6	Matthew 24
12 I looked when He opened the sixth seal, and behold, there was a great earthquake; and the sun became black as sackcloth of hair, and the moon became like blood. 13 And the stars of heaven fell to the earth, as a fig tree drops its late figs when it is shaken by a mighty wind. 14 Then the sky receded as a scroll when it is rolled up, and every mountain and island was moved out of its place.	29 Immediately after the tribulation of those days the sun will be darkened, and the moon will not give its light; the stars will fall from heaven, and the powers of the heavens will be shaken.

Here we see tremendous phenomena occurring in the heavens, along with a great earthquake. We will discuss that shortly, but first will go to chapter 7 of Revelation, as it contains <u>two very important events</u> which pertain to the 6th seal. The first event is not mentioned in Jesus' teaching, so we will cover it here without the comparison of Jesus' teaching:

2. 144,000 Jews Sealed

In Rev. 7:3 we see the command given not to harm the earth, sea, or trees until the servants of God have been sealed in their foreheads. John heard the number of those sealed. It was 144,000 Jews – 12,000 out of each of the following tribes: Judah, Reuben, Gad, Asher, Naphtali, Manasseh, Simeon, Levi, Issachar, Zebulun, Joseph, and Benjamin (Ephraim and

Dan are omitted). Those Jews sealed are called "the bondservants of God," and the seal they are given will provide special protection from the judgments of God which are about to take place. We will look more closely at this group shortly. The second important event mentioned in Revelation 7 is the third and final event of the 6th seal:

3. The Catching up of the Church

Revelation 7	Matthew 24
9 After these things I looked, and behold, a great multitude which no one could number, of all nations, tribes, peoples, and tongues, standing before the throne and before the Lamb, clothed with white robes, with palm branches in their hands, 13 Then one of the elders answered, saying to me, "Who are these arrayed in white robes, and where did they come from?" 14 And I said to him, "Sir, you know." So he said to me, "These are the ones who come out of the great tribulation…, and washed their robes and made them white in the blood of the Lamb.	30 Then the sign of the Son of Man will appear in heaven, and then all the tribes of the earth will mourn, and they will see the Son of Man coming on the clouds of heaven with power and great glory. 31 And He will send His angels with a great sound of a trumpet, and they will gather together His elect from the four winds, from one end of heaven to the other.

If we peek ahead to Revelation 8, we see the seventh seal removed and the scroll finally opened. Following that, trumpets are given the seven angels which stand before the Lord, and with the sounding of each trumpet, a judgment is released upon the earth, beginning with the trees, grass, and sea -- the judgments that had been held back until the exact number of Jews could be sealed. These judgments are the beginning of the *wrath of God*.

We see then, in summary, that the sixth seal directly *precedes* the Day of the Lord's wrath, and consists of these three events:

1. The great earthquake and cosmic signs and shakings
2. The sealing of 144,000 Jews
3. The gathering and catching up of a great multitude of believers from the earth

Let's take a closer look now at each of these events.

1. The Cosmic Disturbances

Tremendous events will suddenly occur with the 6th seal. There will be a full eclipse of both the sun and the moon. For those in daytime, the darkening of the light will capture everyone's attention; for those on the other side of the earth, the moon will turn red, but lest they are sleeping and miss it, the earthquake will shake them awake. Whether in day or night, the events seem designed to bring all people outside and looking *up*. There will be a shower of stars plummeting from the heavens and whizzing by the earth,[1] and the heavens will disappear, rolling up as a scroll. Here finally, the definition of "apocalyptic" is truly realized! This is a convulsion of apocalyptic proportions of the earth and the heavens, signaling *God's arrival on the scene!*

Revelation goes on to say:

> **And the kings of the earth, the great men, the rich men, the commanders, the mighty men, every slave and every free man, hid themselves in the caves and in the rocks of the mountains, and said to the mountains and rocks, "Fall on us and hide us from the face of Him who sits on the throne and from the wrath of the Lamb!**
> **For the great day of His wrath has come, and who is able to stand?" Revelation 6:12-17**

---

1 Is. 34:4, Mark 13:25, Rev. 6:13, 2 Peter 3:10

It no longer matters whether people claimed to believe in God or not. When these things happen, they know Who is behind it, and their response is one of terror. Luke's account tells us:

> **And there will be signs in the sun, in the moon, and in the stars; and on the earth distress[1] of nations, with perplexity[2], the sea and the waves roaring; men's hearts failing them from fear and the expectation of those things which are coming on the earth, for the powers of the heavens will be shaken. Luke 21:25-26**

> [1]*sunoche* G4928T – straits, anguish, distress, a narrowing of the way
> [2]*aporia* G640S, from *aporeo* G639S – to have no way out, at a loss (mentally)

These are events far beyond human control or human recourse. They could come only from the Creator of the universe; they are His announcement of the *end of the age*. He is about to step onto center stage as the Judge of all, the One to whom every man must give an account.[2]

What is coming will affect *everyone*. For the righteous, it is joy – their redemption has arrived! But for the ungodly, it is the end of all things as they have known them. *Nothing will ever be the same again.* The time of reckoning has arrived, and arrived for everyone, regardless of their standing in society! The Bible tells us that terror strikes all alike – police, paramedics, politicians, the military, the great, the small – there is no recourse, no way to avoid what is coming. From great wealth to political power to nuclear weapons – all of man's strength and resources are as nothing. This will now be every man for himself in a situation *way beyond* anything that the earth has ever had to deal with in the past. Men will collapse not only with what's happening, but with an instinctive fear of what will *follow.* As men themselves declare, "The **great day of His wrath has come, and *who shall be able to stand?*"** (v. 17, emphasis added).

What is the Day of God's Wrath?

The Day of God's Wrath was a time spoken of many times by Old Testament prophets, a time when God would involve Himself personally in the affairs of the earth, righting wrongs, judging sinners, vindicating the godly, and establishing justice and righteousness in the earth. We will look later at details given about it in the Word, but for now, we will simply say that it is God's direct intervention on the earth as He brings this age to a close.

It is also spoken of frequently in the New Testament as "the Day of Christ," or "the day of our Lord Jesus Christ," although we are not always tuned into it, as most of us have not been taught about the Day of the Lord.[3] For example:

> **. . . being confident of this very thing, that He who has begun a good work in you will complete it until the day of Jesus Christ.**
> **. . . that you may be sincere and without offense till the day of Christ. Philippians 1:6, 7**

Sometimes it is referred to simply as "that day":

> **I know whom I have believed and am persuaded that He is able to keep what I have committed to Him until *that Day*. 2 Timothy 1:12**
> **...the crown of righteousness, which the Lord, the righteous Judge, will give to me on *that Day*... 2 Timothy 4:8** (emphasis added)

We have already seen that the Lamb is the One who was found worthy to take the scroll from the Father and to open it. When the seventh seal is removed and the scroll is finally opened (Rev. 8), the Lamb will begin to dispense its contents via seven angels with trumpets. With the sounding of each trumpet, one after another, a judgment of God is released. These are the judgments, which, along with other righteous events, will bring this

---

2   Heb. 4:13b
3   Other references are found in 1 Thess. 5:4; 2 Thess. 1:10, 2:3; 2 Tim. 1:12, 18; 2 Tim. 4:8.

present age to a close and cleanse the earth for the coming age. Because the Lamb is presiding over all of this, it is appropriate that in the New Testament the Day of the Lord's Wrath is known as "the Day of Jesus Christ."

The Day of the Lord – the Whole Seven Years?

Although some have suggested that the whole seven years of the 70th week make up the Day of Wrath, the Scripture simply does not teach that. The Lord's wrath is contained *within* the scroll and does not begin until *after* the 6th and 7th seals are removed. The prophet Joel confirms that these phenomena in the heavens *precede* the Day of Wrath:

> **The sun shall be turned into darkness, and the moon into blood,** *before* **the great and the terrible day of the Lord comes. Joel 2:30 KJV** (emphasis added)

If we are willing to go with the simple truth of the Word, we can see this very plainly. Like all the other groups of seven, the seven seals are chronological and sequential. The 6th seal, involving these cosmic phenomena, does not take place until the previous *five seals* have occurred. To try to place these cosmic disturbances at the beginning of the 70th week in order to say that the whole seven-year period constitutes the Day of the Lord, is simply incorrect and means one is wresting the Word to get it to say something it isn't saying! No, in harmony with both Jesus' teaching and Revelation, these cosmic and seismic disruptions don't happen until the other seal events have preceded them, and until God is ready *to intervene directly in the affairs of the earth!* But before that intervention begins, He must take care of two other things. That brings us to the second event that pertains to the sixth seal.

2. God Seals the 144,000

Scripture speaks of this group of Jews only twice, here in Revelation 7 and later in chapter 14. We have already noted that this group is comprised of 12,000 Jews from each of the twelve tribes, and they are called "the servants (slaves) of God" (v. 3). When they are mentioned in chapter 14, we are told that they:

    a. Were redeemed from the earth,
    b. Have the Father's name written in their foreheads (this is apparently how they were sealed),
    c. Are virgins, being not defiled with women,
    d. Are the *first fruits* unto God from among men,
    e. Have no guile in their mouth, and – by that time -
    f. Are standing faultless *before God's throne.*

When we put all this together, a picture begins to form of this group. Remember, the whole 70th week is a time of *turning* for the Jews – turning from centuries of hardness and spiritual blindness toward God. Some turn sooner than others, and this group here is called *the first fruits.* They are the beginning of the harvest of the righteous from among the Jews. The full harvest will come later in the seven years. These are God-fearing Jews, true servants of God in their hearts, but not born again and therefore not caught up in the rapture of the church. Knowing they are part of His elect, God seals them before His wrath begins, signifying ownership of them and protection from the judgments about to fall.

Some have thought these are men who were never married; it's more likely that God is saying they are *spiritual virgins.* God frequently used the picture of an unfaithful wife to refer to Israel in her idolatries, as in this lament:

> **"I have seen your adulteries . . . and the lewdness of your harlotry, Your abominations on the hills in the fields.**
> **Woe to you, O Jerusalem! Will you still not be made clean?" Jeremiah 13:27**

And again,

> **"How has the faithful city become an harlot!" Isaiah 1:21 KJV**

To God's great sorrow, Israel's spiritual harlotry went on and on, century after century. But at the end, when Israel has been cleansed and forgiven, God again refers to her as a virgin:

> **Again, I will build you, and you shall be rebuilt, O virgin of Israel!**
> **You shall again be adorned with your tambourines,**
> **And shall go forth in the dances of those who rejoice. Jeremiah 31:4**

This 144,000 are people pure of heart and mouth, sincere in their love and faithfulness to God, who have refused the mark of the beast even at their own risk, but who at the 6th seal do not yet have the revelation of their Messiah. They appear before God's throne in heaven *between the two series of seven* which constitute God's wrath. From that, we are led to believe that God takes them to heaven before the final seven, the bowl judgments.

144,000 -- 12,000 from each tribe -- is such an unusually precise number that we might wonder about it. I believe that God speaks of this group with such precision – such perfect knowledge of *each one*, first, because they are *His*, and second, because they are coming through such an enormously treacherous time where issues of life and death and heaven and hell hang in the balance. Jews who don't know Jesus are being killed during this time, and yet God is saying, "I know *each one* that is Mine, even though they don't yet know Me. I am *preserving* each one with perfect care and precision, and *not one will perish*, but everyone will come through this dangerous time and will come to faith in Me. I know every tribe (though they may not know their tribe), and I know exactly how many from each tribe is mine and am preserving and protecting the exact number from each tribe. "Twelve" represents that perfect number of God's government – His oversight and jurisdiction of His people. (I think it's unlikely that it's a literal number, because for that to be true, there would have to be a manipulation of people's hearts to get the right number, and that's just not how God is.)

Mercy to the 144,000
I have a personal theory about this group. They are worshipping God under the Old Covenant in the rebuilt temple; they are not familiar with the New Testament writings -- with the warnings and indicators of Christ's return or of the greatness of the dangers posed by Antichrist. The terror of the midpoint takes them by surprise, but they undoubtedly know immediately that Antichrist is a false leader and they must flee for their lives. Furthermore, they are not aware of how soon after Antichrist rises to power, Christ will return and His wrath judgments begin. But Christians, "awake" and aware, knowing what is going on and what will happen at the midpoint, have made preparations; because they are ready, they will provide a place of refuge not only for fellow Christians, but also for Jews who refuse to submit to Antichrist.

> **. . . for as ye also once did not believe in God, and now did find kindness by the unbelief of**
> **these: so also these now did not believe, that in your kindness they also may find kindness.**
> **Romans 11:30-31 YLT**

Even as God's mercy was turned toward us Gentiles through the unbelief of the Jews, so there will be a time when we the church share with them the provision and sufficiency given us through faith in Christ. Although that may have been happening all along to a certain extent, I believe that when Christians take them in and care for them during this coming time of trouble, that will be the fullness of this word coming to pass – the beginning of them returning to God and receiving mercy from Him.

They will not only receive material help from the church, but will hear the witness of their Messiah Jesus, and that He is returning soon to catch up those who believe in Him. The testimony will be so clear that when *the event – the rapture -- happens,* I suspect the whole 144,000 will be converted to Christ. Scripture tells us the whole group comes to faith between the beginning of the trumpet judgments and the beginning of the bowl judgments, so that they apparently experience their own "rapture" in the middle of the wrath of God. This is a lovely thing. It's very possible that it's this group that God is speaking to in Isaiah:

Come, my people, enter into your chambers, and shut your doors behind you. Hide yourself for a little moment, until the indignation is past.
For, behold, Yahweh comes forth out of his place to punish the inhabitants of the earth for their iniquity. The earth also will disclose her blood and will no longer cover her slain.

Isaiah 26:20-21 WEB

With the church about to leave, this group, now representing "the people of God" on the earth, will receive God's special attention and care. They will bring the testimony of Christ to fellow Jews in the same way that the church brought it to them. We notice in Rev. 14:6, that once they are in heaven, an angel "flying in the midst of heaven" continues the preaching of the gospel, bringing more people yet – probably Jews - to faith in Christ.

It is said frequently about this 144,000 that they are tremendous evangelists. But these two passages that speak of them say nothing about that. I think some have been forced to conclude this because of the great multitude who are saved out of the Great Tribulation (Rev. 7:9ff). And it makes sense that having come to faith in their Messiah, they would share that whenever possible. However, we do not see validation for the tremendous numbers of converts that are attributed to them. In actuality, this great multitude is brought to heaven before the 144,000 have even confessed Christ. (If they *had* confessed Christ, they would have been part of that multitude and would not have remained on earth as God's wrath began.) We will look next at this great gathering that appears in heaven.

3. The Gathering of the Saints

In Matthew Jesus gives this event from the perspective of earth – people are being gathered from *the whole earth*. John sees it in Revelation from the perspective of heaven; a great multitude of believers come out of the Great Tribulation on the earth and appear, standing before the throne in heaven. Luke agrees with Matthew and with Revelation – that this great gathering happens *right after* the cosmic signs. Earlier we quoted verses 25 and 26 of Luke 21 that speak of the cosmic signs (the 6th seal) and their effect on people. Luke then goes on:

27 Then they will see the Son of Man coming in a cloud with power and great glory.
28 Now when these things begin to happen, look up and lift up your heads, because your
    redemption draws near." Luke 21:27-28

Jesus instructed the church that when these cosmic signs occur (as well as the indicators which precede them), His people are to *look up and lift up their heads, because their redemption is near!* What is this redemption? It is receiving our new, immortal bodies!

As mentioned before, if we were to look ahead at Revelation 8 when the wrath of God begins to be released by the angels, we would see that the portions of the earth that come under judgment first involve the trees, the grass, and the sea -- the very portions that the angels were temporarily restrained from hurting. It is clear that before the wrath begins, God will give the protecting seal to those Jews, and then *pull the church to safety in the rapture.* This coincides perfectly with Paul's words:

For God did not appoint us to wrath, but to obtain salvation through our Lord Jesus Christ.

1 Thessalonians 5:9

The chronology of Jesus' teaching in the Olivet Discourse ends with His coming and the rapture. He does not continue with the Day of Wrath, which follows, so our comparison of Matthew 24 with Revelation also ends here. When we pick up our chronology again in a couple of chapters, we will rely on the sevens of Revelation, which is the only portion of Scripture which sets forth the Day of the Lord systematically. But first, there is much to say about the rapture of the church, and we will continue with it in the next chapter.

CHAPTER 15

The Rapture
of the Church

Let's begin with a few basics and then proceed to the timing of this event, which for most Christians is the issue most in question.

The catching up of the church is frequently called "the rapture." This word is derived from the classic Scripture on the rapture, 1 Thessalonians 4:

> **15 For this we say to you by the word of the Lord, that we who are alive and remain until the coming of the Lord will by no means precede those who are asleep.**
> **16 For the Lord Himself will descend from heaven with a shout, with the voice of an archangel, and with the trumpet of God. And the dead in Christ will rise first.**
> **17 Then we who are alive and remain [shall be caught up][1] together with them in the clouds to meet the Lord in the air. And thus we shall always be with the Lord. 1 Thessalonians 4:15-17**

[1]*harpazo* G726T – to seize, to snatch out or away

NOTE: In the Latin Bible, this word *harpazo* is translated *rapere*, and it's from that word that we have derived "rapture." It's become widely used and accepted to refer to this catching up of the church at the end.

The rapture includes the resurrection of the righteous, whom Jesus will bring with Him when He returns. This resurrection will be immediately followed by the catching up of those saints still alive to join Jesus and the resurrected saints in the air. Paul speaks again of this event:

> **51 Behold, I tell you a mystery: We shall not all sleep, but we shall all be changed[1] —**
> **52 in a moment, in the twinkling of an eye, at the last trumpet. For the trumpet will sound, and the dead will be raised incorruptible, and we shall be changed.**
> **53 For this corruptible must put on incorruption, and this mortal must put on immortality.**
> **1 Corinthians 15:51-53**

[1] *allasso* G236T - to change: to exchange one thing for another; to transform

He again mentions the two parts to this event – the rising of the dead and the *changing* of those yet alive. For both groups, this means the clothing of our spirits and souls with new, incorruptible bodies. Paul tells us that it is for *this very purpose* that God has redeemed us and worked fully in our lives to conform our souls to the image of Christ – that we might finally be fitted with a new body that will never know corruption.[1]

Paul speaks here of a mystery. The whole concept of the church – "the Body of Christ" – was a mystery in the Old Testament, so the various aspects of the church, including the rapture, are only unveiled in the New Testament, particularly in the epistles. The mystery spoken of here is not the fact that saints will be resurrected, but that saints alive at that time will be caught up and their bodies *changed*.

As these rapture events became known, revealed by the Holy Spirit to the apostles post-Pentecost, the church was taught to look and long for this return of Christ, when our redemption would finally be completed with resurrected bodies.[2] Paul gave voice to this longing in his letter to Titus:

> . . . **[looking for][1] the blessed hope and glorious appearing of our great God and Savior Jesus Christ, who gave Himself for us, that He might redeem us from every lawless deed and purify for Himself His own special people, zealous for good works.**
>
> Titus 2:13-14

[1]*prosdechomai* G4327T- to receive to oneself into companionship; to expect (the fulfillment of promises)

The tremendous hope associated with the glorious appearing of Jesus had been received by Paul into his heart – he had *embraced the substance of hope* associated with seeing Jesus and becoming like Him, and the visualization of the glory of it was a reality inside him. It is this same hope, *internalized*, that is normative for us, God's people! This is our primary goal in studying the prophetic Scriptures!

Here are the main aspects of the rapture, compiled from various Scriptures:

Elements of the Rapture

1. Jesus Himself will appear in the heavens (He *is* "the Sign").[1]
2. He will come in the clouds.[1,3,6]
3. He will appear against a blackened sky with great power and great glory.[1,2]
4. He will bring a great number of saints and angels with Him.[1,8,9,10]
   He will bring with Him those who are 'asleep' in Jesus - their bodies will be resurrected as new.[6]
5. Jesus will descend with the rousing shout of the archangel.[6]
6. Every eye shall see Him.[3]
   They also who crucified Him (the Jews).[3,4]
7. All peoples of the earth shall wail (in utter distress) when they see Him.[1,3]
8. There will be the sound of a great trumpet, also called "the last trump."[1,5,6]
9. The dead in Christ will rise with resurrected bodies.[6]
10. The angels will begin to gather the living saints – the elect – from the four winds, from the uttermost part of the earth to the uttermost part of heaven.[1,2,5,6]
    a. As the elect are gathered, they will be *changed* from mortal to immortal, receiving resurrected bodies like Christ's.[5,7]
    b. This happens in a moment – in the 'twinkling of an eye!'[5]
    c. Like Christ's, these will be bodies of great glory![11,12,13]

---

1   2 Cor. 5:4-5
2   1 John 3:2

11. We shall all meet the Lord in the air.[6]
12. We shall ever be with the Lord![6]

[1]Matt. 24:30-31   [8]1 Thess. 3:13
[2]Mark 13:26-27   [9]2 Thess. 1:7-10
[3]Rev. 1:7   [10]1 Thess. 4:14
[4]Matt. 26:64   [11]Ro. 8:18
[5]1 Cor. 15:51-52   [12]1 Cor. 15:42-54
[6]1 Thess. 4:15-17 (Luke 17:37)   [13]Matt. 13:43
[7]1 John 3:2   I encourage you to read these for yourself.

What an *utterly glorious* appearing! As all eyes are looking up, shocked and awakened by these great cosmic events, Jesus, surrounded by saints and angels, will appear in stupendous power and brilliant glory against the blackened sky. It is *the Second Coming* of Christ! -- that great event the church has been looking forward to since Pentecost. It includes the resurrection of the saints and the catching of up those who are still alive.

The *Coming* of the Lord

The night of the Last Supper, Jesus said He was going away to prepare a place for them, promising, "I will come again, and receive you to Myself, that where I am, there you may be also" (John 14:3). Just days before that, the disciples had asked Jesus,

"What will be the sign of Your coming,[1] and of the end of the age?"

[1]*parousia* G3952T – presence; the coming, arrival; to be near
--from *pareimi* G3918T – to be near, at hand, to have arrived, to be present; hence, not merely an
     arrival, but a remaining presence with

Jesus' response to this question makes up the Olivet Discourse, which we've been following in Matthew 24. This Greek word for "coming," *parousia,* is the one used most frequently in Scripture to refer to Jesus' return. Tracking Jesus' answer, as we have been doing, we understand that He is telling the disciples about <u>a series of events that will take place leading up to His parousia.</u> In v. 6 of Matthew 24, after warning of war, He clarifies, "But the end (His coming) is not yet." He goes on with more events, finally arriving at *His coming* in v. 30:

Then the sign of the Son of Man will appear in the heaven, and then all the tribes of the earth will mourn, and they will see the Son of Man *coming* on the clouds of heaven with power and great glory. (emphasis added)

What follows next, of course, is the gathering of the elect from the four corners of the earth and heaven. At this point in Matthew 24, the *listing of events* ceases. Why? Because Jesus has arrived at the end and the *time of His coming!* This is what the disciples asked Him about, and this is His answer. The long-promised *return of Christ* takes place in Matthew 24, and follows the series of events which He lists there, including the Great Tribulation, which we know begins at the midpoint of the 70th week.

NOTE: See Appendix 4 for Aimee Semple McPherson's vision of the rapture.

The Timing of the Rapture

When it comes to end-time prophecy, the timing of the rapture is probably the issue of greatest disagreement and controversy within the church. I know there are probably some of you who have questions – even problems – with the timing being presented here. We are at a point in our study that requires *very careful attention* to the Word and to the Holy Spirit. This is not a time to hold stubbornly to something because "that's what I've always heard and always believed (and it's what I *want* to believe)." If what you believe is correct, it will stand up to the words of Scripture! If it doesn't stand up, then for your own sake, you need to be willing to reconsider your position. The issues are too important for anyone to hang onto a belief because it is what he or she *personally prefers* or "has always been taught." We are going to take a careful look at various Scriptures that speak of the timing of this event. We want to look for agreement *within* Scripture – harmony between all the relevant passages. It actually is spelled out very clearly in Scripture, so there shouldn't be a need for disagreement if we all want what the Word sets forth. There *are* loose ends, but even they can be tucked safely into a harmonious picture of what is to come.

The Correlation of the Rapture with His Coming
Let's begin where we just left off – with the issue of *His coming*. Notice the following verses:

> **For as in Adam all die, even so in Christ shall all be made alive.**
> **But each one in his own order: Christ the first fruits, afterward those who are Christ's *at his coming*. 1 Corinthians 15:22-23**
>
> **For this we say to you by the word of the Lord, that we who are alive and remain *until the coming* of the Lord will by no means precede those who are asleep. 1 Thessalonians 4:15**
>
> **I pray God your whole spirit and soul and body be preserved blameless *unto the coming* of our Lord Jesus Christ. 1 Thessalonians 5:23 KJV**
>
> **Therefore, be patient, brethren, *until the coming* of the Lord. See how the farmer waits for the precious fruit of the earth, waiting patiently for it until it receives the early and latter rain.**
> **You also be patient. Establish your hearts, for *the coming* of the Lord is at hand. James 5:7-8**
>
> **And now, little children, abide in Him, that when He appears, we may have confidence and not be ashamed before Him *at His coming*. 1 John 2:28**
>
> **Now, brethren, concerning *the coming* of our Lord Jesus Christ and our gathering together to Him . . . 2 Thessalonians 2:1** (emphasis added to all of them)

We see that each of these verses indicates that the church will be here until *His coming*: the dead in Christ will be resurrected at His coming; we who are alive will remain until His coming; we are to be preserved blameless until His coming; we are to be patient and stablish our hearts until His coming; and we are to abide in Him until His coming. Then finally, the last verse specifically links His coming with "our gathering together to Him," i.e., the rapture. In other words, the *rapture* takes place *at His coming*. **This harmonizes perfectly with Matthew 24, which, again, teaches clearly that the gathering of the saints takes place *at His coming*; and that His coming directly *follows* the events Jesus laid out for us, including the Great Tribulation.** Scripture says that in the 'mouth of two or three witnesses, let every word be established.'[3] Way *more* than two or three witnesses, these passages provide an overwhelming body of evidence, *clearly establishing the testimony of Scripture as to the rapture and the second coming!*

The Correlation of the Rapture with the Day of the Lord
Remember that in Revelation, the Day of the Lord begins when the 7th seal is removed and the scroll is opened. That, of course, follows directly after the 6th seal events, which include the great multitude which appears in heaven, having come out of the Great Tribulation. In other words, the cosmic phenomena occur, followed immediately by the rapture (the great multitude in heaven), which is *immediately followed* by the Day of the Lord. We see this correlation of the rapture with the Day of the Lord in these verses:

---

3 2 Cor. 13:1

Being confident of this very thing, that He who has begun a good work in you will complete it *until the day of Jesus Christ.*

. . . that you may be sincere and without offense *till the day of Christ.* Philippians 1:6, 10

. . . for I know whom I have believed and am persuaded that He is able to keep what I have committed to Him *until that Day.* 2 Timothy 1:12

From now on, there is stored up for me the crown of righteousness, which the Lord, the righteous judge, will give to me *on that day.* 2 Timothy 4:8 WEB (emphasis added to all)

In other words, God will continue His work in us until the Day of Jesus Christ; we are to be sincere and without offense until the Day of Christ; God is able to keep what we have committed to Him until that Day; and the crown of righteousness will be given on that Day. Therefore, the Day of Christ is virtually synonymous timewise with the rapture – in actuality, following immediately after it.

And finally, see how this next verse shows that we will be here until <u>the coming</u>, <u>the end</u>, and <u>the Day of Christ</u>, therefore connecting all three with the <u>rapture</u>:

So that you come behind in no gift, waiting for *the coming* of our Lord Jesus Christ, who shall also confirm you unto *the end,* that you may be blameless in *the Day of our Lord Jesus Christ.* 1 Corinthians 1:7-8 (emphasis added)

Another Timing Issue

Let's review the simple chronology of these events and see what, if anything, is said about the length of time from the midpoint (the beginning of the Great Tribulation) to the Day of the Lord, i.e., the rapture. We see in Matthew 24 that when the midpoint of the 70th week occurs (v. 15), the "Abomination of Desolation" takes place in Jerusalem and immediate persecution breaks out against the Jews. V. 21, of course, uses the term "Great Tribulation"[4] to refer to this time period under the Antichrist.

We have seen that this will be a difficult time for believers. Although His *coming* has not yet occurred, at this point in Jesus' narrative it is right around the corner! Believers who are spiritually alert will know this. When we arrive at v. 29, approaching the cosmic disturbances, there are a couple of little words that are significant for the believers of that coming time.

Immediately[1] after[2] the tribulation of those days, the sun will be darkened. . . v. 29

[1]*eutheos* G2112S – directly, at once, soon
[2]*meta* G3326S– denotes accompaniment; with, amid

When we see the word "after," we get the impression that as soon as the Tribulation is over, then the cosmic signs will occur. But that would place us all the way at the end of the 70th week, because the Bible teaches clearly that Antichrist will hold his position for 3 ½ years. Jesus speaks earlier in Matthew 24 of a *shortening* of these days of intense tribulation:

And unless those days were shortened, no flesh would be saved; but for the elect's sake those days will be shortened. Matthew 24:22

If God left everything alone, no one would survive the rule of Satan on the earth. But for the elect's sake – those chosen by God to be His – He tells us the days would be shortened. However, as we just pointed out, Antichrist's rule lasts for the whole second half of the seven years. So how is it *shortened*? It is shortened by the

---

4   Please note that Scripture never refers to the 70th week of Daniel as "the Tribulation." There is only "the Great Tribulation" which begins at the midpoint and lasts for 3½ years.

intervention of the Day of the Lord – the 6th and 7th seal events. It is shortened for the saints, *the elect* (v. 31), when the rapture takes place and they are removed right before the Day of Wrath begins.[5]

Let's look more closely at these two words in v. 29. In this context, they are both *time* words. The first one is simple and means just what it says: *immediately* – right away, at once, soon. But the second word, *meta*, needs a closer look. It is a word which means something happening *along with* something else -- two things happening at the same time. But the two events may not *begin* at the same time. In this case, the Great Tribulation begins first; and then, "immediately after," the sun is darkened, etc., the people of God are *taken to safety,* and the Day of the Lord begins *while* the Great Tribulation is continuing to happen. So rather than "after the Tribulation" in the sense of the Tribulation is over and then the next events occur, we could read it, "immediately along with." That is, soon after the Great Tribulation begins, the 6th seal takes place *alongside it, as the tribulation is continuing to occur.* [6]

We see from this that the rapture takes place so soon after the midpoint, that Jesus used the word "immediately." We don't have any way to know specifically how long a period that will be – just that it apparently won't be "long." This is the *shortening* of the Great Tribulation which Jesus spoke of. It is *not* the Lord's desire that all His people be martyred (or that they starve to death)! The multitude that is raptured is described in Revelation 7 as a "multitude so great that no man could number it" (v. 9), telling us that the number of those raptured alive is much greater than the number of those martyred.[7]

This would be a good place to mention the martyrs who appear in heaven with the 5th seal – the marker of the Great Tribulation in Revelation's chronology. From their place in heaven, these martyrs cry out to God *how long* will You "wait to bring relief to the righteous and judgment to these wicked ones!?" That is certainly the question we would all ask. The answer is given them to wait a little longer "until the number of their fellow servants and their brothers should be complete, who were to be killed as they themselves had been."[8] God, who is working with exquisite carefulness in the lives of each of His children, knows exactly *whose* sanctification will be perfected by means of martyrdom, and again, is simply using this tyrant for His own good purposes. His answer here tells us that when the number of those who are to give their lives for Him is complete, He will move on immediately to the 6th seal, bringing this persecution of His saints to a full and decisive end. The wisdom that He gives us here equips us to bear up in full faith in His workings and His timing.

One or Two Comings?

There's been confusion over two apparent "comings" depicted in the New Testament. There is an earlier 'coming' of Christ for the church, and then there is 'the coming' which occurs in Revelation 19. This has been perplexing, as everyone agrees that Scripture speaks of only *one* Second Coming. Pretribulation rapturism solves it by their "secret rapture," which they don't call a coming.[9] However, we've already demonstrated clearly that the Word associates the catching up of the church with *the* (one and only) Second Coming of Christ. Marv Rosenthal dealt with this question very satisfactorily in his landmark book, *The Pre-Wrath Rapture of the Church.* I will give you my understanding of this issue.

It is interesting to notice that the disciples asked Jesus for the sign – singular – of His coming. In response, Jesus laid out a whole series of events which would lead up to His return, which we could call 'precursors' of His coming. His people would know of these events and be alert to them as they took place, and in that way, be aware

---

5 Note that it is also shortened for the 144,000 Jewish faithful who are brought to faith in Jesus upon seeing Jesus at the rapture, and then raptured themselves between the Trumpet and Bowl Judgments. It is softened for the remaining elect Jews, as the rule of Antichrist is weakened by the intervention and terror of the Day of the Lord events.

6 The very timing issue presented here confirms this definition of *meta*. We know that the reign of Antichrist will last for the full second half of the 70th week (Dan. 7:25, Rev. 13:5). If these cosmic signs (which we have seen signal the beginning of the Day of the Lord's wrath – Rev. 6:12-17) were not to occur until the END of the Great Tribulation, there would be no time left in the last seven years for the Day of the Lord judgments. Just one judgment alone, we are told, will last for five months (Rev. 9:10). Therefore, the darkening of the sun, etc., of Matt. 24:29 must begin within the 70th week, and run alongside the Great Tribulation, even as *meta* would lead us to understand. Interestingly, *meta* is used around fifty times in Revelation, most frequently as a simple preposition; in nine of those, it is used as a timing word and yet is translated "after," indicating, again, events that don't begin at the same time and yet occur concurrently.

7 Some have thought that perhaps this number includes those whom Jesus brought with Him who were raised from the dead, but we are told specifically in Rev. 7:14 that this great multitude are those who "came out of the Great Tribulation."

8 Rev. 6:11 ESV

9 One teacher of pre-tribulationism has called it, with absolutely no Scriptural basis, a "translation coming." If the Word were taken simply, at face value, there would be no need to invent terms and ideas not found in Scripture.

that His coming was right around the corner.[10] But He didn't call any of them a sign, or rather, *the* sign, until He arrived at v. 30, when He said, "Then the sign of the Son of Man will appear in heaven…." This was His answer to the request for "the sign of His coming." It isn't that He will be carrying a sign when He appears in the heavens. Rather, He Himself will BE the sign. His glorious appearance in the heavens will be <u>the sign to the unbelieving world that His coming has arrived!</u>

Believers won't need "the sign." They are ready to go with Him. They are alert to all that has been happening – the precursors – and they have already been looking up, lifting up their heads, ready to see Him and to go when He appears. "Unto them that look for Him shall He appear the second time, without sin, unto salvation."[11]

The reason the sign of His visible presence is needed at that point, is because He will *not remain visible* to those upon the earth. Nevertheless, it is His time of visitation; He is very near the earth, even as we defined *parousia* – **an arrival and resulting presence with or near.** He is the One worthy of opening the scroll and dispensing the contents, personally supervising the release of judgment after judgment in the retaking of the earth. His presence, though not visible, will continue throughout all the judgments of the Day of the Lord, until at the end of the seven years, He will again *become visible* – shining forth with splendor and magnificence:

> **. . . the lawless one…, whom the Lord will consume with the breath of His mouth and destroy with the brightness[1] of His coming.[2] 2 Thessalonians 2:8**

[1]*epiphaneia* G2015 – appearance(T), manifestation (S), "the shining forth of the glory of the Lord Jesus" (V)[12]
[2]*parousia* – an arrival and subsequent presence with

At this second manifestation at the end of the 70th week, Jesus will step down upon the earth for the Battle of Armageddon and for the final defeat of all His enemies.[13] The whole span of time, from the cosmic signs to the end of the seven years (and beyond), is the *parousia* of the Lord. This is how we have only one Second Coming, even though these *appearances* take place several years apart.

---

10   See Matt. 24:32-33, Luke 21:28-31
11   Hebrews 9:28
12   This word *epiphaneia* is also used to refer to Jesus' initial manifestation at the rapture: "Waiting for the blessed hope and *epiphaneia* of the glory of our great God and Savior, Christ Jesus" (Titus 2:13); "Blameless until the *epiphaneia* of our Lord Jesus Christ" (2 Tim. 6:14); and "All who love his *epiphaneia*" (2 Thess. 2:8). These references tell us, that like the Rev. 19 appearance, His glorious appearance in the sky for the rapture will also be an *epiphaneia*.
13   See Rev. 19:11ff, Zech. 14:4, Is. 63:1ff.

CHAPTER 16

Why Not a Pre-Tribulation Rapture?

The pre-tribulation viewpoint is probably the most prevalent one in evangelical circles today. Because the view we are setting forth here is so different, this is a section focused on addressing those aspects of the pre-tribulation view that we feel are unscriptural. It is my hope that any reader whose convictions lie in the pre-tribulation camp will take the time to investigate, carefully and prayerfully, the thoughts and Scriptures set forth here. With humble hearts, open to the Lord and His Word, may truth be the ultimate goal of each of us, His children.

The Secret Rapture…

Pre-tribulationism teaches that the rapture occurs before the 70th week begins; that is, it occurs *before* the Olivet Discourse (and the seals) even begin. It is claimed that it is a "secret rapture" – believers will be caught up and simply disappear – no one else will see Jesus or apparently hear the great shout or the blast of the trumpet![1] The problem with this secret rapture is it's so secret we can't even find it in Scripture! We can't even see this rapture in Jesus' primary teaching on His return! How could this event – the most looked-for and longed-for event in all of church history -- *not even be found* in Jesus' primary teaching on end-times? Nor can we find it before the 70th week in the *chronology of Revelation's "sevens"* – it is not to be found in the letter to the seventh church, nor in the first seal.

… Or, All Will See Him

In fact, all these verses we have just looked at in the previous chapter make it abundantly clear that the church will remain on the earth until *the coming* of the Lord, and Jesus taught us just as clearly in Matthew 24 that these listed events will *precede His coming.*

The last event to precede it will be the great cosmic and seismic phenomena which we have already spoken of and which pertain to the 6th seal. These events are undoubtedly designed and sent by the Father *to get the attention of the whole world:* We have already mentioned the supernatural darkening of the sky – whether it's a daylight sky or a nighttime sky. There will be an earthquake so great that *every mountain and island will be moved out of their place*[2] -- never mind the homes and buildings that will be shaken! Added to all that will be the heavens passing away with a *tremendous noise!*[3] If one of these doesn't wake a person up, another will be

---

1 1 Thess. 4:16
2 Rev. 6:14
3 2 Peter 3:10

sure to! *The whole earth will be awake and looking up!* Even one of these phenomena would be frightening, but all together, they will be utterly terrifying. No wonder Scripture says, "Every eye shall see Him, and they also who pierced Him," and, "Then shall *all the tribes of the earth* mourn."[4] They will all see the Lord Jesus appearing in stunning power and glory against the blackened sky, surrounded by the glory of the angels and the returning saints. All will hear the great shout and the sound of a trumpet calling His people to Him. They will *see* Jesus and see the gathering of God's people take place at this *great Second Coming of the Lord Jesus Christ!* This is the clear testimony of Scripture.

And yet, Scripture also indicates that it's in *seeing* Him that we will become like Him:

> **Beloved, now we are children of God; and it has not yet been revealed what we shall be, but we know that when He is revealed, *we shall be like Him, for we shall see Him as He is.***
>
> 1 John 3:2 (emphasis added)

If we are saying that <u>all will see Him</u> (i.e., *it's not a secret rapture*), then why don't all people become *like* Him and go with Him? I have had to process this question and resolve it for myself.

I believe the answer is that the unbelieving won't see Him the same way believers do. The difference lies in the spiritual dimension; it lies in the belief of the heart which precedes His appearing. Perhaps a good example is found in Anna and Simeon, Jews of deep prayer and consecration who were looking for the Messiah. They were in the temple when Mary and Joseph brought Jesus for His dedication, and upon seeing Him, both *knew* who He was![5] They knew because they had *heard from the Lord* out of that prayer relationship with Him. That baby was revealed to them as *the Messiah*. There were many Jews in the temple that day who saw Mary, Joseph, and Jesus, yet did not see Him *by revelation*. None of them knew that this baby was the Messiah they had been long awaiting. They saw Him with physical eyes, yes. But not with the eyes of revelation and faith.

Likewise, when Jesus returns, it isn't seeing Him with physical eyes that will transform us. *All* will see Him with physical eyes, but those looking and longing for Him will see Him on a different, a deeper level. He will be *revealed* to them. There will be a connection, heart to heart and spirit to spirit, and via that connection, *grace* will come. Peter said that grace comes to us at the unveiling of Jesus Christ.[6] That is happening even now, every time we get a deeper glimpse of who Christ really is; as we grow in our knowledge of Him, we grow correspondingly in grace. When He returns, there will be a *complete revelation of Him* – there will be nothing more hidden, and in that moment, grace will be given to us *for the transformation to incorruptible bodies!* In seeing Him fully as He is, we will *become like Him!* We are told in Heb. 9:28:

> **So Christ was once offered to bear the sins of many; and unto them that look for him shall he appear the second time without sin unto salvation.** KJV

The "looking" mentioned here is a very patient, persistent, focused expectation that will result in tremendous joy and glory at Jesus' appearing. The rest who see Him, who are *not* looking for Him, will be deeply distressed, for His appearance will be not unto salvation, but *unto judgment*.

> **Behold, He comes with clouds, and every eye will see Him, and they also who pierced Him. And *all peoples of the earth will wail because of Him*.** (Cf. Matt. 24:30)
>
> Revelation 1:7 (emphasis added)

Because of completely different *preparations of the heart*, His appearance will mean different things to different people. To all the evil doers of the earth, it signals the beginning of great anguish, tribulation, and wrath, and their response is not rejoicing, but universal terror.[7]

---

4   Rev. 1:7, Matt. 24:30
5   Luke 2:25-38
6   1 Pe. 1:13
7   Rev. 6:15-17

Further Thoughts on a Secret Rapture

Some have said that the latter part of Matthew 24 refers to the "secret rapture." But even that portion is talking about *His coming*:

> 37 As the days of Noah were, so will be *the coming* of the Son of Man.
> 38 For as in those days which were before the flood they were eating and drinking, marrying and giving in marriage, until the day that Noah entered into the ark,
> 39 and they didn't know until the flood came, and took them all away, so will be *the coming* of the Son of Man.
> 40 Then two men will be in the field: one will be taken and one will be left;
> 41 two women grinding at the mill, one will be taken and one will be left.
> 42 Watch therefore, for you don't know in what hour your Lord *comes*.
>
> Matthew 24:37-42 WEB (emphasis added)

This is the same *coming* that Jesus spoke of previously in the chapter. It is not a different or separate coming! There *is* only one coming! Just because one is taken and the other left, doesn't make it a secret rapture. It simply means that the dividing line between those who make it and those who don't is very fine. This indeed is the *same* "taking" that occurred in v. 31 of the same chapter. There is no textual basis for saying it is a different event.

Even First Thessalonians 4, the classic rapture passage, contains within it a reference to *the coming* – the *parousia* – of the Lord:

> For this we say to you by the word of the Lord, that we who are alive and remain until *the coming* of the Lord will by no means precede those who are asleep.
>
> 1 Thessalonians 4:15 (emphasis added)

The testimony of Scripture is so strong and so consistent on this issue, that to set forth *a different timing* for the rapture requires *conscious, deliberate twisting* of verses and *ignoring* of others. This is a very serious problem for those who knowingly and deliberately engage in this kind of tampering with the Word. And it is a serious problem also for those who trustingly (and gullibly) accept this way of thinking, tempting though it may be to do so. Peter himself gave a warning much stronger than I could ever give. Referring to the return of Christ and our readiness for that return, Peter said:

> . . . as also our beloved brother Paul, according to the wisdom given to him, has written to you, as also in all his epistles, speaking in them of these things, in which are some things hard to understand, which untaught and unstable people *twist to their own destruction*, as they do also the rest of the Scriptures. 2 Peter 3:15-16 (emphasis added)

This is an issue of importance for every believer. After going through the chronology of events that will lead up to His return, Jesus went on for the rest of Matthew 24 and on into chapter 25, warning and teaching about *being ready* for His return. If one isn't ready, isn't *aware*, Scripture warns us repeatedly that His coming will be like a "thief in the night."[8] With the extreme craftiness and deceptiveness that Antichrist will use to veil his true identity, if a Christian is going along serenely, expecting to be raptured with no previous signs to look for, and no Antichrist to worry about, he could very well waltz inadvertently into a dark corner of deception (which looks, of course, like the real thing), and find himself utterly unprepared at the return of Jesus! We cannot afford simply to grab the interpretation that we're most comfortable with personally. It's going to happen *only one way,* and that is the way set forth in Scripture. We need to *know* that way and take it seriously, along with the warnings God gives us.

---

8 Matt. 24:43; 1 Thess. 5:2, 4; 2 Peter 3:10; Rev. 3:3, Rev. 16:15

Conclusion

We see from the testimony of all these Scriptures that this is not a secret rapture, but one witnessed by all the people of the earth! A secret rapture simply cannot be found in Scripture. There is only this magnificent gathering of His people found in v. 31 of Matthew 24; this gathering which holds the place of *glorious pre-eminence* in Jesus' account of the end-times -- a pre-eminence worthy of so great an event.

NOTE: Some also divide "the blessed hope" and "the glorious appearing" (Titus 2:13) into two events, a secret rapture and His coming at the end of the seven years. For comments on this, see Appendix 5.

Imminence

Let's continue now with the issue of imminence. Besides claiming that it's a secret rapture, pre-tribulationists would have us believe that it could occur at any moment with no identifiable signs or required prophetic events preceding it. This is known as the Doctrine of Imminence and is a foundational tenet of this viewpoint, so it's important to understand it, especially in the light of Scripture.

Let's begin with a look at what Jesus said we couldn't know regarding the timing:

> But of that *day and hour* no one knows, not even the angels of heaven, but My Father only.
> **Matthew 24:36** (Cf. vv. 42-44)

> Watch therefore, for you know neither *the day nor the hour* in which the Son of Man is coming. **Matthew 25:13** (emphasis added to both)

That is a pretty clear message: we cannot know *the day or the hour* in which Christ is returning. But the day or hour is a much smaller time frame than "times" and "seasons," and it's a different story when it comes to the general time and the specific *season* for His return. Look at Paul's instructions to the Thessalonian saints:

> But concerning the times and the seasons, brethren, you have no need that I should write to you. For you yourselves know perfectly that the day of the Lord so comes as a thief in the night. **1 Thessalonians 5:1-2**

First, we notice that there *are* "times and seasons" related to Christ's return which Paul assumed to be knowable and recognizable to God's people. Why did he not need to write to them about times and seasons? Because he had already taught the Thessalonian saints about them.[9]

Second, what did he mean by Jesus returning "as a thief in the night"? He was saying the same thing as the previous verses from Matthew -- that no one would know ahead of time the exact day. There isn't a "calendar date" which he or anyone else could point to, identifying the date of Jesus' return ahead of time. Jesus is going to return on a day that is unknown and *unknowable,* and He's going to do that *on purpose.*

But before we take that as an endorsement of imminence, Paul went on:

> But you, brethren, are not in darkness, so that this Day should overtake you as a thief.
> You are all sons of light and sons of the day. We are not of the night nor of darkness.
> Therefore, let us not sleep, as others do, but let us watch and be sober.
>
> **1 Thessalonians 5:4-6**

Just because no one knows the exact day ahead of time *does **not** mean that it should take them by surprise,* because being of the *day*– i.e., being capable of *seeing clearly,* they – we -- have been called to *be aware ahead of time.* For the very reason that there is not a calendar date to be broadcast, they would need to be *watching*, as he says in v. 6. This watching pertains to *the times and the seasons.* For those watching, the Day would not come as

---

9 See, for example, 2 Thess. 2:5.

a surprise; for anyone *not watching*, the day would come as a thief in the night – completely unexpectedly, and *to their harm!* And yet if imminence is true, there is nothing to be watching!

Jesus also speaks of watching. Hear His words from Luke's account of the Olivet Discourse:

> **28 Now when these things begin to happen, look up and lift up your heads, because your redemption draws near.**
>
> **31 So you also, when you *see these things happening*, know that the kingdom of God is near.**
> **Luke 21:28, 31** (emphasis added)

What specifically are "these things" that they will be able to see *happening*? They are all the events that we have been tracking that Jesus said would take place leading up to *His coming* – events of "the time and the season"! For example, we look to see the global empire, with ten divisions and leaders in place, and we look for a charismatic, seemingly benevolent world leader to make a seven-year treaty with Israel. Once the treaty is made, we know that exactly three and one-half years later the Great Tribulation will begin, and it won't be long after that midpoint marker that the rapture and Day of the Lord will occur. When the temple is rebuilt and the Old Covenant worship is reinstated there, that will be another key marker. He gave us these events so that we could be aware of what was coming – so the day would not overtake us *as a thief*.

Those for whom it arrives like a thief will be in *deep trouble*. The simple and repeated warnings (*to the saints*) throughout the New Testament regarding this issue, make it very clear.[10] We need only look at the examples Jesus used of Lot and of Noah to understand why it is essential to know *beforehand*.[11] Think for a moment about the situation with each of them. Neither Lot nor Noah would have escaped had they not known ahead of time. The destruction would have been inescapably upon them before they realized it. Scripture is clear that it will be the same when Jesus returns: if the day "overtakes us as a thief," it will be too late. We will not escape. Look at Jesus' closing words from the same place in Luke:

> **34 But take heed to yourselves, lest . . . that Day come on you unexpectedly.** (as a thief)
> **35 For it will come as a snare on all those who dwell on the face of the whole earth.**
> **36 Watch therefore and pray always, that you may be [counted worthy][1,2] to escape[3] all these things that will come to pass, and to stand before the Son of Man.**
> **Luke 21:34-36** (comma added to v. 36)

[1]*katischuo* G2729T – to overpower, prevail against, be superior in strength
[2]*kataxioo* G2661T – to be judged worthy
[NOTE: Ancient manuscripts differ – some use *katischuo*, some *kataxioo* – both meanings have value]
[3]*ekpheugo* G1628T – to flee out from, to escape

Like Paul, Jesus is urging us to be *spiritually awake* and sober, so that we will overcome *to escape out from* all these things going on in the earth at that time, (as well as all that is coming following the rapture), and to "stand before the Son of Man."[12] What is coming? -- the Day of God's righteous judgment and wrath on sinners! Paul used this same word for escape when speaking of those who *won't* escape at this time:

> **For when they shall say, Peace and safety, then sudden destruction cometh upon them, as travail upon a woman with child; and they shall not escape.[1] 1 Thessalonians 5:3**

[1]*ekpheugo* G1628T – to flee out of, to escape

---

10 Matt. 24:43; Luke 12:39-40; 1 Thess. 5:2, 4; 2 Pe. 3:10; Rev. 3:3, 16:15
11 Matt. 24:36-44; Luke 17:26-30
12 Jesus speaks here of escaping the tribulations on the earth, and standing before the Son of Man. This is, indeed, what Revelation says of the great multitude which appears in heaven: "I looked, and behold, a great multitude . . . *standing before the throne and before the Lamb* ..." (Rev. 7:9, emphasis added).

One group will escape – the other won't. What determines the difference? This is a KEY QUESTION. Notice what the second group is *saying*. Their words make clear they *do not see* what is just around the corner! The group that escapes sees what is coming, is intimate with Jesus, and is ready *to go* when He returns. As tough as this may be to digest, Jesus is saying here in v. 36 that the rapture is not automatic for believers! The same destruction that will overtake the unbeliever *could* overtake the believer who is not *watching and staying closely connected to the Lord in prayer.* As these verses from Luke say, when we are aware, there will be a specific time when we will *look up and lift up our heads in expectation,* knowing that our redemption draws near! This very fact tosses imminence out the window![13]

It is astonishing that in the face of so much Scripture, there are still so many who believe in and teach imminence. Unfortunately, in our attempt to make things easier for ourselves – convincing ourselves that we will be taken out of here before things get too difficult – we are blinding ourselves to the very things we need to be aware of in order to be prepared! The seriousness of this error can hardly be overestimated. It will be a dire situation for anyone who believes that there are no prior signifying events he needs to be watching for before Jesus will return. Failure to see these events means the Day could come upon him as a thief and he would not be ready!

Paul Refutes Imminence

We've been looking at some of Paul's teaching to the Thessalonians. Paul had taught these saints about end-time events when he was with them in person. But someone had arisen claiming that the rapture had already taken place (implying, therefore, that these saints had missed it), and the Day of the Lord had already begun. In his second letter to them, Paul reassured them and reviewed the order of events as he had already taught them.

> **Now, brethren, concerning the coming of our Lord Jesus Christ and our gathering together to Him, we ask you not to be soon shaken in mind or troubled, either by spirit or by word or by letter, as if from us, as though the day of Christ had come.**
> **Let no one deceive you by any means; for that Day will not come unless the falling away comes first, and the man of sin is revealed, . . . 2 Thessalonians 2:1-3**

Now here are these saints, and someone had gotten them all shaken up, thinking that the Day of the Lord (and therefore the rapture) had *already come.* The simple question we ask is *how did Paul reassure them?* He reassured them by reminding them that two unmistakable events have to happen *before* the rapture/Day of the Lord will take place! He reminded them that the Day of the Lord *will not come* until AFTER the apostasy and the revealing of the Man of Sin at the midpoint of the 70th week (two events listed, as we've seen, in the Olivet Discourse preceding Jesus' return).

The clarity of this Scripture is incontrovertible and brings the whole imminency house of cards tumbling to the ground! The consistent testimony of portion after portion of the prophetic Scriptures is that there will be a whole series of events – including these two mentioned here by Paul – that will be observable and that will play out before the coming and the rapture of the church. Let us be wise as God's people and rightly divide the Word on this issue.

Notice, incidentally, in v. 3, the warning Paul gave leading into his clarification of these two events: He said most emphatically, "*Let no one deceive you by any means!*" Paul must have sensed by the Holy Spirit how this *very issue* would be targeted with lies and distortion by the enemy of our souls. Be careful, dear Saint, that you yourself have not been deceived on this issue, and that you are not leading others astray!

Conclusion

It is true that we don't know the day or the hour, but we can – and will – know the "time and the season." We will *know* when to look up and lift up our heads; we will *know* when our redemption draws near; we will know because we are of the light and of the day and we will be *watching* – prayerfully and expectantly tracking events as they happen! When the day comes, we will be ready - it will *not* come as a snare, as a thief in the night.

---

13   And if some say this – the Olivet Discourse – was written just for the Jews. . . well, it isn't the Jews who read the New Testament – it's the church! The unconverted Jews do not listen to Jesus nor look for His coming -- they don't believe in Him. Jesus was informing those who would be looking for Him – His disciples, and all who would believe on Him through their testimony. The idea that this is speaking to the Jews here is sheer nonsense. Besides which, the same message to be watchful is given repeatedly to the church throughout the New Testament, including the 1 Thess. 5 passage we looked at above.

When the disciples asked for the sign of His coming, Jesus didn't say, "There will be no sign. I will return for you completely unexpectedly!" Instead, he began to go through the events which He said would precede His coming, ultimately arriving at what He called "the sign." If there are no precursors to His return, why did Jesus go through all those events and say, "This will happen, and then that, but the end isn't yet. Then this will happen, and then this, and *then* you will see the sign of the Son of Man in heaven." If those events will not all happen before He returns for us, then He was lying to the disciples and us also, telling us there will be prior events when there won't be! (And there is *no question* that the Olivet Discourse, with the instructions that follow it, is spoken *to His disciples* – those who believe in Him – as those who will *need* it and *heed* it when the time comes.)

On the other hand, if His appearing in Matt. 24 was at the end of the 70th week, why then did He need to give all those lead-in events? Everyone would have already known that it was the time and being ready would no longer be relevant. Why are none of the wrath judgments mentioned, if they all happen during that time? And what would that gathering of the saints in vv. 30-31 be, except the church? There has been *no other mention of a gathering* – no mention of a *prior* gathering. And when Jesus returns at the end of the 70th week, He *brings the saints with Him!* He is no longer "gathering" them. No, Jesus doesn't lie. His Word IS true, and the doctrine of imminence, as well as that of a secret rapture, are false doctrines. Scripture does not bear them out.

The Whole 70th Week – Day of the Lord?

We have alluded to this previously but will mention it again. Apparently because the Word is so clear that the rapture occurs right before the Day of the Lord's Wrath, proponents of pre-tribulation rapturism identify the whole 70th week as the Day of the Lord. This, however, violates the clear sequence of events seen in the Olivet Discourse, where those cosmic signs occur well *into* the 70th week, after the midpoint, in fact; and in chapter 6 of Revelation where the peoples of the world are indisputably alerted to the imminent Day of Wrath by those same cosmic signs. As is *clearly* set forth in Revelation 7, the wrath is delayed until the two great events of chapter 7 can take place, and then it begins with the removal of the 7th seal and the opening of the scroll in Revelation 8. Clearly, the Day of the Lord is not the whole 70th week but begins at some point after the midpoint. This order – the signs in the heavens *preceding* the Day of the Lord - is also stated clearly in Joel:

> **The sun shall be turned into darkness, and the moon into blood, *before* the great and the terrible day of the Lord comes. Joel 2:30 KJV** (emphasis added)

Again, since these heavenly signs occur well inside the 70th week, it is clear *that the Day of the Lord also begins well inside the 70th week.*

Satan's Wrath and God's Wrath

Revelation speaks both of Satan's wrath and God's wrath. It's been the inclination of some to equate these two as being the same, and also equate them with the whole 70th week - that is, include the seal events as part of God's wrath. As we've pointed out a number of times, the seal events are not directly generated by heaven, but by sinful men complicit with the kingdom of darkness. They are not something unprecedented for the people of the earth, but are consistent with millennia of human history liberally sprinkled with the sorrows of war, famine, disease, and injustice. They manifest the work of Satan in the earth, particularly at the midpoint, when (according to Revelation 12) *Satan's wrath* begins. We are told there that his wrath is triggered by the heavenly battle which leads to his casting down from heaven and confinement to the earth. His wrath, expressed in the constricting control of the Great Tribulation and continuing to the end of the 70th week, is characterized by his customary malevolence and lies. There is absolutely no truth, justice, or righteousness to be found in it.

God's wrath, on the other hand, begins *after* the midpoint, and (obviously) does not perpetrate wickedness, but instead pours out His righteous judgment upon a rebellious earth whose wickedness has come to utter fullness. These judgments are supremely beyond anything that man and even Satan would be *capable of generating.* They are poured out *from heaven* – from the sovereign Creator and Ruler of all things - and are such as have never before been seen on the earth, as we will see when we get to them in this book. It must be emphasized that His wrath is *not* to be equated with Satan's wrath!

In conclusion, we must say emphatically that there's no Scriptural basis for making the whole 70th week the Day of the Lord. Instead, that day is contained *within the scroll,* thus beginning at some point *inside the second half* of the 70th week, after all seven seals are removed.

The Restrainer

Before we leave pre-tribulationism, we need to address the issue of 'the restrainer.' Paul speaks in his second letter to the Thessalonian church of one who restrains the full development of "the mystery of iniquity." Speaking of the antichrist, he says:

> **Now you know what is restraining[1] him, to the end that he may be revealed in his own season. For the mystery of lawlessness already works. Only there is one who restrains[1] now, until he is taken out of the way.**
>
> **Then the lawless one will be revealed. . . 2 Thessalonians 2:6-8 WEB**

> [1]*katecho* G2722T – to hold back, detain, retain, restrain, hinder (the course or progress of); to hold fast, keep secure, get and keep firm possession of

Paul teaches here that a hidden work of sin, fomented by Satan within the church, was already going on at that time. Hidden, because if people knew what was *really* going on "behind the curtain," they would see Satan at work, be appalled, and try to deal with it, or at least flee from it. Satan desires to increase this hidden work until it reaches a place of fullness where he can bring it out in the open and it's too late for any protest or prevention. By then, he will have gained the desired place of power and control. Paul explains that God, ever in ultimate control, will restrain this secret work of iniquity from coming into fullness until this Man of Sin's "own season" arrives; that is, the time determined by God when Satan will finally be allowed to achieve his long-held goal of total world domination. Then, and only then, will the one who is doing the restraining be removed out of the way, allowing the great swelling of darkness and wickedness that will carry the Wicked One to power.

The Holy Spirit as Restrainer

The pre-trib view of the rapture teaches that with the church leaving the earth right before the 70th week begins, the Holy Spirit, being in the church, also leaves. The Holy Spirit in the church has been the One restraining this development of evil all during the church age, and with the departure of the church, the restrainer leaves also, allowing the full development of the evil, all the way to the Abomination at the midpoint.

This might be a neat little package of thought, except for a few problems. Because the rapture is purported to take place before the seals begin, the great multitude which appears in heaven (Rev. 7) must be people who come to faith in a great evangelistic outreach carried out by the 144,000 Jews. This leaves us with a few perplexing questions:

1. If the Holy Spirit has left the earth, *how* did this great multitude of people become born again? Scripture tells us that "No man can say that Jesus is Lord *except by the Holy Spirit.*"[14]
2. Jesus said, "this gospel of the kingdom shall be preached in all the world for a witness to all nations, and then the end shall come."[15] How is it that a group of Jews (who apparently don't have the Holy Spirit? – because He's left the earth?) (and how did *they* become born again?) are able bring to faith a multitude *so great that no man can number them,*[16] when the church,

---

14 1 Cor. 12:3
15 Matt. 24:14
16 Rev. 7:9

filled with the Holy Spirit and fulfilling the Great Commission before the end, was not able to bring them to faith?

Why, in fact, would Jesus not *wait* – a few more weeks or months - for this great multitude of Gentile Christians to be saved so they also could be included in the rapture? It makes no sense to have the rapture and *then* all these people are saved! No, it's after *the fullness* of the Gentiles come in that Israel begins to turn to the Lord, with the 144,000 being *the beginning* of that turning.[17] To say that the 144,000 bring the Gentiles to faith is to have it backward; instead, they are the first fruits of the harvest of *Jews* – the harvest which *begins after* the full number of Gentiles is saved. James agrees also, saying that the heavenly Father waits long and patiently for the precious fruit of the earth [the harvest of souls that completes the church] before the *coming* of the Lord – that is, the rapture -- takes place.[18]

3. These problems force "pre-tribbers" to allow that the Holy Spirit *must* still be active on the earth, and therefore is *not removed*, disqualifying Him as the Restrainer. Either that, or neither the 144,000 nor the great multitude of Rev. 7 can come to faith during the 70th week. This appears to me an insoluble dilemma, the answer to which, is that the Holy Spirit is NOT the Restrainer.

Satan's Goal

Before we look at a different possibility for the identity of the restrainer, let's diverge from the topic briefly to review what happened at the Tower of Babel under the leadership of Nimrod. Nimrod was the first one to organize resistance to God in the earth, giving full human cooperation to Satan's agenda of establishing a false religious system and building a kingdom in opposition to the true God. This was an organized apostasy with the goal of diverting power and worship unto himself instead of God. God, of course, "restrained" it, destroying the unity of the people and scattering them through the dividing of their languages. But this has continued to be Satan's goal - his lust - and he's attempted it over and over down through the millennia, establishing himself in one earthly kingdom after another.

When the church began, he immediately inserted himself secretly into the church (the "mystery" of iniquity[19]) seeking craftily to draw worship and obedience to himself via religious and deceiving spirits. This hidden work of self-will (lawlessness) will come to its fullness at the end, bringing climactic defilement into the church itself, as well as into the Jewish temple, when he steps forward, finally unveiled, to claim *openly* that he is god and should be worshipped and obeyed. This will finally be possible, Paul explains, because the one restraining him has stepped *out of the way*, allowing him a forward path.

A Biblical Identity for the Restrainer

Paul had apparently explained to the Thessalonian church who the restrainer was. Don't you wish he had repeated it – for our sakes? But we will do our best to identify him, believing that his identity is found in the Word. We consider that Israel is the prime target of this whole end-time plan of Satan's: Antichrist's work with the world merely confirms and seals their state of utter spiritual darkness, and his work with the church (following the midpoint) is fairly brief, compared to his role with Israel.

Our best hints as to the identity of this restrainer come from the book of Daniel, where the archangel Michael shows up several times as Israel's advocate and defender. It makes sense that Michael, the angel specifically assigned to guard Israel, would be the one who, through the centuries, restrains Satan in his repeated attempts to eliminate Israel forever as the nation which God will use, finally and utterly, to *overthrow and replace his kingdom of darkness*.[20]

In the beginning of the 10th chapter, we see Daniel setting his heart to seek God with prayer and fasting. After three weeks he receives a heavenly visitation, at which time the messenger who comes to him explains that the

---

17   Romans 11:25-26
18   James 5:7-8
19   E.g., 2 Thess. 2:7, 1 John 2:18-19, 4:1.
20   We will see this when we look at the final events of the 70th week.

prince (angel) of the kingdom of Persia had hindered him from coming in response to Daniel's prayers; but that Michael, one of the chief (angelic) princes, had come to his aid, enabling him to prevail over the Persian kings and to bring to Daniel the message from the Lord. Toward the end of the chapter, the angel asks Daniel if he knows why he has come to him, and then he tells him,

> **"I will show you what is written in the writings of truth; and there is no one who holds[1] with me in these things, but Michael your prince." Daniel 10:21**

[1]*chazak* H2388S – to bind, restrain; to seize, fasten upon, be strong; to strengthen, conquer

This angelic messenger then proceeds to deliver to Daniel, from "the writings of truth," the message that makes up the final two chapters of Daniel. The message pertains to his people Israel, and most of it, to events at the end. This messenger, very probably the pre-incarnate Christ, is aided by the powerful Michael, who was assigned to the nation of Israel as their advocate, protector, and the *only one* who, along with this messenger, *strengthened himself to prevail over enemies on behalf of Israel.* As if the Lord would use this very word to help us identify the restrainer, the word *chazak* appears to be the Hebrew synonym of the Greek word *katecho*, used in 2 Thess. 2:6-7 to describe the work of the restrainer:

> [1]*katecho* G2722T – to hold back, detain, retain, restrain, hinder (the course or progress of); to hold fast, keep secure, get and keep firm possession of

The similarity of the two words is unmistakable!

We now proceed to the last verse of Daniel 11, where we see the end-time ruler (described in vv. 32-39) planting himself in "the glorious holy mountain," the elevation of Jerusalem. The very next verse (there was originally no chapter break), speaking of the midpoint, tells us:

> **At that time Michael [shall stand up],[1] the great prince who [stands][1] watch over the sons of your people; and there shall be a time of trouble, such as never was since there was a nation, even to that time. Daniel 12:1 NKJV**

[1]*amad* H5975T,S – to stand, in a variety of postures: stand, stand aside, stand up, stand still

Amad is used twice in this verse; note the definition of it. Michael's usual posture was to stand on behalf of Israel. At this time something changes so that the usual protection is removed. We conclude then, since *amad* is used in various meanings of the word "stand," that at this time in the future, instead of *standing watch over* Israel, Michael will *stand aside*, allowing this time of great trouble to take place.[21] This is the most direct Scripture that I'm aware of that refers to anyone playing this kind of role as a restrainer of evil on behalf of Israel, and then removing himself as protector *right at this specific time* in the future.

In Revelation 12 we see a further indication of the key role Michael plays at this time, where, with other angels, he engages in a heavenly battle with Satan and his angels. The result of the battle is that Satan and his angels are cast out of heaven and from then on, confined to earth. This takes place *right before the midpoint* of the 70th week, and it is probably at this time that the deadly wound and "resurrection" take place. Satan responds with great fury to being cast out and cast down, undoubtedly precipitating Antichrist's unveiling and his vicious power grab at the midpoint. We won't explore the significance of this heavenly battle beyond mentioning it here, but it is worth considering as a further aspect of Michael's role in stepping aside as protector, and even hastening Satan's rise to power in the earth.[22]

---

21   Marv Rosenthal cites this definition as given by the great Hebrew scholar Rashi: cited by Judah J. Slotki in *Daniel, Ezra, Nehemiah* (London: The Soncino Press, 1978), p. 101. Rosenthal also quotes a Midrash comment on Daniel 12:1: "The Holy One, Blessed be He, said to Michael, 'You are silent? You do not defend my children.'" Marv Rosenthal, *The Pre-Wrath Rapture of the Church* (Nashville: Thomas Nelson Publishers, 1990), p. 258

22   We will take a more in-depth look at these events in *Part 2*.

When we put all these Scriptures together, we have a very strong biblical basis for saying the restrainer is Michael – much stronger than for identifying him as the Holy Spirit.

In Conclusion

We have not addressed Revelation 3:10 in this refutation chapter. This verse is one which seems clearly to support a pre-tribulation rapture. It is a verse which we will address in *Part 2* of this book. This is not an attempt to avoid it. There is, in fact, a different explanation for it that is fully consistent with the Word, but it requires laying a foundation of understanding that is complex enough that we are not going to go into it here. I would add that though this verse might seem to support a pre-tribulation rapture, there is no way that a single verse can bring balance to the scale when there is such an overwhelming weight of evidence placed on the *other* side of the scale - from verse after verse and passage after passage - supporting a rapture associated with *the coming* -- a coming associated with the Day of the Lord, both of which begin *inside the 70ᵗʰ week,* following the midpoint and the great cosmic disruptions. It is never *textually justifiable* to take a large and consistent body of clear Scriptures and overturn them with a few verses which seem not to fit, in order to try to build a case for a doctrine which has been chosen for belief before the biblical basis for it can be established. This is the kind of wresting of the Word which Peter said clearly "leads to destruction." May God spare us from taking such unjustifiable and dangerous liberties with the truth.

Facing Our Fears

Having gone through this list of refutations of the pre-tribulation rapture, we close with a reiteration of one of the strongest admonitions of Scripture related to this false teaching: the command given over and over in the Word, to *"fear not!"* Jesus said more specifically, "Fear not those who kill the body but cannot kill the soul. But rather fear Him who is able to destroy both soul and body in hell."[23] Fear of pain, persecution, and possible death at the hands of men compels many to treat the Word in such a sloppy and disrespectful way as to try to build a case for pre-tribulationism. There is *no place* in Scripture that allows a child of God to tolerate fear in their life, much less to "protect and extend" it by encircling it with false hope and false teaching. God has never promised His people immunity from suffering and persecution. Instead, He has commanded us *not to fear it.* Why? Because fear will cause us to compromise our *walk with God* and the integrity of our relationship with Him. And because the fear of man *brings a snare!*[24] To fall into the hands of the living God in the Day of His Wrath is *far worse* than anything Antichrist can do to a believer.

As we approach the challenges and trials of that time, it is appropriate not just to establish our hearts in faith, but to seek the Lord for wisdom and guidance concerning any preparations – physical, financial, spiritual, relational – that He would have us make. Twice, the Proverbs teach us, "A prudent man foresees evil and hides himself, but the simple pass on and are punished."[25] It is good and wise to anticipate needs and to make appropriate provision as God leads us, provision not only for ourselves, but to share with others. When a young boy's lunch was placed in Jesus' hands, with His blessing it became an abundant meal for thousands of people, with baskets of remnants left over. As we face the evident truths of Scripture and submit ourselves and our loved ones to the Lord, we can become part of the provision and strength of the overcoming Bride.

---

23 Matt. 10:28
24 Prov. 29:25
25 Prov. 22:3; 27:12

CHAPTER 17

Readiness for
the Return of Christ

Before we continue chronologically, we're going to pause and take a look at the issue of readiness to meet Christ. We have alluded to this in the last two chapters, but Jesus Himself makes it such a prominent issue that it's something we can't ignore if we're going to be faithful to the Word.

This is an issue I have wrestled with myself – does the whole church slip away with Him by virtue of rebirth, or is it not that simple? It seemed like it *should* be that simple – rebirth should qualify us for the rapture. But I kept running into portions of the Word that give a different message, so after puzzling over it for a while, the Word has won out for me. Let's take a look.

The Olivet Discourse continues well beyond Jesus' coming, as Jesus goes on to warn of being *ready* for His return.

> **Watch therefore, for you do not know when the master of the house is coming — in the evening, at midnight, at the crowing of the rooster, or in the morning — lest, coming suddenly, he finds you sleeping.**
>
> **And what I say to you, I say to all: Watch!**   Mark 13:35-37

In a way, the warning has simplicity to it: No one will know the day or hour, and if we're not *watching*, it will come upon us as a thief. If it comes upon us as a thief, the result, as Paul said, is *sudden destruction.*[1] This, of course, is the stated future of the unbeliever. It *should not be* what happens to the believer. Nevertheless, as we've said before, the numerous warnings send the clear message that even for believers, it's possible *not* to be watching, *not* to be ready. Why would Jesus warn us, if *not being ready* was not a real possibility? No, we need to be *watching* and in prayer;[2] as Paul said, we need to be awake ("of the day"), sober, protecting our hearts with faith and love, and our minds with the *hope of salvation.*[3] Again, what are we watching? <u>We are watching the events</u> which Jesus said would precede His coming for us. Of course, for those who *have* been watching and tracking events, choices have been clear; the mark has been *refused;* hope is strong, and the wait for Christ's return is a *clear focus!*

---

1   1 Thess. 5:3
2   Matt. 24:42,44; Luke 21:36
3   1 Thess. 5:4-9

We are also watching over our own relationship with Him:

> **So be careful, or your hearts will be loaded down with carousing, drunkenness, and cares of this life, and that day will come on you suddenly. Luke 21:34 WEB**

This issue of our own relationship with Him is the most important one! Let's take a closer look.

Guarding Our Own Relationship with Him

In this section we will look at three groups whose expectations at the end were grievously disappointed, due to issues in their relationship with Him.

1. Those Who "Hang Out" with Jesus - Luke 13:23-30

> **24 Strive to enter through the narrow gate, for many, I say to you, will seek to enter and will not be able.**
> **25 When once the Master of the house has risen up and shut the door, and you begin to stand outside and knock at the door, saying, 'Lord, Lord, open for us,' and He will answer and say to you, 'I do not know you, where you are from,'**
> **26 then you will begin to say, 'We ate and drank in Your presence, and You taught in our streets.'**
> **27 But He will say, 'I tell you *I do not know you*, where you are from. Depart from Me, all you workers of iniquity.'** (emphasis added)

This is a group of people who did not enter the kingdom by the narrow gate – that is, they came in with self and with the baggage that accompanies self. Other relationships, money, family, making their own choices in life, hiding a secret sin – any or all of these, or some similar thing, came before Jesus. Though they attended church and went to conferences, maybe taught Sunday School, they never saw themselves in the light of the cross of Christ – the sentence of death passed upon all that they were and all that they had *apart from Him*. They never fully surrendered to Him. They lived their lives on their own terms – to one extent or another – and never really came under His Lordship. In the end, the verdict from Jesus will be: "I don't know you, where you are from. Depart from Me, all you workers of iniquity!" They were self-deceived; what a shock at the end to find that the door was shut to them and they were left on the outside!

2. The "Many-Wonderful-Works" Gang - Matthew 7:13-23

> **21 Not everyone who says to Me, 'Lord, Lord,' shall enter the kingdom of heaven, but he who does the will of My Father in heaven.**
> **22 Many will say to Me in that day, 'Lord, Lord, have we not prophesied in Your name, cast out demons in Your name, and done many wonders in Your name?'**
> **23 And then I will declare to them, *'I never knew you*; depart from Me, you who practice lawlessness!'** (emphasis added)

This is another group which did not enter at the narrow gate. They came into the kingdom still deeply attached to self, and Jesus identified their problem as never really submitting to the Father's will for them. This is similar to the last group, but Jesus shows the issue as manifesting a little differently. This group went wholeheartedly into service for the Lord – they "prophesied in His name, cast out demons in His name, and in His name, did many wonderful works!" They were very busy operating in the supernatural for the Lord, but when the time of accounting took place, Jesus' sentence upon them is that *He never knew them* (in the intimate way that He longs to know us, as we surrender to Him), and He commands them to "depart from Me, you workers of lawlessness!" Or we could say, "You workers of *self-will*," because even though we may be doing kingdom work, if we do it out of independent *self*, in God's eyes that is lawlessness. It is failure to submit to Him as Lord! Earlier in the passage He identifies them as ravening wolves!! Wow! There they were, doing all these *marvelous* things for His kingdom and in His name, and He *utterly rejects them!* As can be seen in the parable that follows (in Matt. 7), their house will come crashing down! It wasn't founded on obedience to Him. This is a hard thing for us to wrap our minds around. But it does help us identify what Jesus is looking for in His relationship with us. More on that shortly.

3. The "Insufficient Oil" Gang - Matthew 25:1-13

> **6 And at midnight a cry was heard: 'Behold, the bridegroom is coming; go out to meet him!'**
> **7 Then all those virgins arose and trimmed their lamps.**
> **8 And the foolish said to the wise, 'Give us some of your oil, for our lamps are going out.'**
> **9 But the wise answered, saying, 'No, lest there should not be enough for us and you; but go rather to those who sell, and buy for yourselves.'**
> **10 And while they went to buy, the bridegroom came, and those who were ready went in with him to the wedding; and the door was shut.**
> **11 Afterward the other virgins came also, saying, 'Lord, Lord, open to us!'**
> **12 But he answered and said, 'Assuredly, I say to you, *I do not know you.'***
> **13 Watch therefore, for you know neither the day nor the hour in which the Son of Man is coming.** (emphasis added)

This is the Parable of the Ten Virgins, one we're all fairly familiar with. Of course, that doesn't mean we really understand it, as it too, is a passage that is a bit puzzling. We notice right away the number ten. Ten in Scripture signifies testing, discipline, and opportunity. God took the children of Israel through ten tests after they left Egypt. After consistently meeting all ten tests with rebellion and unbelief, the verdict came down from God. They would not go into the land – the door of opportunity closed for them.[4] So also with this parable there is testing, opportunity, and the closing of the door for some.

All ten of these were virgins. We understand from this that they had been cleansed by faith in Jesus' blood – they were ready to be presented as "chaste virgins" to Christ.[5] So we understand that all ten were born again believers, possessing the oil of the Holy Spirit and awaiting Jesus' return.

The difficulty is that only half of them actually went with Jesus at His return. How can this be? How are we to understand this? We are told that the problem was a lack of oil – and when they realized the problem, they left to go find those who *sold* the oil so they could *buy* more. To get to the heart and essence of the problem, and therefore the message of the parable, we must consider the question, "How do we *purchase* the Holy Spirit?" We know that the Holy Spirit has been poured out freely because of Jesus' death on our behalf. We have been cleansed by the blood and are therefore able to receive the Holy Spirit. There is no money that can buy Him into our lives. Why then does this parable speak of *buying*? A similar question arises in Isaiah 55:

> **Ho! Everyone who thirsts, come to the waters; and you who have no money, come, buy and eat. Yes, come, buy wine and milk without money and without price. Isaiah 55:1**

Here the Holy Spirit is spoken of as water – the living water. All are invited to come and buy, even those without money. There is no price, and yet, again, we are to *buy*. So, what is the "medium of exchange" with which we "purchase" spiritual water and oil? Jesus answered this question for us:

---

4 Numbers 14:22
5 2 Cor. 11:2

If anyone desires to come after Me, let him deny himself, and take up his cross, and follow Me.
For whoever desires to save his life[1] will lose it, but whoever loses his life[1] for My sake will find it.
For what profit is it to a man if he gains the whole world, and loses his own soul?[1] Or what will a man give in exchange for his soul?[1] Matthew 16:24-26

[1] *psuche* G5590T – soul; the breath, the breath of life: the seat of feelings, desires, affections; the essence of man which differs from the body and is not dissolved by death

We can read "self" here for "soul." The soul is commonly understood as the mind, the will, and the emotions of the natural self; that is, the self we are born with in natural birth. It is distinguished from *the reborn SPIRIT* in Scripture. Jesus teaches us here to let go completely of the soul. If a person holds onto his own life – his *self*, and gains all that he could want, even to the gaining of the whole world, how would that benefit him if, in the end, he loses his own soul? **What exists that has greater value than his soul, that would be worth giving up his soul in order to gain?** This is the issue here and is the great question for all mankind. Jesus came offering His eternal life, but He is making it clear that to obtain that life – the Holy Spirit – there must be a laying down of our *own* life. The two "lives" will not co-exist peacefully together with both being "in charge."[6] We will yield to and then be controlled by one *or* the other – by our own soulish life, or by His life, resident in our reborn spirit. As we have seen in our two previous passages of Scripture (#'s 1 and 2 above), many will try to have *both*, will deceive themselves, and will lose out in the end. We cannot have both. To have the Holy Spirit, there must be surrender of self and *self-will*. To the extent we yield self, to that extent we have 'purchased' and 'possess' the Holy Spirit.

This is how the virgins purchase their oil. The five foolish virgins were initially born again – had oil – but did not grow spiritually through the *ongoing* yielding of self and self-will. Sadly, when it comes to the end, the foolish virgins, like the Israelites, will not be able to make it over the finish line. In spite of believing in Jesus and heading toward the finish line, they had retained rights to themselves, and in the end, they came up lacking. The verdict for them is the same as the two previous groups: "Truly I say to you, *I don't know you.*"

Why Will Some Not Make It?

So, we see that in all three of these passages, the underlying issue is the same – it is the failure to submit fully to the Lordship of Christ, letting go of the things of self in order to come into the fullness of the Holy Spirit as well as the intimacy that comes with full surrender to Him. As with the Israelites in the wilderness, God continually presents us with opportunities to yield up our own ways and resources, our own fleshly responses, our old natural ways of thinking and acting, etc. Each opportunity is a test of who is really on the throne of our life – Jesus or self.

This what Paul speaks about so eloquently in the third chapter of his epistle to the Philippians. He speaks of all the things of self that he could take pride in. He had reached the zenith of the righteousness that natural (soulish) man is capable of, and yet he throws it all aside, counting it as utterly useless. He explains that whatever honor and value he would retain for himself would mean a loss of glory for Christ. His heart's passion is "to win Christ, and be found *in Him*," not having his own righteousness, which is of the law -- i.e., of the independent capabilities of self. He goes on to say, "That I may *know Him*, and the power of His resurrection, and the fellowship of His sufferings, being made conformable unto His death. . ." We are called to submit to Him all that we are in ourselves – that is, self, with all of its loves and strengths and abilities, its pride, its secret wounds, lusts, and sins, its ambitions and addictions, its blindness and deceptions, its rationalizations and justifications of sin, its good deeds and high moral achievements. Only the wonderful Holy Spirit can see all these often-secret roots in our lives and lovingly and faithfully lead us on the progressive path to repentance and victory over them. We must allow God to illuminate our hearts for us, and let the Holy Spirit work deeply in our hearts, our understanding, and our experience. Our strong and independent soulish life is too deeply embedded in each of us for us to deal

---

6 Romans 8:5-7, Galatians 5:17

with it ourselves. As we cooperate with Him in this process, repenting of and experiencing death to these issues, exchanging *our* life for *His,* we come *to know Him.*

Paul said the end of all this is that "I may attain to the resurrection of the dead."[7] There is coming a resurrection after the Millennium, when ALL who have not yet risen will rise.[8] The one with the rapture is called "the first resurrection" and is the one that Paul is seeking to *attain to.* In the very expression he uses, we can see that being in the rapture is not automatic to those who would call themselves Christians. To teach that all who are born again will make it in the rapture is simply not consistent with Scripture. Jesus' words of indictment to all three of the groups we looked at above (who either were, or thought themselves to be, Christians) were, "I do not know you!" And Paul is showing us here in Philippians *how we come to know Him.* This is about experiential sharing in His death and resurrection. It is about union and intimacy with Him. The five wise virgins had learned this and were doing it -- *purchasing,* and therefore *possessing,* an abundance of oil -- and were ready when Jesus came, attaining unto the resurrection.

The message of these three points is that we are not to take just *the blood* of Christ for our sins, but we are to yield the *source* of sin in our lives, the self, to His *cross.*

"If anyone comes to Me and does not hate his father and mother, wife and children, brothers and sisters, *yes, and his own life*[1] *also,* he cannot be My disciple. Luke 14:26 (emphasis added)

> [1]*psuche* G5590T – soul; the breath, the breath of life: the seat of feelings, desires, affections; the essence of man which differs from the body and is not dissolved by death

If we truly love Him, we will hate our own life as He requires, and we will love His work in us to cleanse us of every hidden sin and every spot of self. This is the full salvation *unto holiness* that He has provided: ". . . holiness, without which no one shall see the Lord."[9]

This holiness includes our hearts fully turned toward heaven and away from the world. We are warned to "remember Lot's wife."[10] All it took was one backward glance, but the glance revealed a connection her heart had yet with *that which was coming under judgment.* Let us be careful not to love anything that God will judge! We must be on guard as to what our heart goes after – what is it attached to – what do we love? Do we love money or a property? Do things have sentimental value that would cause us to cast a lingering look backward? Are there people in our lives we would cling to, reluctant to part with? We must be *ready to leave all* when He comes. Our first love must always be Him – His kingdom and His righteousness. This alertness to the "loves of our heart" is the purity that John spoke of:

> **We know that when He is revealed, we shall be like Him, for we shall see Him as He is. And everyone who has this hope in Him purifies himself, just as He is pure. 1 John 3:2-3**

Notice how John said we purify *ourselves.* This speaks to the personal responsibility we take for ourselves – response-ability we have to the work of the Holy Spirit as He reveals to us things that we need to deal with. We must school our own lives, standing guard over the attachments of our hearts and over our relationship with the Lord. We *work out* our own salvation with fear and trembling as He works *within* us – giving us both the desire and the power to please Him.[11] We respond to His inward work with repentance, receiving the grace we need to make the needed changes. This is all about loving Him and desiring, more than anything else, to please Him.

What About Those Who Miss the Rapture?

I have wondered for years about those 'Christians' who do *not* go in the rapture. What happens to them? Do they get another chance? I have never discerned in Scripture the answer to this, other than what is indicated with

---

7   Phil. 3:3-11 Also termed a "better" resurrection (Heb. 11:35), this first resurrection is extended to include all the saints killed for their faith after the general rapture (Rev. 20:4-5). They are resurrected at the end of the 70th week, and, like the raptured saints, enter the Millennium with glorified bodies.
8   Rev. 20:11-13
9   Heb. 12:14
10   Luke 17:32
11   Phil. 2:12-13

these three groups I have mentioned in this chapter. Someone asked me that question recently, causing me to ponder it again. As I did, light began to come to me.

First, I remembered Jesus' words to the church of Sardis, that they were in a dangerous place spiritually, with much that was already dead, and the few remaining things "ready to die"; and that if they were not careful to repent, He would come upon them "as a thief," meaning they would be *unprepared* and therefore *would not go with Him.* Furthermore, those who would not repent and thus overcome would have their names *blotted out of the Book of Life* (Rev. 3:1-5). Wow! Their only options were to *repent and overcome* <u>or</u> have their names blotted out!

Then the Holy Spirit led my thoughts to the five foolish virgins of Matthew 25. I turned there and read again, and realized, *they were not ready when He came!* They had to retreat to "buy" more oil, and after He had *been there and gone,* they approached Him <u>wanting late entrance</u>! Well, *yes,* I thought, *His coming and leaving was the rapture.* That's always been understood! Yet I had missed the implications: They were not ready when He came, but when they sought *late entrance,* it was *not granted!* They did not get another chance! The fact that they were not ready when He arrived meant that they *did not KNOW Him,* and knowing Him was the "make it or break it" issue!

Then my mind went to the other passage we mentioned above, Luke 13! And I realized, *that's the same situation!* The Master has gathered His people into His house and has "shut fast the door" – *locked it!* And someone calling Him "Lord" arrives *late* seeking entrance! It's the same scenario! They 'present their case' to Him as to why He should let them in and it turns out that they also, did not truly *know Him,* and therefore did not qualify as *His.* The door was not only closed, but locked. Here, He makes it clear that they will end up with "weeping and gnashing of teeth" among all others who are cast out (v.28) as hypocrites.[12]

I would add that I am not aware of any portion of Revelation that indicates there will be a late arrival of 'Christians' who missed the rapture. The Scripture seems consistent that when the door closes for Gentiles, *it is closed for good.* However, we do note that there are those in the second resurrection whose names are written in the Book of Life (Rev. 20:12). Are these just the believers that die during the Millennium, or are there others? That mystery remains to be deciphered at another time. For now, suffice to say, it continues to amaze me how God is able to hide things in plain sight! The answer was right there: the rapture took place, these came afterward seeking entrance, and did not obtain it! We are so dependent on the Holy Spirit as our Teacher to see the things of God!

As we close out our thoughts on readiness, we simply say that the call of the Spirit is always upward toward loving Him, following Him in purity, and watching and waiting with a wholly consecrated heart:

> **To those who [eagerly wait for][1] Him He will appear a second time, apart from sin, for salvation. Hebrews 9:28**
>
> [1]*apekdechomai* G553T – to wait for patiently with great care and perseverance

NOTE: In Appendix 6 I share a dream the Lord gave me a number of years ago about the lack of readiness of the Bride for Jesus' return.

---

12   See Matt. 22:13; 24:51; 25:30

SECTION 6

THE SCROLL
IS OPENED

CHAPTER 18

The Beginning of the Day of the Lord

Chronologically, we have arrived at the opening of the seventh seal, found in chapter 8 of Revelation. Remember that **the seal events bring to fullness mankind's rebellion against God as well as all that man has been able to accomplish apart from God.** Under the mesmerizing global leadership of the false messiah, the whole earth has now become *fully ripe* for the just judgment of God. With the removal of that last seal and the opening of the scroll, we find ourselves in the Day of the Lord's Wrath.

What is the Day of the Lord?

This Day of the Lord has long been a time anticipated by the people of God, who, enduring mistreatment at the hands of the ungodly, understood that this would be the time of the final defeat of all their enemies, and their instatement as God's kingdom people in the earth. We understand it to be what signals *the end* – the end of the age and the end of the *day of man*. The significance of this time can hardly be overstated. This is a time when wickedness is judged and the wrongs and injustices of the ages will be righted. The plans, works, and institutions of the wicked will be destroyed, while the righteous will be resurrected, rewarded, and exalted to *inherit the earth.*[1] The Day of the Lord is for the *purging* of the earth in preparation for the righteous Millennial rule of Christ and His saints.

Remember, the scroll contains the title deed to the earth – the terms for the redemption of the earth and the completion of man's redemption. Two thousand years earlier Christ paid the ransom price. At His second coming He will return to *complete* the redemption and execute the events that will finally bring down Satan's rule over the earth.

For the unsaved of the earth – the rebels – as well as for the saints of Christ, things are pretty well decided and settled by the time the Day of the Lord arrives. We will see that the people of the earth do not repent under the wrath judgments; instead, they seem to become more hardened in their rebellion. And of course, the church, sanctified and set apart by the Holy Spirit, will leave right before the wrath begins.

God's purpose for the Jews during this time is different from that of the world or the church. The Day of the Lord begins the fulfillment of their Feast of Trumpets, when, at the sound of the "last trump,"[2]

---

1 Ps. 37, Matt. 5:5, Gen. 17:8 (Heb. 11:8), Jer. 32:37-42, Jer. 33,
2 For thoughts on the last trump – what and when -- see Appendix 7.

three different groups receive attention from God: The righteous are gathered to God, the wicked are punished, and *the Jews* enter a time (ten symbolic days) of testing and decision. For them, this is a time of **remembrance** – remembrance of Yahweh, His covenantal mercies, and their transgressions – and of **repentance**. The whole 70th week – from the treaty with Antichrist until the final desperate days of Armageddon -- is the time designated by God for the Jews' national turning back to God. From Old Testament times, the plan has been that the Messianic rule of the earth would be executed *with God's covenantal people,* the Jews.[3] The kingdom was promised forever to the house and line of David, specifically as that line came through Christ; participating also in the kingdom would be Christ's Jewish brethren from the rest of the tribes.[4] For those Jews who have any vestige of hope in the kingdom promises given long before to their fathers, now is the time to be serious about them. God has long known that their blindness and hardness of heart is so deep-seated that the dire and painful straits of both the Great Tribulation and the Day of the Lord would be required in order to remove it. He is working with them and wooing them now in the midst of terrible chastenings and trials. (We will see the wooing more clearly when we look soon at the two witnesses.)

So, while the Day of the Lord is a time of terrible judgment upon the wicked, it is a time of tempered mercy for the Jews. The verdict is still out on them during this time. Those who refuse to repent will not survive these wrath judgments. But for those who turn and become the believing remnant, great mercy is available, and these "ten days" will culminate in the fulfillment of the next Jewish feast, *the national Day of Atonement.* God has His eyes and heart set on this remnant. As with the 144,000, He knows and is protecting each one of them as they go through the difficulties of this season. We will look more closely at this turning as we go through the events of this time.

For the Gentiles, there is very little, if any, turning possible; the time of mercy is over, and it is now a time of implacable judgment. We will see that at the end of this time, there are only a handful of people left on the earth, and the earth itself is essentially – and appropriately -- left as a blackened, smoking ruin; appropriate as representing all that Satan was able to accomplish as prince over the earth.

Now the redemption accomplished by Christ 2,000 years ago will come to its full expression: dominion over the earth will transition from Satan to the Lion of Judah and His righteous followers. Now the stone cut out without hands will crash into the great image of Nebuchadnezzar, reducing the kingdom of Babylon into chaff blown away by the wind. Now will the derisive laughter of God against the wicked cease as He moves in purposeful wrath to smash them in pieces like a potter's vessel and set His Son upon the holy hill of Zion. Now will the righteous of all the ages celebrate the greatness of God as they participate in setting up Christ's kingdom on the earth. The Day of the Lord sets fearful things in motion, things never before seen upon the earth -- **things of terror, of fearful holiness, and of glorious victory and unimagined joy. The uniting of heaven and earth in holy celebration will be unlike anything previously experienced by either.** Let's move on to take a closer look.

The Setting in the World for the Day of Wrath

As I studied over the years, attempting to put pieces together in the "big puzzle" of end-time events, one piece that I had trouble with was Paul's statement about the arrival of the Day of the Lord:

> **For when they say, "Peace and safety!" then sudden destruction comes upon them, as labor pains upon a pregnant woman. And they shall not escape. 1 Thessalonians 5:3**

I found myself persistently puzzled by a world that was saying "peace and safety" in the midst of *the Great Tribulation!* I knew the Day of the Lord will begin during that difficult time, and I would think, "How can they feel so safe and be so complacent when there is such a *tyrant* ruling and oppressing the world!?" It made me

---

3 This is what the disciples were referring to when they asked Jesus at the time of His ascension, "Lord, will you at this time restore the kingdom to Israel?" (Acts 1:6).
4 2 Sam. 7:11-16, 1 Chron. 22:9-10, Is. 9:6-7, Is. 24:23, Jer. 23:5-6; 31:6-19, Ezek. 34:23-24; 37:9-14, 24-25, Zech. 14:9, Luke 1:31-33

wonder if I had my facts and times straight. It is something I have continued to ponder, and was recently helped by a verse in Daniel. We have talked already about this, but as it is relevant here, I will mention it again:

Through his cunning he shall cause deceit to prosper under his rule; And he shall exalt him-self in his heart. He shall destroy many in their prosperity.[1] **Daniel 8:25**

[1]*shalveh* H7962B – quietness, ease, prosperity

Shalveh defines the very condition Paul is expressing -- "peace and safety!" The first part of the verse, "he shall cause deceit to prosper," that is, to push ahead and thrive in the earth, helps explain the last part of it. The deception will be so thorough that people will truly believe that *all is well* on planet earth! That *total misperception* makes their doom unavoidable! Oh yes, there is a group of people who are rebellious and resistant to this great leader, and yes, they have to be punished, but they are simply foolish for resisting him. They're the ones who've caused us a prob-lem for a long time, with their stringent morality and narrow views on religion! They deserve whatever harassment they're getting! But really, life is good, and we have no complaints!! *This attitude of "peace and safety" reflects the di-minished understanding of a deceived world,* <u>not</u> the awake and discerning perception of God's own people. It reflects the DEEP DIVIDE in perception between God's people and those who follow the lies of Antichrist.

Jesus spoke in Luke 17 of the sense of complacency that would characterize this time:

26 And as it was in the days of Noah, so it will be also in the days of the Son of Man:
27 They ate, they drank, they married wives, they were given in marriage, until the day that Noah entered the ark, and the flood came and destroyed them all.
28 Likewise as it was also in the days of Lot: they ate, they drank, they bought, they sold, they planted, they built;
29 but on the day that Lot went out of Sodom it rained fire and brimstone from heaven and destroyed them all.
30 Even so will it be in the day when the Son of Man is revealed.   Luke 17:26-30

Notice that Jesus isn't pointing out the great violence and wickedness present during both Noah's and Lot's Day. Rather, **He's pointing out how** *everyday life* **was going on**. Both of these Old Testament judgments were utterly catastrophic – the destruction of human lives was complete. And yet those who were destroyed were completely *oblivious* right up to the moment! They wouldn't have needed to be, particularly those in the flood: the testimony of the ark was in the earth in Noah's day. It is probably safe to say that the whole known world at that time knew about the ark. After all, it was HUGE, and Noah had been building it for one hundred years by the time it was completed. During that time, it had generated plenty of discussion, giving Noah the opportunity to explain that "the reason I'm building this 'monstrosity' is because a tremendous flood is coming that is going to wipe out all living creatures on the earth because of their godlessness, including you, unless you repent. So, you need to repent!" There was no one who could say, in the last moments before succumbing to drowning, that they had *not been warned.*

In the same way, the testimony of the gospel will have reached all the earth by the time Jesus returns. As in Noah's day, the sinners will be *without excuse.* And yet, they will be going on with life as usual: peace and safety, eat and drink, buy and sell, marry, plant, and build. They will be serenely oblivious right up to the moment that signals destruction. We see from these three passages not only the mindset of heedlessness (coming from decep-tion) that will fill the unsaved world at that time, but in the Luke passage we see Jesus setting forth a timing issue.

The Rapture and the Day of the Lord

This passage in Luke is the one that God used quite a few years ago to get my attention regarding the timing of the rapture. Until that day, I had been unsure about when it would occur. That morning, one of my first thoughts upon waking was this passage in Luke. The Holy Spirit was underscoring *the same day* aspect of it; that is, the same day that the righteous were "snatched" to safety, destruction fell upon those remaining. The only teaching I knew on the rapture was the pre-tribulation view; but I knew that the beginning of the 70th week was not a time of tremendous judgment upon the wicked, so the whole *same day* revelation puzzled me. How could the rapture – followed *the same day* by God's destruction on the wicked - be right before the 70th week, when I knew the beginning of the 70th week was not a time of destruction on the wicked, but a time when the antichrist would be going forth to build a following in the earth? It was later that same day that I first read about a <u>pre-wrath rapture</u>. I was familiar enough by then with what Scripture teaches about the end, that I knew immediately that *this was right*. A pre-wrath timing for the rapture answered so many questions - including the one from that morning - and caused so many Scriptures to fall right into place with one another. In time, the few remaining questions I had were also answered and reconciled fully with this view.

The very clear message of Luke 17 is this: The same day that Noah and his family entered the ark, the flood came and destroyed everyone else. The same day that Lot fled Sodom, utter destruction rained down upon the cities. *"Even so will it be in the day when the Son of Man is revealed."* **That is, the same day that the Son of Man appears in the heavens, snatching His people to safety, He will begin to pour out wrath upon those remaining on the earth.**

This then – on the cusp of God's wrath - is where we are in our chronological progression. We have covered the events of the sixth seal – the great cosmic shakings, the sealing of the 144,000, and the glorious appearance of Christ in the darkened sky to gather the elect. And we know from Jesus' words in these Luke verses that *the very day* that great gathering occurs, the seventh seal will come off the scroll, opening it, and the events of the Lord's wrath will begin to be poured out upon the earth.

The Day of the Lord in the New Testament

Since the chronology of the Olivet Discourse ends with the rapture, we now look to Revelation, which provides us with the only source in Scripture for an ordered sequence of events for God's wrath. His wrath, of course, is contained in the scroll, and the scroll events encompass *two* "<u>series of seven</u>" – the judgments of the **seven angels with trumpets**, followed by the judgments of **seven angels with bowls**. With the pouring forth of the seventh bowl, the wrath of God will be completed; great Babylon will be judged and the earth thoroughly purged. There is much in both the Old and New Testaments that supplements Revelation; we are going to begin with a quick look at a few of these passages in the New Testament to get a feel for what this amazing time on the earth will involve.

The Great Tribulation was a time of trial greater than any known before it or that would ever follow it (particularly for the Jews); this time now of God's wrath also involves *judgment* events of such horror and devastation as have never before been seen on the earth. Paul speaks of men with hard and unrepentant hearts "treasuring up unto themselves" wrath for the "day of wrath and revelation of the righteous judgment of God." That day, says Paul, will be one of passion and wrath, squeezing and anguish upon every man who does evil and refuses the truth.[5] We are told men will seek death and will not be able to find it.[6]

Peter tells us that whereas our earth was initially formed out from a judgment of water, the judgment that will conclude this age will be one of fire – fire that will consume both the earth and its contents:

> **But the day of the Lord will come as a thief in the night, in which the heavens will pass away with a great noise, and the elements will melt with fervent heat; both the earth and the works that are in it will be burned up. 2 Peter 3:10**

Jude speaks of the wicked who will come under judgment:

> **14 Now Enoch, the seventh from Adam, prophesied about these men also, saying, "Behold, the Lord comes with ten thousands of His saints,**

---

5   Romans 2:5, 8-9
6   Rev. 9:6

15 to execute judgment on all, to convict all who are ungodly[1] among them of all their ungodly[2] deeds which they [have committed in an ungodly way],[2] and of all the harsh things which ungodly[2] sinners have spoken against Him." Jude 14-15

[1] *psuche* G5590T – soul, soulish; the natural life of man
[2] *asebeia* G764S – impious, wicked, irreverent

Jude repeats "ungodly" multiple times throughout the verse, almost giving the feeling that he is at a loss for words as he speaks of these wicked ones. What is interesting, however, is that the first use of the word (#1) is not the usual Greek word for ungodly but is the word *psuche* – soulish.[7] This speaks of the lawlessness – the *self-will* – which we have seen will prevail both in and out of the church in the last times. But professing to be God's or not, the judgment upon all these sinners includes them being *convicted* of their godless deeds and words. They *could* be convicted *before* Jesus returns, repent, and be made right with God through faith. But their hearts are hard and their ears closed, and it isn't until it's too late, when the terror and judgment are falling upon them, that the conviction and reality of their sin overtakes them. How important it is for us to keep a tender and receptive heart toward the Lord!

Highlights of the Day of the Lord from Scriptures

Here are some high points of what will happen:

1. It is a time *cruel* with wrath and fierce punishment to destroy both people and the earth.[2,3,9,16]
   a. The earth, defiled and cursed by people's sin, is judged along with the people.
   b. The curse has come because of the breaking of God's laws and covenant.[3,4]
2. Profound treachery and deception will precede this time of judgment.[5]
3. It is a judgment on all who are wicked and *proud:*[1,2]
   a. Human leaders
   b. Human kingdoms and governments[9]
   c. Military might[9,16]
4. Judgment will be inexorable and inescapable.[3,12,14]
5. The earth will be almost emptied of people.[2,3]
6. It will be a judgment of fire on both the earth and on people.[3,6,8,11,13]
7. Commerce and economic systems will be brought down and earthly treasures destroyed.[1,9,18]
8. All idols, as well as gold and silver, will be cast aside as useless.[1,16]
9. False religions and all idolatry will be destroyed.[17]
10. People will seek to hide in caves and dens of the earth for terror of the Lord.[1,10]
11. It's a day of darkness and desolation.[12,13,16]
12. At certain times the sun, moon, and stars will be darkened and the heavens shaken.[2,9,10,13,15]
13. The earth will reel, be broken up, burn, and fall under the judgment.[5,6,7,10]
14. God will use supernatural beings to execute judgment.[13,14]

[1] Is. 2:10-21
[2] Is. 13:6-13
[3] Is. 24:3-6
[4] Dan. 7:25, Rev. 11:18, Is. 28:14-18
[5] Is. 24:16-20; Is. 66:4; 2 Thess. 2:8-12; Matt. 24:5,11; 1 Tim. 4:1

[6] 2 Peter 3:7, 10-12
[7] Nahum 1:5-6, 16:18-20, Ps. 46:2,6-10
[8] Mal. 4:1, Is. 30:27, 30
[9] Is. 34:1-8
[10] Rev. 6:12-17
[11] Rev. 16:8-9

---

7 Some manuscripts have *psuche*, some use *asebeia*, the word for the other references to 'ungodly.'

[12] Amos 5:18-20
[13] Joel 2:1-11
[14] Rev. 9:1-12, 13-19
[15] Joel 2:31, 3:15

[16] Zeph. 1:14-18
[17] Rev. 17:1-6, 15-16
[18] Rev. 18

Chronology – The Trumpet Judgments

We turn now to Revelation chapter 8, where we finally see the removal of the seventh and last seal binding the scroll. After a solemn silence lasting about one-half hour,[8] a trumpet is given to each of the seven angels around the throne.[9] The sounding of each trumpet successively will release a judgment upon the earth. We see that *the prayers of all the saints* ascending up before God are the *catalyst* for these judgments to begin to fall. And now the initial judgments of God upon the earth begin – judgments which were held back in Revelation 7 until the specific Jews could be sealed and the saints gathered to heaven.

The Seven Trumpet Judgments:

1. Hail and fire, mixed with blood, are cast to the earth, burning up all grass and one third of all trees.
2. A huge burning mountain, cast into the sea, turns one third of the sea to blood, killing one third of marine life and destroying one third of ships on the sea.
3. A great burning star, named Wormwood,[10] falls upon one third of all rivers and freshwater sources, making them bitter and bringing death to many.
4. One third of the sun, of the moon, and of the stars are struck and wounded, causing darkness for one-third of the daytime and one-third of the nighttime.

These judgments are somewhat tempered, affecting only parts of the earth. We will see that the judgments now intensify in horror and effect, as Scripture itself indicates, designating each of the **last three trumpet judgments as a "woe."** We move now into Revelation chapter 9:

5. In this **fifth trumpet**, a star -- a fallen angel -- is given the key to the bottomless pit. When opened, a great cloud of darkness escapes the pit, along with a horde of supernatural beings called locusts. These beings are given authority to sting men with their scorpion-like tails for a period of five months, causing great agony. They appear as horses wearing armor, with faces like men, hair like women, and teeth like that of lions. They are not permitted to harm grass, trees, or any living thing, other than people who do not have the seal of God in their foreheads. Their king is Abaddon/Apollyon ("destroyer"), the angel over the bottomless pit. This is the **first woe.**

We compare this horde with one spoken of in Joel chapter 1 – a strong, numberless multitude with teeth like the teeth of lions, that lays waste the vine and strips the fig tree of bark. Both the vine[11] and the fig[12] are symbols of Israel in Scripture, so rather than speaking of a literal effect on these two plants, it may be that God is referring to the pain and stripping suffered by Israel from this judgment. (Joel goes on to speak of the temple

---

8   See also Zeph. 1:7.
9   The seven throne angels were well-known to the Jews, and were sometimes called the "Angels of the Presence." Mentioned in the Book of Enoch, they are listed as Uriel, Raphael, Raquel, Michael, Sariel, Gabriel, and Remiel. Tobit 12:15 quotes one of them: "I am Raphael, one of the seven angels who stand in the glorious presence of the Lord, ready to serve Him." I believe we would be on safe ground surmising that these angels with trumpets are these same seven angels.
10   Wormwood (*apsinthe* in the Greek) is a small woody shrub, bitter in taste and acrid in scent. It is a key ingredient in absinthe, a liquor of dubious reputation because of its ingredients and its deleterious effects on people, including hallucinations. Wormwood symbolizes bitterness and calamity.
11   Ps. 80:8, 14-19; Hos. 10:1; Is. 5:1-7; Mark 12:1-12
12   Hos. 9:10; Matt. 24:32-33; Luke 13:6-7; Mark 11:13ff

offerings being cut off, the fields lying waste, the vineyards, fig trees, and *all* trees withered because joy is withered from the sons of men; these conditions could exist because of the scattering under the Antichrist of those who would have tended all these. Likewise, the burned condition of the earth mentioned in Joel 1:19 may depict the results of the first trumpet judgment and/or the army of the next judgment. None of these conditions from v. 8 onward can be directly attributed to this army from the bottomless pit.)

6. With the **sixth trumpet**, the **second woe**, another great army is released upon the earth. This army appears to be under the control of four angels who are bound in the Euphrates River and are released at the sounding of this trumpet. This great army of horsemen is 200 million strong and is authorized, not merely to hurt, but to kill one third of mankind. The horses have heads like lions, and death is inflicted with the fire, smoke, and sulfur that comes out of the horses' mouths. They also inflict hurt with their tails, which are like serpents with heads. This army "had been made ready for the hour and day and month and year," telling us the Lord had long anticipated and carefully prepared for this very specific point in the future.[13] God's wrath against sin has never slumbered, but rather, for the sake of His mercy, has been restrained; when the very specific hour arrives, the judgment will be devastating and inexorable.

Again, Joel has a corresponding vision, speaking of a deadly, invincible army that is part of the Day of the Lord (Joel 2:1-11). Though terrible in its devastation, he calls it "the Lord's army," and gives us even more details of the horrors inflicted by this supernatural host. The fiery destruction unleashed not just on people, but on the earth's surface, brings to mind such apocalyptic movies as *The Reign of Fire,* where the earth is depicted as a blackened ruin. It is helpful to see the "Highlights of the Day of the Lord" above in the light of this judgment. Unlike the fifth trumpet judgment, we are not told how long this judgment will last.

The prayers accumulated at the golden altar of incense were the initial catalyst for the trumpet judgments. Now we see this sixth judgment – climactic in its terror – specifically *authorized by a voice speaking from the horns of this altar*, and we understand, once again, the link between the justice being dispensed and the prayers of the saints; the cries and the faith of the saints release the power of God. His wrath is not the action of a capricious and temperamental God deciding to take personal and vindictive vengeance on sinners, but the action of a God who waited with long-suffering and patience, whose holy and righteous wrath is now being justly dispensed. Horns speak of power. Prayers for God's justice have long been rising on the incense of this altar, and when it's finally the time, the answer comes with all the invincibility of a *just* and *powerful* God.

The Response of People

We are now at the midpoint of the two series of wrath judgments, and we ask, what is the response of the people of the earth to the judgments that have already come?

20 But the rest of mankind, who were not killed by these plagues, did not repent of the works of their hands, that they should not worship demons, and idols of gold, silver, brass, stone, and wood, which can neither see nor hear nor walk.

21 And they did not repent of their murders or their sorceries or their sexual immorality or their thefts.

Revelation 9:20-21

---

13 It is unclear whether this is indeed just a very specific beginning point for this judgment or whether this period of time, adding up to just over 13 months, indicates the total duration of the judgment.

They did not love truth before all this began, and they continue to resist it in the face of the overwhelming vindication of the God of the Bible. That Scripture points out that they did not repent, leads us to believe that if they had the heart and the inclination to do so, mercy would still be open to them. Instead, they continue clinging to idols, lies, and sins, displaying both the true wickedness of their hearts as well as the justice of God in their punishments.

Does that mean God takes pleasure in all this? Creating sons who have free will means that God has subjected himself to the possibility of great pain where these loved ones are concerned. How can we know the depth of pain in the heart of God as His righteous justice is forced to do this? Indeed, we suspect that as all this plays out upon the earth, His heart is even as Jeremiah's was millennia ago:

> **15 Hear and give ear: do not be proud, for the Lord has spoken.**
>
> **16 Give glory to the Lord your God, before He causes darkness, and before your feet stumble on the dark mountains; and while you are looking for light, He turns it into the shadow of death and makes it dense darkness.**
>
> **17 But if you will not hear it, my soul will weep in secret for your pride; my eyes will weep bitterly and run down with tears, because the Lord's flock has been taken captive.**
> **Jeremiah 13:15-17**

These are God's words regarding an erring Israel and Judah who were "His flock" in a unique way; and yet how His heart yearns over all of creation! We cannot pretend to understand the sorrow, mingled with anger, in God's heart as He is forced to bring these final and calamitous destructions upon the rebel sons of Adam!

CHAPTER 19

The Two Witnesses and Mid-Wrath Events

Scripture pauses at this point before the seventh trumpet sounds (releasing the bowl judgments), and we will pause also to give attention to other events taking place at this time.

The Two Witnesses

The two witnesses, two of Revelation's most significant and amazing characters, are found in Zechariah 4 and Revelation 11. Let's look at the highlights:

1. Both accounts of these two are saturated in "Jewishness," and it's very likely that they are indeed Jewish. They are clothed in sackcloth – the traditional Old Testament garb of humility, grieving, and deep repentance before God.[1]

2. Though on earth, they stand in a position of obedience and intimacy before "the God of the earth," receiving a continual flow of light and anointing from Him.

3. This anointing, along with their prophetic testimony (hence, "witnesses"), supplies a crucial flow of encouragement and anointing both <u>to Israel</u> *as it is in the process of turning back to God,* <u>and to the church</u> in its final months and days before the rapture. (We will look below at the timing of their ministry.)

4. They testify in Jerusalem, the hotspot for the events surrounding the midpoint and after.

5. If anyone tries to hurt them, fire comes out of their mouths, with the power to kill. In this way they are protected from the wrath of Antichrist and enabled to carry out their ministry until it's completed.

6. They carry an anointing similar to Elijah's (the power to prevent rain) and Moses' (the power to turn waters to blood and bring plagues to the earth at will).[2]

7. They bring testimony directly from God for 1,260 days (3½ years), and when their work is finished, they are killed by Antichrist and their bodies left lying unburied in the street.

---

1   See such Scriptures as Gen. 37:34; 1 Kings 21:27; 1 Chron. 21:16; Esther 4:1, 3; Is. 37:1-2; Jer. 4:8; Joel 1:13-15; Jonah 3:6-8.

2   Some think it will be Elijah and Moses themselves come back to earth, but these two witnesses have mortal bodies, bodies which would not have survived as mortal if they belonged to Elijah and Moses. Instead, we understand them to carry an anointing similar to Elijah and Moses, even as John the Baptist carried an anointing similar to Elijah's, but was not actually Elijah (Luke 1:17, Matt. 11:14, Matt. 17:10-13).

8. They are seen by peoples, tongues, and nations around the globe (undoubtedly via satellite and internet), and now these same people who were "tormented" by their prophesying rejoice over their death.

9. After 3½ days, God's Spirit raises them from death, they stand up, and in response to a "great voice from heaven, ascend to heaven in the sight of all, causing great fear to all who witness it." In the same hour, a great earthquake destroys one tenth of Jerusalem, slaying 7,000 men.

The Time Frame of the Two Witnesses' Ministry

Identifying exactly when their ministry takes place has been perplexing for many. They assume that since the time of their ministry equals half of the 70th week, that it must coincide with either the first or the second half of the 70th week. But there is nothing that says the 3½ year duration has to fall in one or the other of those time slots. In fact, what we see here in Revelation 11 is that the end of their ministry takes place at the conclusion of the *sixth trumpet judgment*, well inside the end of the 70th week. To have it end at this point would mean that it *begins* at some point before the midpoint.

This bears out the message of Zechariah 4, which is that their ministry as the "sons of oil" is extremely significant for *the church* in the time leading up to the rapture. The power of God preventing their harm or death at the hands of Antichrist is a powerful message to the church that God is with them and holding all in His hands. The flow of prophecy and of the anointing upon these two provides invaluable strength, encouragement, and light to the saints as they head into the Great Tribulation at the midpoint, and then as they walk through those dark days, faithful to the Lord. This is a season in the church when now, more than ever, all that is taking place in the Bride in preparation to meet Christ *must* be of pure gold – must be of the Holy Spirit, and not the flesh of man. As the angel says when he explains the essential message of the Zechariah 4 vision, "'Not by might, nor by power, but by my Spirit,' says the Lord of Hosts" (v. 6). The two "sons of oil" play a crucial role in this final preparation of the Bride.[3] Even as the church's presence on the earth yet spans the midpoint, so also does the ministry time of these two.

Their ministry is also vital for the Jews. We assume that the survivors of this earthquake are Jews, and we notice that unlike the Gentiles' response to judgment, these survivors "were afraid and gave glory to the God of heaven" (Rev. 11:13). They can hardly fail to be aware that the tremendous 3½-year ministry of these two, including finally their resurrection and ascension, sends to the whole world a power-packed supernatural testimony of Jesus as the Jewish Messiah! This is God, honoring the Jewish need for signs[4] by sending the Jewish people a solid, 3½-year long, public witness of who He is, of His presence, and of His power. Even the miracles done by these two are like pages out of their Old Testament, reminding them of the God of their fathers and of their spiritual heritage; God is surely bending over backward in great mercy to woo them back to Himself!

Their ministry of anointing and empowering also continues after the rapture, when the 144,000 – now the sole representatives of the gospel - find themselves not only in the Great Tribulation, but in the time of wrath. What tremendous support these two provide, both to these new believers in Messiah, as well as to Jews who are still in the process of turning back to the Lord. Surely, they are a demonstration of the promise, "When the enemy comes in like a flood, the Spirit of the Lord will lift up a standard against him" (Is. 59:19). God knows exactly what is needed for these Jews to be able to bear up under the pressures and trials of that time!

NOTE: We will be looking at the two witnesses again in *Part 2* when we look at Rev. 11 and Zech. 4 together.

The 'Rapture' of the 144,000

We have mentioned this previously, but will review it briefly here, as it is at this same point – at the conclusion of the first six trumpet judgments – that the 144,000 appear with the Lamb, faultless, before the throne in heaven.[5]

---

3   We will look more closely at this in *Part 2*.
4   1 Cor. 1:22
5   Rev. 14:1-5

They have been redeemed from among men and are the first fruits unto God of the nation of Israel. They will be followed by the full harvest of redeemed Jews at the end of the 70th week. Incidentally, we note that the 144,000 receive incorruptible bodies when they are taken up, whereas the rest of the Jews still alive at the end of the 70th week will enter the Millennium with mortal bodies.

With this Messianic group gone from the earth, v. 6 tells us that the proclamation of the gospel now rests with a mighty angel, which, flying in the "midst of heaven," calls all peoples of the earth to fear and worship God. By this we know that still at this time, "whosoever will call upon the name of the Lord will be saved" (Joel 2:32); people go to destruction, not for lack of opportunity to be saved, but because of the choice of their hearts.

Transition Time Between the Trumpets and Bowls

We have seen now these two significant events – the ascension of the two witnesses and the catching up of the 144,000 – which take place between the two 'series of seven' that make up the Day of the Lord. We sense in Scripture that there is a pause between the trumpet and bowl judgments. This would be appropriate, considering the devastation caused by the huge army which burns both the earth and mankind. Here are a few elements of this "pause":

10. Scripture assesses the response of people (Gentiles) and finds there is no repentance. Instead, they continue in the sins which are bringing God's wrath upon them (Rev. 9:20-21).

11. There is the pause of several 'parenthetical' chapters, where fuller light is given on concurrent events. Although we will look at them more closely in *Part 2* of this book, we will mention them briefly here. Outside of the chronology of the 'sevens,' the time placement of these concurrent events must be determined by the information given in the chapters:

    a. Chapter 10 speaks of "another mighty angel," holding a scroll, which brings a great announcement pertaining to the final wrath judgments. We will look shortly at that announcement.

    b. Chapter 11 deals primarily with the two witnesses, and also contains an announcement which pertains to the final judgments.

    c. Chapter 12 tells us of powerful interactive events between heaven and earth which affect the people of the earth, the church, and the conclusion of the age.

    d. Chapter 13 is our primary New Testament source for the actions of Antichrist and the false prophet during the Great Tribulation.

    e. Chapter 14 informs us of the 144,000, makes a number of pronouncements, and then speaks of the two great harvests of the earth.

The Pronouncements Regarding the Seventh Trumpet

We have mentioned two pronouncements that are made in this interim. In Rev. 10:7, the mighty angel holding the scroll declares:

> . . . there should be delay no longer, but in the days of the sounding of the seventh angel, when he is about to sound, the mystery[1] of God would be finished,[2] as He declared[3] to His servants the prophets. Revelation 10:6-7

[1]*musterion* G3466T – hidden thing, secret, mystery
[2]*teleo* G5055T – to bring to a close, accomplish, fulfil, complete, execute
[3]*euaggelizo* G2097T – to bring good news, announce glad tidings ("evangelize")

In saying there should be no more delay, it isn't certain whether this refers to the very long period of time overall since God began first to prophesy concerning the redemption of the earth and of man,[6] or if the angel is referring to pauses between the previous judgments (making them somewhat intermittent). Either way, the time for pauses and delays is over, and earth is being served notice that the sounding of the 7th trumpet signals *speedy completion* of the work of redemption.

Though foretold by the prophets, the understanding of this redemption remained hidden to them. They spoke in fragments and partial knowledge, longing themselves to understand what it was that they were seeing (1 Peter 1:10-12). Now the mighty angel declares that all that has been hidden will be fully revealed, played out in events of magnificence and power such as have not been seen before on the earth. All these fragments given centuries ago were part of a larger picture of *good news;* they were the gospel in the Old Testament. They promised full restoration of what was lost in the Garden - of God's *original plan.* That is, for man to partake of the Tree of Life (Jesus) and to fulfill, finally, his original mandate of dominion in the earth.[7] In the redemptive plan given to the prophets, this would take place under the kingship of David's greater Son. Heaven rejoices over the great plan coming finally to full realization, and we rejoice with it!

It has been a long and arduous task, and the end of it is triumphantly celebrated once it is in sight. Though not quite yet completed, it is seen as do-able – the hard part is over, all that is left is a wrap-up. These final judgments will play out with such power and speed that even as they begin and the seventh trumpet is yet sounding, the end of them is seen with utter clarity and certainty. We see the same thing in the announcement made at the sounding of the seventh trumpet:

> **The seventh angel sounded, and great voices in heaven followed, saying, "The kingdom of the world has become the kingdom of our Lord and of his Christ. He will reign forever and ever!" Revelation 11:15 WEB**

The first proclamation (above) declared the fulfilling of God's plan for full redemption as spoken by the prophets. This one is similar to a king's herald going before the king to announce his arrival with the blowing of his trumpet and waving of the banners while the king and his entourage are still out of sight behind the last bend in the road. It is to *put all on alert* that *the king* – and in this case, the king *as he ushers in his kingdom* – is here! Though the seven bowl judgments must occur yet, and this transition of power will not be complete until they are finished, the ending of it is so clearly in sight, and the conclusion of the events *so sure,* that the announcement is made beforehand as a *done deal.*[8] Of course, because this 7th trumpet *encompasses all the bowl judgments,* both pronouncements pertain to the full completion of the bowl judgments, and it is ultimately why they are spoken as finished *at the sounding of the trumpet.*

Following this announcement, the twenty-four elders break forth in great thanksgiving to God, declaring that He has taken His great authority and began to reign:[9]

> **Your wrath has come, and the time of the dead, that they should be judged, and that you should reward Your servants the prophets and the saints, and those who fear Your name, small and great, . . . Revelation 11:18**

It is *God,* taking the initiative, who brought things to where *judgment is now taking place* – judgment that is

---

6   This first is possible, as it has been a long time since the promise was first made in the Garden, and Scripture itself speaks of "the delay" – see Matt. 24:48; 25:5; 2 Peter 3:4; James 5:7. However, by the 6th trumpet, Jesus has already returned, so that comment would possibly not pertain to that. Instead, it may be that in looking for anyone repenting yet under the trumpet judgments, God paused between them (Rev. 9:20-21)? Either way, it's now a speedy and inexorable march to the finish!

7   Gen. 1:28, 2:9; Ps. 8; John 14:6; Heb. 2:5-10; Rev. 2:26-27, 3:21

8   The proclamation of Rev. 12:10, "now is come. . . the kingdom of our God," contains the same Greek verb as "has become" in 11:15, and in the same (aorist) tense, indicating something completed. And yet, if the work is not manifestly finished in the chapter 11 declaration, it is even less finished in chapter 12, where we are still at the midpoint of the 70th week. We see, therefore, that what God sees as finished (knowing the end from the beginning) does not mean there are not still events that must play out in time before the conclusion is manifested.

9   The "reigning" referred to here is not His rule in the Millennium but is laid out further in the chapter that follows (12); it is a "taking of authority" that served to catapult events to the intensity of the midpoint.

long overdue (from a human standpoint). This is the time for judgment of "the dead" – that is, the spiritually dead, though physically still alive[10] -- and for reward for the righteous. Paul spoke of this day:

> 5 . . . the day of wrath and revelation of the righteous judgment of God, 6 who "will render to each one according to his deeds": 7 eternal life to those who by patient continuance in doing good seek for glory, honor, and immortality;
> 8 but to those who are self-seeking and do not obey the truth, but obey unrighteousness — indignation and wrath, 9 tribulation and anguish, on every soul of man who does evil, of the Jew first and also of the Greek;
> 10 but glory, honor, and peace to everyone who works what is good, to the Jew first and also to the Greek. Romans 2:5-10

Of course, the punishment aspect is familiar to us now. But there is also a time of reward for the righteous -- "the prophets, the saints, and those who fear God, both small and great," as the elders declared. This giving of rewards is not a scene revealed to us in Scripture, but simply spoken of – even as this Scripture does -- as something that will take place "on that day." Let's proceed to take a look at this.

---

10   The judgment of the physically dead won't happen until they are resurrected at the end of the Millennium (Rev. 20:11-15). Here, "dead" is used in the same sense as in John 5:24-26.

CHAPTER 20

The Judgment Seat
of Christ

L et us linger briefly with the saints who have been taken up, and consider what Scripture says takes place
with them following the rapture.

10 For we shall all stand before the [judgment seat]¹ of Christ.
12 So then each of us shall give account of himself to God. Romans 14:10, 12

¹*bema* G968T – a raised platform, a judgment seat

These words are addressed to believers, letting us know that each of us will stand before Christ – in our resurrected bodies -- to give account of ourselves to Him. This accounting will take place at the Day of the Lord – that is, following the rapture, while the wrath judgments are being poured out upon the earth. It will not be a time of deciding whether one is saved or damned – all present at this judgment seat have already been approved as being the Lord's. The wicked do not partake of the rapture, and those who were false believers, make believers, were separated out of the kingdom *before* the rapture took place (Matt. 13:30, 40-43, 49-50). This judgment is for the giving of rewards, based on service and personal spiritual development.

Insights into the Judgment Seat of Christ

1. In two parables, Jesus spoke of *kingdom goods* being entrusted to God's servants, and there being a subsequent account required of each servant as to how he used what was given him:
    a. In Matt. 25:14ff, a certain number of talents¹ - a portion of the master's goods - was entrusted to each one, based on their varying ability. We would suggest that these talents consisted of gifts and callings issued individually to the servants. Each was instructed to work with and trade with the amount given them in order to bring kingdom increase.

    Following a long absence, the Lord returned, assessed each one, and when the service was seen to be good and faithful, granted the reward of *rulership* to that faithful servant.
    b. In Luke 19:12-26, the master delivered an identical amount of money to each – one *mina*, a

---

1   A talent was the largest unit of weight by which precious metals were measured. One talent weighed about 75 pounds, so had very great value – in a conservative estimate, anywhere from hundreds of thousands of dollars to over a million dollars in today's money.

much smaller amount, about 1/60th the value of a talent – and issued the command to "trade" with it until He returned. Whereas actual "talents" and "minas" had value in the world system, in these parables they represent what is of value in *God's* system, in His kingdom. The mina here would seem to be the "basic spiritual commodities of the kingdom," that is, the Word, the Holy Spirit, faith, love, etc., that are given equally to every Christian.

We note that the Word provides the foundation for our faith, the Spirit leads us in the Word and the will of God, and faith produces the works of God, drawing the power and resources of God into the earth: "This is the work of God, that you believe on Him whom He has sent" (John 6:28-29). This has to do with how we walk with God, trusting Him on a daily basis, in whatever path He has laid out for us.

Again, the Lord returned and called the servants for a time of accounting of their stewardship of His goods. The reward this time is rulership given over a specific number of cities, based on the amount produced by the servant's labors.

In both these parables, the servant who simply sat on the goods and did nothing with them was judged worthless and cast out.

Criteria and Reward - The key issue in both lessons is the faithfulness of the servants to use the goods entrusted to them in order to bring increase for the master. It is not a matter of the inherent abilities of the servant, but simply of his heart willingness to serve and his faithfulness in doing so. In both parables the reward for faithful service is a share in rulership during the coming kingdom era.

2. In response to the disciples having forsaken all to follow Him, Jesus promised that when "all things would be made new," and the Son of Man would sit on the throne of His glory, then they also would "sit on twelve thrones judging the twelves tribes of Israel." In addition to that, whatever they had given up to follow Him, they would receive back with a *hundred-fold increase!* This promise of judging was not given to the twelve alone but is part of the heritage of all who overcome: "To him who overcomes I will grant to sit with Me on My throne, as I also overcame and sat down with My Father on His throne" (Rev. 3:21).

Criteria and Reward - The reward for surrendering all to follow Him was a restoration of all that was lost -- with huge increase -- and also a sharing in the administrations of His throne of glory!

3. The bestowing of *crowns* is part of the reward:[2]

From now on, there is stored up for me the crown of righteousness, which the Lord, the righteous judge, will give to me *on that day*; and not to me only, but also to all those who have loved his appearing. 2 Timothy 4:8 WEB

When the chief Shepherd *is revealed*, you will receive the crown of glory that doesn't fade away. 1 Peter 5:4 WEB (emphasis added)

Notice that these are given in the time frame we're speaking of – "on that day," and when He "is revealed." It is amazing to see the Lord's heart to honor us and to share His glory with us. And He will do it as "the righteous Judge," because we have received His righteousness and clothed ourselves with it! The second crown is promised to those who shepherded and fed the Lord's flock, not for money, but from a heart of love and faithfulness.

Criteria and Reward - The crown of righteousness is for those who *love* His appearing, and the crown of glory for those who served His people with a faithful and willing heart.

---

2 There are more promises of crowns: see 1 Cor. 9:25, James 1:12, Rev. 2:10, Rev. 3:11.

4. In <u>Matt. 10:41-42</u> we see the Lord's promise of reward to those who welcome and *receive* those who come in the ministry and anointing of the Lord. When we receive a prophet *as* a prophet, and a righteous man *as* a righteous man, we participate in their very rewards! How amazing! Jesus goes on to say that simply giving a drink of cold water to a child in the name of a disciple will bring a reward. He desires our hearts to be discerning of opportunities He brings our way to love and serve others. When we love from our hearts, we are loving Him and advancing His kingdom. The reward will be seen on that day!

Finally, we consider this powerful passage from Paul regarding the building of the house of God and the quality of the work produced by different ones:

> **Now if anyone builds on this foundation with gold, silver, precious stones, wood, hay, straw, each one's work will become clear;[1] for the Day will declare[2] it, because it will be revealed[3] by fire; and the fire will test[4] each one's work, of what sort it is.**
> **If anyone's work which he has built on it endures, he will receive a reward.**
> **If anyone's work is burned, he will suffer loss; but he himself will be saved, yet so as through fire. 1 Corinthians 3:12-15**

> > [1]*phaneros* G5318V – to uncover, lay bare, make visible and known
> > [2]*deloo* G1213S – to make plain (by words)
> > [3]*apokaluptoo* G601T – to uncover, to lay open what has been veiled or covered
> > [4]*dokimazo* G1381T – to test, examine, scrutinize, prove

<u>Notice this repetitive emphasis on the *uncovering* of what has previously been hidden.</u> In this age, there is a veil over so many things. The flesh of man, though unable to please God, is capable of being so good and so competent; it is capable of doing many things that appear outwardly the same as what *the spirit man* does. Because of that, there is much in the church that is of counterfeit quality -- that is soulish -- appearing good -- yet not carrying the life of God (the anointing). But in the judgment of *that Day*, veils will be removed and everything will come into plain view. The work that each one has done will *become clear*. Was this one building with material that would endure the fire – that is, *spirit* material? Or was he laboring to build and achieve apart from God -- with merely human materials that will not sustain the fire? All this will be made manifest. The works of many who genuinely love the Lord will be seen to have been wrought in self, rather than in God. Those works will pass through the fires of judgment and will be consumed. The worker himself will be saved, but *so as through fire.* That is, though his spirit is saved, the fire will consume that unbroken part of him that was yet engaged in soulish works. Whatever comes through the fire unscathed has been built with eternal qualities and will bring a reward. Seeing this way of judging the quality of our work and life helps us understand this passage:

> **For we must all appear[1] before the judgment seat of Christ, that each one may receive the things done in the body, according to what he has done, whether good or bad. 2 Corinthians 5:10 KJV**

> [1]*phaneroo* G5319T – to make manifest or visible or known what has been hidden or unknown; to be exposed to view; plainly recognized, thoroughly understood

It can be confusing to hear that we will be judged on the basis of what we did – whether it was good or bad. Aren't we justified by faith, not by works? Yes, we are made right with God by faith, given righteousness as a free gift. But when it comes to *rewards*, God looks at the things we have done "while in the body." How have we "stewarded" our lives as His children? And then beyond the deeds, He looks to the intentions and motives behind those deeds. Notice here the same word again for removing a cover. When we stand before the judgment seat of Christ, there will be no more pretense, no more fleshly works, no more hidden, selfish motives that pass as good. Rather, there will be *an accurate and discerning judgment* of what is good and what is bad.

If so much appears to be good that may not be good in God's sight, how then can we define 'good' and ensure that we are doing good as *He* sees it? Jesus said to Nicodemus,

> **But he who does the truth comes to the light, that his deeds [may be clearly seen],[1] that they have been done[2] in God." John 3:21**

[1]*phaneroo* G5319T – to make manifest, visible, or known what has been hidden or unknown; to be exposed to view; plainly recognized, thoroughly understood
[2]*ergazomai* G2038T – to work, labor, do business, make gains by trading; acquire

He is speaking here of these same things that we are speaking. And here He answers our question. Good deeds are those *that are wrought* – worked – *in God.* He works them *in* us, so that when we *work them out,* they are coming out of our spirit. They do not originate from our independent soul, but are derived from God, coming forth out of our spirit as our will is surrendered to Him. Though they may *employ* our human abilities and strengths, they are initiated and energized by the Holy Spirit in us, and therefore demonstrate those "talents" and "minas" – those deposits of His Spirit and His kingdom goods – that He has entrusted to each of us. We may have to work to bring our souls, with their strong independent life, into obedience to Christ and His will for us. *We welcome His searching light, that anything not of Him will be exposed.* We may have to labor to get to a place of *faith* with the issue we're dealing with so that the power of God can come into the situation; so that rather than wood, hay, and stubble, the materials we're building with are gold, silver, and precious stones.

Knowing all this, we are motivated to please Him in all we do. Just before speaking of our judgment before Christ in the passage above, Paul said,

> **Therefore, we make it our aim, whether present or absent, to be well pleasing to Him.**
> **2 Corinthians 5:9**

Jesus has planted in us the same desire to please the Father that dwells in Him! Following this desire puts us on a good path as we each move toward that day of accountability.

It's possible to feel shame as we give an account on that day. But John encourages us:

> **And now, little children, abide in Him, that when He appears, we may have confidence and not be ashamed before Him at His coming.   1 John 2:28**

Abiding in Him – leaning on Him and trusting Him with every aspect of our lives, will give us *confidence* in that day!

We have covered a lot of ground in this chapter and said a lot of things. Before leaving this topic, let's reduce it to something much simpler. We are all on different paths, as God has led us, but regardless of what we are occupied with on a daily basis, God has brought it all together into simplicity for us who love Him:

> **And whatever you do, do it heartily, as to the Lord and not to men, knowing that from the Lord you will receive the reward of the inheritance; for you serve the Lord Christ.**
> **Colossians 3:23-24**

It isn't an issue of being or not being in ministry; or of having a degree and a very important job; or of doing something that others think highly of and admire us for; or even of doing something that *we* think highly of. It all comes down to the simplicity of accepting where God has put us, and then doing the very best we can *as unto Him,* desiring to please Him. With all our lives, we serve Him from our hearts. This is what brings freedom from human pride, insecurity, or striving. This is what will bring commendation from Him on that day – that we sought with faithfulness, humility, and good cheer to do what was put in front of us to do, and to do it with the grace that He supplied. We come finally to see that whatever we do in His name, desiring to love and please Him, is a good work in His sight, and will bring a reward on that day – an award that will amaze us with its generosity and goodness!

This judgment, besides giving rewards to the saints, enables the administrative development of Christ's earthly kingdom. The saints will serve both as judges and rulers over cities, regions, states, and nations, participating in the authority of Christ as He rules all the earth.

Three Judgments

One of the foundational principles of the doctrine of Christ is the teaching of *eternal judgment* (Heb. 6:2). This is the final judgment of God with which a person enters the next age, following his probationary life on the earth. Just as there are differing times of resurrection for different groups, so there are three different times of eternal judgment. This *judgment seat of Christ* (bema) is the first. The second will occur when the events of the 70th week are completed, and Christ sits upon the *throne of His glory* to judge those (Gentiles) still alive on the earth; that is a judgment based upon how they treated the Jews during the last 3½ years. Some will be rejected and sent into age-lasting punishment, others will be given eternal life and enter the Millennium (Matt. 25:31ff). (There is, incidentally, a similar judgment for the Jews at this time to determine whether they will enter the Millennium or not – Ezek. 20:33-38.) Finally, the third judgment takes place when the Millennium is over, when all who have not been previously raised from the dead will be resurrected and will stand before God at the *great white throne judgment.* This is a resurrection comprised mostly of the ungodly, but there will be righteous among them, including many who died during the Millennium.

CHAPTER 21

The Jews During God's Wrath

We have referred previously to how difficult things are for the Jews during the Great Tribulation. During the earlier part of it, the church – and then after the rapture, the 144,000 – are there for support and aid. But things become more difficult following the trumpet judgments. The two witnesses, along with the 144,000, were strong supports for the remaining Jews, but are now gone from the earth. Although his effectiveness has been diminished, Antichrist is still targeting the Jews, and the wrath judgments continue. See this poignant lament from the prophet Micah, who seems to be speaking of this time:

> **Woe is me! for I am as when they have gathered the summer fruits, as the grape gleanings of the vintage: there is no cluster to eat: my soul desired the first ripe fruit.**
> **The good[1] man is perished[2] out of the earth: and there is none upright among men: they all lie in wait for blood; they hunt every man his brother with a net.**
>
> **Micah 7:1-2 KJV**

[1]*chaciyd* H2623B – faithful, kind godly, holy one, pious
[2]*abad* H6S – to wander away, lose oneself, vanish, perish

It isn't the purpose of this study to focus on the Jewish feasts, but we will just note that the four spring feasts all pertain to Jesus' first coming, and the three fall feasts to His second coming. The church age takes place over the summer, followed by the harvest in the fall, when the church is gathered to the Lord; the harvest of the wicked is also reaped around that time, the conclusion of that harvest occurring at Armageddon. There is likewise a harvest of the Jews who turn to the Lord, with the 144,000 being the first fruits of that harvest of Jewish converts.

In the passage above, we see that the summer harvest has already taken place, with even *the first fruits* gone. Micah prophetically declares that good men are perished – vanished – from the earth, and there are no upright men left. *Abad* would describe both those who were taken to heaven in a rapture (vanished), and also those upright Jews who were killed by Antichrist. The ones left are vicious and treacherous, complicit in the evil of Antichrist. There is nothing left now for the Jew *but to look to the Lord*:

7 Therefore, I will look to the Lord; I will wait for the God of my salvation; My God will hear me.

8 Do not rejoice over me, my enemy; when I fall, I will arise; when I sit in darkness, the Lord will be a light to me.

9 I will bear the indignation of the Lord, because I have sinned against Him, until He pleads my case and executes justice for me. He will bring me forth to the light; I will see His righteousness. Micah 7:7-9

We saw at the first seal the hypocrisy still present, though temple worship had resumed. The Jews entered the 70th week with a deep need for repentance. But now we are seeing meekness, the acceptance on the part of the speaker of his own guilt. He knows that though the enemy may have the upper hand, he has brought this on himself by his own sin, and it is right for him to submit to the Lord's judgment. Surely this is a prophetic picture of the Jew and is powerful and significant for him at this time. He is no longer looking to Antichrist and to the covenant with him – now in shambles. He is turning at long last and looking, in these dire straits, to the Lord -- laying claim to His mercy and His light. It is that light that will lead him away from his own righteousness[1] and eventually to the righteousness that can be found only through faith in the shed blood of the Messiah.

Notice the reference to "falling" in v. 8. We get a picture here of people who are penitent, yet groping for light, unsure yet of the right way. They are making mistakes yet – but reaching and trusting for mercy from God. This is reminiscent of Daniel:

Some of those who are wise shall fall, to refine them, and to purify, and to make them white, even to the time of the end; because it is yet for the time appointed. Daniel 11:35 WEB

After centuries of blindness, there is an aspect of trial and error in their turning – there is *learning* going on. There is human weakness, which causes slips, followed by repentance and a leaning on God's strength. They will be learning more and more how to rely upon God, instead of on themselves. This is the purification going on – the beautiful thing that God is doing in them at this time.

The call for the Jews to repent is inherent in the Day of the Lord itself:

11 . . . the day of the Lord is great and very terrible; who can endure it?

12 "Now, therefore," says the Lord, "Turn to Me with all your heart, with fasting, with weeping, and with mourning."

13 So rend your heart, and not your garments; return to the Lord your God, for He is gracious and merciful, slow to anger, and of great kindness; and He relents from doing harm.

15 Blow the trumpet in Zion; consecrate a fast, call a sacred assembly;

16 Gather the people, sanctify the congregation, assemble the elders, gather the children and nursing babes; let the bridegroom go out from his chamber, and the bride from her dressing room.

17 Let the priests, who minister to the Lord, weep between the porch and the altar; Let them say, "Spare Your people, O Lord, and do not give Your heritage to reproach, that the nations should rule over them. Why should they say among the peoples, 'Where is their God?'" Joel 2:11-13, 15-17

Notice that even the nursing moms and babies, and the bride and groom on their honeymoon – those who would normally be exempt -- are included in the call to *gather in sacred assembly* before the Lord. This *is the time*, dire and crucial, for Israel to repent. The priests lead the way, weeping between the porch and the altar; that is, making their way spiritually from first turning toward the Lord, to the *place of sacrifice for sin* – that is, the place

---

1 Ro. 10:1-4

of recognition of the sacrifice made for them by the Lamb of God, their Messiah. This is a beautiful, prophetic picture that will be fulfilled during this time in the future.

In Isaiah 27, giving *His* perspective, God speaks of this time of difficulty when they are still in the refining fire. But He *speaks first* of the time when His anger toward them is over, and Israel "blossoms and buds, and fills the earth with fruit" (vv. 4, 6)! Then He goes on to say:

Has He (God) struck Israel in the same way as He struck those who struck Israel? Or are they killed like those killed by Him? Isaiah 7:27

God is making a difference between the Jew and the others on the earth.[2] The others, persecuting the Jews, will be judged unto full destruction, but His dealings with Israel are *in measure*:

In a carefully measured way, when I sent Israel away, I contended with her. v. 8a

The word here for measure is *seah,* which is the equivalent of about 2 gallons; so, a *small* measurement. The wording is "with *seah* and *seah* have I contended with Israel." I.e., the deep trials Israel is passing through have been carefully and *incrementally* measured and monitored by the Lord as being *only what is required* in order to bring the desired results with them. He goes on to explain,

He removes his rough[1] wind in the day of the east[2] wind. v. 8b

[1]*qasheh* H7186B – severe, harsh, cruel, obstinate, intense
[2]*qadiym* H6921B – east, east wind

Although the antichrist is not removed until the completion of the 70th week, his persecution of the Jews is so effectively curtailed by the Day of the Lord, that we could understand that to be what the Lord is speaking of here: the 'rough' wind being the Great Tribulation, and the 'east' wind being the Day of the Lord's wrath.[3] In this transition of winds, we see the Lord **redirecting the focus of the Jews from this treacherous "messiah" and the danger he presents (via the Great Tribulation), to their *true God.*** They should be deeply disillusioned with their false messiah by now, and ready to shift their focus: The wrath events are from the God of their fathers, and it is He they need to deal with. Their sins against Him have brought them to such extremity, and it is His light they need. This changing of focus is very important for them, and will bring them to the next verse:

By this, therefore, will the iniquity of Jacob be purged; and the full fruit of his repentance is the full destruction of all idolatry. v. 9

Through the working of the two winds, Israel's iniquity will finally be purged, turning all who remain of them fully to the Lord. At the midpoint, God made it clear that His deep anger against Israel was being expressed through the ferocity of Antichrist, "in whose hand is the club of my wrath" (Is. 10:5-6). As Israel returns to Him, His anger diminishes; by the end, He declares, "Fury is not in me," saying that those who are left to persecute Israel have now become *His* enemies, and will, in fact, be *easily defeated* when they finally face Him in battle.[4]

Because the woman of Revelation 12 continues throughout the whole second half of the 70th week (constituted of seed who have the testimony of Jesus Christ), we believe there is a constant stream of Jews who are coming to faith in Christ throughout this whole time, particularly after the rapture of the church. We are informed by Zechariah that two thirds of the Jews will perish, but the one third that comes through *will turn to the Lord, finally*

---

2 See Is. 49:25 - 50:1.
3 The east wind in the climate of Judea was usually hot, noxious, blasting and scorching, tempestuous and violent. From *Barnes' Notes* (Electronic Database, 1997). Notes on Is. 27:8. (See also Job 27:21, Jer. 18:17.)
4 Is. 27:4

recognizing their Messiah and repenting.[5] The turning of this one third, completed in the extremity of Armageddon,[6] will lead to both the ultimate deliverance and *the national rebirth* of Israel. Here in Micah, Joel, and Isaiah is this final group, feeling alone in the midst of wicked men and terrible judgments, yet beginning to see their sin and to look to the God of Israel.

Not All Will Turn

The two witnesses have just completed 3½ years of powerful testimony – accompanied by signs and wonders -- right there in Jerusalem. (This is at the close of the 6th trumpet.) Yet notice the stubborn persistence of the Jews' spiritual condition, discernible by how God still sees their city:

> **7 When they finish their testimony, the beast …will make war against them, … and kill them.**
> **8 And their dead bodies will lie in the street of the great city which spiritually is called Sodom and Egypt, where also our Lord was crucified. Revelation 11:7-8**

The tremendous afflictions of the trumpet judgments, added to the trials coming from Antichrist, have not been sufficient to purge Jerusalem. After all the suffering and judgments, the testimony of Scripture is that she remains as proud and as morally depraved as Sodom, and as carnal and spiritually dark as Egypt– as the unsaved world! As the two witnesses and the 144,000 are taken to safety, we see fresh judgment falling upon Jerusalem with a great earthquake (consistent with the pattern that "the same day the righteous are taken to safety, the wicked undergo judgment"[7]). A tenth of the city is destroyed, killing 7,000 men – men that are surely part of the two thirds that do not survive to the end and are not saved. And now the world and what remains of Israel will head into the final series of judgments, the bowl judgments. By the end of these final and devastating judgments, the ungodly will be purged out of Israel, and her turning – her *converting* -- will finally be accomplished, even as God promised through His prophets and in the words of Isaiah:

> **25 And I will turn my hand upon thee, and purely purge away thy dross *(impurities)*, and take away all thy tin *(mixture);***
>
> **26 And I will restore thy judges as at the first, and thy counsellors as at the beginning: afterward thou shalt be called, The city of righteousness, the faithful city.**
>
> **27 Zion shall be redeemed with judgment, and her *converts* with righteousness.**
>
> **28 *And the destruction of the transgressors and of the sinners shall be together, and they that forsake the Lord shall be consumed.***
>
> Isaiah 1:25-28 KJV (emphasis added)

---

5   Zech. 13:8-9
6   Zech. 12:10 – 13:1
7   Luke 17:26-30

COUNTDOWN TO THE END

CHAPTER 22
The Bowl Judgments

The earth and its inhabitants are left reeling following the trumpet judgments, particularly the <u>fifth and sixth</u> (the first two **woes**), with the fifth inflicting terrible pain, and the sixth killing many, as well as burning the earth. Let's reconnect with our chronology now, which we left at the end of chapter 18 (of this book) when we spoke of the pronouncements associated with the seventh trumpet. The latter pronouncement (Rev. 11:15ff) was followed with a view of the ark of the covenant, seen in the temple in heaven. Remember, the ark contained the tablets of stone upon which were inscribed the law of God. As the ark is seen, there are "lightnings, voices, thunderings, an earthquake, and great hail." We are reminded of the original giving of the law at Sinai, when similar phenomena occurred, striking the hearts of the people with terror.[1] The law always pertains to human efforts apart from God's grace; therefore, it carries with it the curse, judgment, and fearful consequences for falling short of God's glory.

Now, in the midst of the wrath judgments, we are given this glimpse of the ark, reminding us of God's high and holy standard; though despised by the sinners of the earth, it has never ceased to be the standard by which they will be judged. Having rejected God's merciful provision of an atoning Substitute for their sins, they are now experiencing "the wine of the wrath of God, which is poured out full strength into the cup of His indignation" (Rev. 14:10). All that is taking place is *the result of broken law*. There was *always* going to be a consequence for humankind's rebellion; the delay simply softened the reality of that. Now the full reality of it has broken forth upon the earth without remedy, and the lightning, thunder, earthquake, and hail remind us of God's terrible, righteous, and inevitable judgment.

The chronology, briefly set aside there at the end of Revelation 11, is resumed in chapter 15; there we again see the tabernacle of the testimony (covenant), and the seven angels holding the seven last judgments come out of the temple. This is a scene of great holiness, as the glory and power of God fill the temple with smoke, preventing anyone from entering the temple until these final calamities are finished.

Since these seven judgments are all released by the <u>seventh trumpet</u>, they all together comprise the **third woe**. Dubbed "the bowl judgments," they are listed in the 16th chapter of Revelation and will be dispensed with rapidity – like finishing a long job of washing dishes: the hard work of scrubbing is done; all that's left is to rinse and swish the residue around the sides of the bowl and swirl out down the drain – job done and dispensed with! This is no great task for God. He has it well in hand and is just about TO BE DONE.

---

1 Exodus 19:10-25, Heb. 12:18-21

Except for one more event at the *end* of the Millennium,[2] Satan's usefulness to God will be finished by the end of the bowl judgments. The purging of the earth will be complete, as will the transition of the rulership of the earth. The Jewish remnant will have turned fully to the Lord, the armies of the earth will be decimated, and great Babylon utterly judged. Let's look now at the bowl judgments.

Chronology – the Seven Bowl Judgments

1. A painful and malignant ulcer is inflicted upon all who have the mark of the beast and who have worshipped his image.
2. All the seas become as stagnant blood, killing all sea life.
3. All the fresh-water sources become as blood. A voice from heaven declares the righteousness of God in doing this, because those forced to drink this blood have shed the blood of saints and prophets.
4. This fourth bowl is poured upon the sun, greatly increasing its heat and scorching men. Scripture notes that men curse God in response, rather than repenting. Along with the great army that scorches the earth (6th trumpet), this explains how the earth and people are burned.
5. This judgment is poured upon the throne of the beast, filling his kingdom with a supernatural darkness which causes them to gnaw their tongues for pain. This also brings further blasphemy toward God.
6. This angel pours his bowl on the Euphrates River, drying it up to open the way for the kings of the east.[3] Three frog-like demons, *working miracles*, come out of the mouths of the dragon, beast, and false prophet to induce the kings and armies of the whole world to assemble and go up against Israel for the final battle, Armageddon. And they are assembled.
7. This enormous battle takes place, accompanied by an earthquake of a magnitude never before seen on the earth. All the great cities of the earth collapse, every island disappears, every mountain is *leveled,* and hailstones weighing about 100 pounds drop from the sky upon people. And Babylon is judged!

The final bowl judgment brings the rule of Antichrist to an end. His 3½ years are completed, bringing us to the conclusion of the 70th week of Daniel. There are details that need to be filled in, especially with this final bowl judgment. We will begin in the next chapter with a look at Babylon – what does it represent? And why is it given so much attention in Revelation?

---

2 Rev. 20:7-10
3 It's interesting that about 2600 years before this event will take place, the prophet Jeremiah foresaw the ultimate downfall of Babylon (Jer. 50-51). After writing it all out, he gave his servant Seraiah instructions to stand at the Euphrates, read the full prophecy at the river, and declare, "O Lord, you have spoken against this place to cut it off, so that none shall remain in it, neither man nor beast, but it shall be desolate forever." Seraiah was then to attach a stone to the prophecy and cast it into the Euphrates, declaring, "Thus Babylon shall sink and not rise from the catastrophe that I will bring upon her." This prophecy of the final destruction of Babylon, facilitated here by the drying of the Euphrates, will be fulfilled at the final bowl judgment.

CHAPTER 23

What's Up with Babylon?

As we begin a look at Babylon, we might well ask ourselves why two whole chapters in Revelation are given over to this ancient city – which for all practical purposes doesn't even exist any longer – and nothing is said of the destruction of the beast or the great global empire by which he controls the earth. The answer is simple and evident when we look away from the physical location of the ancient city of Babylon, and look instead at Nebuchadnezzar's mighty image with the head of gold (Daniel 2). Then we remember, with an "aha!" moment, that, "Of course! The smashing of the great end-time kingdom *is* the smashing of Babylon, for the nature and character of the head of gold, Babylon, is the nature and character of the *whole image* -- all the subsequent kingdoms!" *All* of those kingdoms have ever and only been <u>a manifestation of the essence of the original kingdom</u>. The stone, not cut by human hands, which crashes into the ten-toed kingdom of the end, demolishes and brings down *Babylon*.

The Nature of Babylon

The destruction of Babylon is mentioned more than once in Scripture, and in the context of great rejoicing on the part of the righteous. To understand why God is so strongly set against it, we need to understand its essential nature; and to understand that, we must understand its origins. For that, we must look earlier than the great kingdom of Babylon. We must look past Assyria, which predated Babylon, and even past Egypt, all the way back to Babylon's origins at the Tower of Babel. When we understand what took place there, we will understand the essential nature of the great Babylon which is judged at the end.

There is more to be said about Babylon's origins, which we will address later; we will keep it fairly brief here. Following <u>the great flood</u>, there was general knowledge of the true God among the people of the earth. They had seen up close His hatred of sin and experienced His mighty power both to save and to destroy. But all too soon, as people began to multiply again on the earth, there again rose rebellion against the true God. The rebellion was spear-headed by Noah's great grandson Nimrod.[1]

Nimrod arose as a "mighty hunter," possibly hunting animals first, but then men. He became the first *kingdom builder* in the earth, amassing people and territory unto himself, and training others in the arts of warfare and conquest. Not only did he build a military and political kingdom, but he developed an organized system of false religion in a deliberate strategy to lead people away from the true God. He inserted himself between God

---

1 Daniel J. Elazar, *Government and Polity in Biblical Israel* (New Brunswick, NJ: Transaction Publishers, 1998), pp. 117-118. Josephus, *The Antiquities of the Jews*, from *The Works of Josephus, Complete and Unabridged* (Peabody, MA: Hendrickson Publishers, Inc., 1987), Book 1, Chapter 4, pp. 109-119.

and men, gathering them unto himself and fostering a dependency upon him; he did this "before God," or, we might say, "in God's face" – in flagrant flaunting of God's person and authority. He was the ringleader in the open rebellion of the Tower of Babel. Babel, which originally meant "the gate of God" (as in, "we will make our *own* way to God – our *own divinity*"), came to mean *confusion* after God confounded their labors with the confusing of the tongues.

This whole work and effort of Nimrod was instigated by Satan with the goal of gaining a foothold, a stronghold, in the earth for himself; that is, a whole kingdom, society, and religious framework through which he could operate and work *his* purposes in the earth in opposition to God's purposes. [2]

This then, is how Babel (i.e., Babylon) is the head of Nebuchadnezzar's image; that is, it is the foundation and essential nature of the image. We have looked previously (chapter 10) at the succession of kingdoms which comprise the image, and we know that they were all called "beast kingdoms," bearing characteristics of Satan. Of course, it's always been more advantageous for the names and characters of other gods, false gods, to be on display and in the forefront of things, rather than the name of Satan. Hence, these were often called "mystery religions," even as in the chapter we are about to deal with, John was told that the woman he saw riding the beast was "*Mystery* Babylon. . . "

The Three-fold Aspect of Babylon

Seeing the Babylon of Revelation (chapters 17-18) from the point of view of Nebuchadnezzar's image takes us a long way toward understanding it. But we must look at how it is depicted in Revelation itself to understand it fully. There we see the kingdom as it is manifesting at the end and as it is when it comes under God's judgment, and we perceive three discernible aspects to it: the woman – i.e., the religious aspect; the beast – i.e., the political aspect; and the economic aspect. We will discuss each of these.

The Woman

In chapter 17 (please read it), John is given vision of a lavishly clad, decadent woman sitting upon a beast, the one previously described. We assume she is riding it, and therefore has a relationship of mutual dependency with the beast – it is carrying her where she directs it to go, and when she gets to where she's going, so also does the beast. We are given information about both the woman and the beast she rides. The woman, decked in wealth and holding a gold cup full of filth from her fornications, is called, "MYSTERY, BABYLON THE GREAT, THE MOTHER OF HARLOTS AND OF ABOMINATIONS OF THE EARTH." She is drunk from the blood of the saints and the martyrs of Jesus. There has always been deep evil and vicious malice in the whore – the very malice of Satan – but it's been kept carefully veiled behind religious order, pseudo piety, and natural goodness (the *good* of the Tree of the Knowledge of Good and Evil). Why *mystery* Babylon? Because the vastness of her network in the earth, as well as the malevolent presence of Satan within her, were almost completely veiled from human sight. And, in fact, her presentation to the world (whether from within the church or out in the world) is always presented in a cloak of deeds and words that are *attractive* to mankind. This too is part of her mystery – her *occult hiddenness*.

We are told that when John saw her,

> **. . . he marveled[1] with great[2] amazement.[3] Revelation 17:6**

> [1]*thaumazo* G2296V – to wonder at, to marvel, to be astonished
> [2]*megas* G3173T – large, great
> [3]*thauma* G2295T – a wonder, marvel

John's mind "was blown" – he simply could not grasp and comprehend what he was seeing. *Thauma* is used almost exclusively in Scripture to refer to an occurrence which taps into the supernatural and which is therefore beyond the natural understanding of man. Whether it is God or Satan behind the event, it confounds human

---

2   We will look more closely at Babylon's origins in *Part 2*, chapter 42.

understanding and is therefore often translated a "wonder" or a "marvel." This is John's reaction – he has trouble comprehending what he is seeing. Interestingly, students of this passage have also struggled to understand who exactly this woman is and what she represents. The angel proceeded to explain to John the mystery of the woman.

Because they are often depicted as the wife or bride of Christ, God's people are frequently depicted in the feminine. They are those who are joined to God in spiritual union through faith. Here is a woman, but a *harlot* – one who has joined herself indiscriminately and unlawfully to false 'lovers' – false gods. Not only has she joined herself, but she's the mother, the originator, of all spiritual harlots – ALL FALSE RELIGION -- of the earth.

We understand her, therefore, to be the *religious* aspect of Babylon. We are told her fornication has been with the kings of the earth. Rather than being joined to the true God in consecration and faith, she has chosen the way of collaboration with and dependence upon earthly powers and stratagems. This religious system which rides the beast is the one that has been present *all along* – since the inception of Babylon – as we see from the seven heads (heads representing all those prior kingdoms plus the end-time kingdom). It is false religion, instigated and empowered by Satan. <u>This is "the broad path" Jesus taught of. It is all religion except the "narrow way" which passes through His cross and requires death to sin, self, and the world.</u>

The mighty angel proclaims that Babylon the great "is fallen, is fallen." This is not a reference to her judgment, but to her moral and spiritual collapse, for in her fallenness, she has become the home and the *prison* of every unclean and detestable spirit. Because of this, John sees her in the wilderness – the place that is dry, devoid of life. Scripture tells us that the "rebellious dwell in a dry place."[3] The woman and her constituents are *lawless;* that is, they may have laws of their own making, but they do not submit to the laws of God and His way to righteousness.

There is endless variety in the woman; because she constitutes that broad path, all manner of beliefs, practices, institutions, prophets, doctrines, and followers are found in her. But the great common denominator in all the variety is that she is apart from God and the truth of His Word. Jesus is God's way *to life* – to reject Jesus is to end up in a dry, barren, and desolate place in the soul. It is also to lose one's way, for He is the way to the Father; there is no path in the wilderness.[4] This woman appears to be enormously wealthy, but the wealth is an illusion; in reality, she is bereft of life, blessing, and true prosperity.

The angel explains that the woman is "that great city" which rules over the kings of the earth (v. 18). To claim a direct line to divinity gives power over men's souls -- in this life and presumably in the next -- and it is *the enemy's trump card over all earthly authority.* The woman has wielded this false claim with great craftiness and effectiveness, manipulating men, armies, and kingdoms for her own purposes. As we will see when we move into Revelation 18, the reference to a city goes far beyond any one geographical location in the earth. Even if the ancient city of Babylon were to be rebuilt before the end, it could in no way represent all that is being said here of *this city.*

This city is the spiritual counterpart of Jerusalem, which, though located on earth, has a spiritual link with heaven. Jerusalem is the city from which the kingdom of God will be administered on the earth in the Millennium. It will be the center of worship as well as of the political administration of Christ's kingdom. It is the earthly counterpart of the Jerusalem which is from above, which is comprised of the saints of all the ages. The spiritual Jerusalem is a mother, portrayed in Rev. 12 as the woman clothed with the sun. Mystery Babylon is also a mother – her offspring being harlots, even as she is. The godly seed of the heavenly Jerusalem have been in pitched conflict with Babylon and her seed down through the centuries. The conflict of these two "women"-- one faithful to God, and the other a harlot -- was foretold by God right after the fall, and it reaches climactic proportions as the age comes to a close.

Each of the successive seven heads of the beast have been the manifestation, at that point in history, of the spiritual kingdom of darkness which encompasses the earth. The rulers of this kingdom live in the heavenly sphere surrounding the earth[5] and answer to Satan. Until we see the city and kingdom of Babylon with this clarity, we have not yet understood what it really is. Their seers and soothsayers, prognosticators and priests, are, and have always been, in direct spiritual connection with the kingdom of darkness. Accessing a level of spiritual

---

3 Ps. 68:6
4 Ps. 107:40
5 Eph. 6:12, Col. 1:16, Rev. 12:7-9

reality, albeit false, has enabled them to provide divine backing for the kings of the earth, enabling them to consolidate their power over the people in a way that mere armies never could. Truest obedience comes from the heart, and for a people to believe from their hearts that their king has divine backing brings the greatest compliance and servitude a king could expect. The king, on the other hand, backs up the spiritual authority of the priest and prophet (i.e., soothsayer) with his civil authority, thus cementing his union with them and sealing their complicity in devilish power and oppression over the people.

Although Scripture unites her specifically with these seven, she has been linked with countless other lesser kingdoms, governments, and peoples – many waters[6] -- down through the millennia. The civic and political entities have transitioned from one to another, coming and going, rising and falling, but the whore has remained constant in her idolatry, lies, and spiritual darkness. It is appropriate that these two chapters in Revelation dedicated to the fall of Babylon should begin with the religious component, this "mother of harlots." It is she who bears the greatest responsibility for evil before God; even while claiming to speak authoritatively for God, she has deceived these countless peoples, multitudes, nations, and tongues with her lies, making them "drunk with the wine of her fornication," her spiritual and moral filth.[7]

The Beast
The angel then goes into detail regarding the mystery of the beast carrying her – the end-time kingdom.

> But the angel said to me, "Why did you marvel?[1] I will tell you the mystery of the woman and of the beast that carries her. Revelation 17:7

[1]*thaumazo* G2296T – to wonder at, marvel

We might ask, what is the thing we don't yet understand about the beast? We understand what the mystery is *by what the angel proceeds to explain.* The angel says of him that "he was, and is not, shall ascend out of the bottomless pit, and go into perdition." Revelation 13 told us that one of the heads on the beast would be "as it were, wounded to death, and his deadly wound healed" (v. 3), causing all the world "to wonder" about him, even as John himself had when he saw this vision of the woman and the beast. The Lord wanted John and us to understand more fully this "mystery" which will daze the minds of those on the earth when this man undergoes this (apparent) death and return to life, and behaves so differently afterward.

The angel proceeds, explaining that the beast John is actually seeing here "was, and is not; and shall ascend out of the bottomless pit, and go into perdition." In other words, Antichrist's own spirit will not return to his body (assuming it left, upon 'death'); but *another spirit* would enter it -- one which had (presumably) lived previously on the earth and was now (at the time of John) in the bottomless pit. This spirit would ascend out of the pit for the purpose of providing a pseudo-resurrection for this man's body at this time in the future,[8] and thereby 'impress' people, deceive them, and silence any opposition. His arrogance and wickedness will know no bounds. But God is letting us, His people, know ahead of time so we will not be thrown by this. The final destination of this wicked spirit is *perdition.* We will not be intimidated or bewildered by this. God has shown us ahead of time and is in complete control.

The angel explained further: the seventh head will continue only "a short time." This is Antichrist in the very brief time that he heads up the kingdom *in the first phase,* before the midpoint. At the midpoint the seventh head will transition into *the eighth* (v. 11) via this "death and resurrection." There will still be only seven heads, but the seventh will have undergone an identity change. The vision we see here is after that change, in the second half of the 70th week. We might add that at this point, the purpose and agenda of the beast is no longer a mystery – he is conducting a clear and blatant power-grab and worship-grab. And the 10 regional leaders, now *of one mind* with the beast, are putting their full power and authority at his disposal to assist in his agenda. This now is the global kingdom in complete unity, prepared to fulfill the purpose of the beast.

---

6 Rev. 17:1,15
7 Rev. 17:1-4, 15
8 We will look at this more closely in *Part 2.*

We said earlier that when the woman gets to where she is going, the beast also gets to where *he* is going. We are now at the point of seeing where both are going, for both are under the direction of Satan, and the goal, of course, is complete domination of the earth. That domination extends to all *worship,* as well as to all *political and military* power. The political/military domination will now come *to one man* and be extended *through him* to all the earth. The worship, coming previously to Satan more indirectly – that is, via many different beliefs and practices -- must now be condensed and refocused to come to him *solely through this one man* – the false messiah. All other ideas, avenues, beliefs must be eliminated. This one false christ must receive *all power and worship;* this, of course, means *war* with anyone who resists. We will see this in the next chapter when we see the woman *destroyed by the beast.*

The Commercial Aspect

Chapter 18 is largely devoted to Babylon's link with commerce, with the goods of the world. She is a mighty city that has not only committed fornication with kings, but has glorified herself, lived in luxury, and made rich -- beyond all imagination -- *the merchants of the earth.* It is interesting here to look at a few verses specifically:

> **3 The kings of the earth have committed fornication with her, and *the merchants* of the earth**
>   **have become rich through the abundance[1] of her luxury.[2]**
> **7 In the measure that *she* glorified herself and lived luxuriously,[3] in the same measure give**
>   **her torment and sorrow.**
> **9 The *kings* of the earth ... lived luxuriously[3] with her ...** (emphasis added)

[1]*dunamis* G1411T – strength, power, ability
[2]*strenos* G4764TS – excessive strength which strains to break forth; that is, the impetus and
       straining for luxury; strenuousness
[3]*streniao* G4763T – to be wanton, to live luxuriously (the adverb form of *strenos*)

Strenos, found in all three of these verses, is difficult to translate with one word. It speaks of the strength and power of LUST; of the powerful motivation – the *willfulness* – involved in the pursuit of wealth, luxury, and all that would allow for complete self-gratification. The thing desired may not even in itself be wrong; but when we lust, we *want* the thing (whether God wants us to have it or not), we *must have it,* and we must have it *now.* This power of lust provides a three-fold cord of purpose shared by the merchants of the earth (v. 3), the religious whore (v. 7), and the kings of the earth (v. 9). The three working together provide the driving mechanisms for the rise and fall of governments, religious systems, and economic systems. Working together, they lead to much buying and selling, to feeding the flesh, to the accumulation of great power and great wealth, and to whatever control and manipulation of people, armies, and governments is needed to gain *and maintain* these. We see the great banking systems; the huge companies that wield power through their wealth; the ships, the merchants, the sailors and the traders; the stock companies and stock brokers, as well as the kings, rulers, and politicians. This chapter encompasses all who operate *outside of the realm of trusting God* in order to obtain their desired goal in life. The pursuit of money has always been a powerful motivator of men, and here we see it exposed as part of the great kingdom of Satan by which he ensnares people.

We say again, the whore seems to be held the most responsible for the iniquity involved in this, for she is the one who claims spiritual knowledge and authority. She is the one who puts the stamp of false "divine approval" upon the departure from the true God, as well as upon whatever means is used to gain this tremendous accumulation of power and wealth. To satisfy her lusts, she trades in all the precious and valued commodities of the earth: gold, silver, precious stones, pearls, fine linen, purple, silk, ivory, valuable creations of wood, brass, iron, and marble; cinnamon and other fragrances, ointments, wine, oil, fine flour, wheat, beasts, sheep, horses, chariots, and *slaves, and SOULS OF MEN.* And when we read at the end of the chapter that "in her was found the blood of prophets, of saints, and of *all that were slain upon the earth,*" can we doubt at all that **she is indeed the manifestation of the kingdom of Satan on the earth, where every principality and ruler of darkness, down to** the smallest demon, obeys her bidding? We may see wicked men behind the evils of the earth, but God looks farther, and sees this great, wicked city and the spiritual entities that act upon men, pressuring and enticing them into wickedness.

On this three-legged stool, then – the religious, political, and commercial -- rests the great kingdom of Babylon, the kingdom "of this world," which will be brought down at the end of the age to make way for the kingdom "of our Lord and of His Christ."

The Pervasiveness of Babylon

We have seen that all false religion – all that is outside of the narrow way of Jesus – makes up Babylon. When we understand it with that clarity, we see that Babylon intrudes even into the church. Of course, the tares – the make-believers – are part of Babylon, being plantings of the devil in the kingdom.[9] But as we saw clearly in our study of the church ages, Babylon is constantly pitted in deadly opposition to God's people and, whether using force or subtilty, is always seeking to encroach upon and gain entrance to the true church and the true believer, often with great success.

We become vulnerable to Babylon – as opposed to *Jerusalem* -- whenever we begin persistently to put ourselves or self-interest before the Lord. Whenever we have an area of our lives consistently not surrendered to the Lord Jesus, that area is no longer under kingdom authority; as that area begins to control us, it becomes ground in us for the demonic and a "Babylon area" in our lives. This can happen in whatever way a believer's complete consecration to the Lord is compromised by other interests in his life – whether a love of money or material possessions; relationships with others, such as spouse, children, or other loved ones; a religious heritage or training or ministry that we hold to for selfish purposes; or finally, something that is simply an issue of pride and of self or of sin that we hold onto stubbornly. When a whole denomination or a local church follows in the path of tradition or falls under the control of man, they have 'gone into exile in Babylon.' Things may not seem that bad outwardly, but in the spiritual dimension, there is interaction with the kingdom of darkness rather than the kingdom of God. It goes without saying that the antichrist spirit, which we've discussed previously and which is rampant in the church, is a primary agent of Babylon in its subtle work against the church.

John taught us that the love of the world is in opposition to the love of the Father, "for all that is in the world, the lust of the flesh, and the lust of the eyes, and the pride of life, is not of the Father, but is of the world."[10] John was describing the many and varied seductions which are a part of the world system and which can draw hearts astray. These seductions are of Babylon, and there is a repeated call of God in Scripture for God's people to separate themselves from Babylon. [11]

"Come Out of Her, My People"

Babylon works by the power of fear, lies, and lust. As God's people, we have been given power to escape the corruption caused by lust, and instead - by means of great, precious promises - partake of the very nature of God Himself.[12] Nevertheless, because of how subtly Babylon has infiltrated the kingdom of God, and how easily God's people can fall into her clutches, God warns His people in Scripture:

> **Come out of her, my people, lest you share in her sins, and lest you receive of her plagues.**
> **Revelation 18:4**

This is a spiritual call to come out of religious mixture, compromise, and anything that falls short of complete consecration to the Lord Jesus. It is a call to direct, personal surrender to Him, and to withdrawal from any institution or organization of man that would stand between the believer and the Lord. There can be no other allegiance, no other attachment of the heart. God's repeated call for His people to separate from Babylon, that

---

9   Matt. 13:24-30, 37-43.
10   1 John 2:15-16
11   Is. 48:20; Jer. 50:8, 28; 51:6, 45, 50
12   2 Peter 1:4

"you be not partaker of her plagues," is consistent with the many warnings of deception and straying that we see in the New Testament. We've already noted the judgment of the 'tares':

> **The Son of Man will send out His angels, and they will gather out of His kingdom all things that offend, and those who practice lawlessness, and will cast them into the furnace of fire. There will be wailing and gnashing of teeth. Matthew 13:41-42**

The tares appear to be in God's kingdom, but in actuality are part of Babylon, and will therefore partake of the judgment upon Babylon! How *profound* will be the misery and regret! How deep will be the suffering and self-reproach! They were *so close*, and yet missed it!

It isn't just a matter of "coming out of Babylon" as we might envision it, but of ensuring that any vestige of Babylon is cleansed out of us! We have seen that the Day of the Lord will test and *reveal by fire* what we and our work consist of.[13] This includes *all that is in us and in our service, that pertains to Babylon.* The call to separate ourselves from her is one to take with utter seriousness. Speaking of that judgment, Paul said, **"Knowing therefore the terror of the Lord, we persuade men."**[14] And again, **"It is a fearful thing to fall into the hands of the living God."**[15] These are warnings about God's judgment *of His own people.* God grant each one of us *ears to hear!* We would note that separating ourselves from Babylon lies in our *heart* and our *will.* That is, we repent and *choose,* before God, to consecrate ourselves fully to Him and allow Him to *work out* that consecration in any way that He chooses, cooperating with Him! It is an act of faith, followed by walking the *path of faith.*

---

13 1 Cor. 3:12-15
14 2 Cor. 5:11
15 Heb. 10:31

CHAPTER 24

The Judgment
of Babylon

The primary focus of these two chapters in Revelation is, of course, the *final judgment* of Babylon. As the enemy in continual opposition to God, the judgment of Babylon has been long anticipated by God and His people. Jeremiah gave a lengthy prophecy of her downfall at the very time that King Nebuchadnezzar was afflicting Judah and finally destroying Jerusalem and the temple completely.[1] But Isaiah prophesied against her even earlier, before Babylon had arisen as the empire that would succeed Assyria. Ever since the Tower of Babel, God has had an issue with Babylon (and the kingdoms that she gave expression to) and has anticipated her ultimate judgment and downfall. However, in the meantime, these Babylon kingdoms have been important tools in God's hands for the judgment of His people. Inflicting pain is not inherent in God, but with the flesh of man requiring discipline and training, God has used the oppression of the heathen to bring testing and chastisement to His people. When Babylon's usefulness to God will be finished, she will be judged for the overflowing of iniquity and filth found in her.

The confusing of the languages at Babel and the consequent scattering of the families throughout the earth made clear God's displeasure with man's attempt to establish *a single kingdom* over all the earth. At the end, God will allow this single kingdom again for a brief time. The renewed Roman empire of the ten toes will be unlike the previous empires in that it will be truly global in nature. But it will be this way in rebellion against God – the spirit present at the Tower of Babel again rearing its head; and the final, consuming judgment of God will not be long in coming.

This judgment appears to take place in two stages: the first is the judgment of religious Babylon, and the second is the judgment of political Babylon.

The Judgment of 'Mystery Babylon the Great'

The judgment of Mystery Babylon, the harlot, is spoken of in Rev. 17-18. In chapter 17 she is depicted as the whore riding the political system, and in chapter 18, as "that great city by which the merchants of the earth have been made wealthy" (18:15). The judgment of the whore takes place earlier in the seven years than that of the political kingdom: first, because there is time for the merchants, who up until then have been prospering, to feel the loss of her business and to lament it; and second, although it is the Lord God who judges her, He uses the

---

1 Jeremiah 50-51.

ten regional kings to execute the judgment (18:8, 17:16). That is, He causes the *political* arm of Babylon to turn on and to judge the religious arm. Therefore, the judgment of the whore *must* precede the judgment of the beast and his political kingdom. We note that although the judgment is not directed at the merchants, they are dealt a devastating blow with the loss of their greatest customer.

The ten kings, then, are of one mind with the beast and give their power and authority to him to carry out his agenda:

> **And the ten horns which you saw on the beast, these will hate the harlot, make her desolate and naked, eat her flesh and burn her with fire.**
> **For God has put it into their hearts to fulfill His purpose, to be of one mind, and to give their kingdom to the beast, until the words of God are fulfilled. Revelation 17:16-17**

That God uses the beast and his kingdom to execute judgment upon the whore makes complete sense in view of the nature and agenda of the beast:

> **Then the king shall do according to his own will: he shall exalt and magnify himself above every god, shall speak blasphemies against the God of gods, and shall prosper till the wrath has been accomplished; for what has been determined shall be done.**
> **He shall regard neither the God of his fathers nor the desire of women, nor regard any god; for he shall exalt himself above them all. Daniel 11:36-37**

This man used the whore to reach his goal of ultimate power. Having reached it, and having become indwelt by the principality from hell,[2] he will be implacably focused upon himself as the one and only god and will tolerate loyalty to no other god. There will be systematic persecution of all who refuse to worship him, both false religions as well as apostate Christianity:

> **[The false prophet] was granted power to give breath to the image of the beast, that the image of the beast should both speak and cause as many as would not worship the image of the beast to be killed. Revelation 13:15**

As frightful as this sounds, we are reminded from the passage above that this "prophet" is simply carrying out the Word and will of God. Heaven rejoices over the horrific judgment of the great whore; after all, it is not only the blood of *all the righteous* that is found in her, but the blood of *all who were slain upon the earth!* It is the kingdom of Satan – Babylon – that God holds responsible for all murders upon the earth. Here we see God using this terrible (political) kingdom for His purposes, to deal "death, mourning, and famine to her," and to "utterly burn her with fire" (18:8). When the whore becomes the target of God's wrath, she goes down completely, having *no defense.*

But when God's people are the target of the beast, the outcome is different. Remember, this is the Great Tribulation, the time of testing for the whole world. Though the Lamb and His followers are also targeted, the outcome is different:

> **[The ten kings] will make war with the Lamb, and the Lamb will overcome them, for He is Lord of lords and King of kings; and those who are with Him are called, chosen, and faithful." Revelation 17:14**

The war against the Lamb, of course, is carried out on the earth against His followers. It's not just the qualities of the Lamb that make war against Him futile; it's the qualities of those who are undergoing the warfare, for they *share* the qualities of the Lamb! They too, *are kings* under His Kingship. They too, *are lords* under His Lordship. They are *called, chosen, and faithful,* and the power of God rests upon them, a power greater than any angel from

---

2 Rev. 17:8, 10-11

hell! They are *under His authority and covering*. Nothing will happen to them outside of His express will and purpose for them! We already noted with the martyrs of this time, that only those chosen by God for martyrdom will die under the persecution of the beast.[3] Even when they are killed, they are *overcoming* (even as Jesus overcame). Those who are raptured (alive) are a multitude *so great that no man could number it*.[4] Their faithfulness to Jesus Christ under this test is what causes a triumphant victory over the beast, his image, and his mark, and all his intimidation! The true church is put to the same test as the false, and the outcome for the two is entirely different! **It is possible for every believer to be established in the conviction that his life is in God's hands and will end only at the time and in the way that God chooses; and that whatever God's plan is for him, God's grace will carry him through to victory! This brings peace and security to the believer.**

We believe this separation of the false from the true is taking place before the rapture occurs and the Day of the Lord begins. In other words, this time of separation and judgment takes place (or at least begins) while the church is still present on the earth. Remember, we have seen that at the end of the age, those who make up the whore will gather together around their particular false teachers/beliefs, whether Islam, Buddhism, humanism, communism, false Christianity, etc.[5] The tares, also part of the whore, will be separated out from the kingdom into bundles and cast into a furnace of fire. "*Then* shall the righteous shine forth as the sun in the kingdom of their Father"[6] (emphasis added). So, we see that the rapture occurs and the righteous shine forth as the sun directly following the judgment of the whore.

Exactly how long this judgment takes isn't clear. In chapter 18 it's said to occur both in "one hour" (v. 19) and in "one day" (v. 8). Similar terms are used in chapter 17 to describe the duration of the beast's reign: "a short space" (v. 10), and the ten kings' rule: "one hour" (v. 12). So, we see that these terms are used to show a relatively brief period of time but are not to be taken literally. We would guess that to bring all the members of the whore to accountability would take some time, possibly a year at least. Although the tares are (of necessity) separated out of the kingdom before the rapture, it's very possible/likely that the full judgment of the whore continues even after the rapture of the church, as Antichrist continues to enforce worship of himself alone.

Therefore, to sum up, this judgment of the religious Babylon appears to take place during the second half of the 70th week under the direction of the beast, the antichrist.

NOTE: A prophecy from Dumitru Duduman seems to speak of this time, presenting a picture of the separation process as well as of the protection and power upon the church at this time. See Appendix 8.

The Judgment of Political Babylon

The seventh trumpet heralds the time for God to "destroy those who destroy the earth" (Rev. 11:18c). It is popular today to worry about human responsibility for 'climate change,' the 'destruction of the ozone layer,' and other 'green' issues. Some might read this verse through those lenses. But the prophet Jeremiah ascribed responsibility for the earth's destruction to another source, the kingdom of Babylon:

> **"Behold, I am against you, O destroying mountain (kingdom), who destroys all the earth," says the Lord. Jeremiah 51:25**

How can this be laid at the feet of Babylon? We have already seen the responsibility for the blood of all the saints, as well as of all the slain of the earth, resting upon Babylon. Isaiah clarifies further:

> **The earth is also defiled under its inhabitants, because they have transgressed the laws, changed the ordinance, broken the everlasting covenant.**
> **Therefore, the curse has devoured the earth, and those who dwell in it are desolate.**
> **Therefore, the inhabitants of the earth are burned, and few men are left. Isaiah 24:5-6**

---

3 Rev. 6:9-11
4 Rev. 7:9
5 Matt. 24:24-26, 28. It's interesting to note that the 'Jezebel' of Thyatira, which we identified as being the Roman Catholic system, will be punished at this time. Jesus said that because she had failed to repent, He would "cast her. . . and those who commit adultery with her into great tribulation. . ." (Rev. 2:22). We see clearly that this system is part of the whore.
6 Matt. 13:40-43 (Col. 3:4, Phil. 3:21, 1 John 3:2, Rev. 1:16)

It is the iniquity of man that brings the curse, and the curse brings destruction. Under the leadership of Antichrist, the rebellion and iniquity of the earth is brought to fullness, and with the sixth bowl judgment, the time arrives for the vengeance of the Lord upon Babylon. It is His proclamation that He has "opened His armory and brought forth the weapons of His wrath." No one will escape – from foundations to storehouses to wall to inhabitants, Babylon will be *utterly destroyed.*[7] Now all the kings and armies of the earth will assemble for "the battle of that great day of God Almighty." The trap is laid,[8] and Antichrist and all the forces of the earth will walk straight into it with the intention of finally and ultimately destroying Israel – Israel who has remained vulnerable and defenseless in her separation from God. But they have failed to reckon on the *turning* that is taking place with Israel. As Israel completes her turn and cries out to God, *everything changes.* God has been waiting – millennia – for that cry, and with a mighty roar, the Lion of the tribe of Judah will break forth from heaven in such a display of God's power and glory as to leave us stunned and breathless. It is the time long awaited – the time for the wicked of the earth to drink to the bottom the "cup of the fierceness of the wine of His wrath."[9]

The bloodbath that ensues will bring the ultimate decimation of the beast kingdom. Not only are the armies completely destroyed, as the closing verses of Revelation 19 tell us, but both the beast and the false prophet are captured and thrown alive into the lake of fire. This then brings the wrath of God to a stunning conclusion, as all His enemies are either destroyed or captured. Jesus has retaken the earth in such a way as to stagger the mind, as we shall see in the next chapter.

---

7   Jer. 50:15, 26, 29; 51:49
8   Jer. 50:24
9   Rev. 16:13-14, 19

THE ROAR OF THE LION OF JUDAH

CHAPTER 25
The Battle of Armageddon

The Battle of Armageddon is completely entwined with Israel and impossible to separate completely, but the two issues together are so great that we will focus on the battle in this chapter and on Israel in the next.

There's one thing we must credit the devil with, and that is his consistency. He never deviates from his goal of utterly destroying Israel. Even when he knows what the Word says – that his final attempt will be his downfall - he *must* move forward with the attempt! And so, as we have seen, the invitation goes forth:

> **12 Then the sixth angel poured out his bowl on the great river Euphrates, and its water was dried up, so that the way of the kings from the east might be prepared.**
> **13 And I saw three unclean spirits like frogs coming out of the mouth of the dragon, out of the mouth of the beast, and out of the mouth of the false prophet.**
> **14 For they are spirits of demons, performing signs, which go out to the kings of the earth and of the whole world, to gather them to the battle of that great day of God Almighty.**
> **15 "Behold, I am coming as a thief. Blessed is he who watches, and keeps his garments, lest he walk naked and they see his shame."**
> **16 And they gathered them together to the place called in Hebrew, Armageddon.**
> **Revelation 16:12-16**

The gathering place for all these armies is "Har Megiddo" – the mountain of Megiddo. Megiddo is a plain (Esdraelon) in the northwest of Israel and in the Jezreel Valley, just north of the Megiddo mountains. It lies in a strategic crossroads, and has been the site of numerous battles in the past:

- 1400's BC – a battle between Egypt and the Canaanites
- 1200's BC - Gideon defeated a huge coalition of Amalekites, Midianites, and others (Judges 6-7).
- 609 BC – a battle between Egypt and Judea
- 1914 – a battle between British forces and the Ottoman Empire

Notice that Joel sees *God* calling the armies:

1 For behold, in those days and at that time, when I bring back the captives of Judah and Jerusalem,

2 I will also gather all nations and bring them down to the Valley of Jehoshaphat;[1] and I will enter into judgment with them there on account of My people, My heritage Israel, whom they have scattered among the nations; they have also divided up My land.

9 Proclaim this among the nations: "Prepare for war! Wake up the mighty men, let all the men of war draw near, let them come up.

10 Beat your plowshares into swords and your pruning hooks into spears; let the weak say, 'I am strong.'"

11 Assemble and come, all you nations, and gather together all around. Cause Your mighty ones to go down there, O Lord.

12 "Let the nations be wakened and come up to the Valley of Jehoshaphat; for there I will sit to judge all the surrounding nations.

13 Put in the sickle, for the harvest is ripe. Come, go down; for the winepress is full, the vats overflow — for their wickedness is great."

14 Multitudes, multitudes in the valley of decision![2] For the day of the Lord is near in the valley of decision.[2] Joel 3:1-2, 9-14

[1] *yehoshaphat* H3092B – yah is judge
[2] *charuwts* H2742TS– sharp-pointed, incised, cutting; having sharp teeth, a cutting instrument

Here we see a call from God for the nations to gather, and for them to garner their utmost armaments with which to come against both Him and the *mighty warriors* that He will bring with Him. Here in this valley of "God is Judge," they will be judged and executed; here also is mentioned the great winepress of the wrath of God (v. 13), a metaphor we will encounter repeatedly in reference to Armageddon.

Preceding this in heaven, the Bride has stood before the judgment seat of Christ for the giving of rewards, probably around the same time that all false religions ('Mystery Babylon') are continuing to undergo judgment on the earth. Following this destruction of the great whore (Rev. 19:1-5), the marriage of the Lamb to His Bride is announced (vv. 7-9); then we see *the Lord Jesus,* prepared to leave heaven and engage this final battle:

Now I saw heaven opened, and behold, a white horse. And He who sat on him was called Faithful and True, and in righteousness He judges and makes war.
His eyes were like a flame of fire, and on His head were many crowns. He had a name written that no one knew except Himself.
He was clothed with a robe dipped in blood, and His name is called the Word of God.
And the armies in heaven, clothed in fine linen, white and clean, followed Him on white horses.
Now out of His mouth goes a sharp sword, that with it He should strike the nations. And He Himself will rule them with a rod of iron. He Himself treads the winepress of the fierceness and wrath of Almighty God.
And He has on His robe and on His thigh a name written: KING OF KINGS AND LORD OF LORDS. Revelation 19:11-16

This now is the second *manifestation* ("shining forth") of Christ which pertains to His second coming. The first manifestation was at the rapture; this one is now for the rescue of Israel and the destruction of Antichrist and his armies. It is *with the word of His mouth* and the shining glory of His person that He will slay His enemies.[1] With Him are the armies of heaven: the saints, shining with glory, and a mighty host of angels.

---

1 2 Thess. 2:8 We note that the first manifestation led to the salvation of the 144,000; this second one brings the salvation of the remaining remnant of the Jews; a lovely thing. To see Jesus is to live.

The evil purpose of Satan and the armies – to destroy Israel completely - is what fills the cup of their iniquity to the uttermost. In truth, it is God calling them to this "valley of incision" for *their* final destruction:

> **And another angel came out from the altar, who had power over fire, and he cried with a loud cry to him who had the sharp sickle, saying, "Thrust in your sharp sickle and gather the clusters of the vine of the earth, for her grapes are fully ripe."**
> **So the angel thrust his sickle into the earth and gathered the vine of the earth and threw it into the great winepress of the wrath of God.**
> **And the winepress was trampled outside the city, and blood came out of the winepress, up to the horses' bridles, for one thousand six hundred furlongs. Revelation 14:18-20**

Each of these three passages speaks of the great harvest of the grapes of the earth, which will be thrown into the winepress of the wrath of God. We are told here that blood will come up to the height of the horses' bridles for approximately 200 miles![2] This may be difficult to visualize, but this will be a *vast army*, "multitudes, multitudes," in this valley of blood-letting. Revelation 19 tells us that the outcome of this battle is an invitation to all the fowls of heaven to come and feast on the "flesh of kings, of captains, of mighty men, of horses, of them that sit on them, and on the flesh of all men, both free and slave, small and great" (vv. 17-18).

Hear the overflowing power of God's wrath in this:

> **1 Come near, you nations, to hear; and heed, you people! Let the earth hear, and all that is in it, the world and all things that come forth from it.**
> **2 For the indignation of the Lord is against all nations, and His fury against all their armies; He has utterly destroyed them, He has given them over to the slaughter.**
> **3 Also their slain shall be thrown out; their stench shall rise from their corpses, and the mountains shall be melted with their blood.**
> **4 All the host of heaven shall be dissolved, and the heavens shall be rolled up like a scroll; all their host shall fall down, as the leaf falls from the vine, and as fruit falling from a fig tree.**
> **5 "For My sword shall be bathed in heaven; indeed it shall come down on Edom, and on the people of My curse, for judgment.**
> **6 The sword of the Lord is filled with blood. . . for the Lord has a sacrifice in Bozrah, and a great slaughter in the land of Edom.**
> **7 The wild oxen shall come down with them, and the young bulls with the mighty bulls; their land shall be soaked with blood, and their dust saturated with fatness."**
> **8 For it is the day of the Lord's vengeance, the year of recompense for the cause of Zion.**
> **Isaiah 34:1-8**

For years, centuries, *millennia,* God has forborne with the mistreatment of His people, the people of Zion. Zion is the highest, most impregnable part of Jerusalem – the place from which His rule is to go forth. But always, there has been contention over Zion. Who will control it? Will it be *natural* man – independent of God (despite being religious), or *spiritual* man – man redeemed by the Lamb's blood and under the Lamb's authority? The warfare over this issue has existed since the fall in Eden. Those who would walk submitted to God have suffered every persecution, injustice, and death, and God has waited patiently. But now His fury is unleashed without restraint.

Notice that this judgment begins in Bozrah, the capital of Edom, at the southeastern corner of the range of this bloodbath.[3] Edom is Esau, brother to Jacob;[4] but although related to Israel, the Edomites were always at en-

---

2   See Psalm 29, where it is the voice of the Lord executing judgment; and where the scope of the judgment ranges from the wilderness of Kadesh in the south to Sirion (Mt. Hermon) and Lebanon in the north – a distance of about 180 miles. Compare this Psalm with Is. 30:27-33 – "the Assyrian" being a reference to Antichrist.

3   See Is. 63:1-4, also Deut. 33:2 and Hab. 3:3-4; Teman, Seir, and Paran are all references to Edom. It is interesting to consider that this is also the likely location of the wilderness where many of God's people continue to find refuge from persecution (Rev. 12).

4   Gen. 36:8

mity with Israel, hostile to what they represented. They were either subdued by them, or, when Israel was under judgment, they increased the suffering, siding with Israel's enemies.[5] **Beyond that, Esau in Scripture represents** *natural man*: **self-sufficient man making his own way, with all his capabilities, strategies, and strengths,** *apart from God.* As we see in v. 5 above, Edom represents *the "people of my curse."*[6] Always the *lawless one,* there can be no blessing on natural man, but rather, a curse.

As we saw in Revelation 19, Jesus *leaves* heaven with blood: here, His sword is *bathed with blood in heaven.* Is it His own blood that stains His garments and His sword? It *was* the shedding of His own blood that earned Him the authorization for this vengeance! From heaven He comes forth now for *the express purpose* of bathing the earth with the blood of sinners! Those who rejected the death of the Lamb on their behalf will now become the sacrifice *themselves*: lambs and goats, rams, oxen, and bulls – the land will be soaked with blood.[7] **It is the closing of the age of man.**

Under devastating judgment, the earth staggers and its very foundations shake. Islands are moved and mountains disappear as the earth breaks in pieces and totters, swaying like a hammock in the wind. Even the heavens roll up and pass away, to be replaced with new heavens, wherein dwell righteousness.[8]

---

5 Obadiah 1:8-18, Amos 1:11, Ps. 137:7

6 See Jer. 17:5-6.

7 This is probably a reason that this final series of judgments is called "the bowl judgments." Speaking of this time in the future, Zechariah tells us, "The Lord of hosts will protect [Judah and Ephraim], and they shall devour, and tread down the sling stones, and they shall drink and roar as if drunk with wine, and be full like a bowl, drenched like the corners of the altar" (Zech. 9:15) ESV. In the temple worship, the blood of animal sacrifices was drained into two bowls from which the blood was then flung against the four sides of the altar. This could only be done by flinging each bowl full at a corner so it would hit two sides at once.

8 Is. 24:18c-20, Rev. 16:17-20, 2 Peter 3:13 (Ps. 102:5-6, Is. 51:6)

CHAPTER 26

The Final Turning
and Deliverance of Israel

As we consider further this great conflict, we find that though the armies assemble at Armageddon, their intent is to surround and overtake Jerusalem. We saw Antichrist clearly in control of Jerusalem at the midpoint; he apparently loses that control - how and when is unclear; perhaps it happens in the mayhem of the Day of the Lord. In any event, Zechariah depicts this huge, assembled army laying siege against both Judah and Jerusalem. It is a "now or never" situation; the end of the 70th week is approaching, and it is time for the final great showdown. If Antichrist wins now, Israel is removed forever as a nation. Zechariah prophesied that at that time, God would make Jerusalem a "cup of reeling and a burdensome stone" for all those gathered against her; "All that burden themselves with [Jerusalem] shall be cut in pieces, though all the people of the earth be gathered together against it" (Zech. 12:2-3).

We recall God's words to Isaiah at his commissioning, that he was being sent to a people whose hearts were dull, their ears heavy, and their eyes shut.[1] And he was warned that this condition would persist way into the future. They had used their demand for "a sign" – a supernatural indication that something was 'of the Lord' – as an excuse to resist opportunity after opportunity to believe God. They had refused all Jesus' miracles as coming from the Father; they had refused 'the sign' of His resurrection.[2] Paul affirmed in his day that "the veil remained" over their eyes;[3] continuing on down through the centuries, they refused 'the sign' of His Person in the sky at the rapture, though every eye had seen Him, even "those who pierced Him."[4] Though seeing Him *physically* at that time, the resistant hearts, stopped ears, and veiled eyes remained (except, of course, for the 144,000). The many 'signs' given through the two witnesses had availed to turn some, yet not all. Now at the end of the final seven years, their thick, proud hearts have been 'thinned' by the *necessary* suffering they have passed through. In their deep, dire need and under siege, their hearts turn, and we are about to see Paul's words come to pass: "But when it – the heart – turns to the Lord, the veil is taken away."[5]

The Turning of Israel

And so, in the extremity of the siege, Israel *completes her turning* to God and, desperate, cries out to Him. God has both begged and promised regarding this:

---

1 Is. 6:10 (Acts 28:27)
2 Matt. 12:39-40
3 2 Cor. 3:14-15
4 Matt. 24:30, Rev. 1:7
5 2 Cor. 3:16; see also Deut. 4:29-31, Jer. 50:4-5.

O Israel, return to the Lord your God, for you have stumbled because of your iniquity; Take words with you and return to the Lord. Say to Him, "Take away all iniquity; Receive us graciously, for we will offer the sacrifices of our lips. Assyria shall not save us, we will not ride on horses, nor will we say anymore to the work of our hands, 'You are our gods.' For in You the fatherless finds mercy." Hosea 14:1-3

Once the long, hard work of *heart change* has taken place, all that is needed is for Israel to turn to God with words of repentance. The Lord Himself supplies the words with which they return: "Cleanse us, oh God; forgive all our sin by your grace. It is not the Assyrian who will save us. We will not trust in armaments or in our own inventions, but in You the fatherless finds mercy." Having turned their back on their heavenly Father, they have been the "fatherless" nation – the outcast ones. The time for these words has at long last arrived, and God hears their desperate and repentant cry!

God's Response to Israel's Cry

We notice immediately the change in God's behavior! Israel is no longer in need of chastisement. God is done using the beast and the armies of the nations to chastise Israel. He is done pouring out wrath upon them. For *so long* has the Lord restrained Himself, watching as His people were abused and persecuted, hounded from one nation to another. With what sorrow has He had to hold back, waiting until they would again seek His face. Now, He will turn His fury upon all who have hated and persecuted them. He need hold back no more, but at long last, can be Israel's defender. The day of His ultimate vengeance against the wicked has arrived, and He breaks forth with ferocity on behalf of Israel:

> **The Lord shall go forth like a mighty man; He shall stir up His zeal like a man of war. He shall cry out, yes, shout aloud; He shall prevail against His enemies.**
> **"I have held My peace a long time, I have been still and restrained Myself. Now I will cry like a woman in labor, I will pant and gasp at once.**
> **"I will lay waste the mountains and hills and dry up all their vegetation; I will make the rivers coastlands, and I will dry up the pools." Isaiah 42:13-15**

And from Jeremiah:

> 30 **"The Lord will roar from on high and utter His voice from His holy habitation; He will roar mightily [over]¹ His fold. He will give a shout, as those who tread the grapes, against all the inhabitants of the earth.**
> 31 **"A noise will come to the ends of the earth — For the Lord has a controversy with the nations; He will [judge] His case with all flesh. He will give those who are wicked to the sword," says the Lord.**
> 32 **Thus says the Lord of hosts: "Behold, disaster shall go forth from nation to nation, and a great whirlwind shall be raised up from the farthest parts of the earth.**
> 33 **"And at that day the slain of the Lord shall be from one end of the [land] even to the other end of the [land]. They shall not be lamented, or gathered, or buried; they shall become refuse on the ground." Jeremiah 25:30-33**

¹*al* H5921B – over, above, upon, on behalf of

The Lord *roars* from on high, comes down, and *roars over* His flock. What a description of the Lord's actions! Joel adds:

> **The Lord also will roar from Zion and utter His voice from Jerusalem; The heavens and earth will shake; but the Lord will be a shelter for His people, and the strength of the children of Israel.**

So *you shall know that I am the Lord your God*, dwelling in Zion My holy mountain. Then Jerusalem shall be holy, and no aliens shall ever pass through her again."

Joel 3:16-17 (emphasis added)

Israel's Revelation of Christ

Having cried out to the Lord, their eyes are fixed heavenward. What does Israel now see? Who then is it that roars from heaven, coming to their aid? What do they now *know?* He who appears is *the One on the white horse, called "Faithful and True," with eyes as a flame of fire and crowned with many crowns.*[6] This is a stunning moment – the moment when they know I AM. Jesus had declared to the Jews, "If you believe not that *I am*, you shall die in your sins." And, "Before Abraham was, *I am*." In response, the Jews picked up stones to throw at Him.[7] Their fundamental iniquity was refusal to receive their Messiah – to receive Him as sent by the Father, one with the Father. Now, at this time in the future, *they will stagger at the knowledge of Who has come to their aid -- Jesus Christ, the I AM – the One they crucified!*

Zechariah speaks of this time when the Lord, who descends to fight against those nations, steps down on the Mount of Olives[8] and is revealed to be the One "whom they pierced":

> **10 "And I will pour on the house of David and on the inhabitants of Jerusalem the Spirit of grace and supplication; then they will look on Me whom they pierced. Yes, they will mourn for Him as one mourns for his only son and grieve for Him as one grieves for a firstborn.**
> **14 all the families that remain, every family by itself, and their wives by themselves.**
> **13:1 "In that day a fountain shall be opened for the house of David and for the inhabitants of Jerusalem, for sin and for uncleanness. Zechariah 12:10,14; 13:1-2**

They will *finally* <u>look on Him</u> and *see* Him! And that will bring a cataclysmic, *shattering* realization, that the One they have resisted for 2,000 years – the One *they put to death on a Roman cross* – was actually the One they've been waiting for forever, their Messiah. Stunned to the depths, this brings a mourning so deep – *so profound* – that the men abstain from their wives; a *process* of realization is required. The rebellion and spiritual blindness so deeply entrenched in their national psyche has finally been broken; and now so many things must change internally.

The Anointing Upon Israel

It is not only internal change for the Jews that occurs, but this deep grieving and repentance and the consequent cleansing in the fount of Messiah's blood *changes everything from God's perspective*; it opens the way for the Spirit of God to come upon them as a people. It is not simply now that Israel is *rescued* by the Lord, but that *Israel is transformed* to participate in the astonishing display of power over these enemies. The Spirit of God now falls upon Israel – even as in the days of old. No, *more* than in the days of old:

> **4 In that day . . . I will open My eyes on the house of Judah . . .**
> **6 . . . and I will make the governors of Judah like a firepan in the woodpile, and like a fiery torch in the sheaves; they shall devour all the surrounding peoples on the right hand and on the left, but Jerusalem shall be inhabited again in her own place.**
> **8 In that day the Lord will defend the inhabitants of Jerusalem; *the one who is feeble among them in that day shall be like David, and the house of David shall be like God, like the Angel of the Lord before them.***

Zechariah 12:4,6,8 (emphasis added)

---

6 Rev. 19:11-12
7 John 8:24, 58
8 Zech. 14:3-4

Isaiah explains:

> **It shall come to pass in that day that his burden will be taken away from your shoulder, and his yoke from your neck; and the yoke will be destroyed because of the anointing oil.**
>
> **Isaiah 10:27**

Empowered from on high by the Spirit of God, tiny Israel arises with invincible power to cast off the yoke of Antichrist and this huge assembled army:

> **Now also many nations have gathered against you, who say, "Let her be defiled, and let our eye look upon Zion."**
> **But they do not know the thoughts of the Lord, nor do they understand His counsel; for He will gather them like sheaves to the threshing floor.**
> **"Arise and thresh, O daughter of Zion; for I will make your horn iron, and I will make your hooves bronze. You shall beat in pieces many peoples; I will consecrate their gain to the Lord, and their substance to the Lord of the whole earth." Micah 4:11-13**

Participating in this harvest bloodbath, Israel is now "a new, sharp threshing instrument" with which the armies and nations will be threshed and beaten small, and the peoples will be made like chaff which the wind will carry away (Is. 41:15-16). This is the beginning of the great national restoration of Israel.

The Fury of the Lion of Judah

At Jesus' ascension in Acts 1, the disciples were told that He would return in a similar fashion as He had left. In the initial unveiling of His return, He comes in the clouds of heaven to gather the saints, but His feet do not touch the earth. In this second manifestation of His Presence, Zechariah tells us that "His feet will stand in that day upon the Mount of Olives. . . "[9] And in that day, He will go forth and fight against those gathered nations. The picture given us in the Word regarding Jesus' actions at this time is astonishing – He begins to sweep through the land in a whirlwind of judgment:

> **For behold, the Lord will come with fire and with His chariots, like a whirlwind, to render His anger with fury, and His rebuke with flames of fire.**
> **For by fire and by His sword the Lord will judge all flesh; and the slain of the Lord shall be many. Isaiah 66:15-16**

As we've seen before, this whirlwind begins in the south, in the area of Edom (which, incidentally, is interesting, given that this is the likely area of the wilderness that the Jews have sought refuge in as they have fled from Antichrist):[10]

> **3 God is coming from Edom, the Holy One from Mount Paran. His glory covers the heavens and the earth is full of His praise.**
> **4 He shone with brilliant light; rays of power went forth from His hand, there where His power is concealed.**
> **5 Before Him goes destruction and burning flames follow at His feet.**
> **12 You march through the land in fury; you thresh the nations as you trample them in anger.**
> **13 You went forth for the salvation of Your people, for salvation with Your anointed.**
>
> **Habakkuk 3:3-5, 12-13[11]**

The Lord marches through the land, and with great sweepings of His arms,[12] releases devastating power. The power going forth from His hands will bring fiery judgment upon the land and people. Notice that He goes forth

---

9 Matt. 24:30, Zech. 14:4.
10 See also Is. 63:1-4. He steps down on the Mt. of Olives, yet appears coming up from Edom.... It is uncertain where He first appears.
11 Worded by the author from Hebrew definitions (Strong's and Brown Driver Briggs).
12 Is. 25:11

with His people *for* their salvation. A more complete reading of this chapter of Habakkuk shows the turbulence upon the land as mountains and hills shift and rivers of water go through upheaval and rerouting. In the destruction, all the armaments of Antichrist and his armies are laid level with the ground. Babylon is uncovered from the foundation to the neck, and is mortally wounded in its head, Antichrist. Isaiah speaks of this time:

> **4 For thus the Lord said to me, "As a lion or a young lion growls over his prey, . . . so the Lord of hosts will come down to fight on Mount Zion and on its hill.**
> **8 And the Assyrian shall fall by a sword, not of man; and a sword, not of man, shall devour him;**
> **9 declares the Lord, whose fire is in Zion, and whose furnace is in Jerusalem.**
>
> **Isaiah 31:4, 8-9 ESV**

What sword – not of man - devours Antichrist? Christ leaves heaven with a sharp sword going out of His mouth, and with it, He will *smite* the nations. Paul tells us that Christ will *consume* "that lawless one" with the breath of His mouth and with the shining manifestation of His *parousia*.[13] "In that day," says the Lord, "all who do wickedly will be stubble… and you shall trample the wicked, for they shall be ashes under the soles of your feet on the day that I do this" (Mal. 4:1,3).

Revelation sums things up for us. After John saw Antichrist, kings, and armies gathered for war, he also saw Antichrist - the Assyrian - taken, along with the false prophet and all those who worshipped the image. The two were cast into the lake of fire, and the rest were slain by the words coming out of the mouth of Christ.[14] This then, along with the final earthquake -- which levels the cities and mountains of the earth -- and the plague of the 100-pound hailstones, brings to a conclusion the reign of Antichrist.

> **The heavens and the earth shall shake, but the Lord will be the hope of His people, and the strength of the children of Israel.**
> **So shall you know that I am the Lord your God, dwelling in Zion, my holy mountain. Then shall Jerusalem be holy, and there shall no strangers pass through her any more. Joel 3:16-17**
>
> **And the Lord shall be King over all the earth; in that day shall there be one Lord, and His name one. Zechariah 14:9**

This now is the end of the old age. Once Israel completes her return to God, there are no more restraints on God bringing down everything raised against Him. The old earth and heavens undergo shaking, shattering, burning, and devastation. God's wrath is poured out to the uttermost, bringing to a close the age of man. The kingdom of this world has now become the kingdom of our Lord and of His Christ.

---

13 Rev. 19:15 (Is. 11:4), 2 Thess. 2:8 (This is the second *epiphaneia* – manifestation - of His coming, the first occurring at the rapture – Matt. 24:30, 1 Tim. 6:14.)
14 Rev. 19:19-21

THE WRAP-UP AND
THE MILLENNIUM

CHAPTER 27

Transition
Events

At the close of the book of Daniel (12:11-12), the Lord adds thirty days onto the end of the 70th week, and then adds an additional forty-five days, saying, "Blessed is he who . . . comes to [that 75th day after the 70th week."] Marv Rosenthal is quite helpful here with these two additional periods of time.[1] He points out that thirty days was the usual period of mourning in Israel,[2] so it is likely that these thirty days are Israel's time of national mourning spoken of by Zechariah (12:10-12). When Antiochus Epiphanes defiled the temple, the full cleansing was accomplished in seventy-five days, which is the exact span of time between the Day of Atonement (the day of Israel's national repentance at the close of the 70th week) and Hanukkah, the day which celebrates the *completion* of the cleansing. If this is accurate, we would guess that the coronation and instatement of Christ as King of the earth would follow these two periods of time.

The Renovation of the Earth and Heavens
With the conclusion of the Day of the Lord's Wrath, the heavens are destroyed and the earth left in shambles. We know also that the earth's seas and rivers have been polluted, and all that is in them destroyed. Peter speaks of the burning judgment upon both the heavens and the earth: "The Day of the Lord. . . in which the heavens will pass away with a great noise, . . . being dissolved, being on fire; and both the earth and the works that are in it will be burned up." Peter adds, "Nevertheless, we, according to His promise, look for new heavens and a new earth in which righteousness dwells" (2 Peter 3:10,12).

So even as Peter prophesies of the deep destruction of the present heavens and earth, he also prophesied in v. 13 of a new – a "renewed, freshly made" - heavens and earth.[3] With the curse exhausted and Jesus now Lord of the earth, God's blessing will abound upon the physical earth and heavens. Ezekiel speaks of water coming out from the temple, flowing to all the waters of the earth, healing the waters and reviving marine life.[4] Paul anticipated the day when all of creation would be delivered from the slavery of corruption and would participate in the wonderful *freedom* of the glory of the

---

1   Marv Rosenthal, *The Pre-Wrath Rapture of the Church* (Thomas Nelson, Inc., 1990), p. 275.
2   Deut. 34:8, Num. 20:29
3   This can be confusing, as we know Revelation says God will make a "new heaven and a new earth" at the close of the Millennium (Rev. 21:1). But Peter, like Isaiah (Is. 65:17), is indeed speaking of a new heaven and earth with which we will *enter* the Millennium. At the beginning (v. 5) of this same chapter in Peter, he spoke of a prior civilization which was judged by water, saying that the *same Word of God* which recreated the earth following that judgment, is *keeping and maintaining* our present earth until the time for its judgment arrives. Therefore, we see that when sinners occupy the earth, God's ultimate judgment upon them affects the earth (and heavens) also, and therefore requires renovation of the earth for the age which is to follow.
4   Ezek. 47:1, 8--9

children of God. How can we imagine what that will mean? Our earth is already very beautiful, but with the corruption in nature removed, as well as the oppression of the devil and his demons, the earth itself will reach a transcendent beauty that we have not known. Psalm 67 speaks of the time when God's way and "saving health" will be known among all nations; a time when the nations will "sing for joy" and God will govern the nations righteously. Then "shall the earth yield her increase." No more will men labor in the sweat of their brow to eke a daily living out of a resistant earth, but the blessing of God will be upon men, their labors, and the earth itself.

Conclusion of the First Resurrection
The first resurrection, including those who are caught up alive, takes place in a number of stages. For the saints, this is the resurrection to be sought for and desired, even as Paul and the Old Testament saints did.[5] The first stage is comprised of the man child of Revelation 12 (which will be addressed in *Part 2*). The main part, of course, consists of the church (which includes the Old Testament saints, saved by faith in the anticipated sacrifice of the Lamb for them), raised or raptured at the coming of Christ. It is followed by the 144,000 and the two witnesses between the trumpet and bowl judgments, and finally, we see the conclusion of it at the end of the 70th week, when God resurrects those who were martyred for their testimony to Christ after the rapture of the church (Rev. 20:4-5). We assume this latter group is primarily - if not exclusively - Jewish, as we don't see evidence of Gentiles repenting after the church is gone.[6] We are told there in Revelation 20 that "the rest of the dead lived not until the thousand years were finished," at which time they will be judged (vv. 11-15). With the ending of the first resurrection, the number of saints with glorified bodies that will enter the Millennium is now complete.

Judges and Judgment

Included also in this chapter of Revelation is John's simple statement that he "saw thrones, and they sat upon them, and judgment was given unto them" (v. 4). Cryptic it is, and we must consult other places in Scripture to understand *who* exactly sat on them. For this information, we refer to such verses as Ps. 122:5, Ps. 132:12, Luke 22:28-30, 1 Cor. 6:2, 2 Tim. 2:11-12a, Rev. 2:26-27, and we conclude that it is the *saints* who are now seated on thrones, participating in the judgment that we shall look at shortly. It is likely that these judging positions have a correlation with the 'Judgment Seat of Christ' and the rewards handed out at that time. Jesus will share this authority to judge with those who have walked under His Lordship. This is a small glimpse we are given of "the meek inheriting the earth." These thrones of rulership and judgment will, of course, proceed into and be a part of the Millennial rule of Christ.

So, who is judged at this time? There is only a handful of people remaining on the earth (Is. 13:12; 24:6). These, of course, were not believers, since they did not go in the rapture. On the other hand, they also did not receive the mark of the beast, or they would not stand the possibility of entrance into the kingdom (Rev. 14:9-11). Remarkably, they survived the Great Tribulation without the mark, and also survived the judgments of the Lord's wrath which brought death and destruction to so many. Just surviving all that, however, does not qualify them to enter the kingdom of God which is now to be set up on the earth. Both Jews and Gentiles, therefore, must stand before the King and undergo His scrutiny.

The Judgment of the Gentiles
At the end of the Olivet Discourse in Matthew 25, we see the "Sheep and Goats Judgment" (vv. 31-46). We are told at that time, Jesus will sit upon "the throne of His glory" with all those remaining alive gathered before Him, and He will separate them into two groups as a shepherd divides the sheep from the goats. This judgment will not be on the basis of faith – faith in His shed blood for forgiveness; but it will be based solely on how they treated *Him* throughout the duration of this difficult time, presumably from the midpoint until that time. Did they care for Him – feeding Him when hungry, giving drink when needed, clothing Him when naked, visiting Him when sick or in prison. Both groups will be bewildered by the criteria - neither group was aware of having helped or not helped Him. Whatever goodness was shown was given from a heart of genuine mercy, not with ulterior motives.

---

5   Phil. 3:8-11, Heb. 11:35
6   References for these phases of the first resurrection: Rev. 12:5; 7:9-17; 11:11-12; 14:1-3; 20:4-5.

But now their merciful hearts are made manifest, as He asserts that whenever they helped "one of the least of these, His brethren, they were helping Him."

Those who gave this help – the sheep – are beloved of the Lord, and in helping, they qualify themselves as children of the kingdom and are received as such into Jesus' Millennial kingdom. Little did they know, when they were moved with compassion, the place they were gaining for themselves in the kingdom! What a lovely little glimpse this gives us into Jesus' heart yearning over His people, as they go through such difficulties at that time. On the other hand, because of hard and unmerciful hearts, the 'goats' will be sent into everlasting punishment and will not enter the kingdom of Christ.

The Judgment of Jews

We are given a look at a similar test for surviving Jews. We know that Jews are at this time gathered from all around the earth and brought to Israel.[7] God's intention for them is *so good*, and yet He must ascertain their willingness to accept His Lordship and Kingship over them, or there will be trouble down the road. So, they are put to the test:

> **33 "As I live," says the Lord God, "surely with a mighty hand, with an outstretched arm, and with fury poured out, I will rule over you.**
> **34 "I will bring you out from the peoples and gather you out of the countries where you are scattered, with a mighty hand, with an outstretched arm, and with fury poured out.**
> **37 "I will make you pass under the rod, and I will bring you into the bond of the covenant;**
> **38 "I will purge the rebels from among you, and those who transgress against Me; I will bring them out of the country where they dwell, but they shall not enter the land of Israel. Then you will know that I am the Lord.**
> **40 "For on My holy mountain, on the mountain height of Israel," says the Lord God, "there all the house of Israel, all of them in the land, shall serve Me."**
> **Ezekiel 20:33-34, 37-38, 40**

Even now, the Lord's goodness will not be manifested until all hearts are obedient to Him. Not an individual will escape scrutiny. There is *no room for rebels* in the kingdom of the Lord. Receiving the New Covenant will be mandatory for all who enter the kingdom. Those who refuse will be slain. Whether Jew or Gentile, Jesus has declared regarding this time:

> **"But bring here those enemies of mine, who did not want me to reign over them, and slay them before me." Luke 19:27**

All of these being scrutinized are, of course, still in their mortal bodies. Those received into the kingdom will repopulate the earth and live long lives, though their bodies will still be subject to death. They will be ruled by Christ and the resurrected saints. Incidentally, whenever Scripture refers to Millennial rule with a rod of iron, the word in the Greek for "rule" is *poimaino* – to tend as a shepherd.[8] This speaks not of fleshly, authoritarian rule, but of compassionate nurturing, backed up by the authority of righteousness, as the true needs of people are tended to – an entirely new kind of rule on the earth!

Spirits of Darkness Imprisoned

The twenty-fourth chapter of Isaiah is about the Day of the Lord, concluding with these verses:

> **And it shall come to pass in that day, that the Lord shall punish the host of the high ones that are on high, and the kings of the earth upon the earth.**

---

7 Is. 11:11, Jer. 23:5-8; 30:8-11; Ezek. 11:16-20; Joel 3:5-7; Amos 9:14-15; Zech. 10:5-10
8 Rev. 2:27; 12:5; 19:15: "rule" *poimaino* G4165S. In the Old Testament (Ps. 2:9), it is breaking with a rod of iron – apparently with a view to the destruction of the wicked before the kingdom is established: "break" *ra'a* H7489B.

> **And they shall be gathered together, as prisoners are gathered in the pit, and shall be shut up in the prison, and after many days shall they be visited.**
>
> **Isaiah 24:21-22 KJV**

At the same time that the Lord deals with earthly kings, He will deal also with the powers of darkness who have empowered so much evil from behind the scenes. The rebel angels and demons will be rounded up and thrown into 'the pit' (presumably a holding place in Sheol). Revelation confirms this, with these verses immediately following the debacle at Armageddon:

> **Then I saw an angel coming down from heaven, having the key to the bottomless pit and a great chain in his hand. He laid hold of the dragon, that serpent of old, who is the Devil and Satan, and bound him for a thousand years; and he cast him into the bottomless pit, and shut him up, and set a seal on him, so that he should deceive the nations no more till the thousand years were finished.**
>
> **Revelation 20:1-3**

Decades ago, my husband worked at the giant General Motors Plant in Ypsilanti, MI. One morning, as he arrived at work and stepped out of his car, the parking lot disappeared; instead, he saw a vision of a faraway village, set in a valley, with numerous church spires visible. He heard all the church bells ringing, pealing and pealing in joyous abandon, one church after another, throughout the village and out across the countryside. People were out in the streets, celebrating and rejoicing. He knew this was a picture of what was happening all around the world, and that it was the beginning of the Millennium. He said the sense of joy was indescribable. What a day that will be -- there will be an absence of oppression that we cannot even imagine now – a lightness of joy in the very atmosphere! The vision of a new, renewed earth, filled with such beauty, gives new joy to the promise, "the meek will inherit the earth" (Ps. 37). What a hope we live with!

A Reflection on the Sevens

Having arrived now at the completion of the 'sevens,' we reflect briefly on the finished work represented by each.

- The seven church ages brought the full number of Gentiles into the kingdom. By the close of the 7th church age (at the sixth seal), the Bride is brought into full spiritual maturity, prepared for Christ's return, and the 144,000 are brought to readiness to receive Christ.
- At the same time, by the sixth seal, wickedness on the earth has reached fullness and sinners are ripe for the Day of God's wrath.
- With the completion of the trumpet judgments, the 144,000 are spiritually prepared for their rapture, and the ministry of the two witnesses has come to completion. Both are taken to heaven.
- And finally, by the end of the bowl judgments, the turning of the Jewish remnant back to God is fully accomplished, as is also the full and final destruction of earth's rebels.

By the end of the 'sevens,' those who were destined for heaven are there, the Jews who would enter the Millennial kingdom of Christ are set apart for Him, the earth itself is purged from wickedness, and the principalities of Satan's kingdom are bound and removed from activity on the earth; and all this has been accomplished in the perfect righteousness and justice of God. To His great glory, God's intricate and matchless redemptive purposes have all been completed within the context of the 'sevens.'

CHART OF THE COMPLETED WORK OF REDEMPTION IN THE SEVENS

SEVEN CHURCH AGES (spanning the gap between the 69th and 70th weeks of Daniel):

1. Ephesus
2. Smyrna
3. Pergamos
4. Thyatira
5. Sardis
6. Philadelphia
7. Laodicea

By the completion of the **7th church age at the 6th seal/the rapture**, the Bride has been brought to her full number and to full spiritual maturity; and the 144, 000 have been brought to full readiness to receive Christ.

----------------The 70th week of Daniel: The Seals, Trumpets & Bowls----------------------

SEVEN SEALS ON THE SCROLL:

By the end of the **6th seal**, the earth also has been brought to fullness of iniquity, ready for God's just judgment.

1st Seal
2nd Seal
3rd Seal
4th Seal
5th Seal - Midpoint — the Great Tribulation.
6th Seal - The rapture.
7th Seal - The scroll is opened — GOD'S WRATH BEGINS:

SEVEN TRUMPET JUDGMENTS:

1st Trumpet
2nd Trumpet
3rd Trumpet
4th Trumpet
5th Trumpet
6th Trumpet - the 144,000 and the two witnesses are taken to heaven — God's work with them is completed.
7th Trumpet

Throughout the first six trumpet judgments, the 144, 000 are tested and matured, prepared for their own rapture.

The ministry of the two witnesses is completed, their testimony to the Jews, Antichrist, and the world is fully delivered!

SEVEN BOWL JUDGMENTS:

1st Bowl
2nd Bowl
3rd Bowl
4th Bowl
5th Bowl
6th Bowl
7th Bowl - The last of the Jewish remnant turns in repentance; Antichrist is defeated; the earth is purged.

With the last bowl judgment, the turning of the Jews to the Lord is completed and God's judgment and destruction of the wicked is finished.

---------------**The 70 weeks of Daniel are now complete, with God's stated purposes** -------------
for that period of time having been fully accomplished!

The way forward into the Millennium is now open!

CHAPTER 28

The
Millennium

According to Scripture, the present age will be followed by a period lasting one thousand years, in which Christ Himself will rule the earth from His throne in Jerusalem.[1] This will be, finally, the fulfillment of countless promises made in the Old Testament to the descendants of Abraham, Isaac, and Jacob; and the arrival of *the political* kingdom promised to David and his Seed. There are several aspects of this new age which we will look at briefly. Scripture does not speak of it at length, but does give us a few blessed glimpses.

We have seen how severely the Lord will deal with those Jews who are resistant to Him. In contrast, Jeremiah gives us a lovely picture of the regathering of the Jews to Israel:

> **8 Behold, I will bring them from the north country, and gather them from the ends of the earth; among them the blind and the lame, the woman with child and the one who labors with child, together; a great throng shall return there.**
> **9 They shall come with weeping, and with supplications I will lead them. I will cause them to walk by the rivers of waters, in a straight way in which they shall not stumble;**
> **10 . . . 'He who scattered Israel will gather him and keep him as a shepherd does his flock.'**
> **12 Therefore they shall come and sing in the height of Zion, streaming to the goodness of the Lord — for wheat and new wine and oil, for the young of the flock and the herd; their souls shall be like a well-watered garden, and they shall sorrow no more at all.**
>
> **Jeremiah 31:8-9, 10, 12**

Great blessing and prosperity will be poured out upon this believing remnant, the one-third left at the end of the 70th week. Now we will see Jerusalem, the city of the great King, become the "joy of the whole earth"[2] and the center of worship and teaching in the earth:

> **Now it shall come to pass in the latter days that the mountain of the Lord's house shall be established on the top of the mountains and shall be exalted above the hills; and peoples shall flow to it.**

---

1   Rev. 20:4d, Is. 32:1, Jer. 23:5, Luke 1:32-33
2   Ps. 48:2, Matt. 5:35

Many nations shall come and say, "Come, and let us go up to the mountain of the Lord, to the house of the God of Jacob; He will teach us His ways, and we shall walk in His paths." For out of Zion the law shall go forth, and the word of the Lord from Jerusalem.

Micah 4:1-2

In the Millennium we see the fulfillment of the final redemptive feast, the Feast of Tabernacles. It is the uniting of all the earth under the banner of the Jewish Messiah, the Son of David. They will come from afar every year to worship and be taught and celebrate this feast together:

And it shall come to pass that everyone who is left of all the nations which came against Jerusalem shall go up from year to year to worship the King, the Lord of hosts, and to keep the Feast of Tabernacles. Zechariah 14:16

Though so many times disappointed, now, finally, God's great heart of love is satisfied – His desire from the Garden of Eden onward:

For the earth will be filled with the knowledge of the glory of the Lord, as the waters cover the sea. Habakkuk 2:14

There will be a righteous enforcement of peace upon the earth. From that safety will come prosperity:

3 He shall judge between many peoples, and rebuke strong nations afar off; they shall beat their swords into plowshares, and their spears into pruning hooks; nation shall not lift up sword against nation, neither shall they learn war anymore.
4 But everyone shall sit under his vine and under his fig tree, and no one shall make them afraid; for the mouth of the Lord of hosts has spoken. Micah 4:3-4

The peaceful and prosperous reign of Solomon typed the Millennial reign of Christ (even as the warfare reign of David typed the church age), and **Psalm 72** gives us a picture of this reign. Here are a few highlights:

- His rulership will be under God's authority, hence filled with righteousness and justice.
- The leaders and governments of the nations will be under *His* authority, therefore bringing peace and righteous rule to the peoples of the earth; all nations will serve Him.
- The poor will be cared for, oppressors punished.
- The blessings of His grace and His life will come down upon the earth like showers.
- His dominion will be from sea to sea, and from the river to the ends of the earth.
- His enemies will bow before Him, and Gentiles will come to worship, bringing gifts.
- There will be great abundance in the earth.
- All nations will be blessed in Him and will call Him blessed.
- The whole earth will be filled with His glory!

Such glory! We add a few highlights from Isaiah's picture of this time:

- Bringing restoration from the Day of the Lord, God will make a new heavens and new earth, and "the former" will not come to mind.
- God will rejoice in Jerusalem and her people will be a joy. There will be no more weeping.
- The human lifespan will be greatly extended. There will not be early or premature death: Infant mortality will be unknown; death at a hundred years old will seem like a child dying – it will be as though that person was a sinner, accursed. It appears that the normal length of life will be

similar to the pre-flood era, when men lived to be seven, eight, nine hundred plus years. "As the days of a tree will be the days of My people" (v. 22).

- People's labor will be blessed and they will enjoy the fruit of their hands.
- Prayers will be heard and responded to instantly.
- Nature itself will come into rest, and there will be no more prey and predator: the wolf and lamb will feed together, and the lion will eat straw like an ox. There will not be pain or destruction throughout the kingdom. Isaiah 65:17-25 (Cf. Is. 11:2-9, Zech. 8:3-8)

<u>And a couple more highlights from Isaiah:</u>

- God will destroy *the covering* over all the nations that hides the knowledge of God from them.
- God will remove the rebuke – the scorn and reproach -- of His people from all the earth. (Cf. 2 Cor. 3:13-16; 4:3-4) Isaiah 25:7-8

Both of these issues – the veil over people's minds and the reproach upon God's people – are present now in the earth because it's under the rulership of darkness; to be in darkness is to be "normal." When Satan and all his minions are removed, light and truth will shine and those who love righteousness will be held in honor, rather than reproach. This is glory beyond our present imagination!

This then, is a little glimpse of the Day – the Millennium – of rest when "God's sabbath" prevails upon the earth. Beyond that lie the ages that will unfold in the future, beginning with the vision of John found in Revelation 21 and 22. There are glorious things ahead for God's people who love Him!

Chart of the Sevens of Revelation

The Seven Church Ages						
From Pentecost to the Return of Christ – Revelation 2 - 3						
1 Ephesus Apostolic Age AD 32-98	2 Smyrna Persecution Age AD 64-313	3 Pergamos The State Church AD 315-590	4 Thyatira The Papal Church AD 590 – End	5 Sardis The Reformation Church AD 1517 To End	6 Philadelphia The Missionary Church AD 1730 – End	7 Laodicea The Lukewarm Church AD 1900 – End
These dates are approximate.						
The Seventh Church Age Contains/Releases the first six Seals						

The Seven Seals
Events Preparatory to the Scroll Opening – Revelation 6

Seal #1	Seal #2	Seal #3	Seal #4	Seal #5	Seal #6	Seal #7
WHITE HORSE Antichrist going forth **The 70th Week of Daniel Begins**	RED HORSE War	BLACK HORSE Famine and In-equity	PALE HORSE Death & Hell One fourth of the earth slain by sword, hunger, death, & wild beasts.	MARTYRS **The Great Tribulation Begins** Abomi-nation of Desolation **Midpoint of 70th Week**	COSMIC SIGNS in Dark-ened Sun, Moon, and Stars, Great tempest and Earthquake **SIGNALS - The Great Day of the Lord's Wrath!** **Before the Wrath Be-gins:** 144,000 Jews are sealed and Jesus returns for the church – **Rapture** takes place, Rev. 7.	**Scroll is Opened:** Now begins the redemption of the earth – the Day of the Lord's Wrath. Rev. 8

The Seventh Seal Contains/Releases the Seven Trumpet Judgments

The Day of the Lord's Wrath in Revelation

The Seven Angels with Trumpets – Revelation 8 - 11

Angel #1	Angel #2	Angel #3	Angel #4	Angel #5	Angel #6	Angel #7
One third of grass and trees are burned.	One third of the sea turns to blood.	One third of fresh waters become embittered.	One third of the sun, moon, and stars are darkened.	Army of locusts re-leased from bottomless pit to tor-ment men five months (Rev. 9). WOE #1	200,000,000-man army released – kills 1/3 world population (Rev. 9). Two witness-es complete their ministry (Rev. 11). WOE #2	Signals the fall of earthly kingdoms as it releases the 7 angels with bowls. (11:19 is linked to 15:6-8, continuing the chronology.) WOE #3

The Seventh Trumpet Contains/Releases the Final Seven, the Bowl Judgments

Additional Events Contained in Parenthetical Chapters:

Revelation 11

The ministry of the two witnesses begins sometime before the midpoint, lasts for 3½ years, and ends with their death, resurrection and ascension. Then follows a tremendous earthquake, signaling the end of the 6th angel with trumpet (the 2nd WOE).

Revelation 12

The woman, man child, dragon, war in heaven, casting down of Satan and his angels – all happen right before the midpoint. At the midpoint the persecution of the woman begins, lasting for 3½ years.

Revelation 13

Details of Antichrist, False Prophet, and their 'reign' - 3½ brief and bitter years – the Great Tribulation.

Revelation 14

The 144,000 appear in heaven with the Lamb - apparently raptured between the trumpet & bowl judgments.
The preaching angel goes forth with the Gospel – salvation is still possible! (Joel 2:31-32).
Judgment is pronounced on Babylon and the Beast-worshippers.
The harvest of the earth is reaped and humanity goes through the winepress of the wrath of God (under the 7th bowl).

The Seven Angels with Bowls – Revelation 15 - 16 The Third WOE

Bowl #1	Bowl #2	Bowl #3	Bowl #4	Bowl #5	Bowl #6	Bowl #7
Terrible sores on those with the mark of the Beast.	Sea becomes as stagnant blood – kills all in it.	Rivers and streams become as blood.	Sun scorches men.	The throne and kingdom of Antichrist is filled with darkness and pain.	Euphrates River is dried up to prepare the way for the kings of the east. Kings of the earth are enticed by Satan to gather together against Israel for that great last Battle at Har Megiddo.	Completes judgment – Tremendous earthquake, cities fall, islands and mountains disappear, 100# hailstones fall from heaven! Babylon is judged! Antichrist and false prophet are captured and judged.

In the days following the final bowl judgment, the 70th Week of Daniel is concluded.

Revelation 17 - 18
Description of the identity, nature, activities, and judgment of Mystery Babylon the Great Whore and the Beast she rides.

Revelation 19
Marriage of the Lamb & the Bride. Jesus' glorious manifestation with the armies of heaven to rescue his people Israel from all the nations gathered against her – part of bowl #7. The earth has now been cleansed for the Millennial rule of Christ.

Afterword to Part 1

As the end draws closer, things will grow darker in the world. We will see the rise of the beast kingdom and the labor pains that Jesus identified – first the early ones and then the more intense ones -- that are leading to the close of this age and the birthing of a new one. The question might arise, where do we seem to be timewise in this progression to the end? This was not something I had planned to discuss, but as this manuscript nears readiness for publication, we are in the summer of 2021. I am going to put out a few thoughts as possibilities.

Long ago, in the Lord's displeasure with Israel's unbelief, He declared these words:

14 **For I will be like a lion to Ephraim, and like a young lion to the house of Judah. I, even I, will tear them and go away; I will take them away, and no one shall rescue.**

15 **I will return again to My place till they acknowledge their offense. Then they will seek My face; in their affliction they will earnestly seek Me."**

1 **Come, and let us return to the Lord; for He has torn, but He will heal us; He has stricken, but He will bind us up.**

2 **After two days He will revive us; on the third day He will raise us up, that we may live in His sight. Hosea 5:14-6:2**

We spoke of these verses at the close of chapter 6. How, with the Lord stopping the 'clock' at the end of the 69th week, He *left them*, "tearing them," with no one to rescue. And how in a future time of affliction, they would *earnestly seek Him* with words of repentance. The Lord declares that this return and God's subsequent *reviving* of them would occur after two days, and on the third day, they would be raised up to live 'in His sight.' We spoke of Peter's "formula" -- how "with the Lord, one day is as a thousand years, and a thousand years as one day" (2 Peter 3:8).

Taking now a closer look, this not only gives us 2,000 years from when the Lord "left" Israel, but we see, more specifically, that since His 'departure' from them occurred in AD 32 (established in our study of the 70 weeks, chapter 2), the *third* millennium from His departure **would begin in AD 2032**. For the Millennium to begin at that time, *the 70th week of Daniel*, initiated by the treaty with Israel, *would need to begin in the year 2025*. That is a mere four years from now! This is not something I am stating with confidence; it is just a processing of Scripture to give a possible scenario, using certain times and events that we are already aware of. Meanwhile, we *will* keep our eyes open for that treaty!

Covid-19 and Vaccines

In 2020 we labored through months of covid-19 and witnessed the out-of-the-ordinary response to it on the part of leaders, which caused it to affect negatively almost every aspect of human life. With the "vaccine" coming out earlier this year, we are hearing an increasing number of doctors and specialists expressing deep concern over these injections being urged upon people on a global scale. These vaccines have not been adequately tested and verified as safe, and health authorities are sounding the alarm on a whole range of health issues present in them. Although I am by no means an expert, it appears that an issue of concern is the *suppression, by the vaccine,* of the very resilient and adaptable immune system each of us has been born with, and which is able to fend off, on its own, an endless *variety* of viruses and bacteria, etc. At the same time, with how rapidly viruses replicate and mutate, the very limited immunity provided by a vaccine will not protect against future, mutated viruses, and particularly not viruses that have grown much more virulent by *surviving* and mutating to become stronger than the vaccines. We are being warned that this could result in "monster viruses" that are much more dangerous and virulent to the human population – both to the immunized as well as the non-immunized -- and which could result in death for millions of people.

With all this, it has become much clearer to me how one fourth of the earth will suffer death from the various causes, including disease, mentioned in Revelation 6 and Matthew 24. I couldn't understand how that would happen with all the knowledge and skill of modern medicine available to the world. It hadn't occurred to me that there might come a time when the science that should help keep us all healthy would come into the hands of globalists and would actually be used *against* us. And now here we are, with those seal events possibly as little as five, six, and seven years away!

Held by God

As we see all this around us, let us remember Jesus' words, "See that you be not troubled" (Matt. 24:6). We will guard our hearts from strife, worry, and accusation, and remain established in the love and the grace of God. We have exceedingly great and precious promises to lay hold of and stand on which *are not* affected or diminished by anything Satan does!

It is not by chance that God used the analogy of labor pains. When a woman goes into labor, she knows that the pains will intensify greatly before the birth takes place; she is willing to undergo that in order to have, finally, that new life in her arms. So also, the Lord knows that this will be a time of great intensity and testing for His people. Like a woman in labor, this is not something to resist -- *to fight.* A woman has to *let her body hurt,* knowing the pains are working to bring about the birth. So, Jesus said, "He that endures to the end shall be saved" (Matt. 10:22). "Endures," *hupomone,* means literally, *to abide under.* It is a time to remain in God's hands, held by Him, fully trusting Him, knowing all is moving toward a foreordained place where wickedness is utterly defeated, and the new order is fully and surely birthed. The trouble and pain will be worth the end result! This is the "patience and the faith of the saints"; ('patience,' again, is *hupomone)* (Rev. 13:10). We will walk in that patience and faith *unto death*, if needed.

I like to think that God gave us Daniel and Shadrach, Meshach, and Abednego as forerunners and examples for us who would make up the final generation. There they were, exiles and captives in the midst of a tyrannical beast kingdom, faithfully serving the Lord even while serving the king in whatever capacity they could. I love how they had already established in their own hearts Whose they were, before the test came along. They were strong, steadfast, unwavering, because they had already settled the issue of their first priority and highest loyalty – it was to the God of heaven, not the king on the earth. So must we do also, dealing even now with other loves, fears, and a divided heart. If we will do that, then, following their wonderful example, we too will stand fast when the tests come; we will know God can deliver us, but will be fully prepared to lay down our lives if He doesn't.

The best and surest way to get through anything difficult in our lives is to position ourselves with the Lord in it – to seek to understand *His purposes* in it and then align ourselves with that, making it our perspective and focus. This ensures that we *tap into His grace.* It ensures we will come through victoriously! As we study Revelation and the other Scriptures, we catch glimpses of ways that we *as God's people are to help facilitate and accelerate His return.* As we see and understand, we are able to take our place as His kingdom people, aligning ourselves in submission to Him to flow with His purposes. This is one of the great reasons why we study end-time Scriptures, and the call to enter into this will become more evident as we go through *Part 2* of this book. May God bless each of us as we seek Him and walk with Him!

PART 2
FILLING IN THE GAPS -
THE PARENTHETICAL
CHAPTERS

CHAPTER 29

Why
PART 2?

We have followed the chronology of the Sevens so far. But there are whole sections of Revelation that are not directly a part of the Sevens. These portions have been called *parenthetical,* as they supply further explanatory information that completes the picture of events. They round out the bare outlines, supplying more details and digging more deeply into causes behind the scenes. These parenthetical parts are found primarily in chapters 10-14 of Revelation, and they are the main, although not exclusive, focus of this second portion of the book. Because they are not given as part of the chronology, we will be jumping around timewise; but since maintaining an accurate order of events remains crucial, we will pause occasionally and mesh events with the chronology in order to keep the big picture. I will supply a basic timeline of events before we end this chapter, just for reference and review purposes.

We will be looking primarily at chapters 10, 11, and 12 of Revelation. These chapters play a significant role in the whole scheme of things at the end, and we will bring in a few other resources and Scriptures as we look at them. The way they fit into the timing of things *has to be determined from their content.*

It is exciting for me as I launch into this portion of *Sevens,* looking more closely at details and causes. *PART 2* will not be as lengthy as *PART 1,* but with the help of the Holy Spirit, we will draw the veil aside and go deep into God's heart and the work He is doing on the earth during this time of the end. As I contemplated working on these subjects the question arose in my heart, "Lord, why are these things important – important enough to write a book about?" I didn't know the answer. I knew the basic reasons: That there's benefit in *all* of God's Word; that it's important for us as God's people to know what He wants to do and is planning to do as the age ends; and that Revelation promises, "Blessed is he that keeps the saying of this prophecy. . . "(Rev. 22:7). But I felt there was something beyond those basic reasons that I didn't yet know. As I began to work on the material and take a closer look at it, the Lord brought the answer to me. It unfolded before me again and again. We will see this answer already in the next chapter, as we take a quick second look at chapters 4 and 5 of Revelation.

A few of the things that I will share will include my personal path to a particular truth or insight, so it will almost be like a story of "this, and then that, etc." After all, when the Holy Spirit is allowed to be our teacher – which is what we all desire – He will take us down a path of increasing light using a variety of means and methods. He is a skilled Teacher -- very creative and timely with where He leads us, what He shows us, and how He does it – and One with many resources at His disposal! He desires that in the end we be confident that, yes, this is the Lord opening His Word to me and confirming it in this way or that way. It is part of the adventure of being His and walking with Him! The story almost always begins with a question, because that's how learning takes place

– with questions and puzzlement and an awareness that I lack knowledge about some issue. It's so important in our personal study of the Word that we recognize the things we don't understand, so we can ask Him questions! The questions *create a place in us* for that truth – for the answer! God may *try* to give us knowledge we haven't sought, and it's like being in a restaurant and the waiter comes up and hands you a plate of food that you didn't order – you look at it strangely, thinking, "What is this? I didn't order that!" But *seeking* God for answers and then having Him show us, is like ordering something you really want and are hungry for, so when the plate arrives you are filled with recognition, receptivity, and delight.

Having said that, let me take the opportunity again to encourage *you* to continue to pursue understanding of the things of His Word and His kingdom in the same way! He loves to sit with us and teach us and open our understanding! It is a private and secret thrill of belonging to Him! We can sit under a teacher and gain knowledge, and that's important, but it is a slightly more advanced thrill to know these things truly and deeply by studying them for yourself. Start with something taught by someone else, and use it as a springboard for your own personal pursuit of the Word! Get into the Word and let it become a part of your own relationship with the Lord - let Him show you things one on one. Let Him show you why these things are important, and important for *you*. He wants to build things in you for the purposes He has for you in the Kingdom! And He wants to build confidence in you, no matter what the future holds! As you go through this material, ask Him to be teaching you and showing you things from what you read! Let *Him* be your teacher!

TIMELINE REVIEW OF THE 70ᵀᴴ WEEK OF DANIEL

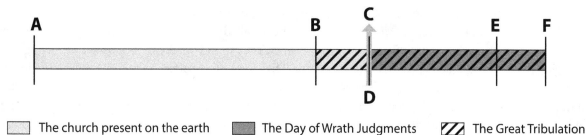

The church present on the earth   The Day of Wrath Judgments   The Great Tribulation

A - 70th week begins. The church present on the earth.

B - Midpoint — Abomination of Desolation — the Great Tribulation begins, lasts 3 ½ years.

C - 6th Seal — Rapture occurs (We don't know the exact placement in this second half of the 7 years.)

D - 7th Seal (This occurs the same day as the 6th seal.) — GOD'S WRATH BEGINS, trumpet judgments.

E - The 7th trumpet sounds, releasing the bowl judgments. (Again, the exact placement in the dark gray area is uncertain.)

- -

Review Highlights:

A. The 70th week begins; peace treaty between Antichrist & Israel; temple worship resumes.
B. Midpoint — 5th seal: Antichrist unveiled as the Man of Sin.
C. 6th seal: cosmic events; 144,000 sealed; rapture/resurrection.
D. 7th seal: scroll is opened; Day of Lord commences, releasing the 7 trumpets.
E. 7th trumpet sounds, releasing the seven bowls.
F. 70th week is concluded. All enemies are defeated. Israel is fully turned. Christ, the Most Holy, is anointed in the Most Holy Place as King over all the earth. Daniel 9:24 is fulfilled, the Millennium about to begin.

The 6,000 "years of man" have been completed. During that time man's free will has played out fully and choices have been made. God has sorted out the wrong from the right, the godly from the ungodly, and has separated unto Himself a people of faith with which to set up *His* thousand-year reign on the earth. Reflected in the repetition of *seven*, all has been completed *to His satisfaction* and by His standards of righteousness. Earth, blessed and flourishing, will now see the full and righteous dominion of man as God had originally envisioned it, *under His authority.* The old Satanic territorial "principalities and powers," given freedom to oppress because of man's independence from God, have now been displaced by the overcomers of the Old and New Covenants, displaying, "by means of the church, the multi-faceted wisdom of God" (Eph. 3:10).

THE LAMB
AND THE SEVEN

CHAPTER 30

The Lamb &
the Seven

Chapters 4 and 5 of Revelation provide scenes of the throne room, including the search for a man worthy to take the scroll and open it. We spoke of the scroll and what it signifies in *Part 1*, but there are other insights to be gained here that we are going to look at now. You will recall the vision of Christ in the midst of the burning lamps, and Jesus' explanation of what the lamps represent:

The mystery of. . . the seven golden lampstands: The . . . seven lampstands which you saw are the seven churches. Revelation 1:20

As we've mentioned before, a "mystery" in Scripture is something hidden that has been true – and part of the plan -- all along, but which had not been revealed. It is primarily *the church, the spiritual kingdom*, which is spoken of in the New Testament as previously being hidden. There are multiple aspects of this kingdom which the New Testament identifies as mysteries and then proceeds to unveil. Here, Jesus says that until now the identity and meaning of these seven golden lamps was not revealed. The seven-branched Menorah (lampstand) which stood in the Holy Place of Moses' tabernacle comes to mind. Unlike all the other articles found in the tabernacle, the menorah had never been given a redemptive significance, other than simply to supply light to an otherwise dark room. It was, in a sense, a mystery already back then. It was a single piece, with the seven branches coming off a main stem. These lamps of Revelation are apparently free-standing, each on their own stand. Nevertheless, we are inclined to see, most remarkably, that Jesus here is revealing that *the seven churches*, making up the whole of the Gentile Bride, are the revelation and fulfillment ("antitype")[1] of the Menorah of the tabernacle! How amazed I was when I first realized that there we were – the church -- in the center of God's heart as He met with Jewish worshippers so many millennia ago!

But Jesus isn't finished pulling back the veil on these reborn sons and daughters!

Seven lamps of fire were burning before the throne, which are the seven Spirits of God. Rev. 4:5

---

1   That is to say, that the menorah is a pattern (a 'type' - tupos) representing the reality ('anti-type' - anti-tupos) as it was later fulfilled by the church, as seen here in Jesus' words. Peter calls baptism the "anti-type" which fulfilled the example/pattern set forth in the deliverance of Noah and his family via the ark (1 Peter 3:21). The type occurs earlier and points to the thing it represents, which usually comes later. Paul says that the experiences of the Israelites in the wilderness were examples and patterns (types) supplied by God for our instruction and encouragement (1 Cor. 10:11).

Here we see seven lamps of fire burning before the throne, identified as "the seven Spirits of God." Some have understandably linked these spirits with Isaiah 11:2. However, only six spirits are identified there; and, in fact, we don't need to go so far afield for the answer, because *further* clarification is given to us in just the next chapter:

> **And I looked, and behold, in the midst of the throne. . . stood a Lamb as though it had been slain, having seven horns and seven eyes, which are the seven Spirits of God sent out into all the earth. Revelation 5:6**

Here are the seven spirits mentioned again! And here, we're told that they are the seven horns and seven eyes seen in the Lamb, and furthermore, that they've been sent out into all the earth! So, they are both before the throne *and* sent out "into all the earth"! Most remarkable! What does all this mean? We move in a kind of 'if A=B, and B=C, then A=C' reasoning. If the seven churches are the seven lamps, and the seven lamps are the seven spirits, and the seven spirits are the seven horns and seven eyes, then *all of them are depictions of the church!* The horns and eyes seen on the Lamb represent the seven churches -- that is, the churches organically and eternally joined to the Lamb! He is the Head, they are the Body—inseparable! This is the Lamb in His "postgraduate" depiction – the Lamb successful in His mission – that of bringing *many sons unto glory.*

The Lamps, the Eyes, and the Horns

Let us move forward with that understanding, seeing, moreover, that these different depictions represent different aspects of the church. The flaming aspect of the lamps is the living, burning Holy Spirit of God dwelling in union with the believers of each age, who are indeed spread throughout the whole earth. From the Spirit of God comes their *life* and their *living testimony.* Alive in the spirit, they transcend earthly limits and are *present continually* before the throne of God! God "has made us alive together with Christ . . . and has raised us up together and made us sit together in heavenly places in Christ Jesus" (Eph. 2:5-6). Here we see that organic unity – His life *is* our life.

And from that same Spirit of God comes the spiritual vision of the seven, their eyes; they *see* and perceive beyond appearances, with the discernment and heart and priorities of God. **The ability *to see* and perceive as God does is *the key* to all the ways in which we cooperate with Christ in bringing His kingdom to the earth.** This cannot be emphasized enough. How can we cooperate, unless we have His perspective? Seeing with His eyes, His discernment, and His compassion, 'the seven' *represent God* in the earth.[2] We will see this from the Word again in a later chapter.

Horns represent power and dominion.[3] The Lamb's horns represent *kingdom* power and *kingdom* authority exercised in the earth by the church. The kingdom of Antichrist has multiple heads. The Lamb has *One Head,* and all those working together under that Headship have one goal and purpose -- to release the Lamb's will and authority in the earth. <u>In the coming age, it will include an outward authority of sharing Christ's rulership in the earth.</u>[4] <u>For now, in its present form, it is a spiritual authority, which in Ephesians 1 is linked inseparably with spiritual vision.</u> In v. 17 Paul prays specifically for the spirit of wisdom and *unveiling*:

> **"...that the God of our Lord Jesus Christ, the Father of glory, may give to you the *spirit of wisdom and revelation* in the knowledge of Him, the *eyes of your understanding being enlightened. . ."* Ephesians 1:17** (emphasis added)

Paul goes on to set forth what he desires the saints *be able to see,* including "the exceeding greatness of God's power." He states that this power is accessed *by faith* (which comes when we *see* it), and that it has placed us *in heavenly places* (before His throne), "far above" all the principalities of darkness which surround the earth. Furthermore, it is power which has placed *all things* under His feet (His feet are in the Body on the earth) and has made Christ to be the Head over all things **to the church.** This is a KEY Scripture and a key to understanding

---

2   We catch a glimpse of this in Zechariah's prophecy of the Messiah: "...behold, I will bring forth my servant the BRANCH. For behold the stone that I have laid before Joshua; upon one stone shall be seven eyes: behold, I will engrave the graving thereof. . ." Zech. 3:8-9. Here is the Stone that the builders rejected, the Headstone and chief cornerstone, having seven eyes.
3   Ps. 89:17-24; Dan. 7:8, 20, 24; 8:5-9
4   See Luke 19:17-19.

this depiction of the Lamb. Christ was already the Head over all things before He ever came to earth. He didn't need to come to earth and die to become the Head over all things. But to become the Head over all things *to the church!* Now, *that's a whole different matter.* It has always been the Father's intention to restore redeemed man to his originally-designed place of dominion over all the earth! It's important to note that the power/dominion that the church has comes through our union with Christ's death and our personal participation in both His death and His resurrection. In our submission to Christ and union with Him, our dominion is reinstated.

The Significance of the Horns and Eyes

Here, in *the horns and eyes of the Lamb,* we are seen in that place of restored dominion. In each of the ways the churches are characterized here, whether as burning lamps, spirits, eyes, or horns, the *key* is the indwelling Spirit of God. Believers operate in these ways as *spiritual men:*[5] that is, as men and women who have *identified* with Christ in His death and resurrection – submitting all of the old life to Him in order to share now in *His newness of life;* men submitted to the Spirit of God in them, no longer operating independently and in the natural; men and women who don't have SELF – with all of its past issues and present struggles – as their orientation, but who have settled all that by entrusting it to Him, and now look at life with His eyes, having what is important *to Him* as the thing that is important to them! Paul affirmed that he "served with his *spirit*" in the gospel of Jesus Christ (Rom. 1:9 emphasis added). All is dependent upon the believer's oneness with Christ! How absolutely essential is it that the church always keep Jesus as Lord, while honoring and utterly relying upon the precious Holy Spirit!

So then, here in Revelation 5 is the Lamb, taking the scroll, about to set in motion *actions and events which will bring about the completion of redemption and the close of this age!* He will be taking on the entrenched powers of Satan's kingdom, both in the spiritual dimension *and* as they manifest in Antichrist and his earthly empire. This will not be the Lamb coming to die again. He may appear as the slain Lamb, but He has been announced as "the Lion of the Tribe of Judah, who *has prevailed.*" This will be the Lamb going forth *with overcoming power,* yet <u>not alone, but with seven horns and seven eyes</u>! Here is the Head, in heaven, with His Body here on the earth being His eyes and His authority in all the earth; and yet, this Body *also present in heaven* in the midst of the throne, the living creatures, and the elders. **Here is the church – the people of God in the spirit – at the heart of the key activity of heaven: sharing in the counsels of God and serving to enact those counsels in the earth!** This is the first hint in Revelation of further discoveries that we are going to make of *our role* in the taking back of the earth; the first hint of the enormous significance of us studying and learning and knowing these events that are coming!

Active Participants in God's Plan

Why do we study and learn all this? This is the question the Spirit was leading me to ask, *because He wanted **this truth*** to be communicated clearly and resoundingly: We study and learn because it is crucial that we *come to understand the essential role that we, the church, play with Christ as He moves to bring this age to its conclusion!* The seven horns and seven eyes will be *there* in the coming conflict – the final conflict between the seed of the serpent and the Seed of the woman that will determine who will possess the earth. It is the season of the wrapping up of the Genesis 3 prophecy that in order to restore what Adam lost, the Seed of the woman will *crush* the head of the serpent. Of course, Jesus won the crucial, foundational battle. But He won it on *our behalf,* so we would be equipped to share in the vision and labors; to join the battle as co-combatants with Christ; and, finally, to share the victory and the spoils. This is "a new mankind" – a new race, brought forth by "the Second Man"[6] – taking the earth *back* from the usurper and taking rulership of it along with the Head and Originator of that race. This is God's glory and man's glory *joined.*

THIS is what God showed me when I asked Him why it was important to write this sequel. We are not passive onlookers. We are *active participants* in God's plan! **The workings of God in the earth are always linked with man and man's faith**, and even though Jesus Himself is the FOCUS of His mighty return in glory, the saints are an *integral part* and play an essential role in the events that take place! That is why it's imperative that we study and understand the plan -- so we can actively and intelligently cooperate with Him in all that is going to take place.

---

5   1 Cor. 2:14-16
6   1 Cor. 15:45-50

"You are My friends if you do whatever I command you. No longer do I call you servants, for a servant does not know what his master is doing; but I have called you friends, for all things that I heard from My Father I have made known to you."[7] He desires to *take us into His counsel,* that we might see our place and understand our role, and then be fitted for and *take our place* in the events that play out.

This is His plan for all His people, and yet not all will fulfill it. It is again, as Jesus said so frequently, those with *ears to hear* who will receive it and walk in it. Let us love Him and give our hearts to Him as He reveals what is important to Him, and then let's make it what is important to us.

In everything that God allows – no, <u>determines</u> – in these end-time events, but especially for His people, the question must always be, 'What is God's purpose in this for His people, and then, more specifically, for *me*?' Nothing is random with Him. I seek and receive light; I let Him work in me to fit me for His purposes (I am His workmanship); I align myself with His purpose, to cooperate with it and to fulfill it. This puts me in the flow, not only of His purpose, but of the grace and empowerment He supplies for that purpose to be accomplished. It puts me personally in the flow of the Sevens. It is my destiny as His child to fulfill the works He planned for me from the foundation of the world. This is our goal as we move forward in this study. By His great grace, may He grant us light to see His purposes and to walk in them, taking our places in His great end-time plan. His keeping and covering power are great. We have nothing to fear, except to fail of His grace and His purpose. Let's seek Him and surrender ourselves afresh to His purpose!

I marvel personally, that of all the beautiful and powerful persons that are undoubtedly to be found in heaven, when the Spirit gave to John the vision of Revelation 4, He highlighted a limited number of basic features – that is, the throne, the One upon it, the twenty-four elders, the living creatures, and the *seven spirits of God* before the throne. The next chapter is also essentially simple, with the Lamb being the focal point – the Lamb with *seven horns and seven eyes, which are the seven spirits of God.* It's as though the Father deliberately simplified everything so that we wouldn't *miss* the thing He was trying to show us – that it isn't just the Lamb, it's the Lamb *with the seven;* and that these seven are continually *before the throne* and *joined to the Lamb.*

Before we leave these chapters in Revelation, we notice that as the Lamb takes the scroll, the twenty-four elders, representing all saints of all time, fall down before Him in worship. As they do this, they are holding golden bowls full of aromatic incense, which, we are told, is the *prayers of the saints.* They break into song to the Lamb, declaring that "You have redeemed us to God by your blood out of every tribe, tongue, people, and nation; and have made us **kings** and **priests** to our God" (5:9-10). This mention of the church in her role as a "royal priesthood"[8] provides an additional clue as to how the seven horns and eyes work together with the Lamb and it takes us forward now to a look at the prayer ministry of the saints, specifically at the end of the age.

It has been said that the church can't be found after the end of Revelation 3. We are going to see it repeatedly, and this is our first glimpse of it. Of course, it *looks different* than it did in Revelation 2 & 3, where it was seen from the vantage point of earth. From Revelation 4 on, it is seen from the vantage point of heaven, as *spirit,* not wearing earthly garb, though still present on earth to begin with.[9]

Connecting with the Chronology

At this point in the chronology, we are still in the 7th church age (Laodicea). The removal of the 1st seal in the next chapter of Revelation signals the beginning of the 70th week, marked by the signing of the 'covenant' between Israel and Antichrist. Remember, the 7th church age *contains* the first 6 seals, the rapture not occurring until the 6th seal. [Continuing also to the end, along with Laodicea, are the churches of Thyatira (Roman Catholic), Sardis (Protestant churches), the missionary-minded Philadelphia (the evangelical, Pentecostal, charismatic, etc., churches) and Laodicea (the deceived church).]

---

7 John 15:14-15
8 1 Peter 2:5,9
9 Finally, at the 6th seal, following the rapture, we see the church in heaven in bodily form (Rev. 7); that is, with incorruptible bodies.

THE PRAYER MINISTRY OF THE CHURCH

CHAPTER 31

Faith on
the Earth

Acontinual prayer connection with God is always to characterize the people of God. In describing our on-going conflict with powers of darkness, Paul said we are to "pray at all times in the Spirit with all prayer and petition, and to this end, be alert with all perseverance and requests for all the saints" (Eph. 6:18). In Luke's account of the Olivet Discourse, Jesus said that a *continual connection with God in prayer* is essential to *prevailing* over all the difficulties of the seal events and finally being *counted worthy* to escape all those things and stand before the Son of man (Luke 21:36). A few chapters earlier in Luke, Jesus gave us something more specific regarding our prayer at that time in the future.

A New Kind of Prayer

A number of years ago I was reading the Parable of the Unjust Judge in Luke 18. When I got to the end of it, I paused, puzzled as I read Jesus' concluding statement: "When the Son of Man comes, will He find faith on the earth?" I thought, 'How can He question whether He will find faith or not? A multitude so great that no man can number it will be taken by Him to heaven at that time, and they will all be people of faith!" It puzzled me for several years every time I read it, until the light slowly began to dawn.

For one thing, I realized with more clarity that this parable of a widow pleading with the judge for justice is an end-time Scripture. It directly follows Jesus' teaching on *the rapture*, found at the end of Luke 17, and when Jesus spoke these things, there was no pause for a new chapter. He went right from the saints being caught up in the air to this teaching regarding a widow seeking justice and vindication from an uncaring, hard-hearted judge. I.e., this is going to be a very difficult time, a time when the 'natural' tendency will be to faint and give up under the pressures. So, He started off with the specific *reason* He's giving the parable: to show us that (in this difficult time in the future), we *"ought always to pray, and not to faint."*

Second, I went on to realize that Jesus wasn't speaking of faith in general; He was speaking of faith for a very *specific thing*. He not only says that *prayer* will sustain and fortify us, but furthermore, that we are to pray for **the very thing the widow was asking -- reward for the righteous** *and justice and retribution for all the wrongs done to them* -- through the centuries, but ***particularly*** *being done in this season which directly precedes His return.*

This second point caused me to begin to process the parable differently. This wasn't just a general teaching on persevering faith. Jesus was likening the church to a widow whose husband was gone. A husband looks out for the interests of his wife and protects her from those who would abuse her or steal from her. This woman's husband was absent, even as our "husband" is in heaven during this season. We, the church, often suffer greatly from the one who sends 'agents' (whether human or demonic) against us to kill, steal, and destroy. We are commanded not to retaliate, but to *forgive* and leave the justice to God. We are conditioned to respond this way particularly when it's a situation that we can't remedy on our own. We are to love our enemies, bless those who curse us, and do good and pray for those who treat us spitefully and persecute us. And that is all well and good – it's what Jesus taught us. But I realized there is a time coming, and perhaps sooner than we realize, when our prayers need to transition from acceptance and forgiveness to a cry for God to come and execute judgment on the wicked and vindication for His people; to come bringing justice and punishment upon evil and unrepentant sinners! This is not a personal cry for vengeance on the part of His people. This is a cry of *faith* from a people who are *seeing* that it is God's ordained time for His wrath to be poured out; it is *the season for vengeance – for removing the wicked from the earth* as He brings this age to a close.

About this time, the Lord provided additional light on the subject. I was studying Psalm 68 and reading in Spurgeon's *Treasury of David* as I attempted to understand that rather challenging psalm. In the various authors quoted, Alexander M'Caul commented on vv. 1-2:

> **Let God arise! Let his enemies be scattered! Let them who hate him also flee before him. As smoke is driven away, so drive them away. As wax melts before the fire, so let the wicked perish at the presence of God! Psalm 68:1-2 WEB**

M'Caul points out that David was quoting the words used by Moses in the wilderness, when, after a time of rest, it was time for the Israelites to resume their journey, the ark leading the way.[1] And yet, here's David centuries later pointing us toward something that is *yet future,* as he repeats the same prayer. M'Caul identifies that future time as the return of Christ, when *once for all,* His enemies will be scattered and utterly overthrown, not to return; it is the time of the restoration of Israel, the establishment of universal peace, and the conversion of all nations. M'Caul goes on to challenge the church to join David in making this prayer one of the "subjects of our addresses at the throne of grace..."; that *our faith* "take up the language of the text, saying, 'Let God arise, let his enemies be scattered; let them also that hate him flee before him.'" Says M'Caul: "It is a prayer for the universal church, for everyone who loves the Savior, and desires to see 'the King in his beauty,' for everyone who mourns over the state of the world and the church."

The Cry of the Martyrs
Added to these passages is the weight of the cry of the martyred souls seen in the 5th seal:

> **"How long, O Lord, holy and true, until You judge and avenge our blood on those who dwell on the earth?" Rev 6:10**

Here are these precious saints, well aware that this period of intense persecution under Antichrist – this period during which their own deaths had occurred -- is still continuing on the earth, and also keenly aware that the hour for God to arise in great fury and vengeance upon the wicked is near at hand. Their hearts are longing to see justice executed, and their cry is, *"How much longer, O Lord!?!"* They are zealous for the suffering of the righteous still taking place, and for the just punishment of the wicked.

The Lord's response reassures them that the time is not far off now. But our focus is particularly on their prayer. This – a prayer from heaven! -- is not a typical prayer found among God's people. It is a cry for God to move with vengeance and justice against the wicked of the earth. This is a timely cry and teaches us who are alive in the last days, that the time is coming when our own prayers will need to transition to this same cry. When those souls appear, the time will be *right around the corner* when vengeance will be *God's express will.* He will look at that time for the prayers of the saints in order to carry out that will on the earth.

---

1 Numbers 10:35

M'Caul speaks also of these saints:

It is remarkable that only one prayer of the departed saints has been made known to us, and that this one should be a prayer to the same effect. In the 5th Chapter of the Revelation, the Lord is pleased to give us a view of the state of those who have died as martyrs. St. John says, "I saw under the altar the souls of them that were slain for the word of God, and for the testimony which they held: and they cried with a loud voice, saying 'how long, O Lord, holy and true, dost thou not judge and avenge our blood on them that dwell on the earth?'"

Though removed from this scene of woe and misery, safe from all the attempts of the wicked, and in the enjoyment of God's presence, their happiness is not yet complete, and they still find subject matter for prayer and supplication. They still long for that day when the Lord shall arise to judgment, and put an end to the triumph of the wicked.... We cannot, therefore, doubt, but that it is our duty to join in a prayer which the Holy Ghost has dictated, which our Lord has appointed, which the saints in heaven use, and which the beloved disciple offered up....

We are bound to pray for those things which promote the honor of Christ and the eternal happiness of his people. But never shall the honor of Christ be complete, nor his people happy, nor the righteous be glad and rejoice exceedingly, until God arise and his enemies be scattered.[2]

The insight and instruction we receive from this cry of the martyrs is remarkable, and, along with these other passages, will surely be a strong signal when that time comes in the future, that *it is time* for the saints to cry out for Jesus' return to judge the earth <u>and</u> to make that cry *with faith!*

Prayers are the Catalyst!
One final thing needs to be noted: When it comes time for Jesus to pour out His wrath, this is what Scripture says:

> **2 And I saw the seven angels who stand before God, and to them were given seven trumpets.**
> **3 Then another angel, having a golden censer, came and stood at the altar. He was given much incense, that he should offer it *with the prayers of all the saints* upon the golden altar which was before the throne.**
> **4 And the smoke of the incense, with the prayers of the saints, *ascended before God* from the angel's hand.**
> **5-6 Then the angel took the censer, filled it with fire from the altar, and threw it to the earth. And there were noises, thunderings, lightnings, and an earthquake. So the seven angels who had the seven trumpets prepared themselves to sound.**
>
> **Revelation 8:2-6** (emphasis added)

Here we see the final catalyst for the long-withheld wrath of God: It's the prayers of the saints -- of ALL the saints – the saints of all ages, who have suffered with patience, refused retaliation, entrusted their sufferings to God, and *trusted Him* for His ultimate justice.[3] They have died, not seeing justice done, committing that *to Him*. But all those prayers have been saved up in heaven; they join with the believing cries of the saints still suffering on earth and with the martyred souls, so freshly come from the suffering; and **they all come together at this climactic moment in the future and play a crucial role in unleashing God's wrath upon the wicked**. At long last, the time has come for God to lift up His mighty arm of justice. But it is more than that; **it is the saints *playing a crucial role* in the establishing of God's righteousness in the earth!** God has placed the earth *under man's dominion* and He *needs* the faith and prayers of the saints for His will to be brought to this earth. God spoke in the Old Testament of the tremendous ways that He will restore and bless Israel in the future, adding, "I will yet for

---

2 From *Plain Sermons on Subjects Practical and Prophetic*, by Alexander M'Caul, D.D., 1840, quoted in C. H. Spurgeon's *Treasury of David*, Psalm 68.

3 The live coals with which the incense is lit (v. 5) are taken from the brazen altar – the altar on which the sacrifices for sin were made. In the reality of things, it represents the cross, on which the true Sacrifice was made, and which lit the fires of the Holy Spirit for all prayer and consecration of believers. When atonement from this altar is not received by the sinner, then wrath, linked to that altar by fire, will come upon him.

this be inquired of by the house of Israel, to do it for them" (Ezek. 36:37). God is waiting yet for Israel to *see their great need for Him and for what only He can do for them.* May we, as God's people, pray about this, meditate on it, and be quick to see His purposes and the part we play in bringing them to pass![4]

The faith of the Son of God resides in us – He has equipped us to partner with Him in His purposes for the earth. And yet for us to cooperate with God with our faith requires that we *know* His purposes, His plan. There is a *hearing* of His Word that is required: *We must see clearly "the Day of the Lord" – what it entails, and what its purpose is.* If we don't see it clearly, our faith will lack confidence, it will be tentative. Behind the cries of the widow and of the martyrs in heaven was the *knowledge* that God is the great Avenger and Vindicator, and that He plans to return to earth for that purpose. That's the *faith* behind their cries. As we continue into the next chapter, we will see more clearly how we get to that place of confident and powerful faith.

> Oh, that you would tear the heavens,
>
> That you would come down, that the mountains might quake at your presence, as when fire kindles the brushwood, and the fire causes the waters to boil;
>
> To make your name known to your adversaries, that the nations may tremble at your presence!
>
> Isaiah 64:1-2 WEB

---

4   In fact, the salvation of the earth will depend upon the prayers of both the church and Israel. The establishing of the Millennial kingdom hinges not only on the Day of the Lord (that is, Jesus' return), but on the full turning of the Jewish remnant back to God; the kingdom Jesus will establish is a Jewish kingdom, in Israel, centered in Jerusalem. It is this full turning of Israel that will bring forth the King and bring "deliverance to the earth" (Is. 26:18).

SECTION 12
OUR MANDATE

CHAPTER 32

Revelation 10

With the scroll playing such a key part in the events of Revelation, we ask whether it is mentioned again after Revelation 5. And indeed, it makes a significant appearance again in Revelation 10, where it is seen in the hand of "another mighty angel." This angel is the focus of this chapter in Revelation: He takes a sovereign position, makes a stirring proclamation, and then gives a strong charge to John. We will take a closer look at all of these: the angel, the position, the proclamation, and the charge.

The Angel

We begin with a search to find the identity of the angel. The word "angel" (*aggelos)* simply means <u>a messenger, one who is sent</u>. It may be a spirit, dwelling in heaven and created directly by God (our usual concept of an angel), it may be a human being used as a messenger (see Rev. 22:8-9), or it can be the Lord Jesus Himself, who is seen repeatedly in the Old Testament as "the Angel of the Lord" or "the Angel of the Covenant." That leaves our options pretty wide open for the identity of this angel, so we will look at his description and see what that tells us. We mentioned in *Part 1* how the Word itself is the greatest code-breaker for the things of Revelation that puzzle us. Here, the identity of the angel isn't openly stated, and yet the clues in the Word are there for anyone who looks. Let's take a look:

1. The angel was <u>clothed with a cloud</u>. Repeatedly in Scripture, God clothes or hides Himself in clouds.
   a. In leading the Israelites from Egypt, as well as manifesting in His glory in the tabernacle and later in the temple, God clothed Himself with a cloud. (E.g., see Exodus 13:21, 16:10, 19:16, 24:16, Lev. 16:2, Num. 10:34, 12:5, 1 Kings 8:11.) Ezekiel's visions of God also included "a great cloud" (Ezek. 1:4).
   b. In the New Testament, both the Father and the Son are seen clothed in a cloud: The Father, at the Mount of Transfiguration (Mark 9:7) and Jesus at His ascension and return (Acts 1:9, Luke 21:27, Rev. 14:4).
2. Upon his head was 'the' rainbow. The rainbow, a sign of mercy from the time of Noah, is usually seen in the clouds, and is always associated with God in Scripture. When Ezekiel saw God enthroned, he said the brightness around Him was "like a rainbow in a cloud" (Ezek. 1:28). In John's earlier vision of God enthroned (Rev. 4), he saw a rainbow around the throne. This is undoubtedly *the* rainbow that John sees now upon the head of the angel – a rainbow clearly associated with God Himself.

3. His <u>face was like the sun</u>. This takes us directly back to the description of Jesus in Revelation 1, "His face was like the sun shining in its strength," and of Him in the Transfiguration, "His face did shine as the sun" (Matt. 17:2).

4. His <u>feet were as pillars of brass</u>. Again, this takes us to the vision of Jesus where we are told "His feet were like fine brass, as if they burned in a furnace" (Rev. 1:17). Brass symbolizes judgment; this is a judgment *finely and perfectly* weighed and dispensed by the One to Whom the Father has committed all judgment. As we saw in the bowl judgments, Jesus will tread the earth, crushing all enemies and claiming all for Himself; we will see a hint of that coming judgment in just a few verses.

Could this mighty angel be anyone but Christ Himself, though His identity be slightly veiled with the term "angel"? But in case there's doubt, we go on.

We see Him holding in His hand a "little book," that is, a *biblion*, the very term used to describe the scroll of Revelation 5. The scroll *is open* in His hand, which is fitting, as we know the scroll has been open since the 1st trumpet, and this encounter with the angel is placed toward the close of the 6th *trumpet* and right before the 7th begins (in 11:14-15). It makes no sense for this little book to be anything other than the scroll, and that anyone other than Jesus should be holding it. Revelation is not the unveiling of random and unconnected events, but of a very powerful, purposeful, and cohesive narrative! Ever since the Lamb removed the last seal (Rev. 8:1), we have been seeing the events of the scroll unfold. Now, at this break between the trumpet and bowl judgments, it is back in view again, still in the hands of the Lord Jesus.

The Angel's Position and Pronouncement

And now see the dramatic and significant action He takes: He places His right foot on the sea and His left upon the land, and gives a mighty shout, as a *lion roaring*. When Israel set out to take Canaan for their own, God told them, "Every place that the sole of your foot shall tread upon I have given unto you" (Joshua 1:3). "For He must reign till He has put all enemies under His feet" (1 Cor. 15:25). In God's ways, to set our feet upon what God has promised us, is how we *take possession* of it. This is now the time, and we see the Lion of Judah *placing His feet on all that He is claiming as His own,* and serving notice to all the earth with a roar. Since the words uttered by the thunders are not revealed, we will pass over them quickly, except to note that words from heaven *can* be disguised as thunder (John 12:28-29). This mighty angel then raises His right hand to heaven (in the gesture of giving oath that is still used today in courts of law) and swears by the One who lives forever, who created all things, that there shall be *no more delay,*

> **… but in the days of the sounding of the seventh angel, when he is about to sound, the mystery of God would be finished, as He declared to His servants the prophets.**
> **Revelation 10:7**

We looked at the significance of this verse previously in chapter 19, so won't go into it again here.

What proceeds next concerns John and, by extension, the reader. For John is instructed by the Holy Spirit to approach the angel and to take the scroll from Him:

> **So I went to the angel and said to him, "Give me the little book." And he said to me, "Take and eat it; and it will make your stomach bitter, but it will be as sweet as honey in your mouth."**
> **Then I took the little book out of the angel's hand and ate it, and it was as sweet as honey in my mouth. But when I had eaten it, my stomach became bitter.**
> **And he said to me, "You must prophesy again about many peoples, nations, tongues, and kings."**
> **Revelation 10:9-11**

It is always a sweet thing to hear and receive God's words. We don't always perceive in that moment the full significance of the words themselves. John is being asked to take the scroll – the seals, the trumpet judgments, and the bowl judgments – and eat them. Jeremiah spoke in a similar way:

Your words were found, and I ate them, and Your word was to me the joy and rejoicing of my heart; for I am called by Your name, O Lord God of hosts. Jeremiah 15:16

Like physical eating when what we eat becomes part of us, eating God's words means to take them into our heart, where they work and grow and become a part of us. They begin to change how we think and what motivates us. They change our outlook on life and how we interact with those around us and with the world. The mighty angel had just spoken of the hidden purposes of God, proclaimed to the prophets as *good news.* Consistent with this, Jeremiah finds God's words to be the joy and rejoicing of his heart, *because* "I am called by Your name, O Lord God of hosts." For the righteous, God is always good, and therefore His words are good and delight our hearts. And yet, Jeremiah is called "the weeping prophet." Perhaps no other prophet brought from God to Israel words of such profound sorrow, anger, and desolation. The judgments that were about to fall in Jeremiah's own lifetime were of a nature that had not been seen, even among the heathen. They were appalling and devastating (e.g., Jer. 19:7-15). His own family and personal friends sought to kill him because of the words he brought from the Lord (Jer. 11:19-23; 12:6). It was a burden Jeremiah could not have stood up under without the Lord strengthening and sustaining him.

Ezekiel, too, was given a scroll to eat and it was to fill him inside. He ate it and "it was in my mouth like honey for sweetness" (Ezek. 3:3). And yet the contents were "lamentations and mourning and woe." As God sent him to *speak* all that He had told him, He warned him that Israel was adamantly hard-hearted and severely obstinate and would NOT listen to his words. What a difficult and painful task and one with *no positive results.* Would Ezekiel have found the grace to obey, except that the glory of heaven and the Spirit "lifted me up and took me away…" Though God carried him, he says,

"I went in bitterness,[1] in the heat[2] of my spirit; but the hand of the Lord was strong[3] upon me." Ezekiel 3:14

[1] *mar* H4751B – bitter, bitterness
[2] *chemah* H2534B – heat, rage, burning anger, hot displeasure; figuratively, poison
[3] *chazak* H2388B – to seize with strength, fasten upon; to conquer, to strengthen, make strong or severe

Ezekiel in his humanness was *not up to this task.* He shrank from it. But God was adamant – Ezekiel was the one for the job, and God Himself would lift, empower, and strengthen him for it. What was this bitterness and heat? Was it the *power* -- the pressure -- of the living word inside him, and the countering pressure – the hostility -- he knew he would receive when he delivered the word? He was stirred up inside – agitated, probably angry. This was not something he would have chosen for himself. We can almost visualize it: to move under the *conviction* of that word and proclaim it to a hostile audience is to stand in a rushing torrent and warn of a ruinous waterfall just ahead, while all are heedlessly jet-skiing downstream, jeering at you as they go and even trying to run you down. All the world, unbelieving and rebellious, are rushing headlong in one direction – toward judgment – while those with God's word stand and call to them to repent – to change direction and go *against* the current! -- proclaiming a dire future if they won't. How small must the prophet feel his voice to be against such powerful forces in the world! It is always a lovely thing to prophesy God's favor and blessing. To issue the call to repent, to prophesy of coming wrath and judgment from God, is not a pleasant, but a bitter thing. And even for God's people, the vision is not just of glory, but of suffering to come.

Jesus spoke of this, amazingly bringing this role of the 'prophet' – one who testifies of the truth – *to each of us as believers:*

> **Blessed are you when men hate you, and when they exclude you, persecute you, and say all kinds of evil against you falsely for My sake.**
> **Rejoice in that day, and leap for joy! For indeed, your reward is great in heaven;** *for in like manner their fathers did to the prophets.* **Matthew 5:11, Luke 6:22-23** (emphasis added)

Jesus is telling us that we are called to speak His word in the same way the prophets did! And we will experience the same rejection and hostility *for the Word's sake,* that they did! Difficult, yes; but empowered by God, and what a privilege!

The Charge is Not Just to John!

We don't see the scroll again. It disappears with John taking it and eating it. Is there significance in this? J. A. Seiss, in his monumental commentary on Revelation, makes such an eloquent case for John *being a representative of all of us*: that each of us is called to take the Word into us so that *we* can testify to what is coming on the earth. Seiss asks, "*What has been the purpose of all that Jesus did while on earth*, and all that He does with the scroll?"

> What indeed is the great object and intent of all his works and doings, whether on earth or in heaven, to procure rights, titles, and warrants from the throne? Yea, what? but that he may give and impart the same to his apostles and believing people, that they may take them, eat them, appropriate them, preach and prophesy them, live on them, and build themselves up with them unto eternal life? There is no book like the roll which the Lamb takes from the right hand of the Sitter on the throne. It embodies in itself all the prophetic, priestly, and royal rights of Christ, in the attitude of our *Go°el*, or Redeemer. It compasses the very spring and kernel of all sacred prophecy, all evangelic preaching, all true faith, all abiding hope. It is the eternal charter, from the right hand of eternal sovereignty, on which reposes the whole right, authority, work, kingdom, and dominion of Jesus, as the Lord and Saviour of man.
>
> And the grand intent and purpose of all that he has done in reference to that document, for which he has obtained it and freed it of its seals, and for which he holds it open in his hand as he proceeds to take possession of the earth is, **that his people may have the benefit of it--that they may take it from his hand, feed on it, incorporate it with their inmost being, make it the subject of their hopes, their prophecies and their prayers, and in the strength and virtue of it live and reign with him forever.**[1] (emphasis added)

This, then, is the *relevance* of John taking and eating the scroll: because he had to "prophesy again about many peoples, nations, tongues, and kings" (Rev. 10:11); and because John represents each of us – all who have ears to hear – for *we* are called to eat the words, let them fill us and change us, and become those who then proclaim and testify of the message. This is a big part of us being 'the horns and eyes' of the Lamb. This is a key part of our role as we participate in the work of the Lamb; we have *heard* the Word, and faith has come; we have *eaten* the scroll and have become convinced of God's plan, of Christ's return, and of His judgments poured out unto the destruction of this present evil age. The eating of it will cause faith to rise up in powerful prayer and testimony. **This is a key part of our believing intercession at the end and of our testimony: We become not just His eyes, but *His mouth* to the many "peoples, nations, tongues and kings!"** Our faith in His words brings the power and authority found in the horns of the Lamb. This is a charge, a mandate, to *us*. Will we accept it? Will we take His words and study them and internalize them until they change us, and then yield to Him as servants and vessels for His purpose? God looks for the faithful witness, for the one who will overcome. This is a work that can be done only with the grace which the Lamb Who has overcome can supply. May we be good *receivers* of His Word and of His grace to fulfill all He has for each of us!

---

1 J.A. Seiss, *The Apocalypse* (Grand Rapids, MI: Zondervan Publishing House, 1900), p. 228.

CHAPTER 33

The Measuring Mandate

Revelation 11 is a continuation of chapter 10, so is also placed in the narrative toward the close of the 6th trumpet (Rev. 9:13 and Rev. 11:15). With John having eaten the scroll, the next thing we see is him *participating* in things to come! Here the mandate to John involves a prophetic action:

> Then I was given a reed[1] like a measuring rod.[2] And the angel stood, saying, "Rise and measure the temple of God, the altar, and those who worship there.
> But leave out the court which is outside the temple, and do not measure it, for it has been given to the Gentiles. And they will tread the holy city underfoot for forty-two months."
> Revelation 11:1-2

[1]*kalamos* G2563T – a reed
[2]*rhabdos* G4464T – a staff, a walking stick; a rod with which one is beaten; a royal scepter

Though only two verses, these are rich in significance and will be very interesting to examine. Before we look more closely, let's get some background on this. We remember that with the close of the 69th week, God's dealings with the Jews ceased; He no longer acknowledged them as His own or dealt with them as His people. We saw this in the prophecy of Hosea:

> I will go and return to my place, till they acknowledge their offence, and seek my face: in their affliction they will seek me early. Hosea 5:15 KJV

And in the words of Jesus,

> Your house is left to you desolate; For I say to you, you shall see me no more till you say, 'Blessed is he who comes in the name of the Lord!' Matthew 23:38-39

With the beginning of the 70th week, marked by the treaty with Antichrist, we know the 'clock' of God's ownership of them and dealings with them begins again. <u>This is the period of time that the Lord is referring to in these two verses from Revelation 11.</u> The temple is rebuilt and their system of worship and sacrifices reinstituted. Where is Israel spiritually at this time? Lamentably, when worship resumes – near the beginning of the seven years -- with the exception of the 144,000, <u>the rituals and worshippers will be in essentially the same place as when the 69th week ended</u> -- a place of alienation from God (see Is. 66:1-4). God assesses the treaty they have just made with Antichrist:

> **Because ye have said, 'We have made a covenant with death, and with hell are we at agreement; when the overflowing scourge shall pass through, it shall not come unto us: for we have made lies our refuge, and under falsehood have we hid ourselves.' Isaiah 28:15 KJV**

What follows this "because"? God goes on to say:

> 16 *Therefore* **thus saith the Lord God,** *Behold, I lay in Zion for a foundation, a stone, a tried stone, a precious corner stone, a sure foundation:* **he that believeth shall not make haste.**
> 17 *Judgment also will I lay to the line, and righteousness to the plummet*: **and the hail shall sweep away the refuge of lies, and the waters shall overflow the hiding place.**
> 18 **And your covenant with death shall be disannulled, and your agreement with hell shall not stand; when the overflowing scourge shall pass through, then ye shall be trodden down by it. Isaiah 28:16-18 KJV** (emphasis added)

This is such a rich and precious thing. God is saying that when this very important time comes, the covenant they enter into will be such a *disastrous* choice that it will bring upon them an *"overflowing scourge."* This will be a trial of overwhelming proportions; they will simply be undone by it, and the "lying refuge" the treaty was to provide will be swept away. But <u>God has provided a solution</u> – seen in v. 16. God has *already laid* a *sure foundation* in Zion. As everything the Jews know and trust is swept away in the shocking flood of betrayal and tribulation, God will begin *holding out to them* this precious corner stone and sure foundation, the Lord Jesus. God's work, which will endure forever, is grounded and founded on this precious, tested, and sure Foundation – Jesus. *He IS the measuring line of *judgment* and the plumb line of *righteousness*. <u>This 'measuring' will begin once the temple worship resumes and it will continue on past the midpoint, which is when that forty-two months begins</u>. Let's take a closer look.

The Rod and the Measuring

Why measuring? Measuring takes place when a building or room – perhaps one that has not been in use for a while – is being taken in hand, assessed, and renovated. When God was preparing to restore Jerusalem and the temple after their destruction under Nebuchadnezzar, he began *measuring*.[1] Measuring speaks of *ownership, restoration, and taking possession*: changes being made and plans to be carried out according to the purpose of the owner. The temple and its worship have been "out of use" for almost 2,000 years. <u>These three being measured – the temple, altar, and worshippers – all speak to how the Jews approach and relate to God</u>. As God "reclaims" them, there are new guidelines and stipulations for how they must relate to Him.

This measuring is to be done with "a reed like a rod." It's clearly a measuring instrument, yet a rod; the root of the Greek word for rod is, "to rap, slap, or smite."[2] A rod is strong and straight, and its strongest meaning is one of discipline; it is used several times in Revelation, and each time communicates an absolute and inflexible authority. Although it can also refer to a shepherd's staff, it is used most of the time in the New Testament as a rod of authority or a king's scepter. We think of God's dealings with the Jews at this time: the severity will be extreme – first under Antichrist, and then, for those who are not yet turning, under the Day of the Lord. *The rod* is clearly in view; and yet, as they turn, the rod will become a staff of guidance, of protection, of provision in His hand. We will see this much more clearly when we get to Revelation 12. All these dealings will be a tender and skillful demonstration of *His kingly rule* over them.

---

1   Zech. 1:16; 2:2-4.
2   *rhapizo* G4474S

This word "reed" is also revealing. *Kalamos*, the Greek here for 'reed,' is the word used in the Septuagint for the Hebrew *qaneh* ('kanah'), defined as "a reed, a measuring-rod." The root meaning of *qanah* is 'erect, upright.'[3] So, it was a key instrument in construction, apparently providing a perfect vertical measurement as well as having markings on it to measure the horizontal. This Hebrew *kanah* is the source for our English word "canon,"[4] which means <u>rule, used particularly for what has been established by God as divinely mandated</u>. For example, we call both the Old and New Testament scriptures '*the Canon*,' meaning that body of writings which all are agreed upon as inspired and given by God and unchangeable in their message and authority. How now is that relevant for the turning of the Jews during the 70th week? The *measuring* here indicates a *change* from what has gone before. And indeed, changes are required for the Jews' relationship to the Lord. <u>No longer will adherence to the Old Covenant satisfy God – even when it's from the heart.</u> Everything changed with the coming and the sacrifice of Christ. There is a new standard – a new mandate, a new *rule* -- in place now that the Jews must accept in order to be accepted by God. Jeremiah had prophesied,

> 31 "Behold, the days are coming, says the Lord, when I will make a new covenant with the house of Israel … I will put My law in their minds, and write it on their hearts; and I will be their God, and they shall be My people.
>
> 34 No more shall every man teach his neighbor, and every man his brother, saying, 'Know the Lord,' for they all shall know Me, from the least of them to the greatest of them, says the Lord. For I will forgive their iniquity, and their sin I will remember no more."
>
> **Jeremiah 31:31, 34**

We saw in *Part 1* that the transition from Judaism to a Gentile bride at the close of the 69th week was gradual; the Old Covenant did not close out abruptly and then the New begin, but there were various overlaps of the two. One of the overlaps was that the temple with its worship continued another thirty plus years after Pentecost. We see the same thing now. At this time (early in the 70th week), both are again in play: the church is still on the earth and the temple is back again and worship taking place.

The Turning Needed

It was their rejection of that new covenant that caused the clock to stop; that issue must <u>still be faced and dealt with</u>, and there are only *seven years* for that to take place. In this relatively short time, the national iniquity must be brought to an end and atoned for, Israel established in righteousness before God, all prophecy fulfilled, and the Most Holy anointed.[5] All this cleansing and preparation is essential as Israel moves toward the fulfillment of God's promise to Abraham of a "land which he should *afterward* receive for an inheritance."[6] <u>There is no Millennium without Israel's turning and repentance.</u> The Millennium is the fulfillment of *their* kingdom promises. Jesus will rule the earth from an obedient Jerusalem. But the rebellion is deeply entrenched; and the work of breaking and chastising will be deep and severe.

God's heart has always longed for fellowship with man, in spite of how sin damaged man. In the tabernacle of Moses, as well as Solomon's temple, we see the terms provided under which man could approach God and commune with Him. Both of these were constructed under God's strict and specific instructions, after the pattern of things in heaven. God set up this worship very carefully both to satisfy His righteousness, but also so that the worshipper could *have confidence that he was on right terms with God.* <u>The whole system – the building, the furniture,</u>

---

3 *Qaneh* H7070S – a reed (as erect); a rod (especially for measuring), shaft, tube, stem, beam. From *qanah* H7069S – to erect, that is, create
4 J.A. Seiss, *The Apocalypse* (Grand Rapids, MI: Zondervan Publishing House, 1900), p. 238.
5 Daniel 9:24
6 Heb. 11:8 (emphasis added)

the worship and sacrifices, etc. -- every aspect of this approach to God and communion with Him typed – that is, was a shadow of – some aspect of the New Covenant. During the 70th week, *Israel is being called to step out of the TYPE into the reality.* How does this work out?

With the temple rebuilt for the first time in almost 2000 years and worship reinstated, undoubtedly there will be tremendous rejoicing in Israel! Jews will feel they are truly established again in their land! They have triumphed and prevailed over many enemies and obstacles! Surely, this will pave the way for the fulfillment of all the prophecies of their national dominance in the earth – "the mountain of the house of the Lord shall be established in the top of the mountains…" (Micah 4:1). But the whole basis for this reinstituted worship is *their trust in an interloper*, a false messiah! From their own rebellion will come the severity of the chastising rod! From this "covenant with death," the manifestation of their still-present rebellion against God, will come the *full weight* of the chastising rod -- this *devastating storm of evil and tribulation* that will sweep over them at the midpoint.[7] Look what God says, speaking of Antichrist:

> **I will send him against an hypocritical nation, and against the people of my wrath will I give him a charge, to take the spoil, and to take the prey, and to tread them down like the mire of the streets. Isaiah 10:6 KJV**

Throughout this calamity the question will be (even as it has been since the days of Moses), <u>will Israel turn to God and seek Him with humble, penitent hearts </u>so that He can be to them all that He desires to be? This is what God will be watching for and weighing. Will their turning to Him be merely according to form and ritual while their hearts remain far from Him, or will that turning be with all their hearts? As we noted from Daniel in *Part 1,* this all will most certainly be *a process*:

> **33 And those of the people who understand shall instruct many; yet for many days they shall fall by sword and flame, by captivity and plundering.**
> **35 And some of those of understanding shall fall, to refine them, purify them, and make them white, until the time of the end; because it is still for the appointed time.**
> **Daniel 11:33, 35**

Here we see the rod -- the deep and varied chastisements -- and we see the learning and turning.

What is to be Measured?

The new standard, the corrected "dimensions" of worship and of approach to God, pertain to the *temple,* the *altar,* and the *worshippers.*

The Temple

The temple gives us an overall view of *how we approach God and have relationship and fellowship with Him.* Every aspect of it – the dimensions, the materials used, the items of furniture and their placement – all had spiritual significance. We will take a quick look at the <u>furniture</u> (using the greater simplicity of the tabernacle rather than the temple) <u>and what it signified in the New Covenant</u>. The New Covenant spoke of a whole new way of approach to God -- one not based on the blood of animals, but the blood of God's "provided Lamb" which made access into the very Holy of Holies *in heaven* available to everyone who believed and received that blood.

Inside the court of the tabernacle, we first encounter the brazen laver where the priests would wash their hands and feet, required before service was given. For the believer now, this represents the "washing of water by the Word" (Eph. 5:26). The Word cleanses our souls from the deceptions, defilements, and confusion that we encounter in our life on earth. This was required to clear the way for communion with God.

---

7 Is. 28:14-18

Next was the brazen altar, the place of the sacrifice of the animals. The shedding of blood made an approach to God possible. "And according to the law almost all things are purified with blood, and without shedding of blood there is no remission" (Heb. 9:19). This was the only door of entrance unto God – there was no other way that a sinner could approach a holy God, but by blood. All of those many animal sacrifices pointed simply to *the one great Sacrifice* which the Father was to supply at the right time; Jesus, the Lamb of God, offered once for all. This is finally what *the Jewish worshippers* will need to come to see – that the altar of sacrifice has been filled, and fulfilled, by the Lamb of God, their Messiah.

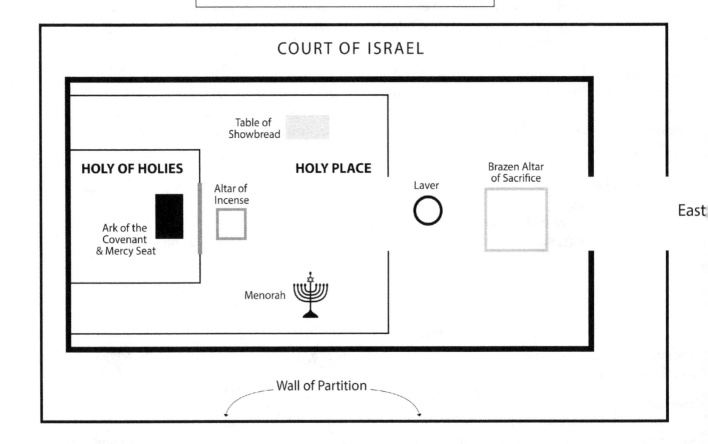

Now entering the Holy Place, to the left was the oil-fed Menorah, supplying the only light in this inner room. The oil always represents the Holy Spirit. Here there was to be no *natural, human wisdom,* but only the wisdom – the light -- of God supplied by the Spirit. We see it now as representing the seven ages of the 'reborn' – those who through faith in the Lamb of God receive His Spirit (the oil) joined with their spirits, bringing inner life and light through that union. More specifically, located here in the sanctuary (the Holy Place), the Menorah gave light to the showbread and the Altar of Incense. This will mean more to us after we look at what each of those represented. Suffice to say here, that the understanding of the believer is to be illuminated by *revelation light from the Holy Spirit,* not from human reasoning or natural knowledge!

To the right was the Table of Showbread upon which sat 12 loaves of bread, flavored with frankincense.[8] This was daily food for the priests and part of their fellowship with God as they served Him there. The bread typed *the Lord Jesus, the Bread of Life*. As believers, we take Him into ourselves and He becomes a part of us. He becomes the way we worship and commune with the Father and our power for living. Jesus promised that if we would *eat of Him, we would live forever* (John 6:51). The fact that there was *only* bread here tells us that Jesus is *all we need* for our own spiritual life and sustenance. "Of His fullness have all we received… and you are complete in Him" (John 1:16, Col. 2:10).

Straight ahead in the Holy Place, right before the veil leading to the Holy of Holies, was the Altar of Incense,[9] typing the prayers of believers. This wood (humanity) altar, overlaid with pure gold (divine nature), was where prayers and intercession and worship were offered. Incense (a type of prayer) was to be burned on it every morning and evening. The altar speaks first of the intercessory work of our High Priest Jesus, then of the intercessory work of the Jewish priests, and now of all believers, ordained by God as a "holy priesthood."[10] We are commanded to "pray without ceasing."[11] Because the once-for-all sacrifice has been made, our worship and prayer now take place *inside the veil* in the very presence of God.[12] We are urged to come with "boldness before the throne of grace" and there find the mercy and grace that we need! (Heb. 4:16). There were horns on this altar, which speak of power. These horns were to be 'cleansed' once a year with blood from the sin offering on the brazen altar. This tells us that the power and effectiveness of our prayers always derives from the shed blood of the Lord Jesus. Now we see more clearly why the Table of Showbread and the Altar of Incense *were illuminated,* not by any natural light, but only by the oil-fed light of the Menorah. Only by *His* light do we see Jesus (our Bread of Life) clearly, as well as see in the spirit to function in our priestly role of worship, prayer, and intercession before the throne!

Finally, there was the Holy of Holies, which contained the Ark of the Covenant. Inside the ark were the two tablets of stone upon which God had written the ten commandments of the First Covenant. This was the very meeting place between God and man, and yet we see that *the righteous requirements of God* could not be left behind, no matter how much He loved the sinner. He would meet with man *in the presence of His righteous requirements!* They hold the place of honor in the 'house' of a holy God. And yet, if God had required perfect and sinless behavior in order to meet with Him, there would have been *no meeting.* But God designed the tabernacle and temple as places for Him to meet *with sinners:* He made provision of *substitutionary blood* shed unto death for the sinner, providing a way to meet with Him in spite of transgression and failure. We might have called these two tablets of stone "the often-broken" ten commandments! And yet, over those very tablets was *the mercy seat,* with the *Presence of God* resting upon it! This was where a God who *loved passionately* in spite of sin, met with those He loved. The only thing required of the sinner was a humble, honest, and repentant heart before God.

This is a brief look at the articles of furniture and what they represent in our present-day New Covenant relationship with the Lord. Jesus has now become the perfection of the law for us. He has become *the mercy seat.*[13] He is the Altar of Incense, the bread on the Table of Showbread, the light of the lamps, the brazen altar and the sacrifice on it,[14] and the water in the laver that cleanses. As this 'measuring' takes place, God will be holding out these truths, and looking for the change from these elements of temple worship as *types,* to them being *reality* for the Jews. The gospel reveals the *realities of Christ;* the types are no longer acceptable when the Reality is here and available. "Nor is there salvation in any other, for there is no other name under heaven give among men by which we *must* be saved" (Acts 4:12, emphasis added). The "dimensions" have changed – no longer is the old temple worship acceptable to God.

---

8   Leviticus 24:1-9
9   Exodus 30:1, 6-10
10   1 Peter 2:5
11   1 Thess. 5:17
12   Hebrews 9:2-4
13   Romans 3:25 1 John 2:2, 4:10
14   Matthew 23:19

NOTE: For a very helpful study on the Tabernacle, its furniture, and all that it signified, see *The Tabernacle,* by M.R.DeHaan.

The Altar

Out of all those items of furniture, the Holy Spirit selects *the altar* for specific observation. And this, of course, is the key to everything else. Because here is reflected the basis upon which worshippers believe they can approach God and be made right with Him. How can the sinner approach a holy God? There are, I believe, two issues here:

1. There must be a restored awareness a.) of guilt on the part of the sinner and b.) that blood is *the only way* to atone for guilt. The one desiring to approach is first confronted with *this altar* – the place of blood-shedding, of sacrifice, because **the one coming *has sinned*.** Is that understood by Jews in this modern day where "sin" is almost a forgotten word? Furthermore, "the soul that sins, it shall die" (Ezek. 18:4). The *altar* tells us there must be *a blood sacrifice* as a substitute for our own death, because of our guilt before God. Is that understood in a day where the concept of "atonement through bloodshed" is so archaic as to be laughed at?

   For the life of the flesh is in the blood: and I have given it to you upon the altar to make an atonement for your souls: for it is the blood that makes an atonement for the soul. Lev. 17:11

   This precept, so foundational to the Jewish mindset, Scriptures, and worship, will need to be retaught to this end-time generation. Perhaps that 'wall of the temple' has fallen and needs to be 'measured' again and rebuilt.

2. Secondly, for those Jews who have accepted their need for a blood sacrifice, there will be the necessity for "the new measurement." That is, they will need to go *beyond* the Old Covenant practice of animal sacrifice, to see how Jesus, the Lamb of God *is indeed* their Messiah and has offered Himself as God's great sacrifice for the sins of all the world. It is their time to forsake the *old* and embrace the *new, the life-giving* gospel of the Lord Jesus Christ. This will be the reviving and then the *forsaking* of centuries-old beliefs in order to receive fresh revelation from the God of the Old Covenant in regard to *the New Covenant!*[15] And all in seven years! This is such drastic "cognitive reorganization," it's no wonder that it's a reed like a *rod* that will be required at that time. And as we know, there will be no lack of the sting of the rod.

The Worshippers

Here now we get down to the individual and his heart; and this is where we process *the worshipper* in terms of the temple and the altar. What is the person's understanding of who God is? Does the worshipper know and accept that he is a sinner seeking to approach a sinless God? This requires first an acknowledgement of God as Creator, to Whom an account will one day be given by all. For the Jew, this can be known through the Torah and the prophets -- does he acknowledge them as coming from God and as truth?

Then is required a certain fear of the Lord, because it's the tendency of the sinner to justify himself and focus on what's good in his life rather than how he has failed God's standard. This is the tendency of all sinners, but particularly *of the Jew:* For Paul said of them, "... being ignorant of God's righteousness, and going about to establish their own righteousness, they have not submitted themselves unto the righteousness of God" (Romans 10:3). The challenge of the Jew at this time will be first to acknowledge God, then to move out of self-justification and self-righteousness in relation to Him. Is the worshipper ready to face how he has sinned personally against God? As the Holy Spirit works to bring conviction, this will require a response of humility and honesty. Is he ready to return to the God of his fathers, making Him Lord of all; to recognize His claim on the whole person; to love Him

---

15 "He is set for the fall and the rising again of many in Israel" (Luke 2:34). Of course, some may respond directly to the gospel, bypassing the return first to Judaism.

with all the 'heart, soul, strength, and mind'? When it comes to this newly reinstated worship, *is the heart engaged* or is the offering of the lamb or the bullock simply a matter of "what the law requires," and the worshipper leaves to go his own way and live his life as he pleases?

The return in truth to the Father will open the way for the revelation of the Son. "Jesus said to them, 'If God were your Father, you would love Me…'" (John 8:42). As back then, the issue will be not just their rejection of Christ, but their rejection *of the Father,* which lies hidden behind their ritual worship.

Who Will Measure?

We ask ourselves now, who will be doing the measuring and how will it be done? Just as we said, it isn't only John who is to take the scroll, eat it, and then testify; so here, the command to measure extends beyond John. This is fairly obvious, since John will not be on earth at that time in the future. Who then? We are again reminded of the words, "He who has ears to hear, let him hear." *All* who are called to be saints receive His Word and are called to testify of that Word! In the previous chapter of Revelation, the call is specifically to take the Word pertaining to these last seven years (the scroll) so that proclamation can be made regarding that coming time. Remember, it is the *seven* -- horns, eyes, spirits of God -- who participate with Christ in the final events of this age. And so, we would understand that it's those same ones – the ones who can *see* as He does, who have the Holy Spirit giving them insight – who are being spoken to here. *We* are being called to be aware of God's work and purposes concerning the Jews and to have a heart and a sensitivity to them at this particular time. We are being called to come alongside them at this time; to hold forth the gospel to them and discern, with prayer, where they are in relation to that gospel and the Christ of the gospel. We are being called to offer them *mercy,* both spiritually and then with material assistance at the midpoint. A 'spiritual Israel' is being birthed during these years, and we are to be midwives, so to speak, in assisting in the birthing of this end-time remnant who will come into salvation.

This requires *knowledge* of what God is doing. It requires an understanding of what measurements are being used. As God's covenant people who understand identification with His death and resurrection, we know that a *death* and subsequent *resurrection* is required of Israel: a death to their own worthiness, to their national tendency toward pride and self-righteousness. They must come to the place of understanding that there will be no exemption or escape from their suffering, loss, and desolation until there has been deep repentance and a whole turning of their hearts to the God of their fathers and His Messiah, Jesus. They must see their own persistent rebellion toward God as the problem, not the hostility of the nations. Our love for them cannot be a natural, soulish love. It is always our responsibility to hold out to them the cross of the Lamb of God as the way to restoration with God. God is looking for nothing less than death to all the OLD as the pathway to Him. Our testimony to them must be nothing less than that, and we must understand that when they suffer, *it is to bring them to the Lord.* That is, we see and discern their situation through the lenses of the prophetic Scriptures and the revelation there of God's end goal for them and *how that will be accomplished.*

This role requires prayer and seeking God so that He can lead us and give us the needed opportunities for relationship across which the Word can be communicated; it requires sensitivity to the Holy Spirit for *discernment* in the 'measuring' process. We have been given the key issues that we need to be skilled in measuring, and we know they all pertain to the knowledge and faith in the Lord Jesus as the Messiah, the Lamb slain and risen again. In this year 2021, it is already happening with Jews and Christians worldwide to an extent not seen since the days of the early apostles. Many ministries and individuals are holding out the Word of Truth with love in their hearts toward the Jews. This will only increase as we move on to the end.

The Court of the Gentiles

> But leave out the court which is outside the temple, and do not measure it, for it has been given to the Gentiles. And they will tread the holy city underfoot for forty-two months.
>
> **Revelation 11:2**

For forty-two months (3½ years, 1260 days) the holy city will be trampled underfoot by those who are desecrating – that is, the antichrist and his group. During this time ALL the city, including the holy places of the inner temple, will be desecrated. There will no longer be faithful worshippers in the temple. But the measuring continues, and this is to be understood spiritually. Though faithful Jews will have fled Jerusalem (Matt. 24:15-21), God's eyes are upon the inward, spiritual progression of hearts turning to Him. God's *claim of ownership* is still upon the temple, altar, and worshippers, even when outwardly they have been scattered. But there is no claim of ownership, no redemptive dealings, with the Gentiles who are trampling. The door of salvation will open progressively for the Jew throughout these seven years; the same door will close progressively for the Gentiles as the fullness of their number comes in and this age closes. The Gentiles have had their opportunity, their choices are largely set by this time. People will receive the mark of the beast or they will not.

The Turning of the Jews

What glimpses of this turning process do we see in Scripture? There are numerous glimpses – we will mention only a couple. We know the 144,000, the "first fruits" of all who will return to God, begin their turning early. God sees them as spiritual virgins already before the rapture. Their seeking and their worship are being offered with sincerity of heart, and God *sees* them. Because of their early turning, He marks them for protection under the Day of the Lord judgments. We know they are not yet born again at that point or they would go in the rapture with the church. They have not yet received the full effects of 'the measuring' – their connection with God is still under the Old Covenant; but we believe they have *heard* the gospel and heard that Jesus Christ is *about to return* to take those who believe in Him, and when that happens, they will know that what they have been told about Him is true! (We will be looking soon at a prophecy in Zechariah that speaks of this.)

In contrast, Hosea prophesied to Ephraim (essentially the Northern Kingdom) of their deep corruption and spiritual whoredoms, warning that their 'iniquity is deeply bound and stored up.' When the time comes for the birthing of the righteous remnant, Ephraim will 'remain long' in the place of childbirth because he is 'an unwise son' (Hosea 13:12-13). He will not turn early in the seven years, but will continue in the place of pain and travail until the end of the seven years because the rebellion is so deeply entrenched. To face his sinfulness and need for the Savior will be a long, painful process; the rod of chastisement will work overtime with Ephraim. But the portion of the righteous remnant that comes out of Ephraim *will* finally turn.

In Conclusion

These two verses in Revelation 11 speak, then, of another very important way in which we, God's people, *participate in the transitional events of the 70th week and the wrap-up events of this age;* and that is, assisting the Jews in their turning back to God. In the next chapter we will proceed further in Revelation 11, and we will see the key and very powerful role that the two witnesses play as this turning takes place.

In the layout of events in Revelation, **chapters 10, 11, and 12** are placed in the middle of God's wrath -- after the trumpet judgments in Revelation 8 & 9 and before the bowl judgments in chapter 16. But what we're going to see as we look at these three chapters is the participation of the saints in the events which take place, *primarily from before the midpoint up until the rapture and, for some, even after the rapture.* That is why these chapters seem to go backward in time - it's because they are like a time out from the chronology to explain what is going on behind the scenes in the progression of events.

THE TWO WITNESSES
&
THE FINAL PREPARATIONS
OF THE BRIDE

CHAPTER 34

The Two Witnesses

This subject is a joyful one amidst some of the darker and more troubling scenes of Revelation. The ministry of these two witnesses is full of the power and presence of the Lord just when things are reaching their darkest point upon the earth; it speaks to us of the tremendous faithfulness and encouragement of the Lord to all His people going through this darkness. The basics of their ministry are clearly and simply spelled out in Revelation 11; we covered them in *Part I*, and won't go over them again here, except for these few points. Their ministry is dynamic, powerful, and based in the fact that they "*stand before the God of the earth*" (v. 4). Though on earth physically, they walk in a deep and constant faith-connection with the enthroned God of heaven. They have undoubtedly been uniquely groomed, prepared, and equipped for this ministry for years before it began. There is a strength in them that was seen in their spiritual counterparts, Moses and Elijah – a strength to stand in the face of extreme opposition, danger, and hostility, and proclaim, without flinching or faltering, *the Word of the Lord*. Many – probably the vast majority – of those they minister to, both among the church as well as the yet-unconverted Jews – do not have this strength. They do not have such a link with heaven firmly established. These two, then, are *their* link with heaven; they look at them – their boldness and courage; they listen to them – to the truth of their testimony -- and *they take heart*. They receive strength to make the right choice and *stand* on that choice in the face of great pressures and dangers. Their ministry leads into and includes most of what Jesus called "the hour of testing," sent from heaven to test all those who dwell on the earth" (Rev. 3:10). These two provide *help from heaven* for all those who desire to be faithful to God and His truth.

Time Frame of the Ministry of the Two Witnesses
As we've said, the time frame for their ministry is somewhat outside the simple progression of the sevens, yet it fits here in Revelation *subject-wise*; that is, we have been looking at <u>the part that the saints play in these end-time events</u>. Clearly, these two play a crucial and highly significant role; as we progress further, we will see a deeper, more hidden message of the saints' role in the overthrow of evil on the earth, confirming the mind of the Lord <u>in placing the subject of the two witnesses so close to the taking and eating of the scroll and to the mandate to measure</u>. As far as the timing issue, the *conclusion* of their ministry (Rev. 11:11-15) occurs at a specific point in the chronology of the sevens. This reminds us, as we mentioned in *Part I*, that their 3½-year (42-month) ministry *begins* at some point during the first half of the 70th week, since it *concludes* at some point during the second half of those seven years, between the trumpet and bowl judgments. (It is interesting to consider, therefore, once

we are in the 70th week and we see the beginning of their ministry, that if we look ahead 42 months, and then backward, estimating the possible length of the trumpet judgments, we now have a general clue as to when the rapture might occur.)

There is further light in Scripture regarding these two which is extremely helpful to us. But first, a prophetic word, gifted to the church almost two hundred years ago, also sheds great light on this time in the future, and is closely linked with the ministry of these two witnesses. Let's take a look at it.

CHAPTER 35

The Vision of Margaret MacDonald

Idiscovered this prophecy in the back of Hal Lindsay's book, *The Rapture,* years ago in my early studies of end-times. From the first time I read it, I was very drawn to it and impressed by it. I must also say that it has been, amazingly, the subject of the most consistent and outrageous misrepresentation by otherwise-reputable men of God (whose names I will not mention) that I think I have seen in all my years of walking with the Lord. I don't think I have ever heard it referred to it except erroneously. The principal misrepresentation is that this prophecy, given to a "misguided, gullible, and rather sickly" young girl, is the origin of the pre-tribulation rapture view. The irony of this viewpoint is that a simple reading of it makes clear that Margaret was giving wisdom to the people of God *as they are present on the earth during the Great Tribulation.* This consistent misrepresentation of it has almost forced me to conclude that God, in His inscrutable and sometimes humorous wisdom, has deliberately chosen *to hide* the treasure that it is until it is His time to release it to His people. It is a great joy and privilege for me to share it in this writing. I share it in the hope that there will be people of God out there who, upon reading it, will recognize the treasure that it is, especially that it *will be* for the final generation of saints who see the rapture. In it is priceless instruction for those who have ears to hear.

Margaret's Vision

The vision was first received in 1830 and published in the Robert Norton publication, <u>Memoirs of James and George Macdonald, of Port-Glasgow</u> (1840). (References to Zechariah 4 are marked with an asterisk.)

It was first the awful state of the land that was pressed upon me. I saw the blindness of the people to be very great. I felt the cry of "Liberty!" just to be the hiss of the serpent, to drown them in perdition. It was just "no, God."

I repeated the words, 'Now there is distress of nations, with perplexity, the seas and the waves roaring, men's hearts failing them for fear—now look out for the sign of the Son of man.' Here I was made to stop and cry out, 'O it is not known what the sign of the Son of man is; the people of God think they are waiting, but they know not what it is.' I felt this needed to be revealed, and that there was great darkness and error about it, but suddenly what it was burst upon me with a glorious light.

Comments

Conditions in the world at the end.

Men respond to the cataclysms of the 6th seal (Luke 21:26), which signal the saint to look for "the sign of the Son of Man."

But what is that sign? What are we actually looking for?

I saw it was just the Lord himself descending from Heaven with a shout, just the glorified man, even Jesus; but that all must, as Stephen was, be filled with the Holy Ghost, that they might look up, and see the brightness of the Father's glory. I saw the error to be, that men think that it will be something seen by the natural eye, but 'tis spiritual discernment that is needed, the eye of God* in his people. Many passages were revealed, in a light in which I had not before seen them.

I repeated, 'Now is the kingdom of Heaven like unto ten virgins, who went forth to meet the Bridegroom, five wise and five foolish; they that were foolish took their lamps, but took no oil with them, but they that were wise took oil in their vessels with their lamps.' 'But be ye not unwise, but understanding what the will of the Lord is; and be not drunk with wine wherein is excess, but be filled with the Spirit.' This was the oil the wise virgins took in their vessels – this is the light to be kept burning – the light of God – that we may discern that which cometh not with observation to the natural eye. Only those who have the light of God within them will see the sign of his appearance.

No need to follow them who say, 'see here,' or 'see there,' for his day shall be as the lightning to those in whom the living Christ is. 'Tis Christ in us that will lift us up – he is the light – 'tis only those that are alive in him that will be caught up to meet him in the air. I saw that we must be in the spirit, that we might see spiritual things. John was in the spirit, when he saw a throne set in Heaven. But I saw that the glory of the ministration of the Spirit had not been known.

I repeated frequently, 'But the spiritual temple must and shall be reared, and the fullness of Christ be poured into his body, and then shall we be caught up to meet him.' Oh none will be counted worthy of this calling but his body, which is the church, and which must be a candlestick all of gold.*

I often said, 'Oh, the glorious inbreaking of God which is now about to burst on this earth; Oh, the glorious temple which is now about to be reared,* the bride adorned for her husband; and oh what a holy, holy bride she must be, to be prepared for such a glorious bridegroom.'

I said, 'Now shall the people of God have to do with realities – now shall the glorious mystery of God in our nature be known – now shall it be known what it is for man to be glorified.' I felt that the revelation of Jesus Christ had yet to be opened up – it is not knowledge *about* God that it contains, but it is an *entering into* God – I saw that there was to be a glorious breaking in of God. I felt as Elijah, surrounded with chariots of fire. I saw as it were, the spiritual temple reared, and the Head Stone brought forth with shoutings of 'grace, grace' unto it.* It was a glorious light above the brightness of the sun, that shown round about me.

I felt that those who were filled with the Spirit could see spiritual things and feel walking in the midst of them, while those who had not the Spirit could see nothing – so that two shall be in one bed, the one taken, another left, because the one has the light of God within while the other cannot see the Kingdom of Heaven.

I saw the people of God in an awfully dangerous situation, surrounded by nets and entanglements, about to be tried, and many about to be deceived and fall. Now will the Wicked be revealed, with all power and signs and lying wonders, so that if it were possible, the very elect will be deceived. This is the fiery trial which is to try us. It will be for the purging and purifying of the real members of the body of Jesus; but Oh, it will be a fiery trial. Every soul will be shaken to the very center. The enemy will try to shake everything we have believed in – but the trial of real faith will be found to honor

It is revealed to her what it really is (Mt.24:3,30). But *the Holy Spirit* will be needed *to see* the Sign. (That is, see it in the spirit, not the natural.)

The danger for the saints will be **a lack of oil – the Holy Spirit.**

Natural knowledge will be insufficient, though one may be born again (a 'virgin').

(The church has been too *natural*, instead of spiritual - 1 Cor. 2:9-16).

The Church referred to as the 'candlestick' (lamp-stand) all of gold.

God's tremendous anointing work with the Bride before Jesus returns.

There will be a *dwelling in the Spirit* which *opens the eyes* of the believer and qualifies him/her for the rapture and enables it.

The people of God will be present during the Great Tribulation and tested to the core (Matt. 24:21-26, 2 Thess. 2:3-9).

and praise and glory. Nothing but what is of God will stand. The stony-ground hearers will be made manifest – the love of many will wax cold.

I frequently said that night, and often since, 'Now shall the awful sight of a false Christ be seen on this earth, and nothing but the living Christ in us can detect this awful attempt of the enemy to deceive – for it is with all deceivableness of unrighteousness he will work – he will have a counterpart for every part of God's truth and a counterfeit for every work of the Spirit. The Spirit must and will be poured out on the Church, that she may be purified and filled with God – and just in proportion as the Spirit of God works, so will he – when our Lord anoints men with power, so will he. This is particularly the nature of the trial, through which those are to pass who will be counted worthy to stand before the Son of man.

There will be outward trial too, but 'tis principally temptation. It is brought on by the outpouring of the Spirit, and will just increase in proportion as the Spirit is poured out. The trial of the Church is from Antichrist. It is by being filled with the Spirit that we shall be kept.

I frequently said, **'Oh be filled with the Spirit – have the light of God in you, that you may detect satan – be full of eyes* within – be clay in the hands of the potter – submit to be filled, filled with God.** This will build the temple.* It is not by might nor by power, but by my Spirit, saith the Lord.* This will fit us to enter into the marriage supper of the Lamb. I saw it to be the will of God that all should be filled.

But what hindered the real life of God from being received by his people, was their turning from Jesus, who is the way to the Father. They were not entering in by the door. For he is faithful who hath said, 'By me if any man enter in he shall find pasture.' They were passing the cross, through which every drop of the Spirit of God flows to us. All power that comes not through the blood of Christ is not of God. When I say, they are looking from the cross, I feel that there is much in it – they turn from the blood of the Lamb by which we overcome, and in which our robes are washed and made white. There are low views of God's holiness and a ceasing to condemn sin in the flesh, and a looking from him who humbled himself, and made himself of no reputation. Oh! It is needed, much needed at present, a leading back to the cross.

I saw that night, and often since, that there will be an outpouring of the Spirit on the body such as has not been, a baptism of fire, that all the dross may be put away. Oh, there must and will be such an indwelling of the living God as has not been – the servants of God sealed in their foreheads – great conformity to Jesus – just the bride made comely, by his comeliness put on her. This is what we are at present made to pray much for, that speedily we may all be made ready to meet our Lord in the air – and it will be. Jesus wants his bride. His desire is toward us. He that shall come, will come, and will not tarry. Amen and amen. Even so, come Lord Jesus.

The two primary areas of trial under Antichrist:
1. outward trial (persecution and the mark),
2. deception.

He will deceive via:
a. revelation (teaching),
b. signs and wonders

There will be a direct correlation between the outpouring of the Spirit and the testing coming from the enemy.

It is only as we yield, with tender hearts, to be filled with the Spirit that we will pass the tests and be kept from failing and falling.

The church will never outgrow or outlive its need for the Cross of Jesus and true, deep repentance. These *precede* and *enable* the filling of the Spirit.

This conformity to Jesus is the end goal – the completion --of our SALVATION.

Summary of the Vision

The primary message is to describe *the challenges* the church will be facing – the material realm is mentioned ("outward trial"), but the greater challenge is on a spiritual level. Margaret referred over and over to various Scripture passages. They were opened up to her in the light of what she was seeing. The vision as a whole, shines a powerful spotlight on conditions at the end for the church, revealing much that is natural – *soulish* – in the church; revealing that the rapture will not be an automatic thing, even for Christians; and revealing, in vividly clear terms, what must of necessity happen for the saints to overcome and be spiritually prepared for the rapture.

There is no hesitation on God's part: we see a great willingness and longing on the part of God to pour out of Himself upon and *into* His people at that time, which alone will conform us to Christ and equip us to go through the testing successfully. So *finely tuned* will be the deceptive strategies of the enemy, that it is *ONLY* by the Spirit of God within us that we will be able to detect the false from the true. Overcoming in that great, final test will require deep faithfulness to the cross of Jesus, continuing hatred of sin, and ongoing receptivity to the Holy Spirit. But our hearts must be receptive and thirsty for what He is giving, or it may pass over us. Because of all that, it is a word to be given careful attention and prayed over and meditated on, so that it reaches the deep places of our hearts. It comes as a precious gift from the heart of a loving God who desires each of us to be a part of that lovely, victorious Bride!

The Vision's Connection with the Two Witnesses

Now, we are looking at this in connection with the two witnesses, and you might wonder what this vision has to do with them. As I studied the vision years ago, I found that *four* of the Scripture references, marked with an asterisk in the vision, were from Zechariah 4! That launched me into a fascinating study of that chapter, where I realized quickly that what Zechariah was prophesying about was linked not only to the subject of Margaret's vision, but *also to Revelation 11, the two witnesses*. This fourth chapter of Zechariah is the only other place in the Scripture (that I'm aware of) that speaks of these two anointed ones who "stand by the Lord of the whole earth." The fact that the two witnesses are *end-time players* (clear from Revelation 11) told me that Zechariah 4 also pertains *primarily* to the end. Through that chapter I discovered a whole window of additional, rich insight – like a "secret and amazing glimpse" – into the church regarding that coming time. So, these three "words" became a kind of three-fold witness of things that are deeply relevant for the Bride immediately preceding the rapture. The rest of what I discovered we will look at in the next chapter as we proceed with a study of Zechariah 4, linking it to Margaret's vision, and by both of them, discerning God's message to the end-time church!

NOTE: Another extremely valuable prophetic word regarding discernment of deceivers at the end is found in Appendix 9.

CHAPTER 36

Zechariah's Vision

The Background of Zechariah's Vision

Zechariah prophesied in Jerusalem to the returned exiles in the 530's and 520's BC, beginning about seventeen years after the initial return to rebuild the temple. This first group to return from Babylonian exile were led by the civil leadership of Zerubbabel (the leading prince and heir of the Davidic line) and the spiritual leadership of Joshua, the high priest. Zechariah's initial prophecies pertained to the restoration of God's favor for Judah and Jerusalem and His determination to start afresh with them in the rebuilding of the temple (which had been destroyed in 586 BC under Nebuchadnezzar). But already by the second chapter of Zechariah, it is evident that far more than just the immediate situation is on God's mind. Over and over, He speaks through Zechariah of events that will take place more than 500 years later at the birth of Messiah, and then thousands of years later at Messiah's second coming.

In the vision of Zechariah 4, we will see this blending of the current situation with events that will be far in the future. The return around 538 BC had been specifically for the rebuilding of the temple at Jerusalem. The temple site, as well as the city itself, lay in ruins from the terrible devastation of 586 BC. Amid much adversity from local enemies, work had begun on the temple and the foundation had been completed, but adversaries had finally succeeded in getting a "writ of cessation" from Cambyses. It wasn't until the second year of the succeeding king, Darius Hystapes, that appeal was made and accepted for them to complete the building of the temple. Two months before this vision of chapter 4, the work had been resumed. But it was still proceeding amid much adversity, and God sent His prophets Haggai and Zechariah to encourage this small remnant in their building efforts.[1] This, then, is the background for the chapter we will be looking at, but there will actually be only a brief portion of it that relates to events at that time. It becomes evident that the weightier issues on God's mind are those of the *future* which *pertain to the church at the very end of this age.* Let's take a look.

Zechariah 4

The Vision

> 1 Now the angel who talked with me came back and wakened me, as a man who is wakened out of his sleep.

---

1   Ezra 3:8 – 6:15

2 And he said to me, "What do you see?" So I said, "I am looking, and there is a lampstand of solid gold with a bowl on top of it, and on the stand seven lamps with seven pipes to the seven lamps.

3 Two olive trees are by it, one at the right of the bowl and the other at its left."

Here is the vision. Zechariah sees the 'Menorah,' familiar to the Jews as the light source in the Tabernacle, with two olive 'branches' or 'trees' which stand on each side of the lampstand. Over the seven lamps is a bowl, into which oil flows from the two olive sources; from the bowl, a pipe runs to each lamp with a continuous flow of oil keeping the flame strong and bright. Although the Menorah is familiar, the olive branches and the bowl are new elements.

There is no way for Zechariah to understand the significance of the Menorah other than as a light source. It falls to John in Revelation to make known the *spiritual reality* and significance of it. Now that we *have* Revelation, we know that the seven lamps represent the seven church ages, which altogether comprise the church of Jesus Christ, from Pentecost to the end of the age.

The Message of the Vision

4 So I answered and spoke to the angel who talked with me, saying, "What are these, my lord?"

5 Then the angel who talked with me answered and said to me, "Do you not know what these are?" And I said, "No, my lord."

6 So he answered and said to me: "This is the word of the Lord to Zerubbabel: 'Not by might nor by power, but by My Spirit,' says the Lord of hosts.

7 'Who are you, O great mountain? Before Zerubbabel you shall become a plain! And he shall bring forth the capstone with shouts of "Grace, grace to it!"'

Zechariah (clearly) does not have understanding of what he is seeing, and so the angel instructing him tells him that the essential message of the vision is: "Not by might nor by power, but by My Spirit." This is a fairly well-known verse, but we have seldom considered the context of it. We will return to this shortly.

Further Message of the Vision

8 Moreover the word of the Lord came to me, saying:

9 "The hands of Zerubbabel have laid the foundation of this temple; His hands shall also finish it. Then you will know that the Lord of hosts has sent Me to you.

10 For who has despised the day of small things? For these seven rejoice to see the plumb line in the hand of Zerubbabel. They are the eyes of the Lord, which [scan to and fro][1] throughout the whole earth."

[1]*shut* H7751S – to push forth; to travel, going to and fro (as to row with oars)

Here we see the brief connection with contemporary events. A word of encouragement is given to Zerubbabel, that even as he had overseen the laying of the foundation, so he would also preside over the completion of the temple.

But there is so much more that pertains to the church age and the conclusion of that *spiritual* temple which is the church. And again, we see a connection with Revelation, with the seven – that is, the seven lamps -- being called "the eyes of the Lord, sent forth into all the earth." Perhaps we would question that we could interpret 'the eyes' that way, except that the Holy Spirit has already done that in Rev. 5:6, 4:5, and 1:20. Continuing the picture, the Lord Jesus *is* the foundation of the true temple, laid primarily by the apostles and prophets[2] during the first church age. It has remained to the successive ages to build on that foundation. And yet as we saw in *Part 1* when we studied the church ages, there

---

2 1 Cor. 3:11, Eph. 2:20

has been *much opposition and error, with the building frequently brought to a standstill.* This temple of Zerubbabel is *a type* of the spiritual temple, the church. Even though the foundation was completed in the first church age, it has been *the exception* rather than the rule, that a *building permit* for the superstructure was given by God in local churches throughout the centuries of the church.[3] As with Zerubbabel's temple, there has been *a delay* in the finishing of the spiritual temple. <u>Although the foundation was laid early, this chapter is giving us understanding as to the timing and the means by which that all-important, spiritual temple will be completed.</u>

Notice the 'plumb line' in the hand of Zerubbabel. Again, he is a type of Christ here – the One who has been supervising the building of the temple. This spiritual temple of the ages, this temple of all temples, must be built according to the *strict and perfect specifications* of the gospel and the covenant Christ instituted at His death and resurrection. In other words, we are reminded of the "measuring" taking place as the Jews make their slow turn back toward God. There is a new covenant, with new stipulations, now required for righteous standing before God. These seven *see* – have revelation of – these righteous requirements of God; that this new temple cannot be built with wood, hay, or stubble – with the abilities and skills of natural man. They *see* that it must be built under an anointing that has been received following repentance and surrender and faith. They *see* this and *walk in it.* Therefore, their building activity in the kingdom is *in the spirit.* It is acceptable to God. The fact that these seven *see* – discern – the plumbline, *identifies them.* There are many in the kingdom who don't belong there. There are many who are deceived; who are counterfeits, pretenders, *busy* in the kingdom.[4] But those who make up the spiritual reality of the church, who truly know the Lord, are those who *have revelation of the plumb line.* They are of the same nature as the chief Cornerstone, they have been tried and tested, and have let Him have His way with them.[5]

The Eyes of the Lord

Here again, as in Revelation 5, those who are joined to the Lord Jesus by faith are identified as "the eyes of the Lord." They are the burning lamps, burning with the Holy Spirit and vision. Their eye is *single* – that is, they have a single heart, devoted wholly to the Lord, that gives them *inner eyes that are full of light.*[6] Luke explains:

> **If then your whole body is full of light, having no part dark, the whole body will be full of light, as when the bright shining of a lamp gives you light." Luke 11:36**

For those who are fully consecrated, there is *no part dark*; we move past seeing merely with natural eyes – with the eyes of fear or doubt, religious tradition, human reason, or simply our own personal needs. Out of our union with Him, increasingly understood and walked in, comes the ability to see, not just ourselves, but others and the world around us, with His eyes. Aligning ourselves with Him and His purposes *by faith* will enable us to see His kingdom and understand His ways; we will become able to assess things with His wisdom and perspective. Our heart, mind, emotions, spirit, and even our subconscious will all become illuminated with the light of God shining throughout, able to give His discernment on any issue as He wills. This is the *spiritual man* who has the mind of Christ; it is the fully mature believer, who, through use and repetition, has *exercised* his 'inner organ of perception and judgment' until he has become skilled at hearing the voice of God and distinguishing that which is of God from that which, though it *appears good*, is *not* of God.[7]

The Two Olive Branches

> 11 Then I answered and said to him, "What are these two olive trees — at the right of the lampstand and at its left?"
> 12 And I further answered and said to him, "What are these two olive branches that drip into the receptacles of the two gold pipes from which the golden oil drains?"

---

3   Heb. 6:1-3
4   See Matt. 13:37-43.
5   See Is. 28:16
6   Matt. 6:22-24 (and the context around those verses)
7   1 Cor. 2:10-16; Heb. 5:14

13 Then he answered me and said, "Do you not know what these are?" And I said, "No, my lord."

14 So he said, "These are the two anointed ones, who stand beside the Lord of the whole earth." Zechariah 4:1-14

Zechariah had one question left. We note the repetition; the original Hebrew writers didn't have a bold font option, so repetition was used to give emphasis. The repetition of the question lets us know we are at a key point in the message – there is *significance* to the two olive 'branches.' Speaking of them now, we wouldn't even know that they were people, except that they are identified here as "the two anointed ones (lit., 'sons of oil') who stand beside (or 'before') the Lord of the whole earth." That tells us they are people, but who exactly they are, anyone could only guess until the final book of the Bible was given. Because there we see again the "two olive trees" and the two "lampstands" that "stand before the God of the earth" – they are revealed to us as the two witnesses: those two with the amazing ministry that is viewed by the whole earth.[8] Both passages – Zechariah and Revelation -- speak of them as standing in the presence of the God of the earth. God's eyes search and oversee ALL that is going on in the earth, and they are His mouthpiece for whatever He would say and do at this time in the future. This stance before God is their greatest and most outstanding characteristic, emphasized by the Spirit to both Zechariah and John. There they stand, in constant and open communion with God, a direct link between heaven and earth, and providing a continual supply of God's current, living words to the earth.

The angel's answer here, that the two olive 'branches' are the "two anointed ones who stand before the Lord of the whole earth," snuggles this *whole chapter* right into Revelation 11! The linking of Zechariah 4 and Revelation 11 via the two witnesses greatly amplifies our understanding of both passages: Zechariah's vision reveals their vital ministry *to the church*; and Revelation 11 explains in much greater detail the nature and setting of their ministry and where and when it will take place – in Jerusalem *during the final seven years* of this age! It confirms that Zechariah's vision is of the completion of that *spiritual* temple, *the church,* begun at Pentecost so long ago. There has been long delay following the laying of the foundation, but at the close of the age, right before the rapture, *the building will be completed.* The full number will be brought in (the Great Commission accomplished), and the purity and maturity that God is looking for (to make it the perfect dwelling place for Him) will be achieved. This will happen in the fires of purification during the brief reign of Antichrist; and the *means* by which it will be accomplished is not by (human) might or power, but *by the Spirit of the Lord!* A tremendous, ongoing, outpouring of the Spirit of God will finally bring to completion the beautiful habitation of God which He has been building for the last 2000 years.

NOTE: Chapter 19 of *Part 1* deals also with the two witnesses.

Summing It Up

So, what it is that we are seeing here?! We have seen that the connection of Zechariah 4 with the two witnesses of Revelation 11 confirms that Zechariah's vision is a word for the end-times, and more specifically, for the end-time *church,* as it is speaking, almost exclusively, to the seven-branched lampstand. Taking it a step farther, even as the Spirit of God applied it through Margaret, it is given to the church for that future time of intense pressures and trials under Antichrist when the Spirit of God is putting the final, finishing touches on the Bride *before the capstone* – the Headstone – is *joined to her in the air at the rapture!*[9] And we are told that her readiness for this will be achieved *only* by *abundance of the Holy Spirit,* not by any natural might or power. Furthermore, we are told that there will be two KEY players who, having a direct and continuous connection to God in heaven, will, by that connection, bring to the church *the necessary supply of the Holy Spirit* at that time!

---

8 Rev. 11:3-12
9 Compare with Luke 17, where, when the disciples ask Jesus where they will be taken, He answers, "Wherever the (living) body is, the eagles will be gathered together." The eagles – those who see a great distance and soar on the wind/spirit; 'will gather together' *episunago* G1996T – "to gather together in the same place where others are already assembled." Jesus will circle the globe, collecting His own and gathering them unto Him in the sky. This is the same word used for the rapture in Mt. 24:31 and Mark 13:27.

This is a signal to the church of that final time to be ready to receive -- *in copious amounts* -- the anointing that God will be pouring forth in great and unrelenting rivers, through these two witnesses! As the time here prophesied arrives, it will culminate in the joining of the church to the Headstone in the air amid great shouts of "Grace, grace!" to it. Here again we see repetition, telling us that this *joining in the air* is GRACE from beginning to end: GRACE will be needed – and given – in abundance, for the joining of the Head to the body! It will not be automatic! Peter spoke of the *grace* that comes to us *at the unveiling of Jesus Christ.*[10] Grace is always supplied whenever we see Him more clearly. At that time, we will see Him with a clarity we've never had before: We will *see Him as He is* – every hindrance and veil removed – and the *grace will be supplied to become exactly as He is.*[11]

Babel Kingdom Defeated

But there is more here, and it is a key part of this message. All of this is taking place in the presence of, and with deadly *opposition from,* an overwhelming and fully manifesting *kingdom of darkness!* The consensus in the world is "who is like the beast? Who is able to make war with him?" This 'great mountain' of the Babylon kingdom, called "the destroying mountain" by Jeremiah,[12] is intimidating, powerful, and, by the standards of this age, clearly *invincible.* And yet this is, at long last, *the time for the overthrow of this kingdom.* This is it. This is the final, climactic clash of the two kingdoms, and it's time for the "stone cut out without hands" to come crashing into that Babel world system, bringing its demise forever! And so, the message is not *just* that the anointing is needed for the final preparations and purification of the Bride. It's also that the anointing is needed *as the church cooperates with Christ in the final and ultimate defeat of the kingdom of darkness* – that "great mountain," which before Zerubbabel – Christ – will be *flattened as a plain.* It's the Lamb with seven horns and seven eyes who will do this; it's Zerubbabel *with those seven.* And **the message to the seven is to be not fearful, but to receive God's tremendous supply of anointing with which** *to prevail against the enemy!* This coming time of great darkness on the earth will be the time of the church's greatest, shining glory. This is the time for the Bride to come forth "beautiful as Tirzah, comely as Jerusalem, and terrible as an army with banners."[13] When 'gross darkness' covers the people of the earth, upon His own people the Lord's glory shall arise, and His beauty will be seen upon them.[14] Before this temple of inestimable beauty, grace, and glory, the *mountain will be razed to the ground!* This is not a time to shrink from, but a time to reach forward toward, for it's a time of the *impartation of the life of God into His people in a way not before known!*

Light for the Jews

Although this vision speaks primarily to the church, we must remember the testimony that the two witnesses will also be supplying to the Jews. With supernatural attestation and powerful words of testimony, they will be giving witness to the God of heaven and His Messiah, Jesus Christ. The church, offering refuge to the 144,000, will also be giving testimony to Jesus Christ. (Remember our role with the Lamb – eating the scroll and testifying?) The joining *in the air* of the house with the Headstone is the *finishing* of the temple spoken of in v. 9: "The hands of Zerubbabel have laid the foundation of this house ... His hands shall also finish it ...." And then the Spirit of Christ, speaking prophetically through Zechariah, adds this seemingly random statement, "... and you shall know that the Lord of Hosts has sent me unto you." Ahhh! The beauty of it all! It's *not* random at all! *At that time* -- when the blackened skies split open and the glorious Lord descends, gathering His people unto Himself, *completing the temple* – the Jews will see all this happening, and **then they will KNOW,** this is **our Messiah – Jesus, *sent to us by the Father 2000 years ago!* So remarkable! It is all so lovely. Beyond words. Mighty God. What glory that will be! Surely, the testimony of the two witnesses, going on both before and after the rapture, will contribute to this recognition of the Messiah. It won't be ALL the Jewish remnant at that time – just the 144,000. The rest will come later in the seven years.

---

10 1 Peter 1:13
11 1 John 3:2
12 Jeremiah 51:25 (Dan. 2:36-44, Rev. 17-18)
13 Song of Solomon 6:4
14 Isaiah 60:1-2

One final note on this: this is also tremendous testimony to *the whole earth*. This is the "time of testing of the whole earth." Here in Jerusalem, the epicenter of the earth, the great, final 'stand-off' is taking place between Satan's seed -- Antichrist and the false prophet -- and (part of) the 'seed of the woman' – the two witnesses who stand before the Lord of the whole earth! All will see! All will hear the words from both sides, and have the final opportunity to make their choice: to *hear* God, repent, and receive the Lord Jesus before it's too late, or to make their final rejection of truth before *final judgment* begins to fall. (We are speaking here primarily of their ministry before the rapture/6th seal takes place.)

Transition to Chapter 12 – Revelation 11:15-19

With the ascension of the two witnesses (Revelation 11:12-13), we find ourselves at the conclusion of the 6th trumpet and at the beginning of the 7th. This, of course, gives us the *time placement* of the two witnesses in the chronology of events, but in terms of the content of Revelation, it doesn't launch us yet into the 7th trumpet. There is more 'parenthetical' information yet; in fact, the chronological account doesn't resume until Revelation 15 and 16! We will not cover all those chapters, but are going to move on now into Revelation 12.

Following the announcement of the kingdom of the world becoming Christ's (imminently), the twenty-four elders are seen worshipping God and saying,

> **"We give thanks to you, Lord God Almighty, who is and who was, for you have taken your great power and begun to reign. Revelation 11:17 ESV**

The action verbs here (referring to God) are in the past tense, and leading us toward Revelation 12, they signal a *backward look* at how God Himself set all the events in motion that have brought things now to this point, on the cusp of the bowl judgments. (Some of those events are listed in v. 18: the anger of the nations,[15] then the wrath of God,[16] God's judgment upon the [spiritually] dead, and the rewarding of the saints, etc.). Revelation 12, which we move into next, gives a behind-the-scenes look at *what powerful action God took* to trigger the climactic Abomination of Desolation. It is one of the most amazing chapters in the book of Revelation, and we look to the Holy Spirit to assist us in understanding it!

---

15 Ps. 2:1-3
16 Rev. 6:15-17

SECTION 14

REVELATION 12

CHAPTER 37

The Players of
Revelation 12

Revelation 12 is a mighty chapter, holding KEY events in the unfolding of God's strategic works at the end of the age. In it both the righteous and the wicked are seen reaching the fullness of maturity; the conflict which we see occurring between them in this chapter reaches to the very heaven of God, depicting powerful confrontation, great danger, and both cosmic and terrestrial battle. Here we see, in epic events which straddle the seen and unseen realms, the battle for the earth played out between the Christ of God and His followers, and the dragon and his followers. The 'power players' of this chapter are presented in symbolic form. This has caused uncertainty and guesswork as to their true identity, leading, in many cases, to theories which are both ridiculous and implausible, and which totally miss the mark as to truth. This symbolism might be puzzling, except that we see it as God in His wisdom veiling precious truth from the superficial glance and natural wisdom. Let's take a look, trusting God for His wisdom and understanding.

> 1 Now a great sign appeared in heaven: a woman clothed with the sun, with the moon under her feet, and on her head a garland of twelve stars.
> 2 Then being with child, she cried out in labor and in pain to give birth.
> 3 And another sign appeared in heaven: behold, a great, fiery red dragon having seven heads and ten horns, and seven diadems on his heads.
> 4 His tail drew a third of the stars of heaven and threw them to the earth. And the dragon stood before the woman who was ready to give birth, to devour her Child as soon as it was born.
> 5 She bore a male Child who was to rule all nations with a rod of iron. And her Child was caught up to God and His throne.
> 6 Then the woman fled into the wilderness, where she has a place prepared by God, that they should feed her there one thousand two hundred and sixty days.   Revelation 12:1-6

The Identity of the Woman and Her Child

The first thing we notice is that the woman, and therefore presumably her child also, is referred to as "a sign." That is, she is not a literal personality, but a depiction which, as any sign does, *points to* someone or something else. We will therefore need to establish what she signifies based on how she is depicted. Before we do that, however, there are a couple things of <u>background</u> and <u>context</u> to consider which will help us establish her identity.

Two Timing Issues

<u>First</u>, remember that **Jesus said this whole portion of Revelation -- from Rev. 4:1 onward, pertains to *the things which will be hereafter*** – i.e., end-time events. We don't have Scriptural 'permission' to take this chapter *out of an end-time setting*. Whatever these events of chapter 12 signify, they are part of the wrap-up events of the end. This end-time requirement eliminates suggestions that the woman could be Mary or Israel giving birth to Jesus. We'll see more reasons shortly against those options.

<u>Second</u>, we have said that with the parenthetical portions, we must look to their content to fit them into the chronology of the sevens. This ability to find the chronological context is provided twice in chapter 12:

1. V. 6 tells us the woman is fed in the wilderness for 1260 days (exactly 42 months or 3½ years), and
2. V. 14 tells us the woman is nourished for "a time, and times, and half a time" in the wilderness; that is, for a year, two years, and half a year, adding up to the same length of time, 3½ years.[1] We combine these times with the rest of the chapter and can see clearly that this time in the wilderness does indeed refer to the second half of the last seven years, i.e., the Great Tribulation. Therefore, the primary events depicted here occur within the last seven years and begin *right before the midpoint*.

Rule with a Rod of Iron

We are told that this child is to "rule all nations with a rod of iron." This is of great help in narrowing down the range of possibilities as to the identity of both the woman and the child. We know that Jesus will rule in this way. Does Scripture speak of anyone else who will rule in this way? There are four references to ruling with a rod of iron:

Ps. 2:9 – Jesus
Rev. 2:27 – the overcomers
Rev. 12:5 – this reference
Rev. 19:15 – Jesus

We see clearly from the second reference that, in addition to Jesus, those who overcome, *sharing Millennial rule with Him,* will also rule with a rod of iron.

Thoughts on the Identity of the Woman and the Child

As far as suggestions as to whom this woman may signify: Some say the woman is Mary giving birth to Jesus; others, that it is Israel giving birth to Jesus or the church.

1. Is the woman Mary?
   a. Mary didn't flee to the wilderness after giving birth to Jesus.
   b. This glorious description of the woman doesn't fit Mary.
   c. If the woman were Mary, she wouldn't be designated as a 'sign,' i.e., representing something.
2. Is the child Jesus?
   a. He wasn't caught up to heaven immediately after birth, but remained on earth to grow into manhood.
   b. There is another possibility for someone who rules with a rod of iron.

---

1 This length of time is repeatedly given in Scripture as referring to the second half of the 70th week: Dan. 11:2, 12:7; Rev. 11:2, 13:5.

3. Is the woman Israel?
   a. None of the glorious features of the woman fit Israel, which is still under the Old Covenant at this point in the future, operating in the shadow of the New Covenant.
   b. We've already seen that the child can't be Jesus. As far as it being the church, how can unbelieving Israel give birth to those who believe in the Messiah?
4. Finally, that this is an end-time scenario *makes all of these impossible.* Both Jesus and the church were "birthed" 2,000 years ago, and neither were caught up to heaven immediately afterward.

If Jesus and the "overcomers" are the only ones identified in Scripture who will rule with a rod of iron, and the child can't be Jesus, that leaves only <u>a group called "overcomers"</u> as the possible identity of the child. So who, then, is the woman?

The Description and Identity of the Woman

Let's back up now and take a closer look at the description of the woman, because the way in which she is described (as well as the *actions* which follow in chapter 12) help us identify her.

"a woman clothed with the sun, with the moon under her feet, and on her head a garland of twelve stars"

The sun and moon are in contrast here – clothed with the one, victorious over the other. What do the sun and moon represent? This is a key to identifying the woman.

<u>The sun:</u>

A heavenly body with its own life and light -- shining as the sun characterizes Christ in His glory:

- Jesus' face shone as the sun at transfiguration.
- "His countenance was as the sun shining in its strength" - Revelation 1:16.
- He is called "the Sun of Righteousness" - Malachi 4:2.

Thus we see the woman clothed with Christ's glory, the very glory of heaven.

<u>The moon:</u>

Unlike the sun, the moon does not have its own light. It shines *only* with reflected light. What part of God's work with man shines only with reflected light? I believe it's the Old Covenant – it shines with the reflected glory of the New Covenant. Everything about the Old Covenant was a shadow *cast* by a reality in the New. The law held up the standard of God's righteousness, but it made no provision for the ability to perform it – it was empty, lifeless.

For the law, having a shadow of the good things to come, and not the very image of the things, can never with these same sacrifices, which they offer continually year by year, make those who approach perfect. Hebrews 10:1

Of necessity, this old provision had to give way to something new and better. Faith in Jesus' death and resurrection brings the very life of Christ into the believer, clothing him with God's righteousness and glory.

We recall also that the whole religious calendar of feasts under the Old Covenant was based on the monthly cycles of *the moon.* The moon, with its cold, reflected glory, is a good way to represent the Old Covenant of the law. This woman stands with all the demands of the law under her feet – demands which minister condemnation, bring a curse, and lead only to death.[2] She has battled and *overcome* every lie that she has her own inherent righteousness, and she has instead received God's righteousness as a gift.

<u>Upon her head a crown of twelve stars:</u>
This is a *stephanos* – the crown of the victor in Olympic games. The glory upon her has not been reached with ease – on the one hand it's a gift ("imputed, positional righteousness"), on the other, it's been hard-fought and hard-won ("out-worked, experiential righteousness"). Stars are heavenly bodies; like the sun, they contain light within themselves. The seven stars in Jesus' hand (Rev. 1) are persons who carry a message from heaven. Abraham's seed – the heaven-born seed – were likened to the stars of heaven.[3] Jesus is called 'the Star of Jacob.'[4] This crown is adorned with twelve stars. <u>Twelve is the number of heavenly authority and administration.</u> When God initiated the human bodies of authority in both the Old Testament (the tribes of Israel) and the New (the apostles), it was with the number twelve. This woman is "a royal priesthood," standing before God in both a princely and priestly function. She is crowned with glory and honor; the beauty of the Lord is upon her.[5] The fact that she is seen crowned in this way speaks to us of the <u>governmental authority</u> of God that is hers; and indeed, that is what we will see in this chapter: **God is using her -- including her -- in His end-time initiatives and actions. The twelve stars she wears link us with the words of chapter 11: ". . . You have taken your great authority and have begun to reign" (v. 17). In chapter 12 we see God, *through the woman*, taking the *first step* to engage and displace the enemy on a cosmic scale.**

The woman, then, clothed with the glory of God's own righteousness and wrapped in that glory, lives by God's eternal life, transcending the law and time and this age. She belongs to Heaven – to eternity. This woman is made up of, is constituted of, *many individuals*. This is how she is a sign; she is a corporate woman; she is all the truly born-again saints. She is not *separate from* them – they *constitute* her. All the saints of all time make up the woman. They are her SEED. Paul says of her, "Jerusalem which is above... is free and is the mother of us all" (Gal. 4:26). He goes on to say that she is "the mother of those who are born after the Spirit" (v. 29). She makes up all the saints who were "chosen by God before the foundation of the world to be holy and without blame before Him in love" (Eph. 1:4). In the future she will be the Bride of Christ, the new Jerusalem coming down from heaven in Revelation 21, providing a dwelling place for God Himself. In coming to Christ, we have come to "Mount Zion, and unto the city of the living God, the heavenly Jerusalem...," to a city that "has foundations, whose Builder and Maker is God" (Heb. 12:22; 11:10). This is the *spiritual reality* of the woman – the *truth* about her. She is depicted from a *heavenly perspective* – the way God sees her, yet she is fighting battles of truth and faith – battles that occur here on earth. We will take a closer look at her travail in a later chapter.

The Man Child

> **And she brought forth a man[1] child,[2] who was to rule[3] all nations with a rod of iron; and her Child was caught up unto God and to his throne. v. 5 KJV**

[1]*arrhen arsen* G730T – a male (in the neuter gender)
[2]*huios* G5207T – a son
[3]*poimaino* G4165T– to feed, to tend a flock, keep sheep; to rule, govern

Notice the words above for "man child." *Arsen*, male, is in the neuter gender, telling us that rather than strictly denoting the *male gender*, the emphasis is on **the general qualities of masculinity – that is, strength, power, and**

---

2   In a broader sense, we could say that the moon represents ALL false religion, because it is all founded on man's own efforts to help himself. Only in Christ is provision made for such sure and spotless righteousness.
3   Gen. 15:5-6
4   Numbers 24:17
5   Psalm 8:5; 90:17; John 17:22

vigor.[6] This is no ordinary child, but, as we shall see, one with extraordinary maturity that has attained the highest virtues that man is capable of.

In being "birthed," the child has become *separated and distinguished from* the rest of the believers. From that moment the child is in danger. But God has birthed this child for a heavenly rather than an earthly purpose, and before the dragon can destroy it, God catches it up to His throne in heaven.[7] As we progress in the chapter the reason for this will become evident.

We can assume that, like its mother, this child also is *a sign*, signifying – also like its mother – a corporate group. As Seiss has observed, because this child, "is collective and composite, the same as the mother, … it likewise includes people of both sexes."[8] Since overcomers in the church are the only ones other than Jesus identified as ruling with a rod of iron, we surmise that this child constitutes a group of *overcomers*. And indeed, as we see here, it is the overcomers who will share rule with Jesus in the Millennium:

> **And he who overcomes and keeps My works until the end, to him I will give power over the nations.**
> *'He shall rule them with a rod of iron; They shall be dashed to pieces like the potter's vessels'*
> **-- as I also have received from My Father. Revelation 2:26-27** (emphasis added)

We note briefly *poimaino* (above) – to rule and govern, but as a shepherd does his flock – with kindness and care, nurturing, protection, and provision. But since this shepherding will be done with a "rod of iron," it will be an *absolute authority*.

Michael

Michael is probably the least mysterious of the characters presented here. He's one of the highest ranking of all the angels and is called the archangel ("the chief angel") in Jude 9. Although the definite article is used, there were a number of archangels. Michael is one of the seven archangels that stand at the throne of God; in Jewish teaching those seven are called "the Angels of the Presence."[9] As we've seen, he's the angel who stands on behalf of Israel:

> **… there is none that holds with me in these things, but Michael your prince. Daniel 10:21 KJV**

> **At that time Michael shall stand up, the great prince who stands watch over the sons of your people. Daniel 12:1**

Though Michael has been Israel's special angelic protector, he has not been able to prevent the great suffering of the Jewish people down through the centuries. They have endured great hounding, homelessness, and persecution, even unto death. And yet the race has never been in danger of extinction. God's promise was that they would endure as a people *to be restored to Him at the end*.

Michael is the key angelic player in this intense drama of Revelation 12. His actions here, as we shall see, will serve not to protect Israel, but instead, to precipitate Israel's *time of greatest trouble*,[10] at the same time as they initiate the beginning of God's take-back of the earth.

The Dragon

> **And another sign appeared in heaven: behold, a great, fiery red dragon having seven heads and ten horns, and seven diadems on his heads.**

---

6   An observation on v. 5 from *Vincent's Word Studies* in the New Testament (Electronic Database. Copyright © 2006 by Biblesoft, Inc.).

7   It's interesting to notice that the Greek word for "caught up" is *harpazo*, the same word used for the rapture in 1 Thess. 4:17; it is a 'catching up' very similar to the rapture.

8   Joseph A. Seiss, *The Apocalypse* (Grand Rapids: Zondervan Publishing House), p. 298.

9   Tobit 12:15. Enoch 20:7 names the seven as Uriel, Raphael, Raquel, Michael, Sariel, Gabriel, and Remiel. These are undoubtedly the seven referred to in Revelation 8:2: "And I saw the seven angels which stand before God."

10   We will discuss the implications this has for Michael as the restrainer in the next chapter.

His tail drew[1] a third of the stars of heaven and threw[2] them to the earth. And the dragon stood before the woman who was ready to give birth, to devour her Child as soon as it was born.

[1]*suro* G4951T– to drag, draw (present tense)
[2]*ballo* G906T– to throw or cast something without concern as to where it lands; to scatter (past tense)

His Identity

Identifying the dragon is simple: Rev. 12:9 tells us he is "**...that serpent of old, called the Devil and Satan, who deceives the whole world.**" Granting his power to the 'white horse rider' of the first seal, who went forth 'conquering and to conquer,' the serpent in the Garden has now become 'a great, fiery dragon' with a global following and great authority in the earth. With the amassed forces of darkness joined with the cooperating nations of the earth, the serpent is on the cusp of his greatest power. He is about to transition from being the *unseen* "prince of this world"[11] to being the *visible and revealed* "king" who will usurp the place of Christ in the very Holy of Holies, asserting himself as god. We see him here with seven crowned heads and ten horns, showing us clearly that we are in the time of the end when the earth has been divided into ten regions, regions which are giving their allegiance to the dragon.[12] The heads and horns are what is visible of his kingdom on the earth – the governmental structures and the humans who fill them. In a short time, upon reaching the midpoint, we will see crowns on the 10 horns (Rev. 13:1), signifying imperial rule and their absolute power with the antichrist. So, in the dragon we see not only the *earthly kingdom* of darkness, but Satan himself as he expresses himself through this fearsome kingdom. Somehow the dragon knows that what is about to be brought forth with this birth poses *an enormous threat* to his dominion in the earth; he stands before the woman prepared to devour the child at its birth.

The Tail

The tail of this huge dragon reveals to us the *unseen* part of his kingdom: the dragon is dragging one third of the stars of heaven. As we've said, stars refer to heavenly beings, created in beauty and glory; Satan himself was originally called Lucifer, "the day star."[13] These stars are being dragged by Satan, having *already been cast down*. (Notice the verb tenses given with the definitions above.) Though we are seeing the things which shall be at the end, we are being given insight regarding the angels under Satan's control – members of Satan's kingdom of darkness and wickedness. Through rebellion they had been previously cast down from their high place of purity to a lower place, inhabiting now the atmosphere around the earth. This group of 'fallen stars' undoubtedly constitutes the unseen "principalities, powers, rulers of the darkness of this world, the spirits of wickedness in high places,"[14] which execute and enforce Satan's plans in the earth. John sees these fallen stars being *dragged, hauled* by the dragon's tail. We can visualize the tail sweeping back and forth in the earth, flicking these powerful agents of evil here and there, using them to inflict devastation and suffering upon humanity.

> devil – *diabolos* – slanderer, blasphemer
>
> *satan* – *satanas*– from the Hebrew satan - not a proper noun, but an enemy, someone who obstructs or opposes

---

11   John 12:31; 14:30; 16:11; Eph. 2:2
12   Daniel 2:41-44; 7:7,24
13   Job 38:4-7, Isaiah 14:12
14   Eph. 6:12

In Conclusion

What additional insight does Scripture give us of this? As we've mentioned, the birth, the catching up, and the great heavenly battle evidently take place *right before the midpoint.* What does the *chronological* account of events (from the series of sevens) tell us is occurring late in the first half of the 70th week? In fact, that is the time of the seals (Rev. 6), and the terrors of the red horse rider and the black horse rider – war and famines – are upon the earth; also, from Jesus' teaching, rampant plagues and earthquakes. And finally, from the rider of the pale horse, Death and Hell are covering one quarter of the earth, "killing with sword, hunger, death, and the beasts of the earth." Along a different line, the enemy is working both within and without the church with great subtlety and deception. Surely there is direct a connection between these fallen 'stars' on the dragon's tail and all the suffering and evil happening on the earth at this time. The correlation of the dragon and his malignant tail with events we already know will be occurring is a powerful one!

The Woman, Her Seed, and the Serpent -- Perspective

The woman, her seed, the dragon – these players of the near future are characters and terms which take us back to the very beginning of man's time on the earth. Following the fall, God made it clear that the enduring conflict in the earth would be between the seed of the woman and the serpent with its seed; and that ultimately, the woman's seed would win the victory, crushing the head of the serpent.[15] This would mean *redemption* – the *buying back* of lost man and of his dominion over the earth. In Revelation 12, the conflict has now reached fullness. It is time for the *full execution* of the victory that Jesus, *the Seed,* won in His death and resurrection. We see the glorious corporate woman and her seed facing off in conflict with the fully developed seed of the serpent – the dragon and all who make up his kingdom. Here, behind the scenes, is carried out the amazing drama between the woman, the child, the serpent, and God – a drama which serves to catapult events into the final, climactic battle for the rulership of the earth. In this chapter we see the maturation of the offspring of the Seed Christ, and the maturation of Satan in his kingdom followers: the single woman (Eve/Mary), by bearing a multiplied Seed, has become a glorious *corporate* woman, and the single serpent has become a ferocious dragon with all the might of an earth-wide kingdom behind him. **This is the stage being set for the final showdown which will resolve the issue of *who will rule earth.*** The serpent, through his seed Cain, killed the first promised seed, Abel. Through Herod, Satan sought to kill the baby Seed Jesus; he finally succeeded when Jesus reached adulthood, but *only* when his murderous action fulfilled God's great plan for his ultimate defeat! But here again, now at the close of the age, we see a seed, the man child, about to be birthed, and Satan attempting again to murder the seed that will be instrumental in his downfall. Let's continue now with our study of this chapter in Revelation.

We have said that contrary to the pre-tribulation position that the church is not to be found in Revelation after chapter 3, the church *is* seen later in Revelation, although *from a heavenly perspective*. Here is one of those times. The woman (the church), along with her child (also members of the church), is seen on the earth *inside the 70th week.*

---

15   Gen. 3:14-15; 4:25; Gal. 3:16,19,29; 4:4-7

CHAPTER 38

War in Heaven and the Overcomers

The birth and catching up of the man child are followed by certain actions:

6 Then the woman fled into the wilderness, where she has a place prepared by God, that they should feed her there one thousand two hundred and sixty days.

7-8 And war broke out in heaven: Michael and his angels fought with the dragon; and the dragon and his angels fought, but they did not prevail, nor was a place found for them in heaven any longer.

9 So the great dragon was cast out, that serpent of old, called the Devil and Satan, who deceives the whole world; he was cast to the earth, and his angels were cast out with him.

10 Then I heard a loud voice saying in heaven, "Now salvation, and strength,[1] and the kingdom of our God, and the power[2] of His Christ have come, for the accuser of our brethren, who accused them before our God day and night, has been cast down.

11 And they overcame him by the blood of the Lamb and by the word of their testimony, and they did not love their lives to the death.

12 Therefore rejoice, O heavens, and you who dwell in them! Woe to the inhabitants of the earth and the sea! For the devil has come down to you, having great wrath, because he knows that he has a short time." Revelation 12:6-12

[1]*dunamis* G1411T – power, strength, ability
[2]*exousia* G1849T – authority, ability, power, liberty, and privilege to act; ability and strength to give commands that must be obeyed by others

We will deal later with the woman in the wilderness. For now, our focus is on this amazing cosmic battle in the heavens. The message is fairly clear: there is a great battle between the archangel Michael and his angels, and the dragon and his angels. The dragon is cast out of heaven *down to the earth*. We see from v. 10 that he has been in *God's heaven*, standing before the throne *accusing the saints*.

Why Is Satan in Heaven?

This is rather astonishing to us, that *Satan* should be in God's heaven! We always speak in terms of Satan ruling the earth, but through this amazing glimpse of workings in the heavenlies during the 70th week, we see his nasty presence not just on earth, but in heaven itself and on an ongoing basis – "day and night"! We get a glimpse of this from the book of Job, where we see the "sons of God" – that is, mighty angels[1] -- holding counsel with God in heaven. Satan also is there, giving God a hard time over Job. He's there to accuse Job – to expose some kind of sin or weakness in him; it doesn't seem clear to him that there's anything wrong with Job, but he's trying very hard to find something and expose it! In fact, he works continually as the adversary of God's redemptive work with us -- looking to expose sin, weakness, and unbelief—to point it out to God and perhaps even taunt God about it. And yet, God has declared His people righteous with His own righteousness, declaring, "Who shall bring a charge against God's elect? It is God who justifies. Who is he who condemns? It is Christ who died, and furthermore is risen…" (Romans 8:33-34. This is *divinely established truth* which God knows and Satan knows!

What then allows him to accuse continuously those who've been declared righteous? Where is the breakdown that gives him such – what we might call, *outrageous* access? Surely, we must admit with chagrin, the weakness is in us, God's own people: The doubts, fears, unbelief, and outright disobedience, etc., going on in the hearts, minds, and lives of the saints are what give Satan a place to accuse us before God!

In our world, where the physical largely serves as a visual block and veil to the spiritual, we tend not to see the spiritual insecurities in one another (and sometimes even in ourselves). But in the spiritual dimension there is no veil; and doubts and fears, as well as faith, are well-known to God and, to a certain extent, Satan. And we know that **when it comes to the effectiveness of God's salvation in our lives, truth alone is not sufficient; truth must be** *believed* **and** *received* **before it benefits us.** This means that our fears and unbelief serve both to slow God and to enable the enemy, whereas our unwavering faith shuts down the enemy and empowers God.

What Is Taking Place Here?

In this chapter of Revelation, we see God *beginning* His end-time "face-off" with Satan *not on the earth,* but right here, before His very throne! What is going on?! How does this take place? And why *now?* With the accusation having taken place for so long – since the time of the fall – what has caused this great *battle* and the casting down of Satan to take place now -- around the midpoint?

Notice the "they" in verse 11. Although the battle is with Michael and the angels, they are not the 'overcoming ones' referred to here! They do not lay claim to *the blood of the Lamb,* nor does the rest of that verse pertain to them. We realize, then, that "they" refers to this man child – this group – which has been caught up to the throne! And it is confirmed to us that they are overcomers: "They overcame him…" **God has brought them up before His throne – the place where the accusations occur – at this time and for this very purpose: to confront the Accuser** *face to face and to prevail over him!* Has there never before been a group such as this, who came to such a full victory over the enemy's lies and accusations, traps and stratagems? We don't know; at any rate, there is this group *now,* and *now* is the time to cast the enemy *out* and *down* from this high place of continual accusation. These are not shrinking, shamed supplicants. In them, Satan meets *prevailing authority.* In this unexpected encounter before the throne, they step forward, shining with glory, radiant with holiness; he is stunned and falls back; all he can stammer is, "<u>Who</u> <u>are</u> <u>these</u>???" And as my husband expressed it when we were first making this thrilling discovery, their response is simply, "*Hit the road, Jack!*" There is no secret vulnerability due to hidden sin or shame – they are clothed and filled, from inside to out, with the righteousness of their Father. Representing humanity – the group originally entrusted with authority over the earth[2] – this group 'reads Satan the riot act' and tells him, "NO MORE! You are OUT OF HERE!" ***Authorized* in this way by this group,** <u>Michael and his angels</u> **act immediately to enforce the human declaration by engaging Satan in battle and casting him out!** Satan will no longer have access to God's heaven.

---

1   See Ps. 82, where God holds a heavenly council, calling the "gods," that is the "sons of the Most High" (v. 6), to account for failing to administer justice and judgment in the earth.
NOTE: The term "son of God" is used in Scripture for anyone who is a direct creation of God, e.g., Adam, the angels, and those born-again through faith in Christ.
2   Genesis 1:28, Ps. 8:5-6

This is the beginning of the *reduction of Satan's sphere of influence.* And it is executed through this group of overcomers, caught up to heaven at this time in the future. *This then,* is the spiritual backdrop for the Great Tribulation! This is God Himself initiating the crisis period of the Great Tribulation, even as the elders in Revelation 11:17 praised Him because *He "had taken His great power and had begun to reign."* How did He begin to reign? *Through His people* – with their words of authority *directed to Satan before the throne* and carried out by the powers of heaven, Michael and his angels.

This, of course, precipitates events that Satan had been planning all along, except that he is not the one in control; *God Himself* thrusts Satan into the action by casting him out from before His throne! God now will continue to move ahead with His purpose *to unseat Satan* from his place of dominion in the earth. Before He does that, there will be this brief season when tremendous, unprecedented power on the earth is given to this enemy. Of course, we know that even in that, God is simply using the dragon as a tool to carry out His purposes!

The Three Elements of Overcoming
What has enabled this group of saints to release such prevailing authority? Scripture makes it very clear to us. And, we might add, since Jesus came, these have always been, and forever remain, *the keys* to overcoming, in whatever situation we find ourselves.

> **And they overcame him by the blood of the Lamb and by the word of their testimony,[1] and they did not love their lives to the death. Revelation 12:11**

> [1]*marturia* G3141T– testifying; a testimony, as before a judge

We see three elements identified in their overcoming:

1. The blood of the Lamb
This hardly needs to be discussed, for we all know that the only way for sin and guilt to be removed is by the Lamb's blood. If in any area we think we don't need the blood to cover and cleanse us, in that area we have already lost the battle and the hope of overcoming. Our hope and victory are always in Jesus' shed blood and in His death and resurrection on our behalf.

2. The word of their testimony
The saints of God are those who, like Peter, have received *a revelation* from the Father that Jesus is the Messiah of God.[3] To receive revelation is *to see* in the spirit into God's realm of truth; it's to see with the "eyes of the heart" -- the "eyes of the understanding."[4] It's having the Spirit of God *bear witness with our spirit* regarding truth so that we now *know* things of God.[5] Those things are the foundation of the faith we have toward God; they are the foundation of our life in Him. They become *our reality;* they therefore become what we are called to *testify of.* Sometimes our audience is eager and receptive, with our testimony leading to salvation; sometimes it is non-receptive, leading to rejection and hostility. Whether receptive or not, like Jesus before Pilate, we are called to give testimony to truth. Paul said to Timothy:

> **Fight the good fight of faith, lay hold on eternal life, to which you were also called and *have confessed*[1] *the good confession*[2] in the presence of many *witnesses*.[3]**
> **I urge you in the sight of God who gives life to all things, and before Christ Jesus who *witnessed*[4] *the good confession*[2] before Pontius Pilate, that you keep this commandment without spot, blameless until our Lord Jesus Christ's appearing.**
>

1 Timothy 6:12-14 (emphasis added)

---

3   Matthew 16:16-17
4   Eph. 1:17-18 (Matt. 6:22-24, Rev. 5:6)
5   Romans 8:16; John 14:17, 23, 26; 1 John 2:27, 5:10

¹*homologeo* G3670T – to say the same thing as another; to agree with someone else; assent (verb)
²*homologia* G3671T – one's profession, which is in agreement with another; testimony (noun)
³*martus* G3144T – a witness
⁴*martureo* G3140T – to give testimony; to be a witness; testify

What is this "fight of faith" Paul speaks of here? It is the battle to *lay hold of the Word for ourselves, making it OUR truth.* It is battling against the evidence of the natural realm and of our five physical senses; it is battling against lies from the enemy operating in our minds and emotions; it is battling fear, intimidation, guilt, pride, and every other force, whether inner or outward, that would cause us to disbelieve and cast aside the Word of God. As we engage this battle and stand fast on the Word, we are 'laying hold on eternal life'; that Word now becomes our truth and our testimony. We *speak* what we have seen and know, even as John said regarding 'the Word of life' (Jesus):

> **2 the life was manifested, and we have seen, and bear witness, and declare to you that eternal
> life which was with the Father and was manifested to us —
> 3 that which we have seen and heard we declare to you, that you also may have fellowship
> with us; and truly our fellowship is with the Father and with His Son Jesus Christ.**
> **1 John 1:2-3**

The testimony of "what we have *seen and heard*" has the power to give life to those who believe it, and therefore to bring them into the same fellowship that we have with each other and with the Father and Jesus Himself. What we have seen and heard *is the Word of life*; it is the testimony of the Father which came through His Son, it is the Word given in the Scriptures. We agree with this Word – we confess it; that is, we *say the same thing as God*; that becomes our testimony, even as Jesus' testimony always agreed with what the Father said. When our words agree with heaven, they bring heaven's light and power into the earth -- to us and to the hearers. This is the call to *testify* that Paul gave to Timothy and that the Scriptures give to every believer, and this is the victorious testimony of these overcomers. One day, Jesus will rule "with *the rod of his mouth*" (Is. 11:4). The overcomers are speaking already in this age the "rod of His Word."

Our testimony is directed not just to people or even circumstances. It is also, of necessity, proclaimed to the unseen realm, as that is where our principal enemies are located. To demons, principalities, and powers we declare the victory that is ours in Christ and the truth of His Word which we have *seen* and *know* to be true. This is, again, the very thing that God commissions us to do with the scroll – that is, with the events He has specifically revealed must take place at the end in order to reclaim the kingdom of the earth.

3. They did not love their lives, even unto death.

Jesus taught us right from the beginning that a requirement for following Him was that we not cling to or preserve our own life -- our Self. He taught us that seeking to protect our own natural life would inevitably bring defeat and give ground to the enemy (Matt. 16:21-25). It is in our steadfast identification with *His death* and His resurrection that all ground is taken from the enemy and we overcome him. Although we *reckon* this from the beginning of our walk with Him, *working* this into us – into our experience – is part of the reason for the trials we go through that call forth patience and that bring us into maturity. This was the courage and strength of the Jewish saints in their Babylonian captivity. When faced with hungry lions, Daniel did not flinch; knowing it could mean his death, he continued daily to kneel and pray with his face toward Jerusalem. When threatened with death in the fiery furnace if they did not worship the king's image, Shadrach, Meshach, and Abednego declared to the king, "Our God whom we serve is able to deliver us from the burning fiery furnace, and He will deliver us out of your hand, O king. But even if He doesn't, *we will not serve your gods, nor worship the golden image which you have set up*" (Dan. 3:17-18, emphasis added). And we know God *did deliver them,* providing a stunning testimony of Himself *to that whole Babylon kingdom!*

I believe these four men, staunch in their stand with God, are <u>examples</u> and <u>encouragement</u> for saints of all time, but particularly, for the saints of the end, when the battle will rage so fiercely and the saints again face the formidable power of Babylon under the rule of Antichrist. God always *gives the grace we need to overcome in every situation!* **Whether it's the prospect of a public, fiery furnace, or the 'lesser' battles that take place in the privacy of our own homes and lives, the issue of letting Self go to the cross is always a key ingredient of our victorious walk with Jesus.**

Consequences of the Battle

Cast down and now limited to the earth, Satan is filled with rage. He knows he *has only a short time remaining!* This is great for heaven – that malignant presence is gone! But although heaven rejoices, sympathy is expressed for the earth, for a dire time is about to follow on earth. What is that short time remaining to Satan? We've mentioned that a time period, 3½ years, is mentioned twice in chapter 12. From other places in Scripture, we know that is the duration of Satan's rule upon the earth. So, we see here the ***events that will take place – both in the catching up of a group of overcomers and also in a great spiritual battle in the heavenlies – right before the midpoint of the 70th week.***

Toward the end of Daniel 11, events take place on earth that bring great pressure militarily on Antichrist. We would surmise that the military skirmish mentioned in v. 44 is a reflection of the battle in the heavenlies. We note the mention of his "fury," comparing it with Satan's "rage" in Revelation 12. Daniel 11:45 says that having made his way and planted his headquarters between the seas (Dead Sea and Mediterranean Sea) in 'the glorious holy mountain' (Jerusalem), "yet he shall come to his end, and none shall help him." Is this the deadly wound that we know Antichrist sustains?[6] This appears to be Antichrist positioned – in Jerusalem – for the *hellish resurrection* which follows his death. That resurrection leads immediately to his claim to divinity and his entrance into the Holy of Holies, defiling it and instituting the Great Tribulation. Indeed, "woe to the earth!"

Daniel goes on to say,

> **At that time Michael shall stand up,[1] the great prince who stands watch over the sons of your people; and there shall be a time of trouble, such as never was since there was a nation, even to that time. Daniel 12:1**

[1]*amad* – to stand, in a variety of positions: stand up, stand still, stand aside, etc.

A better translation of this passage would be, "At that time Michael shall stand aside." He has long been standing *watch;* now he changes position and *stands aside.* As mentioned previously in *Part 1,* chapter 16, a restrainer has long been preventing Satan, via a willing human being, from taking control of the whole earth as a counterfeit messiah; in preventing this, the restrainer has *protected Israel,* who will be a particular *target* of Satan once he's removed. Therefore, we see how this passage in Daniel, stating that Michael 'stands aside,' coincides with him being 'removed from the midst' as a hinderer to Satan's purposes;[7] it also coincides with Revelation 12, where we see Michael not only *standing aside* as the protector of Israel, but actually executing the victory over Satan that causes him to be cast out of heaven down to the earth, there to begin his 'reign of terror.'

This cosmic battle, then, becomes the very thing that catapults the earth *into* the Great Tribulation.

Daniel's words here agree with Jesus' description of the Great Tribulation: "Then will be great tribulation, such as has not been since the beginning of the world until this time, no, nor ever shall be" (Matt. 24:21). Both our Scriptures here, Daniel and Revelation, place Michael squarely in the scene at this time, precipitating actions that bring about Antichrist's death. The death is followed by his resurrection, the *revealing of him as the Man of Sin,* and the inauguration of the Great Tribulation.

---

6   Rev. 13:3, 12, 14;17:10-11. We will take another look at this deadly wound and the "resurrection" that follows it, in the last section of this book.

7   2 Thess. 2:6-7

As we close out this chapter, keep in mind the central theme of our study here in *Part 2*: **that the saints are *key participants* in the end-time victory**. In Revelation 12 we see them, via the man child, playing an essential role in activating God's plans for the midpoint and the Great Tribulation. Their *testimony* is powerful and essential in beginning *the reduction of Satan's sphere of influence!*

The Sequence of Events:

1. The man child is birthed and caught up to the throne right before the midpoint of the last seven years.

2. At the throne, these overcomers authoritatively serve Satan notice that his days as accuser of the brethren are over!

3. The great battle ensues and Michael and his angels prevail over Satan and his angels, casting them down to the earth. At this time Michael *stands aside* – moves out of his protective role of Israel, allowing events to proceed:

4. Antichrist receives a deadly wound and comes back to life.

5. He goes into the Holy of Holies and commits the abomination that makes desolate, beginning the Great Tribulation.

CHAPTER 39

Understanding
the Man Child

Before we move on to the woman in the wilderness, we are going to take a closer look at the man child, for there is a level of mystery here that needs to be understood. I am going to share with you the 'progressive unveiling' which God permitted to me when I was first studying this chapter in Revelation years ago. The chapter was pretty much a closed book to me, and reading what others had written wasn't necessarily helping me. I needed the Lord to teach me. And I will add, that if this is something that *you* would like to discern for yourself, it's important that you ask the Holy Spirit to be your teacher. None of these issues of Revelation, including this one, are things to be grasped with the mind; they may be taught by a 'teacher,' but to be truly seen with your inner eyes, they need to be taught to you by the Holy Spirit!

The Overcomers

I began to understand first, that this group spoken of in v. 11, the ones who "overcame by the blood of the Lamb, the word of their testimony, and who loved not their lives unto the death," CONSTITUTES the man child; that **he is *a group of people,* and that they are caught up for the purpose of having this direct confrontation with the Accuser.** They confront him at the throne and *overcome* him in a way that has never before happened in the history of the fallen human race.

But I had to go farther in understanding them. The letters in Revelation all address the overcomers – those in each church age who overcome their own fleshly weakness, the lies and assaults of the enemy, and the challenges unique, perhaps, to that age. In fact, the challenges and instructions of the New Testament are written to all the saints, <u>calling every Christian to overcome</u>. As we mentioned earlier in *Part 1*, it isn't really that overcomers are something special, as much as they are *normal* Christians who learn progressively to walk in the path of victory available to all saints through Christ. It's just that not all avail themselves of that victory, and so although merely "normal," overcomers seem to stand out. Seeing that this was a group of overcomers led me to Watchman Nee, because I knew he had written about the overcomers and what characterizes them. But to rightly grasp Nee's comments, I will first share this:

The Two-Fold Nature of Christ's Atoning Work
1. Man's redemption and salvation -- restoring to man what he lost in the Fall.
2. <u>Satan's defeat by means of the Kingdom.</u>

  • Jesus came *preaching* and *demonstrating* the power of the kingdom of God:

And as you go, preach, saying, 'The *kingdom of heaven* is at hand.' Heal the sick, cleanse the lepers, raise the dead, cast out demons... Matthew 10:7-8
But if I cast out demons by the Spirit of God, surely the *kingdom of God* has come upon you. Matthew 12:28 (emphasis added to both)

- Jesus *legally* crushed Satan's head at Calvary.
- But God is leaving the *executing* of that victory up to us, the church:

And the seventy returned with joy, saying, "Lord, even the demons are subject to us in Your name. And He said to them, "I saw Satan fall like lightning from heaven." Luke 10:17-18

Key Point: If Satan's defeat is through us, and that happens by means of *the kingdom,* then we as believers *need to go beyond a mere "God has saved me" mentality, and take our positions within the kingdom and exercise our authority to help bring the kingdom to this earth!*

Watchman Nee's Comment

This perspective on our part in bringing the kingdom to the earth is something God desires every believer to embrace (although not all do). How does this relate to the overcomers? In his book The Glorious Church, Nee says that **the overcomers are those *with a kingdom mentality*.** I.e., there is a purpose God has in redeeming us which goes beyond the personal benefits to us! Yes, those benefits are real and life-changing, but if we are content to stop there, we are missing *God's greater purpose in our redemption.*

Jane's Dream

It was early 1991, and I was deep in the study of end-time Scriptures. I had been pondering this issue of the man child, and I was considering that it was composed of a group of overcomers. I hadn't shared this with Jane (a friend of mine and an End-Time Handmaiden[1]), and she knew nothing about the man child/overcomer idea. But she had a dream on January 19 which she told me about. I wrote it down at the time exactly as she shared it with me:

> I was in a large gathering of End-Time Handmaidens. Some of the people were suddenly lifted up. The only one I recognized was *Gwen (Shaw* – the leader of ETH). I wondered, "Why am I not going?" Papa Jim (Gwen's husband), who was also left, came over and reassured me, "Don't worry, Daughter. Although we will go through the tribulation, we will be protected."
> In the dream, Jane questioned the Lord: "I don't understand why I've been left behind. I thought I'd made a total surrender." He replied, "Yes, you have. But it's more recent. You only started walking with Me this way in recent years. I've taken them home to help Me put the finishing touches on things before I bring the rest of My people home. You must stay and teach My people and teach them what it is to be totally surrendered."
> Jane said that after He explained it, "I had such a perfect peace."

Notice the implication of the dream – that this smaller group was 'caught up' *before* the midpoint, whereas those who were left, though they loved the Lord, would go through the Great Tribulation. Interestingly, Jane herself was pre-trib in her rapture views, and I don't think she grasped the message in the dream regarding the timing of the rapture. Nor did she have understanding about the man child. She simply shared with me, faithfully, what she had seen and heard in the dream. It was the Lord assisting me in understanding. Notice also, that there's a *maturity* present in those who go up – a maturity that has its beginnings in *a full surrender,* but then has happened *over time*; and also, that there's a promise of God's protection for those who go through the Great Tribulation. This

---

1   The End-Time Handmaidens is an intercessory and evangelism group located in Jaspar, AR. It was founded by Gwen Shaw in 1970, and is now known as the "End-Time Handmaidens and Servants," including men in its global membership.

promise is consistent with what Revelation 12 says about the woman in the wilderness during the last 3½ years. It's neat how when a word is from the Lord, it will be consistent with the Word in every detail.

I knew this was the Lord helping me with further light and confirmation. This became even clearer to me 18 years later, when I was in the midst of teaching a Bible study on end-times.

Gwen's Quote

I was on schedule to teach on the man child the evening of October 9, 2009, and that very day, very randomly, I found myself going through a packet of old papers and notes that I hadn't looked at in years. Quite unexpectedly, I came across this quote from *Gwen Shaw* in regard to the year 2000:

> We must live in anticipation and expectation of the kingdom of God, and daily allow that king-dom-quality lifestyle to take over in our lives. We must press into the kingdom, love it more than we do, long for it – press into that which is available and ready to be given to us. We need to pick up our scepter of ruling authority – kingdom authority – that is waiting for us and begin to use it. This is a year of transition from earth-kingdom to heaven-kingdom and from earth-thinking to heaven-thinking. The high calling of God is a call not to DO, but to BE – be kingdom people, living in the realm and the atmosphere where we are seated in heavenly places in Christ Jesus.

I was amazed, and connected the dots immediately. Here was further confirmation from the Lord: Gwen Shaw was the one in Jane's dream that went up – presumably in the man child rapture – and here she is, giving her *kingdom perspective. . .* with Watchman Nee having taught that a *kingdom mentality* will characterize the overcomers.[2] All three – Nee's comment, Jane's dream, and Gwen's comment – confirmed that the man child is a group of overcomers with kingdom priority; Jane's dream confirmed they are selected by God for His purposes and caught up to heaven right before the midpoint. Because of this, they are not here for the time of testing, the Great Tribulation. I loved how God was giving me more and more understanding.

Revelation 3:10

Born of the Philadelphia Church

But God wanted to give me even more light on it, which came less than a year later while teaching another end-time Bible study! This time it came from a dream I happened to find online at the *Unleavened Bread Ministries* website.[3]

> I dreamt that a woman I knew was going to have a baby by caesarian section. When I rushed to her side to support her, she had already had a natural birth after a labor of only two hours. I held the baby boy for a long time and gazed at his face. He was very mature and could already speak and I discovered he had eight fingers on his right hand. The eighth finger branched off the sixth finger.
> <u>David Eells, the host of the website, gave his interpretation of the dream</u>: A baby by caesari-an section implies a birth by the works of man, which will not happen to this first-born fruit of Christ in these days, called the man child. The sixth finger is the sixth church spoken of in Rev-elation, the Philadelphia Church. Out of this will come the man child, whose number is eight, which represents 'new beginnings.'[4]

It made perfect sense to me that the Lord should depict this group coming out of Philadelphia -- which, of course, continues to the end, fulfilling the Great Commission -- rather than the lethargic and highly-deceived

---

2   Please understand that God was not saying Gwen Shaw would be in this group; instead, He was using her to give instruction as to the quality of maturity and of kingdom commit-ment that would characterize this group.

3   This dream was from Christine Beadsworth, https://freshoilreleases.co.za/, and is shared with her permission.

4   As a note on 'eight' signifying new beginnings: Eight on the ark began a new world following the ruin of the old. Interesting that just as the death and "resurrection" of Antichrist brought forth "an eighth" (Rev. 17:10-11), so, out of the church is being birthed "an eighth," along the lines of a supernatural group beyond the seven church ages.

Laodicea. And it immediately connected me with the verse, *directed to Philadelphia*, that is more in line with a *pre-trib* rapture than a *pre-wrath* rapture:

> **Because thou hast kept the word of my patience,[1] I also will keep thee from the hour of temptation,[2] which shall come upon all the world, to try them that dwell upon the earth. Revelation 3:10 KJV**

[1]*hupomone* G5281T -- to persevere, have patience; literally, to remain under
[2]*peirasmos* G3986T – a trial which puts to the test; adversity, affliction, or trouble which serves to test one's character

Here at last was the Holy Spirit making sense of this passage in Revelation 3! I have never known of any other way to see this than as a group being promised exemption from the time of testing, the Great Tribulation. I could never throw out the pre-wrath rapture because of this verse, because the verse stands alone against a large body of other, clear, pre-wrath Scriptures. And yet, it did need to be answered. It couldn't stand as a lone sentinel and not find its place in the large, complete picture of end-time events. And here it was! More on that in a moment.

The Maturity of the Man Child
Like Jane's dream, this one from the website speaks of the maturity of the child. This coincides with Scripture denoting the masculine *qualities* of strength, vitality, and mature capability. The Holy Spirit began to give me fuller understanding as soon as I connected the man child with this verse in Revelation. Speaking of "the word of my patience," brought James 1 to mind immediately:

> **My brethren, count it all joy when you fall into various trials,[1] knowing that the testing[2] of your faith produces patience.[3]**
> **But let patience[3] have its perfect[4] work, that you may be perfect[4] and complete,[5] lacking nothing. James 1:2-4**

[1]*peirasmos* G3986T – a discipline or trial which tests one's character, faith, holiness, or integrity
[2]*dokimion* G1383V – testing and trial, with a view toward approval upon completion
[3]*hupomone* G5281V –lit., an abiding under, patience; patient endurance and steadfastness, particularly in trials or under chastisement
[4]*teleios* G5046T – complete and mature; full-grown, perfect, finished, having reached its end
[5]*holokleros* G3648T – complete in every part; entire, whole, faultless

God clearly uses the tests and trials we go through to develop and mature us spiritually. That maturity is His goal for all His children. He values this *so highly* that He is willing to send us through trials and tests of all sorts in order to bring us to that place. And the quality *we* need to cultivate to bring those trials to the desired outcome of maturity, is PATIENCE. That is, we *remain under the Lord's hand* even in the stress, strain, and pain of the trial! We don't look for a way around it or try to hop out of it, but with our eyes on Him, we seek to align ourselves with Him and His Word. We seek His wisdom in the midst of it, that we might cooperate with the changes God is desiring in us.

The individuals in the man child group have been taken through a full range of tests and trials and have 'remained under' the Lord's hand throughout; they have therefore arrived at the maturity He desires. This is why we see *maturity* (being "perfect") as a thread running through all these words. **How does the maturity of the man child connect it with this promise in Revelation 3?** This group is not in need of the testing and trials the church will go through under Antichrist. Through godly responses to many trials, maturity has already been produced in their lives, and they are ready – fully equipped -- for the purpose God has in mind when He catches this group up to His throne.

We notice that in this dream, the child is born *speaking*. This is an indicator of maturity. *Nepios,* the Greek word for "childish" or "baby," literally means "not speaking."[5] Just as an immature child does not yet speak, so a spiritually immature child of God has not yet grown into the power and authority inherent in his words as a son of God. Behind the concept of speaking as one who is mature, lies the ability to see beyond appearances to the spiritual realities of God and His kingdom. This seeing *and proclaiming what we see* taps into and releases the authority of God and moves His kingdom forward here on earth.

This group of saints has learned that; they have become skilled in walking by God's word and by faith rather than by feelings or appearances in the natural. They are ready and able to respond to the Spirit's leading and release the purposes of God in their words. Their words carry the truth, authority, and power of God, and it is, in fact, with their words – "the word of their testimony" – that Satan is *blown out of the throne room.* They know fully their authority as sons of God, having learned to operate in it in the probationary trials of life on earth, even as through practice in the field, David knew his authority when facing Goliath. There is no portion of their own life that they are seeking to preserve; if facing the enemy in God's will means death, then so be it. They are not living for themselves, but for Him. They have fully appropriated the *righteousness* that is *theirs through the blood of Jesus.* They are no longer vulnerable to condemnation, but are fully established in His righteousness, which is a gift. They are powerful instruments of God's when the time comes, for they have passed every trial with patience and are now fully equipped for every good work. This is God's full salvation manifest in them; they are prepared and ready for God to use them in this special way.

---

5   See Heb. 5:13: "babe" *nepios* G3516S – literally, not speaking.

CHAPTER 40

Further Thoughts on the Man Child

I had further questions regarding the man child. Why isn't he 'manifested' before the birth – doesn't he have the same character before as after? So why can't the enemy figure out who he is before the birth? Furthermore, what *occurs* to cause him to 'be manifested'? I.e., what separates him from the rest of the church? Light on these questions has come gradually. I will share what I have come to see, while not claiming that it's a full or even fully accurate picture.

Spiritual Conditions in the Church Before the Midpoint

As with the swinging tail of the dragon, it helps to put these questions into the context of what is going on with the church right before the midpoint. The church as a whole is in the age of Laodicea – a time of *complacent deception.* Thyatira (Roman Catholicism), Sardis (the formerly-state churches of the Reformation), and Philadelphia are still present on the earth. Hand in glove with the deception in Laodicea is the deception of Antichrist. At this time, although politically and even militarily active, he is still *the great deceiver* -- the great "man of God," loving holiness, preaching, doing great signs and wonders, etc. Many in the church *are working with him, loving him, following him.* Philadelphia, going *strong to the end,* is continuing to fulfill the Great Commission; she is undergoing great outpourings of the Holy Spirit and moving forward with God, "collecting" the many who are moving on with the Lord. Many supernatural works are also being done by those who are deceived; they are *walking alongside* God's authentic people as both groups operate in the supernatural. Distinguishing between these two groups is a great challenge for God's people. It is this MIXTURE in the church that is the setting for the woman who is in great travail, about to birth a man child.

This situation of mixture in the church -- where some works are true and some are false, and some discern accurately and some don't – is what *the woman of Revelation 12* is dealing with as the chapter begins. For those who *see accurately* to expose this great, godly man as the wicked and fearful *antichrist* when he has such a following and when he appears to be so good, is to go against a very strong tide – a groundswell of great support and enthusiasm which is generated by the enemy and by natural/soulish approval of 'good.' The prophetic call of the Spirit *is for him to be exposed to God's true people so they are warned and protected*; but the enemy is resisting this exposure with a dark, fearful, and ferocious wall of intimidation. Very likely, the *internal struggle* of the woman is being caused, at least in part, by this very issue. Her 'travail' is to bring forth a group that will testify and proclaim, clearly and boldly, the imminent danger that the church is in via deception and apostasy, and particularly in relation to this man! Micah spoke of a similar kind of travail:

Therefore, will he give them up, until the time when she who travails has brought forth; then the remnant of his brethren shall return unto the children of Israel. Micah 5:3

At the end, Israel as a nation will "travail" in order to birth forth those who will finally turn back to God and receive their Messiah; i.e., birth the end-time *remnant* who will be saved and go into the Millennium.[1] This is similar to the woman who gives birth to the child – in both cases, the woman and the child are *corporate* figures; they represent a group of people. Out of the larger group comes the smaller group. For both Israel and the church, the travail consists of the difficulty of the decision-making that is required for the birth. The remnant of Israel will have to turn from millennia of resistance to God, humble themselves, and learn to see the Jesus of the New Testament in a different way than they have been accustomed to. There will be opposition to this turning – there will be struggle; there will be 'counting the cost'; there will be personal, internal arguments, great external pressures from loved ones and powers of darkness who are opposing them; on the other hand, there will be the compelling power of *truth* that is drawing them more and more out from their attachment to the mother. This is the travail. In every birth there is a physical part of the mother that is holding the child back, while there are other physical forces working to bring the child to birth. It's a time of struggle and conflict. The child must finally break away from the mother and take a position *on truth* which is different than that of the mother. And so, at the end, whereas the mother has not yet sorted out the *mixture* within her of the false and the true, this group within her sees the false and knows the urging of the Spirit to step forth and *expose the mixture*. To expose the deception going on under the banner of Christ is necessary for all the true followers of Jesus; they need to recognize the false, that they might reject it and not follow Antichrist into the fullness of error and deception. The enemy *is alert to this group that would expose his man.* He doesn't yet know who they are, but he senses that they are about to come forth, and he is positioned to destroy them as soon as they become apparent. That is, as soon as they publicly step forth from the mother to speak out and say, "This and this and that are *false*. Separate from these!" To be able to do this, these must overcome all condemnation, they must be willing to lay down their lives in the cause of the truth of Christ, and must be willing to step forth and *publicly declare truth that exposes the deception and lies of the enemy.* This is their travail, and they overcome in the struggle and are birthed forth, separate from 'the mother,' ready to accomplish 'the mission.' I suggest this scenario, not as something I am sure about, but as a likely possibility.

Phineas, a Type of the Man Child

As to why the 'child' isn't manifested before his birth, additional insight comes from Watchman Nee again in *The Glorious Church*. In Numbers 25 the Israelite men were seduced into idolatry and whoredom by the women of Moab. God's anger burned; He sent a plague among the people and *called on all the judges of Israel to execute the men in their own tribes who had participated in the idolatry.* Apparently, the judges were slack to do this, finding it difficult to kill their own brethren. In the meantime, a man of Israel brought a heathen woman into his tent right in front of Moses and the weeping congregation. Aaron's grandson Phineas went into the tent with a javelin and thrust both of them through, stopping the plague of judgment against the congregation.[2] Nee compares the man child of the end to Phineas, who, zealous for the Lord and His righteousness, did what the rest of the Israelites were unable to do. He turned against a fellow Israelite in order to stand for God's righteousness; by that single act, done on behalf of the nation, he turned God's wrath away from the people. God honored him by giving to him and his heirs "the covenant of an everlasting priesthood" (Num. 25:6-13).

Putting God ahead of all our loves and attachments, including those within the Body of Christ, is the pathway to overcoming. In this incident, the situation calling for decisive action didn't arise until that specific moment; when it arose, Phineas stepped forth and became that one who *answered the need.* Perhaps the situation at the birthing of the man child will be similar: there will be some kind of transgression and betrayal of God among "God's people" – or perhaps they know a betrayal is imminent -- that *mandates* the stepping forward of this group to speak loudly and boldly against it, and at that time they become evident and identifiable. We will know more as we get closer to the time.

---

1 Is. 10:20-22; 11:11; 28:5; 37:31-32; Micah 4:7; Zeph. 3:12-13; Rom. 9:27
2 See Exodus 32:26-29.

CHAPTER 41

The Woman
in the Wilderness

We now turn our focus back to the glorious woman, who, after her child is caught up to heaven so suddenly, is left here on the earth in dangerous straits. Knowing that as soon as her child is caught up she will be in danger, she flees to "the wilderness":

Then the woman fled into the wilderness, where she has a place prepared by God, that they should feed her there one thousand two hundred and sixty days.

Revelation 12:6

The great heavenly battle follows, with the furious dragon cast down to the earth, and the remainder of the chapter is about the woman:

13 **When the dragon saw that he was thrown down to the earth, he persecuted the woman who gave birth to the male child.**
14 **Two wings of the great eagle were given to the woman, that she might fly into the wilderness to her place, so that she might be nourished for a time, and times, and half a time, from the face of the serpent.**
15 **The serpent spewed water out of his mouth after the woman like a river, that he might cause her to be carried away by the stream.**
16 **The earth helped the woman, and the earth opened its mouth and swallowed up the river which the dragon spewed out of his mouth.**
17 **The dragon grew angry with the woman, and went away to make war with the rest of her seed, who keep God's commandments and hold Jesus' testimony.**

Revelation 12:13-17 WEB

We see the woman pursued and persecuted – and, intriguingly (and reassuringly!), fed by an unidentified group -- for three and a half years. This is, of course, the duration of the Great Tribulation, and we know that during that time, the enemy targets any and all who refuse to worship him and take his mark. The ones who feed her are, to my knowledge, left unidentified.

The Changing Composition of the Woman

Knowing that the church is raptured long before the end of the 70th week, we might be perplexed that the woman is persecuted for that whole period. But it is explained simply by the fact that **the composition of the woman changes as events unfold.** Though the chapter speaks of the woman as a whole, she consists of those individuals who "keep the commandments of God and have the testimony of Jesus Christ." Before the man child is caught up, the woman is the whole church, including the man child. After the man child leaves, the remainder of the believers comprise the woman until the rapture, when they leave the earth. At that time the 144,000, convinced now that Jesus is their Messiah, receive Him and are born again. These 144,000 now make up the woman, and even as the church testified to them before the rapture, *they* now testify to their fellow Jews. As we pointed out in *Part 1,* the 144,000 continue throughout the trumpet judgments, appearing before the throne in heaven between the trumpet and bowl judgments (Rev. 14). Knowing from Revelation when they will be taken, this becomes part of their testimony to Jews who have not yet turned. The fulfillment of their words, along with the ascension of the two witnesses at the same time (Rev. 11:12-15), will impact many Jews. Although their departure from the earth will significantly deplete the number of those making up the woman, there will undoubtedly be Jews who receive their Messiah at that same time, believing the testimony of the two witnesses and the departed Jews. This small but growing number of Jews will now make up the woman. We don't have a way, as far as I am aware, of knowing how many come in at that time. They are in the *process of turning back* to the Lord all during this time, up to Armageddon, when the turning is completed and "all Israel is saved"; that is, the whole remnant that has survived the ravages of Antichrist, the judgments of the Lord's wrath, and the conflict at Armageddon.

Although the number is uncertain once the 144,000 are gone, we know that those being saved are primarily – if not entirely – Jews. From the midpoint to the end, the constituency of the woman transitions from primarily Gentile to Jewish. Additionally, we note that the 144,000, being taken to heaven, now have their new bodies. Any Jews saved after that will enter the Millennium in their physical bodies. Any who *die as martyrs* for their faith in Jesus will be resurrected at the end of the seven years and will participate in the Millennium in their new bodies. That resurrection will conclude the first resurrection (Rev. 20:4-5).

The Woman in the Wilderness

The wilderness is a recurring theme in Scripture, all the way from Moses' forty years to Jesus' forty days. In between we see the forty years of the Israelites' wanderings, Elijah's time when Jezebel hunted him, and John the Baptist's season of preparation. The wilderness is a place of isolation, of separation from normal human activity. It is a place where the normal components of life – particularly social interaction, shelter, and provision – are absent. The isolation may mean we are separated from those who are near and dear to us. Needs for food and shelter must be met in extraordinary ways. Because of that, there is deep spiritual work that God does during the wilderness sojourn. There is no question that at this time in the future, God will do a deep, purifying work in His people.

The Church in the Wilderness

By 'church' here, we mean the primarily Gentile, pre-rapture group of saints. Many of these have been swept into the kingdom in the mighty spiritual outpouring of the Spirit in these final years at the end. The saints have covered the earth – individually, as well as with powerful evangelistic outreaches -- as they finally fulfill the Great Commission. Many of these remaining in the church (after the man child rapture) are young in the faith.

Why the Wilderness?

We ask ourselves, *why* the wilderness and this time of testing and suffering? God could easily have caught the church up in the rapture before the antichrist takes power at the midpoint and spared them the extremity and potential trauma of life with Satan on the throne of the earth. But anyone who has walked with God knows that making life easy for the believer is *not* a priority of God's; rather, He is after bringing many sons into glory by producing the image of His Son in them! And that involves them being built up and developed in the Word, a process which is often intermingled with trials and tests for believers. Because of the short time remaining, there is not *time* for the dealings that God would ordinarily use to bring them into maturity – the trials that develop faith, that ground us more deeply in the Word, and that put patience to work in our lives. Their entrance into the kingdom is followed closely by the rapture, and so God uses this very rigorous time of intense trial to develop the steadfastness, the humility, and the dependence on Him that He would ordinarily develop in His saints over a greater span of time. This is a time of radical breaking of self and self-reliance. It is a time of sanctification, a time of clarifying vision and strengthening of faith, a time of being *separated unto God.*

Jesus Himself had His time in the wilderness. There He "suffered, being tempted," and passing the tests through reliance on the Word and the Spirit, He returned from it in the *power of the Spirit.* If He, being sinless, needed that wilderness testing, how much more do we need it. "If we suffer with Him, we shall also reign with Him!"[1] We *can pass every test by His life in us* – by leaning on Him! There is a deep purification that takes place in the wilderness – hidden pockets of self and of unbelief, of wrong motives and fears, etc., are exposed. This is a work we welcome, because though difficult, it brings greater conformity to the image of Christ.

A great KEY for the saints at the end, but also *for all times*, is that we ask ourselves, "What is God's purpose for me in this?" Sometimes answering that isn't possible – perplexity is part of the trial. But I think that when it comes to this trying time at the end, God has answers for us. In seeking the reasons why we will go through whatever we go through, we are looking for light *so we can cooperate fully with those purposes!* We don't want to shrink from them or rebel against them, but cooperate fully – even unto death: remember, the overcomers *love not their lives unto death.* The suffering is not the point – there is grace from God to endure victoriously! The *end goal* is the point! It is the place of glorious conformity to Christ – *that* will be our identity on into eternity. A brief time of suffering cannot be *compared to the glory which shall be revealed in us!*[2]

Learning the Wilderness Lessons

I tend to think that for the Gentile church, "wilderness" does not mean a primarily physical place. That's not to say that there will be no physical relocating as the saints adjust to their inability to obtain goods in the usual ways. However, I think it likely that many will remain located among the peoples of the world, just getting their needs met by other means than buying and selling – that is, by bartering, having stock-piled, and/or by supernatural provision and by multiplication of the supply they have and are sharing with others. (See chapter 13 of *Part 1.*) We are told that "they" feed her there; here is the wilderness – a place of isolation where supply is coming from other than the usual sources.

This, of course, is the time that Margaret MacDonald described in her vision; it is the time of the two witnesses, when their anointed testimony is supplying great quantities of God's Spirit to the church; and it is the time when God's people are being tested to the core regarding their love for Him and their willingness to trust Him utterly for everything they need. This time of the church in the wilderness is a time for learning new levels of dependence on Him, letting Him purify the heart of all fear, all unbelief, and all other attachments.

This is the 7th horn of the Lamb coming into completion, taking her place as a participant in the defeat of Satan and the taking back of the kingdom of the earth. This is *the church rising!* Rising in victory, in power, in faith, in holiness, in anointing!! She is becoming *all of gold* – the vestiges of flesh are being burned away and she is being filled more and more with the holy Spirit of God. She is *overcoming.* It may not look like that, but the overcoming happens inside. Remember, this is still the age where the kingdom is *within us.* When Jesus comes, He will establish it *outwardly.*

How did Jesus overcome? By emptying Himself and becoming obedient unto death – even the death of the cross. So also, His Bride, like Him in every way, will overcome by holding onto the blood; by faithfully proclaiming the truth and her allegiance to it, even in the face of threat and danger; and by loving not her life, even unto death. *This* is what gains for her the kingdom that Jesus will share with her when He overthrows the present kingdom of this world. The ten horns, along with the beast, will make war with the Lamb, but the Lamb shall overcome them, for He is Lord of lords, and King of kings, and they that are with Him are *called, and chosen, and faithful!*[3]

---

1   Rom. 8:17, 2 Tim. 2:12
2   Romans 8:18
3   Rev. 17:14

The saints will come forth from this time of testing with their robes washed and made white. Wrapped in the perfect righteousness of the Lord, they will stand, ready to be presented to Him all glorious, without spot or blemish.[4] All her passion, devotion, and desire are focused on her Bridegroom. She is reaching up for Him; all else is being forsaken in her heart. All these elements of the Bride's maturity come together into full readiness; that's when we will see the skies rent open and the great Savior descending to take His Bride, and then begin to pour out judgment on those left on the earth.

Once as I rode out into the woods for my health, in 1737, having alighted from my horse in a retired place, as my manner commonly had been to walk for divine contemplation and prayer, I had a view that for me was extraordinary, of the glory of the Son of God. As near as I can judge, this continued about an hour, and kept me the greater part of the time in a flood of tears and weeping aloud. I felt an ardency of soul to be what I know not otherwise how to express, emptied and annihilated; to love Him with a holy and pure love; to serve and follow Him; to be perfectly sanctified and made pure with a divine and heavenly purity.

Jonathan Edwards

Excerpt from *On Prayer,* by E.M. Bounds, p. 299

The Dragon's Persecution and God's Protection

We know from Revelation 13 the details of the dragon's persecution of the woman – requiring the mark to buy and sell and mandating, upon pain of death, worship of Antichrist and his image. This is absolute tyranny on a global scale – unprecedented in human history.

The statements of the serpent sending a flood of water out of his mouth with which to sweep away the woman, and the earth opening her mouth to swallow the flood are a bit cryptic to us:

> **So the serpent spewed water out of his mouth like a flood after the woman, that he might cause her to be carried away by the flood.**
> **But the earth helped the woman, and the earth opened its mouth and swallowed up the flood which the dragon had spewed out of his mouth. Revelation 12:15-16**

We know that the beast will speak great lies and blasphemies against all that is righteous as he wars against God and the saints, and, indeed, overcomes them (or seems to). The saints will need to guard their hearts from being intimidated by the lies and threats of the enemy; it is *God alone* that we fear, listen to, and honor. All else is bluff and can but affect our bodies, not our eternal souls.

It's also possible (likely) that this flood out of his mouth will entail more than words. Scripture refers multiple times to military forces that invade *like a flood*, overwhelming their adversaries.[5] It's entirely believable that forces would be sent in pursuit of those who flee, although they may not be a whole army but just enough to overcome and apprehend the fugitives. The earth "opening her mouth and drinking up the river" could signify just what it says – earthquakes which swallow the pursuing forces. Already in the first half of the 70th week – at the *beginning* of birth pangs – Jesus said there would be "earthquakes in various places"; how much more during the second half when the earth is convulsing in the intense, full-on pains of labor. As Seiss points out, "It is the region and time when there is to be a renewal of wonders."[6] The two witnesses, the church, and the antichrist and false prophet are all sources of mighty supernatural occurrences, and the thought of heaven-sent earthquakes rescuing and

---

4   Rev. 7:14, Eph. 5:27
5   Is. 8:7; Jer. 46:7-8; 47:2-3; Dan. 11:22
6   Joseph A. Seiss, *The Apocalypse* (Grand Rapids, MI: Zondervan Publishing House), p. 318.

protecting His elect fits right into this backdrop of the supernatural.

We know, in fact, of one huge earthquake during this time, mentioned at the very significant 6th seal:

> **I looked when He opened the sixth seal, and behold, there was a great earthquake …**
>
>

Rev. 6:12

Speaking of this same time, Jesus described what is most likely a tsunami resulting from that great earthquake:

> **And there will be signs in the sun, in the moon, and in the stars; and on the earth distress of nations, with perplexity,** *the sea and the waves roaring…* Luke 21:25 (emphasis added)

Of course, *this* earthquake signals the snatching from the earth, and thus from the clutches of the dragon, the entire Bride of Jesus Christ, with the church appearing safely in heaven before the 7th seal is removed from the scroll (Rev. 7:9ff). Perhaps, then, Rev. 12:16 is referring to this very earthquake that signals *the rapture,* and at the same time, does extreme damage to Antichrist's military forces, *swallowing them up!* Although there will undoubtedly be great protection and rescues *all during* this period when the church is under-going the Great Tribulation, this particular rescue seems highlighted, provoking the dragon to renewed wrath against the woman, <u>whose numbers appear then to be diminished</u>:

> **And the dragon was enraged with the woman, and he went to make war with the rest of her off-spring, who keep the commandments of God and have the testimony of Jesus Christ.** Rev. 12:17

It would be the 144,000 Jews now constituting the woman who undergo the dragon's renewed rage at this point, *if* this is an accurate perspective on vv. 16-17. Whether it is or isn't, we are assured of the Father's constant care for the woman and her seed throughout the 3½ years.

A Closer Look at the Wilderness

When God undertook so many millennia ago to deliver Israel from Egypt, the Israelites had only a rudimentary knowledge of Him; they had had no personal interaction with Him and had little or no knowledge of His character. And yet, in covenantal faithfulness to Abraham, Isaac, and Jacob, He was there to deliver them and to lead them to the land He had promised their fathers. **His desire was that in the process of getting them *out* from Pharoah's iron grip and *into* the wonderful land of Canaan, they should *come to know Him,* even as their forefathers had known and trusted Him.** He desired to bring them also into a bond of covenant love and faithfulness. Following their deliverance from Egypt, He said to them, "You have seen what I did to the Egyptians, and how *I bore you on eagles' wings* and *brought you to Myself*" (Exod. 19:4). His supernatural intervention on their behalf had been astounding: His tremendous power against all the gods of Egypt demonstrated in the plagues; their deliverance from the Angel of Death via the blood on their doorposts; their send-off with jewelry, gold, silver, and clothing; His daily and nightly protection of them with His presence in the cloud and the pillar of fire; the mighty, staggering deliverance at the Red Sea, parting and then holding back the waters, followed by the destruction of Pharoah and his army; His daily provision of manna and water; His protection from the attack of the Amalekites – all this lasted three months until their arrival at Sinai. The statement, "I bore you on eagles' wings" meant *every kind of protection and provision --* everything that they needed! **They couldn't access Egypt (though at times they wanted to!) nor could they access the good thing that awaited them – all they had was God. This was the purpose of the wilderness -- that their attention be fully on Him.** He longed to convince them that He was *the* only true God of all; that His power, love, and commitment to them knew no bounds; and that all He *is* and *has* was available to care for them in the most loving and faithful way possible. All of it was *to bring them to Himself.*

Unfortunately, although *Moses* learned his ways, Israel saw only *His acts;*[7] they were never able to come to the

---

7 Ps. 103:7, Heb. 3:9-11

place of *trusting* the greatness of His ability and willingness to meet every need – to be their All in All. And so, He was never able to bring that generation into the trust and intimate bond of love that He desired. When they thirsted or hungered, they accused God of bringing them into the wilderness to die. All the way up to the border of Israel He was patient, until finally, when on the verge of going in to possess the land – just when He was about to deliver them from the wilderness they hated -- they refused to let Him *take them in!*[8] Even after seeing His faithfulness over and over, they were ready to *stone the two who said they were* well able to take the land![9] They utterly rejected His gift of the land and His ability to give them victory over the giants. This was the final test for that generation, and they failed it, closing the door on their chance to possess the land.

God's Care for Her

We note that when Israel left Egypt, heading for the wilderness, other than dough for unleavened bread, *they took no provisions with them...*

> **...because they were *thrust out* of Egypt, and couldn't wait, neither had they prepared for themselves any food. Exodus 12:39 WEB (emphasis added)**

Israel was *forced* out of Egypt by the dread that had fallen on Pharoah and his people after the death of their firstborn. Even so, in this coming time, the urgency of this sudden and dire threat will thrust Jews into the wilderness *with no preparation.* And yet, just as back then, *God* will be the One *caring for the woman:* She has there "a place prepared for her by God and she will be fed there the whole time" (v. 6). Moreover, to her was given "two wings of the great eagle" that she might fly into that prepared place and be fed and cared for there the entire time. We might puzzle over what exactly that means, but again, Scripture provides the perfect description of what that means:

> **You have seen what I did to the Egyptians, and how I bore you on eagles' wings and brought you to Myself. Exodus 19:4**

God's care of Israel at that time was continuous, supernatural, and unconditional. He compares it to the care of a mama eagle for her eaglet – carrying it on her wings as she soars above the earth and providing all it needs.

> **10 He found him in a desert land and in the wasteland, a howling wilderness; He encircled him, He instructed him, He kept him as the apple of His eye.**
> **11 As an eagle stirs up its nest, hovers over its young, spreading out its wings, taking them up, carrying them on its wings,**
> **12 So the Lord alone led him, and there was no foreign god with him.**
> **Deuteronomy 32:10-12**

Here, the description of the mama eagle goes into greater detail: The Lord "encircled" Israel, being a wall of protection around her; He instructed her, seeking to bring her into knowledge of Himself – not just of His limitless ability to meet her needs, but of His *great desire to teach her His ways.* His instruction was to let them appear to lack – to be hungry or thirsty, with no provision *in sight* -- even as the mama eagle pushes baby out of the nest, desiring that it learn to fly. God allowed Israel to experience need, and then *met the need,* looking each time for *progress in their confidence level.* If it holds out the wings, even feebly – i.e., desiring to trust God – that is good. If it isn't ready, she swoops under the falling eaglet, catches it, and bears it back up to the nest to safety. Over and over, God worked with Israel in this way. This, then, is the picture God gives us of that time in the future – of how willing He will be to provide, and of how open His heart will be toward His people as they navigate this difficult time. This is the purpose of the wilderness for God's people – whether it's a spiritual wilderness or a physical one; it's a time of training the heart in looking upward to God for everything. He wants to *convince us of the greatness*

---

8 Exodus 14:11; 16:3; Numbers 14:2
9 Numbers 14:6-10

of His lovingkindness and train us into full confidence in Him!

The Blasphemy Against God's Tabernacle

Revelation tells us that for the full 3½ years, the beast is given a "mouth" speaking great boasts and blasphemies against God, His name, His tabernacle, and those who dwell in heaven.[10] All of that is pretty clear, except I puzzled over "His tabernacle." What is His tabernacle? Obviously, Moses' tabernacle no longer exists, and it doesn't mean His *temple* in heaven; tabernacle tends to refer more to something on earth, as it has the implication of something temporary. Then light came. Psalm 27 speaks of single-hearted passion for the Lord, loving and seeking Him above all else, and a *promise* that follows:

> **For in the time of trouble He shall hide me in His pavilion[1]; In the secret place of His tabernacle[2] He shall hide me; He shall set me high upon a rock. Psalm 27:5**

> [1]*sok* H5520S – a hut (as of entwined boughs); from *sakak* H5526B – to hedge about, shut off, over-shadow, cover; to weave together as a screen
> [2]*ohel* H168B – a tent; a nomad's tent, and thus symbolic of wilderness life, transience

I could *see* this tabernacle – this covering place provided by God that isn't visible in the natural; it's invisible, but completely *real*. It's in the spirit dimension, but its reality extends to the physical: Antichrist won't be able to touch those who are being hidden by the Lord during this time; he will know it and it will *infuriate* him! The Psalmist continues:

> **And now my head shall be lifted up above my enemies all around me; therefore I will offer sacrifices of joy in His tabernacle; I will sing, yes, I will sing praises to the Lord. Psalm 27:6**

Truly, the wilderness will become a place of victory and celebration for the people of God, as they are covered with His feathers and trust under His wings![11]

> **How precious is Your lovingkindness, O God! Therefore the children of men put their trust under the shadow of Your wings. Psalm 36:7**

It will be good for the saints to remember at that time, that the very *faith of the Son of God* resides in them! They *are capable and equipped* to believe Him in any way needed, because the very faith of Christ dwells in them in their spirit.[12] They *are* 'believers.' God commands us to believe: "Have the faith of God" – that is, believing before we see. (Is there any other definition of faith??) If He commands this, it means we can do it. He never requires anything of us that we can't do, but rather, that we are fully equipped and capable of doing! The testimony of the overcoming church in the wilderness is that *God is faithful and will meet every need*. This is her continual proclamation and confession *before* the supply is seen. This is the expression of that faith, and also the way the faith grows. This is her testimony to the world, to heaven, and to the unseen hordes of darkness that would seek to intimidate her with fears and unbelief. *Our God is* <u>always</u> *THE GREATER ONE!*

The Jews in the Wilderness

In Jesus' narrative of end-time events, Matthew 24:15 speaks of the midpoint of the last seven years. This, of course, is when Antichrist goes into the Holy of Holies of the temple in Jerusalem, declares that he himself *is god* and thus inaugurates the Great Tribulation. Jesus' instruction at that time is for all in Judea *to flee immediately*;

When an eagle flies into the wind, he just stretches out his wings and the wind carries him upward.

---

10   Rev. 13:5-6

11   Ps. 91:4. This viewpoint of 'the tabernacle' is supported by the Lord's response to the prayer of the martyrs when He says that His coming will wait until the number of those that "should be killed" as they were, had been completed (Rev. 6:11, emphasis added). For more (an indiscriminate number) to be killed than "should" be would mean there is not protection over them.

12   Gal. 2:16, 20; 5:22; Heb. 2:11-13; Mark 11:22 (literally, "the faith of God," or the God kind of faith, as He had just demonstrated with the fig tree -- releasing faith with our words, calling those things that be not as though they were, Rom. 4:17).

to get as far away from Jerusalem as quickly as they can. We would guess that many of those in Israel flee to the wilderness – a physical wilderness. Most of them are not, at that time, a part of this great woman of Revelation 12, as they aren't born again. Yet their lives are in danger and they will flee. Many have supposed that this will be the wilderness variously known as Sinai or Paran (both in the Sinai Peninsula) or Teman (south of the Dead Sea in the biblical Edom, present-day Jordan). There are large areas of wilderness in this area south of Israel which are presently under Israeli, Jordanian, and Egyptian jurisdiction. In this wilderness place – wherever it will be exactly – God will deal with Israel. There He will woo them and care for them, and there many of them will *turn* back toward Him. God's work with Israel in this future time will be similar to when they left Egypt. They will be fleeing the iron grip of Antichrist and death at his hands. In that suffering God will be seeking again to bring them *unto Himself* as a nation:

> **Therefore, behold, I will allure her, will bring her into the wilderness, and speak comfort to her. I will give her her vineyards from there, and the Valley of Achor[1] as a door of hope; she shall sing there, as in the days of her youth, as in the day when she came up from the land of Egypt. Hosea 2:14-15**

[1]*achor* H5911B – trouble

There is no middle ground, as though any of us can just "belong to ourselves." We are either the Lord's or we are in the domain of the enemy. Sometimes that domain needs to get more intense, as when Israel suffered under Pharoah. It's in those dark times, when we encounter stark needs -- *life and death issues* that we ourselves are utterly helpless to meet – that we are awakened to God. In the extremity of the wilderness, God will allow Israel to suffer the full consequences of her unfaithfulness to Him and her reliance on a false christ. Here, the measuring rod of chastisement and judgment will be applied to them, first under Antichrist and then, additionally, for those not yet turning, under the severity of the Day of the Lord judgments. Throughout this time many will turn back to God *from the heart*; in that turning they will receive the revelation of their Messiah, and as they receive the righteousness of God which comes by faith in Christ, they will become part of the woman:

> **Zion shall be redeemed with judgment, and her converts[1] with righteousness. Isaiah 1:27 KJV**

[1]*shub* – to turn, return; to bring back, restore (See also Ezek. 20:33-38.)

Because God's work with the Jews includes this turning process, we could say there is a <u>dual purpose</u> of God for them in the wilderness: for those who don't know their Messiah, it is to turn them back to God; for those who do, it is to mature them in their faith. As the 3½ year period progresses, more and more of them *become part of the woman*; that is, they become those who "keep the commandments of God and have the testimony of Jesus Christ" (Rev. 12:17. We can certainly include those Jews who *will turn* to God as being among those who are provided for and protected, even though they are not part of the woman the whole time.

Only God sees the depth of the entrenchment of sin and only He understands perfectly – and knows how to provide – the chastisements that will finally bring all Israel back to Him. This is *required* before the earthly reign of Jesus can begin, for the kingdom promises are to the children of Israel, and it's from His *kingdom in Israel* that the Jewish Messiah, the Lord Jesus, will rule all the earth. Nothing less than this will fulfill the promises to the fathers, reiterated so many times, from Abraham to Malachi. Israel's time of great fruitfulness in the earth during the Millennium will come out of God's work in her through affliction and comfort during the Great Tribulation.

The Voice of God in the Wilderness

When we look at various wilderness experiences recorded in Scripture, we can see a common denominator of success:

- <u>Hagar and Ishmael</u> - When Isaac was born, God instructed Abraham to send Hagar and Ishmael away. They headed, alone and vulnerable, into the wilderness. When their water ran out, so did Hagar's hope. But then, as Ishmael wept, **God called to Hagar**, gave her a word for Ishmael's future, and opened her eyes to *the water that was present.* He was establishing a direct connection with Hagar, and hopefully Ishmael (Genesis 21:14-19).
- <u>Moses and the Israelites</u> - Whenever the food or water ran out, it was **the voice of God** giving instruction that caused the provision to appear.
- <u>Elijah</u> - Hiding from Jezebel during a time of drought and famine, Elijah was sustained by **the voice of the Lord** and the instructions he received (1 King 17).

Even so, in any trial, <u>the key to victory is to hear from the Lord</u>. Hearing His voice and following His instructions bring breakthrough and provision every time! The Psalmist wrote of this wilderness time, gleaning the great lesson from it:

Today, if you will hear His voice, do not harden your hearts, as in the rebellion, as in the day of trial in the wilderness, when your fathers tested Me. Psalm 95:7-9

The book of Hebrews repeats this <u>three times</u>:

Today, if you will hear His voice,
Do not harden your hearts as in the rebellion, in the day of trial in the wilderness, where your fathers tested Me,... Hebrews 3:7-9; 3:15; 4:7

There is a reason for the repetition: *the point is a crucial one.* Whether in a wilderness or not, *a tender heart* – one that reaches for God and cries out to Him -- is needed to hear God's voice; and **in His voice is salvation.**

Jesus is always so ready, so available, *so willing* to help in any way needed. When the disciples were out in the ship in the darkest time of the night, "toiling in rowing, for the wind was contrary to them," Jesus came walking to them on the sea, and in His courtesy *would have passed by them.* How amazing! Even though they needed Him so much, He didn't rush to their rescue; He simply came *near, making Himself available.* Why didn't He pass by them? Because they cried out to Him. He *waits* for us to ask! True, they cried in fear, not in faith, but that was all He needed, and *immediately* <u>He talked with them</u> and they allowed Him into the ship; the wind ceased, and they were *at their desired destination.*[13] The reaction of the disciples to all these supernatural aspects of the experience was that they were "greatly amazed in themselves beyond measure, and marveled." Mark explains that their reaction was because they still had *hardened hearts.* This incident on the water follows the feeding of the 5,000, and Mark's concluding observation is that even with seeing that miracle firsthand, their *thinking toward God* had not been affected. There had not been progress toward the supernatural becoming a 'normal' part of their lives with Christ. Nevertheless, in their time of struggle and need in the ship, Jesus was *very near.* The provision was available, just as it will be at that time for the woman: she is taken to the place *prepared for her nourishing*! She will just need to reach out in trust in Him and receive what is being provided.

This is what God is looking for: that *His* 'normal' -- what we call the supernatural -- becomes *our* normal; that we are so one with Him that our problems are His and His resources are ours; that we move as easily in the supernatural as Jesus did. After all, as John explains, "He who says he abides in Him ought himself also to walk just as He walked" (1John 2:6). If that's God's goal for us, then it's our goal for us also. Tests and trials – such as the wilderness – that require the supernatural become our classroom of training in Christlikeness. This will change our perspective on the trials we go through! They are invitations to walk with the supernatural God and become

---

13   Mark 6:47-52, John 6:21

supernatural people! Let's go with Him and flow with Him! He will take us into His dimension of faith and miracles, where the miracles are just our new normal.

Conclusion

As we consider the woman in the wilderness, we realize we are already being told of the supernatural work of God: there is a place for her in the wilderness, *prepared by God, where she will be fed*; when the serpent casts a flood after her, the earth will open its mouth and swallow the flood, protecting her. It's not God's purpose that the woman suffer deprivation: Only those chosen by God for martyrdom will experience it,[14] and His protection will be over the rest. It simply remains for the seed of the woman to open their hearts and ears to be led and to receive of God's great provision.

Psalm 63 - A Psalm of David, when he was in the wilderness of Judah.

1 O God, You are my God; I shall seek You earnestly; My soul thirsts for You, my flesh yearns for You, In a dry and weary land where there is no water.

2 Thus I have seen You in the sanctuary, to see Your power and Your glory.

3 Because Your lovingkindness is better than life, my lips will praise You.

4 So I will bless You as long as I live; I will lift up my hands in Your name.

5 My soul is satisfied as with marrow and fatness, and my mouth offers praises with joyful lips.

6 When I remember You on my bed, I meditate on You in the night watches,

7 For You have been my help, and in the shadow of Your wings, I sing for joy.

8 My soul clings to You; Your right hand upholds me.

9 But those who seek my life to destroy it will go into the depths of the earth.

10 They will be delivered over to the power of the sword; they will be a prey for foxes.

11 But the king will rejoice in God; everyone who swears by Him will glory, for the mouths of those who speak lies will be stopped. NASU

---

14 Rev. 6:11

SECTION 15

ANTICHRIST
&
HIS KINGDOM

CHAPTER 42

The Spiritual Roots
of Babylon

We have touched several times in our study on the ways in which Satan's "kingdom of this world" manifests at various times. God revealed the essence of that kingdom, as well as its demise, in Nebuchadnezzar's dream in Daniel 2. At that time, five kingdoms were revealed in the gold head, silver torso and arms, abdomen and thighs of bronze, iron legs, and finally, ten iron/clay toes. These kingdoms would manifest *in time,* one after the other, with the iron legs being the Roman empire of Jesus' day, and the ten toes being the final empire that will be in play when the whole image comes crashing down. When God gave the Revelation to John, depicting the same end-time kingdom, the look was *backward* and He included two others that predated Daniel's time – Egypt and Assyria:

> **The seven heads are seven mountains on which the woman sits.**
> **There are also seven kings. Five have fallen, one is, and the other has not yet come.**
>
>

Rev. 17:9-10

With mountains depicting kingdoms, and kings basically treated here as synonymous with their kingdoms, we see that there were five kingdoms (not three, as we would think from Daniel) which preceded the *present one*; which, at the time, was the Roman empire, still in power this late in John's life. That Roman empire, the "one that *is,*" would, at the end, rise up again in the *final Roman empire.* (We know this from Gabriel's words to Daniel, that "the armies of the prince that will come" will destroy Jerusalem [in AD 70]. Those were Roman armies, making the 'prince,' the antichrist, a *Roman* leader.)

The significant issue for us here is the head – the head of gold – that dominates, directs, and gives its character to each of the kingdoms that follow it. Although that head was identified as the neo-Babylonian kingdom of Nebuchadnezzar contemporary with Daniel, the origins of that head were much earlier in time. The head began under the leadership of a grandson of Noah not long after the great flood, on the same Sumerian plains along the Euphrates River. This is what we want to take a closer look at, because understanding the roots of Babylon will help us understand the final end-time kingdom that we and our children will be facing.

Pre-Flood Rebellion

Scripture, particularly Genesis 6, makes it clear that following creation, as mankind proliferated on the earth, there was a *corrupting* that took place in the human race. The corrupting was that the "sons of God" saw the "daughters of men," that they were attractive, and, according to their own whim and fancy, and *deliberately transgressing,* they *took* wives from among them. Now this Scripture has been much debated, and I will simply say that the term "son of God" is used in Scripture to refer *only* to someone who has come forth directly from God. Therefore, Adam is "a son of God" (Luke 3:38); angels are "sons of God" (Job 1:6, 38:7), Jesus is "the Son of God" (in a unique way) (Luke 1:35, 22:70, John 1:34); and the saints – believers in Jesus – are "sons of God" (John 1:12, Eph. 2:10, Phil. 2:15, 1 John 3:1). No other *humans* in the Old Testament are ever called that. On that basis (and since born-again believers are not possible until after Jesus' death and resurrection), we understand Scripture to be saying that angelic beings allowed themselves to be drawn into sexual relations with women, and offspring were produced which were literally "larger than life":

> **There were giants[1] on the earth in those days, and also afterward, when the sons of God came in to the daughters of men and they bore children to them. Those were the [mighty men][2] who were of old, men of renown. Genesis 6:4**

> [1]*nephylim* H5303T -- the plural form of *nephiyl,* derived from *naphal* H5307B – to fall; thus literally, 'the fallen ones' (morally, as *apostate*); those who are overthrown, failed, fallen (as to the earth); those who fall upon others (overpowering them)
> [2]*gibbor* H1368S – powerful; by implication, warrior, tyrant

Is there any support in Scripture for the idea that angelic beings co-habited with women? And how would that be possible, seeing Jesus Himself said that there will not be marriage in the future life, but that we will have bodies like angels – not marrying or being married.[1] Peter gives a clue, speaking of angels that are being restrained with "chains of darkness" in Tartarus (the deepest abyss of Hades) until the day of judgment.[2] We know that most of the fallen angels are still loose, comprising the "principalities" and "powers of darkness" that occupy the atmosphere around the earth.[3] So who are these bound angels? Jude provides further insight regarding these angels:

> **6 And the angels who did not keep their [proper domain],[1] but left their own abode,[2] He has reserved in everlasting chains under darkness for the judgment of the great day;**
> **7 as Sodom and Gomorrah, and the cities around them in a similar manner to these, having given themselves over to sexual immorality and gone after strange[3] flesh, are set forth as an example, suffering the vengeance of eternal fire. Jude 6-7**

> [1]*arche* G746T – beginning, origin, first place
> [2]*oiketerion* G3613T – a dwelling place; used of the body as a dwelling place for the spirit
> [3]*heteros* G2087T – other, different; something not of the same nature, class, or kind

These angels are spoken of as leaving the place they were created to occupy – the role God created them for. Leaving it involved a *physical change* – a change to their bodies, which, as we see in v. 7, enabled them to engage in sexual immorality with someone *not of their kind* -- that is, with human women. *Oiketerion,* for "abode," is used only one other time in the Word:

> **For in this we groan, earnestly desiring to be clothed with our habitation[1] which is from heaven,… 2 Corinthians 5:2**

> [1]*oiketerion – same as above*

---

1   Matt. 22:30
2   2 Peter 2:4
3   Eph. 1:21, 6:12, Col. 1:16, etc.

Here, the word is used to speak of *the spiritual body* that we will acquire after death. With those angels, it speaks of the spiritual body they were created with *and which they abandoned* in order to take on the physical capacity of sexual interaction with women. Exactly how they could do this we don't know, except it *is* clear from Genesis that angels could "materialize" in order to interact with humans, even as angels came in physical form to warn Lot and his family. The reality of their physical bodies was such that the men of Sodom demanded access to them for sexual activity with them![4] And so here Jude compares this illicit sexual activity on the part of angels to the forbidden sex going on in Sodom and Gomorrah – men between men; and he uses *both examples* as a warning to those 'creeping into the church,' associating themselves with the people of God while secretly engaging in sexual immorality. Genesis tells us that this took place not only before the flood, but "also afterward," providing a possible clue to issues present at the forming of Babel (Babylon).

The restraining of the angels by God makes sense in order to prevent them from continuing this physical interference with the human race. The writings of Enoch (which both Jude and Peter seem to be familiar with) speak at length of this interaction of angels with human women and the judgment of God upon them for doing so.

The Offspring of the Angels

Let's look more closely now at what Genesis says of the offspring of this illicit union. We have seen that Scripture calls them *nephylim*. In the simple definition of *nephylim* as the plural form of "one who is fallen or cast down," we see the *moral* condition of these offspring: they were 'fallen,' even as Adam and Eve "fell" in the Garden of Eden. They could also be seen as "fallen" from the heavenly place of their fathers and now bound to earth.

Looking further at the word, the Septuagint translates *nephylim* as *gigantes,*[5] which literally means "earth-born" (*gi* – earth; *gantes* – related to genetic, gender, generation, etc. – pertaining to procreation). The use of this Greek word gives insight into the Jews' understanding of what took place back then, as it connects the fact that they are *fallen* (as from heaven) with their conception and birth *on earth*. This is significant, as it is an unremarkable fact that *all humans* are born on earth. This confirms to us that this race of beings was not purely human, but a hybrid mix. Because these hybrid offspring were much larger than humans, the Septuagint word for them, *gigantes,* eventually gained a new meaning – *giant*. Which is, in a kind of circular reasoning, the word used for *nephylim* in the King James Version, rather than the more accurate translation, "fallen ones."

These fallen ones were morally corrupt, as well as beings of great physical size and power; and as time went on, there was a corrupting of the human race because of their moral influence and because of the continued mingling of the genetic seed. (This mingling was very likely an attempt by Satan to corrupt the human gene pool so that no 'seed of the woman' could arise that would defeat him.) Furthermore, they are described not just as *gibbor* – powerful and tyrannical, but as mighty men *of old* – *men of renown*. That is, these literal demi-gods ('half-gods'), interacting with each other and with humans down through generations, became the stuff of *myths and legends*. Claiming divinity (or descent from divinity), they carried out violence and evil with impunity and subjugated tribes and nations, drawing allegiance and worship unto themselves. In the very next verse of Genesis, God speaks of this moral degeneration and of His sorrow over the depravity to which humans had sunk.

> **5 Then the Lord saw that the wickedness of man was great in the earth, and that every intent of the thoughts of his heart was only evil continually.**
>
> **6 And the Lord was sorry that He had made man on the earth, and He was grieved in His heart.**
>
> **7 So the Lord said, "I will destroy man whom I have created from the face of the earth, both man and beast, creeping thing and birds of the air, for I am sorry that I have made them."**
>
> **Genesis 6:5-7**

---

4   Gen. 19:1-11
5   *Keil and Delitzsch Commentary on the Old Testament* (New Updated Edition, Electronic Database, by Hendrickson Publishers, 1996), Genesis 6:4. (This Greek translation of the Hebrew Old Testament was completed ca 250 BC.)

As God contemplated the judgment needed to purge the earth, yet not wanting to exterminate the human race, he looked for a godly man whose genetic line had not been mixed (Gen. 6:9). We know the story of the flood, which follows. But we also know that as stated earlier, this sexual intermingling of angels with humans occurred again *after the flood*. That is where our story moves now.

The Post-Flood Rebellion

From Noah's three sons and their wives, the earth was rapidly repopulated following the flood. The listing of their children and grandchildren and the families they "begat," is found in Genesis 10. This is often called "the Table of the Nations," as many of these offspring – particularly the grandsons of Noah -- gave their names to geographic areas and the people-groups that settled there following the demise of the Tower of Babel. The sons of Japheth are listed first, vv. 2-5; the sons of Ham in vv. 6-20; and the sons of Shem in vv. 21-31. This chapter in Genesis is basically a simple genealogy, giving us names of sons, grandsons, etc., but also linking families in a general way with geographic locations.

There are two significant deviations from this basic genealogy: One is the special commentary on Ham's grandson Nimrod. We will speak more of him in a moment. The other is the mention of Peleg (v. 25), the great grandson of Shem. *Peleg* means "to split, to divide."[6] We are told that he was given that name because "in his days was the earth divided." I puzzled over that statement for a long time, as it seemed to speak of the dividing of the continents from one great land mass – the *pangaea* concept; and yet, that geophysical division seemed unlikely to occur in one man's lifetime and would be so potentially cataclysmic to human life, that I was never really convinced. I tend now to think that the verse speaks of the Lord dividing the nations and sending them to specific geographical locations at the scattering of the people at Babel, as alluded to here:

> **When the Most High divided to the nations their inheritance, when he separated the sons of Adam, he set the bounds of the people according to the number of the children of Israel. Deut. 32:8 KJV**

Considering the context of the Peleg verse, Genesis 10, which <u>is</u> the dividing of the earth among the descendants of Noah, I believe the verse provides timing of when this dividing occurred.

To determine that timing, we look more closely at Peleg. The specific lengths of these generations of Shem and his descendants are given in the middle of Genesis 11, and if we do the math, we learn that Peleg was born 101 years after the flood and lived for 239 years. Given that he was *named* Peleg (presumably at birth), **we would guess that this dividing was already going on at the time he was born; i.e., around 100 years after the flood.** From this we get an idea of the timing of the Tower of Babel incident following the flood. Let's go on now to consider this other notable deviation from the genealogy, Nimrod.

Nimrod

Scripture's brief mention of Nimrod, made in the rather unusual context of this chapter on genealogy, may leave us a little puzzled. I tend to think that Scripture doesn't tell us *more* about him because he was such a well-known figure back in the time of the Old Testament; and, in fact, not only in Bible times, but continuing down into contemporary times. His name has made it into the English language as both a derogatory term and to indicate a hunter; its use in a proverbial sense was present already at Moses' time, as indicated in v. 9 below. He is spoken of in the following verses in Genesis 10:

> 6 The sons of Ham were Cush, Mizraim, Put, and Canaan.
> 7 The sons of Cush were Seba, Havilah, Sabtah, Raamah, and Sabtechah; and the sons of Raamah were Sheba and Dedan.

---

6   Gen. 10:25 *peleg* H6389B – division. Usually used of streams or channels cut in the earth physically; may also be used to refer to the division of the earth into families. *Jamieson, Fausset, and Brown Commentary* (Electronic Database, Biblesoft, Inc., 2006)

8 Cush begot Nimrod[1]; he began[2] to be[3] [a mighty one][4] on the earth.

9 He was a mighty[4] hunter before[5] the Lord; therefore it is said, "Like Nimrod the mighty hunter before the Lord."

10 And the beginning of his kingdom was Babel, Erech, Accad, and Calneh, in the land of Shinar.

Genesis 10:6-10

[1] *Nimrod* H5248B – "rebellion" - most scholars take his name, *mrd,* to signify "rebellion, we will revolt"

[2] *chalal* H2490SB – to bore or pierce through, that is, to wound, dissolve, violate; figuratively, to profane (a person, place, or thing); to break; to begin (as if by an opening wedge)

[3] *hayah* H1961B – to become, to arise, to appear, to come into existence; to be instituted, established; to abide, remain, continue

[4] *gibbor* H1368SB – strong, mighty, powerful; by implication, a warrior, tyrant; having force to win mastery

[5] *paniym* H6440B – face, in front of, in the presence of, in the face of

We have already mentioned Nimrod's significance in being singled out for personal mention in this chapter. Taking a closer look, we see that he is not included in the *list* of Cush's sons, but in the next verse is singled out for a separate mention, as if even in his birth he has a special significance and stands apart from the usual tracing of the genealogy. We will seek to understand this.

A casual reading informs us that he was a mighty hunter, hunting "before the Lord," literally "before God's face," or, we might say, *in* God's face. We go on to see that he built a *kingdom* which included a significant number of cities, first in the land of Shinar (the fertile crescent of Mesopotamia, the land of the Euphrates River and the Tower of Babel), and following that, along the Tigris River farther north in the area of Assyria. The fact that he built cities and a kingdom would lead us to suspect that he wasn't merely a mighty hunter of animals, but also of people; that he gathered people unto himself and gained a power base by doing so. That he did this "in God's face" speaks of resistance to God on his part. This fits with the meaning of his name.

As is so often the case with Scripture, a more careful scrutiny is very helpful. We notice that *gibbor* is mentioned twice in describing him, and we recall that was the term used to describe the offspring of the sons of God and daughters of men mentioned in Genesis 6. Those offspring were mighty and powerful, larger than humans. Scripture tells us that this union of angels with humans would take place "again afterward" – that is, *after the flood.* This means that *again,* unusually large, hybrid persons would exist – and multiply -- on the earth.[7] Is this how Nimrod came about? If so, it may provide a clue as to why he wasn't listed with Cush's other sons. If Nimrod came from such an illicit union, how was he *Cush's* son? Old myths speak of gods having female consorts – were there female angels who could co-habit with human men? If so, the Scripture doesn't speak of that, so we conjecture instead, that Cush may have had a daughter who conceived Nimrod with an erring angel. Either way, Cush is accounted the father, and apparently (from historical and perhaps mythical accounts) exerted much influence upon Nimrod.

Nimrod's Accomplishments

We spoke of Nimrod in chapter 23 when discussing the nature of Babylon: his abilities as a mighty hunter, first of animals, then of men, becoming the first *kingdom-builder* in the earth. Using his "hunting" abilities, he gathered men unto himself by a variety of means, but primarily by either deception or force; that is, by using *words* (deception) and weapons. "Began" in v. 8 is surprisingly revealing when we look at the Hebrew definition; the word signifies *a violation causing a wedge to open in something previously strong and established.* What was 'strong and established' following the flood? When the waters of the flood receded, the small number who came off the ark were strong in some basic, unifying convictions: *The God of the heavens was the one*

---

7   The Old Testament has numerous accounts of these post-flood giants: Gen. 14:5; Num. 13:33; Deut. 2 & 3; 1 Sam. 17:4; Amos 2:9; Deut. 2:21; Josh. 12:4, 13:12; 2 Sam. 21:16; 1 Chron. 11:23.

true God, He hated sin, and He was to be feared and honored. They also knew that He was a God of mercy, upholding and protecting the righteous, and that *He was a God of His Word:* everything He had promised their father Noah *came to pass exactly as He had said.* It would have made sense and been a lovely thing if the earth could have been repopulated in the knowledge of *those very principal truths!*

But along came Nimrod, who *"began to be a mighty one"* in the earth. That is, he *drove a wedge* into that solid knowledge of the Lord, and *took on the identity* of someone who was *larger than human, a mighty warrior and leader.* In so doing, he inserted himself *between* God and the people (much as the serpent did in the Garden with Eve) and became the one they looked to rather than God. This is the first mention of a *kingdom* in the Word; building this kingdom required building a dependency among the people upon him, and that required building *fear* – fear based on *lies.* V. 10 tells us that the beginning of his kingdom was *Babel.* This story, of course, is found in the very next chapter of Genesis, the story of the Tower of Babel. The Jewish historian, Josephus, is very helpful in giving us a behind-the-scenes glimpse of what took place there. Here is a summary of his comments:[8]

1. As their numbers began to increase after the flood, God instructed them to disperse, that the whole earth could become populated and be cared for and there would be sufficient provision for all.
2. Nimrod influenced them not to obey, but to stay there together, telling them that God just wanted to control them and could do that more easily if they were separated and scattered. Their disobedience to God's instruction led to guilt and helped foster the idea that God was against them. (See the wedge being built?) He told them the reason they were prosperous and happy came from their own doing and not God's blessing, fostering the idea that dependence on God was weakness and independence was strength.
3. In this way, by increasing mistrust and disobedience toward God, Nimrod gradually brought people into dependence on him rather than God; his promise of protecting them brought them under his control. Josephus says, "He gradually changed the government into tyranny." This human rulership became their source rather than God, and because it was rebellious authority, Satan was actually behind the government.
4. Nimrod convinced them of the need to build a great tower that would reach high into the heavens in case God decided to send another flood. In their doubt of God, they no longer believed His promise that He would never send another flood, and, in fact, they were persuaded by him to see submission to God as weakness. So, they all set together to build the tower, making it exceedingly high, and using bitumen as mortar to keep water out.
5. Nimrod assured them that in that way they could escape any future flood and at the same time, *avenge themselves on God for the death of their forefathers.* (emphasis added)

I looked in the Word to verify these thoughts from Josephus and was amazed to see that yes, in building the tower, they had used *pitch/asphalt* for mortar! They had made the tower water-proof![9] I had never heard that before! This was *deliberate defiance toward God and disbelief of His promise that He would never again send a flood!*

This, then, was the wedge that Nimrod drove into the knowledge and fear of God that was upon the human race following the flood. Knowing the innate tendency of humans toward independence from God (ever since the fall), he lied to them about God, portraying Him as cruel and vengeful in His destruction of so

---

8   Josephus, *The Works of Josephus, The Antiquities of the Jews* (Hendrickson Pub., 1987), Chapter 4.
9   It's very interesting that Scripture speaks of three arks: the ark of Noah, the ark of Moses, and the ark of the covenant. All three represented a place of safety from danger and judgment. Noah's ark, built under God's supervision, was sealed with pitch (Gen. 6:14). Moses' little ark made of bulrushes was also made waterproof, sealed with "slime and with pitch" (Ex. 2:3). The Hebrew word for 'pitch' in the Bible is *kaphar,* which means "to cover." The first time Scripture uses this word is in reference to the ark of Noah where God instructed him to build the ark and "pitch it within and without with pitch." This provided a thorough *covering* and protection from the waters of the flood; without it, the waters of judgment would have engulfed Noah and his family, just as they did the wicked.
Kaphar went on to become the word used over and over in Scripture for 'atonement' – the covering and removal of sin; a covering that, by God's requirement, was always achieved by means of shed blood. Here we see *the root* of Nimrod's rebellion – that he presumed to provide for people his own fabricated way of avoiding sin's guilt and consequences. This he did knowingly, in defiance of God. (From M.R. DeHaan's book, *The Tabernacle* (Zondervan, 1983), p. 120.)

many fellow-humans, encouraging unbelief and mistrust toward Him and inciting them to disobedience. This brought guilt, which led to fear of this vengeful God. He made the wedge larger by offering his power and ideas as *protection* from this vindictive and uncaring God.

The wedge was completed in the extensive system of false religious belief that Nimrod developed as a substitute for the truth of God. In sync with drawing people to himself away from God, Nimrod himself took the central place in this system, eventually receiving worship to himself. He patterned it in a counterfeit fashion after the redemptive plan God had revealed in the Garden: that a seed of the woman would defeat the seed of the serpent, crushing the head of the serpent while having his heel bruised. Nimrod's "theological" system involved himself, his wife Semiramis, and himself as the seed of his wife, killed and then come back to life.[10] Various other giant offspring of angelic/human unions played various roles as "gods" in this false system, taking leadership over various people groups as they scattered. This is where the claim arose of kings (such as the pharaohs of Egypt) who descended from such and such a god. They probably *were* physically descended from these giants. When God confounded the languages and dispersed the families to various locations in the earth, the people carried this system of idolatry and false belief with them. Hebrew scholar and commentator, Malbim, said, "In ancient time the rulers of countries were the sons of the deities who arrived upon the Earth from the Heavens, and ruled the Earth, and married wives from among the daughters of Man; and their offspring included heroes and mighty ones, princes and sovereigns." These stories, Malbim added, were about the pagan gods, "sons of the deities, who in earliest times fell down from the Heavens upon the Earth... that is why they called themselves 'Nefilim,' i.e., 'Those Who Fell Down.'"[11] I would add that God Himself called them "fallen ones" (Gen. 6:4), implying (in my opinion) primarily a *moral* fall, even as 'the fall' of Adam and Eve and Lucifer.

To return to Nimrod, all of these strategies he used established him as a *gibbor* – a powerful man, a ruthless and revered *king* -- in the earth. Building kingdoms on the earth and gathering men into dependence upon another man was never God's idea; the idea came from Satan. He knew how easy it would be to find men and, playing on whatever their weakness – their greed for power or money or revenge, etc., entice them to make a pact with him (as we get a glimpse of in Satan's temptation of Jesus) to gain power in the earth. Introducing the concept of kingdoms ruled over by godless *gibbors* <u>opened to Satan a vast opportunity for his own rulership in the earth.</u> *His* invisible kingdom -- consisting of a hierarchy of principalities and powers and spiritual rulers of wickedness, down to the lowest demons, etc. -- would be the spiritual power behind such empires, and through these empires, he now had a means to *directly oppress and control* the peoples of the earth. The kingdom-building of Nimrod was just the beginning, the prototype, for this.

The Relevance of Nimrod for Today

Why does any of this matter? Why are we revisiting something that happened thousands of years ago on the other side of the world? What does it have to do with us who are *nearing the close of the Laodicean church age;* who are nearing the close of *the 6,000-year "age of man"* and are looking for *the return of Christ?* We are looking at this because this incident at Babel was *the beginning* – the head and the foundation -- of the great image which Nebuchadnezzar saw in his dream (Daniel 2); at Babel are found the roots of the great world system which is the manifestation of Satan's kingdom and which is on the rise even now to a place of global power at the end. The restraint will be removed, and God will *finally* allow Satan *power and worship* over all the earth, the thing he has lusted for since *before the earth as we know it came to be.* <u>How that will come about</u> will be a <u>repeat of how it happened back then.</u>

The SEALS of Revelation 6, occurring in the early part of the 70th week, will provide the traumatic human dilemmas which *will provide a point of entrance* for Antichrist. He will exploit and use these crises even as Nimrod exploited the great flood that was imprinted on the minds of the 8 persons (and their children) who came off the ark. Antichrist will be the great leader, the great 'savior' who will consolidate power to provide global solutions to these great and difficult human problems of *war, oppression, disease, starvation, poverty, and death.* He will come

---

10   Alexander Hislop's book *The Two Babylons* (published by the Loizeaux Brothers, Neptune, NJ, 1959) provides extensive information from nations around the earth on the religious beliefs present in those cultures, all derived originally from Babel and Nimrod.

11   Zecharia Sitchin, *The Twelfth Planet, Book I of the Earth Chronicles* (New York: Avon Books, 1976), p. 172 (Chapter 5).

seeming good, godly, compassionate, and so very *wise;* so very *just* and *fair.* So very *anointed* – doing great signs and wonders, even as Jesus did. But all along, he will be going forth "conquering and *to conquer." His goal, as was Nimrod's, is* CONQUEST.

All the nations of the earth will come together to form the kingdom he will preside over; this kingdom will implement, execute, and enforce his power. Although this part won't become clear until the midpoint, the goal will be to direct all allegiance and all *worship* to him, and as Satan's proxy, *to Satan himself.* Needless to say, a *kingdom* requires absolute adherence and allegiance *to the king.* It cannot bear division, and from this necessity for *unity* comes propaganda, intimidation, forced conformity, persecution, subjugation, and finally the attempted (though not successful) destruction of anyone who deviates from complete loyalty that kingdom. This is what Jesus was hinting at when He said that the saints would be "delivered up to be afflicted and killed" and many would "be offended, betray, and hate one another" for His name's sake (Matt. 24:9-10).

In all the kingdoms which made up Nebuchadnezzar's image, there was complete unity of the religious system with the political system, i.e., union of "church and state." In spite of the strong emphasis on a separation of those two in our own nation (a consequence of the Christian roots of our nation), the fact is, that when viewing the whole of human history, our policy of separation is the deviation from the norm. The much more common practice has been complete union between the political and religious -- each served the purposes of the other: the military might of the civil government backed up and enforced the religious mandates, and the presumed connection with divinity on the part of the religious enabled the "priesthood" to bestow the blessing of "rulership by divine right" upon the king.[12] This, in fact, will be in play in the final kingdom; we will see the religious interplay more and more with the political as the ten kings and Antichrist move onward in their quest for absolute power in the earth. It's what we see with "Mystery Babylon, the Great Whore" *riding* the beast, the political aspect of the kingdom. Remember, the whore consists of *all religious beliefs* <u>outside of faith in Jesus Christ</u>, including apostate Christianity; the whore *is* 'the broad path.' But more and more, in the progression to the *midpoint,* the paths will seem to lead to Antichrist himself. The beast and the whore will each serve the other until the midpoint is reached, at which time Antichrist has reached his goal of absolute and complete power. Now, all other beliefs and doctrines must go, and Antichrist alone must be worshipped. At this point God will use the ten kings *to judge* the whore.

Nimrod Rises Again in Assyria

What happened to Nimrod after God confounded the languages and dispersed the peoples? Scripture doesn't spell it out clearly, but we do know from v. 10 that Babel was only *the beginning* of his kingdom, and

> **From that land he went to Assyria[1] and built Nineveh, Rehoboth Ir, Calah, and Resen between Nineveh and Calah (that is the principal city). Genesis 10:11-12**

[1]*ashshur* H804B – "a step"; apparently from *ashar asher* – to go straight on, walk, advance, make progress, advance

When the account says "from that land" (Shinar), we surmise that with a certain amount of *disgrace* on his head, Nimrod left Babel and the other cities that he had founded in that area. There was nothing more for him there – the great gathering of people had been dispersed.

From that area he went forth to "Asshur," and *began kingdom-building again!* I find this verse a bit cryptic, but we'll look at it and see what we can make of it. Apparently *making progress* (see the 'Asshur' definition above) in spite of his crushing defeat at Babel, he went on and started again. From then on, <u>Nimrod became identified with Assyria and the cities which he founded there, notably Ninevah</u>, named after *Ninus* (another name for Nimrod).[13] *Asshur* was one of the descendants of Shem (Genesis 10:22). *Asshur* is also the name of a fallen angel, which we

---

12   Remember, this – "the state church" -- was the great sin of Pergamos, and it remained throughout that age and continued on in Thyatira as well as Sardis.
13   Ninus, *niyn,* is Hebrew for "son." It is used less frequently in the Old Testament than *ben,* but can be found (Gen. 21:23, Is. 14:22). This is probably reflective of the system Nimrod developed with himself as the "seed" of the woman (Semiramis, his wife), as well as her husband. Does his identity as Ninus also reflect this second stage of his life: after a "death" of sorts at Babel and now a new beginning – a "resurrection" -- at Ninevah – the place of "the son"? We can only speculate.

will look at in a moment. Was Assyria named *after* Nimrod arrived there and began to kingdom-build, or was it already called 'Assyria,' perhaps after Shem's son Asshur or after the principality Asshur, the territorial angel given jurisdiction there? Did Nimrod move to a new area and begin to identify himself with the presumably more righteous name of *Asshur* in an attempt to <u>reinvent</u> himself after the Babel debacle? Or did Nimrod begin a new collaboration with the fallen angel *Asshur*, eventually becoming identified with *Asshur's power and persona?* Are BOTH true: taking on the name of a more righteous man, but also linking up with a fallen angel (perhaps even his father??) Let's look at a few more clues:

> **Behold the land of the Chaldeans; this people was not, till the Assyrian *(ashshur)* founded it for them that dwell in the wilderness: Isaiah 23:13 KJV**

Here we see *Ashshur* -- the Assyrian, apparently synonymous with Nimrod, the kingdom-builder of the region of Chaldea (i.e., Shinar, Mesopotamia, 'the fertile crescent,' Sumer, etc.).

> **They shall waste with the sword the land of Assyria *(ashshur)*, and the land of Nimrod at its entrances; thus He shall deliver us from the Assyrian *(ashshur)*, when he comes into our land and when he treads within our borders. Micah 5:6**

Here we see the "land of Assyria" as synonymous with "the land of Nimrod." It is interesting to note that though Nimrod is in the *past,* the context for this verse – for the Assyrian treading within our borders -- is end-time. Not only is the *kingdom* yet future, so also is *the Assyrian,* which we will see more clearly in the next chapter.

CHAPTER 43

Asshur –
'the Assyrian'

The term we use most often to refer to the end-time "beast," the "prince that should come,"[1] is the antichrist. As we mentioned in *PART 1,* he is called that only once in Scripture:

Little children, it is the last hour; and as you have heard that the Antichrist is coming, even now many antichrists have come, by which we know that it is the last hour. 1 John 2:18

Let's look now at another term used more frequently for Antichrist.

The End-time Ruler, the Assyrian

This term is used more than once in the Old Testament for this ruler:

**5 Alas, Assyrian, the rod of my anger, the staff in whose hand is my indignation! WEB
24 Therefore thus says the Lord God of hosts: "O My people, who dwell in Zion, do not be afraid of the Assyrian. He shall strike you with a rod and lift up his staff against you, in the manner of Egypt. Isaiah 10:5, 24**

**24 The Lord of hosts has sworn, saying, "Surely, as I have thought, so it shall come to pass, and as I have purposed, so it shall stand:
25 That I will break the Assyrian in My land, and on My mountains tread him under-foot. Then his yoke shall be removed from them, and his burden removed from their shoulders. Isaiah 14:24-25**

"The Assyrian will fall by the sword, not of man; And the sword, not of mankind, shall devour him. Isaiah 31:8 WEB

5 And this man shall be the peace, when the Assyrian shall come into our land: and when he shall tread in our palaces, …

---

1 The term used for him in Revelation 13:3-4 and Daniel 9:26.

6 And they shall waste the land of Assyria with the sword, and the land of Nimrod in the entrances thereof: thus shall he deliver us from the Assyrian, when he cometh into our land, and when he treadeth within our borders. Micah 5:5-6 KJV

For through the voice of the Lord the Assyrian shall be shattered, smitten with a rod.
Isaiah 30:31

Interesting, isn't it, that he is called "the Assyrian," given our studies in the previous chapter, and that the *head* of the whole world system that will collapse at the end (Daniel 2) has its origin in Nimrod/the Assyrian! Of course, the Assyrians *as a people* were present in the Old Testament scriptures, and are the ones who crushed the Northern Kingdom of Israel and took them into captivity in Assyria. So, in looking at any Scriptures involving this name, we have to consider the content and context to see if it's a contemporary reference to that nation back then, or a reference to the end-time leader. At any rate, there is no other name given this end-time ruler that is used as frequently in the Word as this term, "the Assyrian" (except perhaps "beast"). We will see now if there are any other links in end-time prophecy with 'the Assyrian.'

The Beast from the Bottomless Pit

Three times in Revelation the end-time kingdom is referenced. The second passage speaks of the deadly wound that Antichrist will suffer (Rev. 13:3, 12c, 14d) and then "resurrect" from. This death and resurrection, of course, is a key aspect of his efforts to counterfeit the Lord Jesus and persuade the world that he is indeed the messiah, worthy of worship and obedience. The third passage (Rev. 17) depicts this political kingdom as *carrying* the great whore of false religion. False religion has always had its spiritual link to Satan, obscured though that link may have been. Like the mystery religions of Babylon (and later, other nations such as Rome and Greece) instituted by Nimrod, Antichrist will be proficient in the occult arts, having a ready and strong link with Satan and his realm of dark spirits.[2] Bringing forth probably the greatest of Satan's supernatural feats, this third passage gives us details on how the king of this kingdom will revive from the deadly wound. Speaking of this beast that carries the woman, the angel explained to John this greatest of occult secrets:

> 8 The beast that you saw was, and is not, and will ascend out of the bottomless pit and go to perdition. And those who dwell on the earth will marvel, whose names are not written in the Book of Life from the foundation of the world, when they see the beast that was, and is not, and yet is.
> 9 Here is the mind which has wisdom: The seven heads are seven mountains on which the woman sits.
> 10 There are also seven kings. Five have fallen, one is, and the other has not yet come. And when he comes, he must continue a short time.
> 11 The beast that was, and is not, is himself also the eighth, and is of the seven, and is going to perdition. Revelation 17:8-11

As we have seen, v. 10 is taking a backward look at the great kingdoms that constitute the beast. At the time of John, five of those kingdoms had already passed away; one was in existence at that time, the Roman Empire; and one, the end-time revived Roman empire (the 10 toes of Nebuchadnezzar's image), was yet future. When that final king (the seventh) arises, he will continue only a *short time* before he will be killed, and then *resurrected*. When he is resurrected, he becomes *the eighth*.

We are told that this "eighth," the beast that is carrying 'Mystery Babylon, the great whore,' existed in the past, but *is not* (at the time John was writing this). However, at some point in the future, he will ascend <u>out of the bottomless pit</u>, and then proceed into perdition. But before he proceeds into perdition, he will become the eighth

---

2   Dan. 8:23, 2 Thess. 2:9-11, and other mentions of Antichrist's supernatural acts - (see also Acts 8:9-11 as example, and Acts 13:10)

head on the beast that carries the whore. Eight is the number of resurrection, of a new beginning after the completion of 'seven.' This spirit that 'revives' Antichrist will be released from the bottomless pit for that very purpose.

This will take place just before the midpoint, as we discussed when we looked at Revelation 12. This spirit will utterly take over the man, Antichrist, and seize the helm of the world with great aggression and cruelty, being empowered by the dragon Satan. Because this 'eighth' is *already* seen in Revelation 17 (v. 8), we know that the depiction here of the beast carrying 'Mystery Babylon' is taking place in the second half of the 70th week, after the midpoint.

Ezekiel 31

Who is this beast that arises from the pit, coming from the past back into the stream of current events before going on permanently into perdition? We are told in v. 11 that he is *of* – that is, *out from* – the previous seven. Does this mean a *return* of one of those seven? Perhaps a "return" not unlike the return of Christ? Is there any hint in Scripture of such a personage? In a rather obscure chapter of Ezekiel, we find the Lord warning the pharaoh of Egypt against *pride,* and using a previous *prince* as an example of the dangers of greatly exalting himself. It's probably better to read the chapter for yourself, as it's rather lengthy. But we will extract some of the key points from Ezekiel 31:

1. The message is directed to Pharoah using 'the Assyrian,' i.e., *ashshur,* as an example.
2. Throughout, the Assyrian is spoken of as a beautiful cedar tree, taller than all the other trees.
3. He was *in the garden of God,* and was taller and more beautiful than all the other trees.
4. *The waters*[3] made him great; in his beauty, influence, and power, he was the envy of all the trees of Eden.
5. The birds of heaven, the beasts of the field, and *all great nations* found covering under his shadow.
6. In his greatness his heart became lifted up in pride.
7. Using strong, heathen nations, God judged him and brought him down because of his wickedness:
   A. He was cut off and his power base broken;
   B. All peoples of the earth left his covering and abandoned him;
   C. God delivered him over to death, to the 'nethermost' (lowest) parts of the earth;
   D. There he joined "all the trees of Eden," for they are "all delivered unto death, to the nether parts of the earth, in the midst of the children of men..."
8. God's message to Pharoah: Like the Assyrian, you too – and all your multitude - will be brought down with the trees of Eden unto the lowest parts of the earth and lie in the midst of the uncircumcised...

From this chapter in Ezekiel, we see a personality, Asshur, depicted as a *tree;* there were other trees in the garden, all of which also represented *persons.*[4] These were "the gods," the *Elohim,* the angels. We aren't given much specific information about them, but we might surmise that many of these were 'jurisdictional' angels; that is, as the earth later became populated (especially after the flood), they were assigned specific tribes and nations (and therefore certain portions of the earth) over which they served as covering angels.[5] This is what we see Asshur to have been – the jurisdictional angel over Assyria, with many nations finding covering under his "shadow" at the height of Assyria's power. Psalm 82 shows us that these angels, originally created holy and given this "covering" responsibility by God, were not faithful in fulfilling this responsibility. They failed to execute judgment and justice on behalf of men, and instead became oppressors. They were 'sons' – direct creations – of God, created to live

---

3   We might wonder what 'the waters' are. We know Eden was well-watered, with four rivers flowing through it. In all likelihood, the water is a reference to the life, blessings, and gifts of God which lead to great abundance, prosperity, and beauty. (See, for example, Isaiah 55:1.)

4   I have long understood that the two trees of the Garden of Eden that we are most familiar with are, or represent, *persons:* that is, the Tree of the Knowledge of Good and Evil represents the enemy, and the Tree of Life, Jesus. Ezekiel 31 confirms the term "trees" to represent persons, i.e., angels, "gods," present in the Garden of Eden. (See Ps. 82 and John 10:34-35.) In fact, Scripture frequently depicts people as trees: e.g., Ps. 1; 37:35; 52:8, 92:12; Song of Songs 2:3; 7:7; Jer. 11:19; 17:8; Ezek. 17:24; Dan. 4:10-26; Matt. 7:17-20.

5   See also Job 1:6 & 2:1, where we see the 'sons of God' – the *elohim* -- assembling before God, ostensibly to bring a report and give account of their 'jurisdictions.' In Dan. 4:20-22 these are called "watchers" and "holy ones" and they bring decree from heaven regarding Nebuchadnezzar; the command seems to have come by their request.

forever, but God's sentence on them was that for their sins, they would "die like men." This helps explain their presence in the depths of hell.

It is rather amazing that the present "status" of the one fallen angel that we have such clear information on is Ashur/the Assyrian -- the very name that is given to Antichrist repeatedly in the Old Testament: We are told he's been sent to the deepest parts of hell – the pit – in consequence of his excessive arrogance. Then Revelation tells us that a leader that was *previously on the earth -- one that is* <u>of</u> *the seven tyrannical beast kingdoms --* will again *come forth from the pit* and re-enter the flow of human history in a counterfeit resurrection of Antichrist's dead body! And when this leader – called 'the Assyrian -- is finally crushed, it means the devastation of the *whole kingdom* that this fallen angel helped establish.

In Conclusion

It makes biblical sense to conclude that most likely Asshur, the jurisdictional covering angel over the region of Assyria back at the height of Assyria's power, *is* the one from the bottomless pit who will come forth to resurrect and inhabit Antichrist's dead body at the midpoint.

The link between Nimrod and Asshur is still unclear to me. It seems unlikely they are the same person – that Asshur is just Nimrod "reinvented"; if that were the case, then Nimrod was not fathered by Cush, but was actually an angelic being *in Eden* before the fall, a "son of God." It seems more likely that Nimrod began to associate very closely with Asshur, the covering angel assigned to the region which ended up bearing his name. (OR was the region originally settled by Asshur, grandson of Noah and son of Shem, and then named after him?) The Book of Enoch speaks of the angels that sinned with women and of their offspring, and reveals how both came under judgment from God: the angels were sent to the abyss to await final judgment that would come much later; after death, however, the spirits of their *offspring* (the giants) were left to roam the earth and cause misery and wickedness on the earth.[6] That the angels were sent to the abyss agrees with both Jude and Peter.[7] If the Book of Enoch is correct, and if Nimrod was indeed the offspring of a fallen angel, it would seem he was not confined to the abyss as Asshur was, but his spirit was left to operate as a principality of wickedness in the heavens around the earth (Eph. 6:12). In that case, he would not be the spirit which comes out of the pit to inhabit Antichrist at the midpoint. We are left without a definite conclusion, but whatever the exact connection between these two, it was undoubtedly a close one! Their pride knew no bounds, and they were united in their rebellion against God and their solidarity with the enemy's purposes in the earth.

As we conclude this rather brief look at 'the Assyrian,' we are again reassured that *all* of this is ordained and being engineered *by God* for HIS purposes:

> **12 Therefore it shall come to pass, when the Lord has performed all His work on Mount Zion and on Jerusalem, that He will say, "I will punish the fruit of the arrogant heart of the king of Assyria, and the glory of his haughty looks."**
>
> **13 For he says: 'By the strength of my hand I have done it, and by my wisdom, for I am prudent; ...**
>
> **14 My hand has found like a nest the riches of the people, and as one gathers eggs that are left, I have gathered all the earth; and there was no one who moved his wing, nor opened his mouth with even a peep.'**
>
> **15 Shall the ax boast itself against him who chops with it? Or shall the saw exalt itself against him who saws with it? As if a rod could wield itself against those who lift it up, or as if a staff could lift up, as if it were not wood!"**

For this arrogance and sin, the Lord declares He will send judgment that will destroy in one day, leaving those loyal to Antichrist so few in number "that a child could count them" (v. 19). *Then* will be seen *the righteous fruit* of the terrible work of Antichrist:

---

6 The Book of Enoch (available online) - Chapter 15 & 18:14 – 19:3
7 Jude 1:6, 2 Peter 2:4

20 And it shall come to pass in that day that the remnant of Israel, and such as have escaped of the house of Jacob, will never again depend on him who defeated them, but will depend on the Lord, the Holy One of Israel, in truth.

21 *The remnant will return, the remnant of Jacob, to the Mighty God.*

22 For though your people, O Israel, be as the sand of the sea, a remnant of them will return; *the destruction decreed shall overflow with righteousness.*

Revealing God and His purposes in all that 'the Assyrian' does, the Lord concludes:

24 Therefore thus says the Lord God of hosts: "*O My people, who dwell in Zion, do not be afraid of the Assyrian.* He shall strike you with a rod and lift up his staff against you, in the manner of Egypt.

25 For yet a very little while and the indignation will cease, as will My anger in their destruction."

26 And the Lord of hosts will stir up a scourge for him like the slaughter of Midian at the rock of Oreb; as His rod was on the sea, so will He lift it up in the manner of Egypt.

27 It shall come to pass in that day that his burden will be taken away from your shoulder, and his yoke from your neck, and the yoke will be destroyed because of the anointing oil.

Isaiah 10 (emphasis added)

The Lord has explained to us here His purpose for Israel in all this, and He reassures us, "It won't *take long*" (v. 25). Therefore, even as He has commanded us *not to fear,* **we will not fear!** We will not *pull against Him* with fear or resistance or denial, but receive His Word and rejoice in His greatness and goodness as *He works His plan.* As He says above, "the destruction decreed will *overflow with righteousness!*" What glory that will be! Hallelujah!

CHAPTER 44

The Iron
and the Clay

Our covering of Antichrist and his kingdom is not complete here, but rather is an attempt to fill in gaps. Before we leave the subject, there is one more incidental issue to address, and that is the description of the feet of Nebuchadnezzar's image. We know that the whole image represents the kingdom of Satan as it manifests on the earth at various times in history and as it will again at the end in the feet and the toes, which, as we've seen, are ten regions in the earth that all together comprise the global kingdom of the end, with each being ruled by 'a king.' Numerous other Scriptures agree with this.

The description of the *mixture* in the feet and toes is puzzling:

> **40 And the fourth kingdom shall be as strong as iron, inasmuch as iron breaks in pieces and shatters everything; and like iron that crushes, that kingdom will break in pieces and crush all the others.**
> **41 Whereas you saw the feet and toes, partly of potter's clay and partly of iron, the kingdom shall be divided[1]; yet the strength of the iron shall be in it, just as you saw the iron mixed with ceramic clay.**
> **42 And as the toes of the feet were partly of iron and partly of clay, so the kingdom shall be partly strong and partly fragile.**
> **43 As you saw iron mixed with ceramic clay, they will mingle with the seed of men; but they will not adhere to one another, just as iron does not mix with clay. Daniel 2:40-43**

[1]*pelag* H6386B – to divide, to split

None of the previous kingdoms contained such mixture. We ask, what is the clay? And what is the iron? Since all these beast kingdoms (Daniel 7 and Revelation 13:1-2) are represented by the *metals* that constitute the whole image, we would assume that the metals represent the influence of Satan on the human hearts, removing their humanity and replacing it with pride and a ruthless malevolence that causes them to oppress and dominate others. In this way Satan can rule *through* them, using them as the arms and hands of his own will and lust to dominate. Put simply, the iron represents people who've given their hearts over to Satan's purposes and his agenda in the earth. Whereas, in their God-given humanity, humans are spoken of in Scripture as clay: E.g., Adam was formed of the clay of the ground and the Lord implores Israel to be as clay in His hands, that He might shape and fashion them as He desires.[1] From this, it appears that the iron would be those individuals who come under the power of Satan and yield themselves to be used by him in this end-time kingdom, whereas the clay are those who retain their humanity.

The Iron

So how does the iron come in among men? Some have suggested that just as the 'sons of God came in unto the daughters of men' leading to the birth of giants before the flood, so angelic beings will again visit earth and "mingle with the seed of men" by having sexual union with human women, causing them to bring forth hybrid offspring again. And yet the impression this passage gives is that the mixture of clay with iron will characterize the whole kingdom. For these offspring to be dispersed throughout the earth right at the end seems rather unlikely.

On the other hand, choices of the heart, when made consistently over time, will progressively place an individual more and more into the enemy's hands. Satan comes with his myriad of demons to empower individuals who submit (whether knowingly or unknowingly) to his ways, his agenda, his plans and purposes: that is, *to him.* Whom we yield ourselves servants to obey, *his servants we become* (Rom. 6:16). The close of the age is the time when the kingdoms of God and of darkness reach the climax of conflict. Paul warns us that as the age draws to a close, this will have a powerful effect on humanity, bringing about dangerous and difficult times. He speaks of this in his letter to Timothy. What will cause things to become so difficult? V. 2 starts out answering this question with the little word *for* -- "because." Things will be difficult *because* men will be this way! A close look at the Greek definitions is enlightening:

1 But know this, that in the last days, grievous[1] times will come.

[1]*chalepos* G5467T – hard to bear, dangerous, fierce, harsh, difficult

2 For men will be lovers of self,[1] lovers of money,[2] boastful,[3] arrogant,[4] blasphemers,[5] disobedient[6] to parents, unthankful, unholy,

[1]*philautos* G5367T – fond of self, focused on pleasing and pursuing self, selfish
[2]*philarguros* G5366T – greedy, covetous, loving money (synonymous with idolatry – Col. 3:5)
[3]*alazon* G213T – an empty pretender, a braggart (no substance in the boasting)
[4]*huperephanos* G5244T – showing oneself above others, treating others with superiority and contempt, placing oneself in the limelight
[5]*blasphemos* G989T – speaking lies and hurtful slander of others; unrestrained, abusive speech; untrue and unfair accusations made against another to damage and destroy his reputation
[6]*apeithes* G545T – unpersuadable; stubborn, willful

3 without natural affection,[1] unforgiving,[2] slanderers,[3] without self-control,[4] fierce,[5] no lovers of good,

[1]*astorgos* G794T – without normal human affection
[2]*aspondos* G786T -- literally, "without the drink that accompanies a treaty or covenant"; without a treaty or covenant – that is, refusing to enter into compromises that resolve conflict and establish a way forward; implacable (this one is a cumulative result of previous characteristics)
[3]*diabolos* G1228T – one who lies and falsely accuses another
[4]*akrates* G193T – without self-control, intemperate
[5]*anemeros* G434T – not tame, savage, fierce, beast-like

---

1   For more references, see Isaiah 29:16; 45:9; 64:8; Jer. 18:4-6; Romans 9:21.

4 traitors,[1] headstrong,[2] conceited,[3] lovers of pleasure rather than lovers of God;

[1]*prodotes* G4273T – literally, giving forward into another's hands; a betrayer, traitor
[2]*propetes* G4312T – plunging forward precipitously headlong; rash, reckless in falling downward
[3]*tuphoo* G5187T – to be enveloped in a mist, to raise a smoke; to be puffed up and blinded with
haughtiness; to make foolish or stupid with conceit and pride; beclouded, besotted

5 holding a form of godliness, but having denied the power thereof. Turn away from these, also. 2 Timothy 3:1-5 WEB

Considering these adjectives is like putting a magnifying glass on the inner life of these people – and there are people that already at this present time are clearly showing forth many of these qualities. The first and the middle words in this list are keys. The first is that they are lovers of self. Whereas Jesus' call to discipleship is that we *deny* self and put God first, these people will put Self ahead of all others. This will put them (whether knowingly or unknowingly) in agreement with Satan -- who exalted himself above God -- and in agreement with Antichrist, who will exalt *himself* above "all that is called God or that is worshiped" (2 Thess. 2:4). This agreement with Satan will *lead to* the middle word *astorges* – that is, without normal and natural human affection: not loving or caring for others even in family relationships or within the human family. This will make them *beast-like* and inhuman. This is the end result of Satan's influence on the yielded soul; it makes them tools in his hands, bringing compatibility with his kingdom. ***This is the iron*, this quality of implacable, immovable evil**. These people will take on the very nature of Satan and become as beasts, all the way from administrators holding power in this end-time kingdom to people on the street who will agree with the beast and become betrayers of friends and loved ones. This intermingling of the iron with the clay will make these coming times very difficult. At this time, in the year 2021, we can already see clearly many taking their position with 'the metal,' displaying character qualities that are implacable, ungodly, hardened, and impervious to human compassion.

Is this how the iron will infiltrate humanity – primarily on the heart level, with resulting demonization of personalities? Or is there some other way that is more physical? The statement, "they will mingle with the seed of men" has certain implications. First, who are *they?* The text doesn't tell us. That in itself sounds suspect. Second, all humans are "the seed of men," so to mingle human seed with something *else* sounds like some kind of interference with human genetics. In this day when the human genome has been explored and all manner of questionable experiments are being done behind the scenes, the issue is left open to unknown possibilities, which, at the moment are not clear. Satan really does love his methods of invasion into humanity, both subtle and open.

Possibilities of Technology

Perhaps we find the statement in Scripture vague and difficult to grasp because the means of accomplishing this "mingling" would not even be possible until the very end. With the development of nanotechnology and its use in vaccines, a scenario never before heard of presents itself: the possibility that via injected nanoparticles, alterations could be made to a human being's genetic code. It is, in fact, what we are seeing with the mRNA (messenger RNA) being injected in the recently released covid-19 "vaccine" injections. This mRNA has the capability to penetrate and mingle with the person's own DNA. It isn't yet clear what this could/would do: probably influence the moods, choices, and thoughts of man, and probably even more than that. This makes possible, on a frightening scale, the words, "They shall mingle with the seed of man." Again, "they" isn't specified, but we can be quite certain that the pronoun refers to powerful and evil angels of darkness, released to do their full wickedness at this testing time at the end.[2]

Via the nanotechnology, electronic particles are likely being injected that are linked to a digital control system. This could happen particularly with repeated injections of these particles, as they serve essentially as an operating system that hooks people up to the cloud. This would enable digital identification and tracking of people according to their financial activity, enabling centralized control of people. The online Oxford Dictionary gives us the term for this:

---

2 I note, with a touch of amusement, that here is an unidentified "they," and we saw another in Rev. 12:6 where the woman fled to the wilderness and "they" fed her there for the duration. Both are pronouns with no antecedent; God feels no obligation to our rules of grammar. Perhaps both refer to angels – the first group evil and the other good?

transhumanism – and defines it as "the belief or theory that the human race can evolve beyond its current physical and mental limitations, especially by means of science and technology." This is essentially a fancy and clouded way of laying out Satan's end plan for control of all peoples, with the result being the replacement of *democracy* (as generally accepted around the world) with *technocracy*. It makes science the new god, behind which Satan's face lurks, even as it lurked in the Garden behind the Tree of the Knowledge of Good and Evil. This technology is probably similar to that of "the mark" itself, which at the midpoint will finally inaugurate the more complete control. However evil this strategy appears to us, we remember that God's great power and covering are ever *over His own people,* protecting and caring for them, granting them discernment and the ability to be "wise as serpents."

The Clay

Verse 41 (see above) tells us that there will be a division in the kingdom between these two elements. The Hebrew word for "divide," *pelag*, always signifies "an unnatural or violent division arising from inner disharmony or discord."[3] The implication seems to be that the clay element, retaining its humanity, will not agree with what is being done by 'the iron.' We ponder that the clay are not God's people, because God's people are identified with the great stone that rolls into the image, finally destroying it.

> **You watched while a stone was cut out without hands, which struck the image on its feet of iron and clay, and broke them in pieces.**
> **Then the iron, the clay, the bronze, the silver, and the gold were crushed together, and became like chaff from the summer threshing floors; the wind carried them away so that no trace of them was found. Daniel 2:34-35**

Here we see that in spite of the clay's lack of cohesiveness with the iron, it appears *to come under judgment along with it.*

A Remaining Question

A question remains as to how the clay will be in strong disagreement with the kingdom and yet apparently be judged with it. Although these verses include the clay in the downfall of the kingdom, is it possible this is meant in a more general way? I.e., perhaps this clay element is present in the kingdom but is not part of the structure and *administration* of the kingdom, and so does not participate directly in it *or* in its judgment? In this scenario, although the whole entity is brought down, the clay consists of people who disagreed with what was going on and who never took the mark of the beast. They were scattered (perhaps in great numbers) throughout the whole kingdom, weakening the strength of the iron because they fought to retain their personal freedom and humanity. Perhaps these were individuals who encouraged and supported one another with supplies and with a kind of underground communication system. Although not born again, they had resilience, creativity, and resources to survive; they eluded Antichrist's grip, remaining on the earth through everything, surviving all the dangers. If that is a possibility, is there any indication in Scripture of who they might be?

> **All who dwell on the earth will worship him, whose names have not been written in the Book of Life of the Lamb slain from the foundation of the world. Revelation 13:8**

The only ones who will *not* worship the beast and take his mark are those whose names are written in the Book of Life. We are compelled to ask who, then, have their names written in the Book of Life and yet are not born again at the time of the rapture?

The apparent answer is found in a very interesting teaching of Jesus in Matthew 25 that was actually the conclusion of the Olivet Discourse – the Sheep and Goat Judgment. Rather than print it all out I will summarize the

---

3 *Keil and Delitzsch Commentary on the Old Testament.* (New Updated Edition, Electronic Database, 1996 by Hendrickson Publishers, Inc.), Daniel 2:41.

high points. (I encourage you to read it.) We have mentioned it before, but we're going to revisit it briefly in this context. This judgment takes place following the collapse of Satan's kingdom (that is, after the stone destroys the image) at the Battle of Armageddon, when Jesus has come to earth in all His glory and is in process of 'sorting out' all those who are still left on the earth. We are told that He separates them from one another as a shepherd separates the sheep from the goats.

The criterion for His judgment is what surprises us. We are accustomed to entrance into His kingdom based on the garment of righteousness which we acquire through faith in Jesus' shed blood. But nowhere in this whole judgment process is *faith* or the *cross* or *blood of Jesus* or *repentance* mentioned! Instead, the criterion is <u>how these people treated 'His brothers.'</u> I long debated internally whether He means His spiritual brothers, the saints or His physical brothers, the Jews. I have come to believe He means *both!* Both will suffer deprivation under the oppression of Antichrist because they will not take the mark. The 'sheep' of this judgment also will not take the mark or worship the beast, but perhaps they will be better situated to make it through this time than many of the others who are suffering. At any rate, when they see others in need, they extend vital help simply because of *natural human kindness.* Obviously, this will be at great risk to themselves, for they will be defying the authority of Antichrist and his minions. In spite of the extremity of the times, and expecting no kind of payback, they live with personal integrity and common sense, helping others out of simple compassion; in doing so, they will *un-knowingly help Jesus!* To their great amazement, their reward is entrance into His Millennial kingdom!

> **Then the King will say to those on His right hand, 'Come, you blessed of My Father, inherit the kingdom prepared for you from the foundation of the world.' Matthew 25:34**

Jesus calls them "righteous" (v. 37), and says that they will go "into life eternal" (v. 46). Here we see the 'names written in the Book of Life' inheriting the kingdom *prepared* for them from the foundation of the world, and yet not entering into that life until the very end! This is an amazing glimpse into the compassionate heart of God and into the high value He places on the love and care He has placed in us for one another. This group of righteous individuals, gathered out of every nation, have survived the scourge of Antichrist and the horrors of God's wrath; they will enter the Millennium as mortals and, along with the saved Jewish remnant, will repopulate the earth. Although they are not classed with the overcomers who participate with the Lamb in His redemption of the earth, they nevertheless play an assisting role -- one that is highly valued by the Lord Jesus!

Could it be that they are 'the clay'? It's possible; and yet we are told that the clay, along with all the metallic elements of the image, became like chaff and was carried away with the wind, so that no trace of them was left! If they aren't the clay, who is? It's a puzzle!

Conclusion

I've presented thoughts on this passage of Daniel which I hope are helpful to the reader. We will see what the future brings and will undoubtedly gain greater clarity then on this intriguing passage of Scripture.

CHAPTER 45

The End
of the Kingdom

In chapter 24 we saw the judgment of God on the kingdom of this world – the religious aspect of in Revelation 17 and the political at Armageddon. We noticed that before it is judged, the <u>political</u> arm, via the ten kings, is used by God to judge/persecute the <u>religious</u> of the earth:

> **12 The ten horns which you saw are ten kings who have received no kingdom as yet, but they receive authority for one hour as kings with the beast.**
> **13 These are of one mind, and they will give their power and authority to the beast.**
> **14** *These will make war with the Lamb*, **and the Lamb will overcome them, for He is Lord of lords and King of kings; and those who are with Him are called, chosen, and faithful."**
> **15 Then he said to me, "The waters which you saw, where the harlot sits, are peoples, multitudes, nations, and tongues.**
> **16 And the ten horns which you saw on the beast,** *these will hate the harlot, make her desolate and naked, eat her flesh and burn her with fire.*
> **17 For God has put it into their hearts to fulfill His purpose, to be of one mind, and to give their kingdom to the beast, until the words of God are fulfilled. Revelation 17:12-17**
> (emphasis added)

The ten kings, as the execution arm of the beast, will come against *all* who refuse to worship the beast. When they hate and destroy the harlot, the harlot goes down and is destroyed; this is God's judgment on all false religion. When they come against *the Lamb*, notice that the Lamb *overcomes them*. <u>Why</u> does He overcome? Is it because He is the Son of God? Is it because He already overcame 2000 years ago? Both those things are true, but they are not given as the reason why He will overcome the ten kings. He will overcome because *He is Lord of lords and King of kings*.

What is the significance of this? What does it mean? Who are these lords and kings that He is master over and to whom *this victory over the beast is attributed*? <u>Early in the book of Revelation</u>, grace and peace are spoken to the reader from "Him who is, who was, and who is to come; and from the seven spirits before His throne; and from Jesus Christ, the faithful witness, the first begotten of the dead, and *the prince of the kings of the earth*" (1:5). The next verse declares how He has made us "**kings and priests** unto God and His Father." The letters to the churches speak again and again to those who have an 'ear to hear'[1] and to those who *hearing,* finally *overcome*[2] amid the tests and assaults that challenge the church. (Note below the correspondence of the verses on *hearing* with those on *overcoming.*) Then, <u>as Revelation nears its conclusion,</u> we read of the great and beautiful new Jerusalem – the tabernacle of God -- which will come down out of heaven to dwell among men. The beauty and glory of that city is hardly to be described in human language. John declares of this city that "the nations shall walk in the light of it and **the kings of the earth will bring their glory and honor into it**" (21:24). The kings are again mentioned! And we are told that these kings will *enhance* the glory of that city with their very presence! They will walk the streets, adorning the city with the stellar character and virtue of Jesus Himself.

Who are they? We know now, don't we? They are the ones on the earth that are feeling the pain of the persecution (as well as all previous generations of saints that suffered and died via the agents of Satan's kingdom.) They are God's elect, who are "called and chosen and faithful." They hear that call and respond; they follow Him in all things, even unto death. They are *disciples,* trained to be *'as the Master.'*[3] Suffering with Him, they qualify to reign with Him. In this we see their pathway to 'kingship' and 'lordship.' He triumphs **with them. Here then, in the fiery trial of the deceptions and persecution of the Great Tribulation, is the triumphant church, shining through the darkness and pain, shining with the glory of God and with faithful and patient endurance.** Here she is, receiving the overcoming life and power of the Lamb to prevail in her darkest hour and come through to victory. This is the grace of God upon her – grace available to *every saint* – to be faithful no matter what the path ahead, because Jesus walks with us every step of the way, holding us up, giving wings to our feet and strength to endure. We see the goal; we see the prize; and we hold to Jesus to get us there, leaning hard on Him.

And furthermore, these are the saints of all the ages. Though stumbling, weakness, and failure are found in our lives here, God has worked ceaselessly and *successfully* through many dealings and disciplines and graces to form us into the image of Christ; and all the beauty from that will shine forth, unveiled, in the time to come as we walk those streets. There will be honor, formed in times of dishonor; there will be integrity, formed in the personal pain of betrayal; there will be abiding faith, perseverance, and humility, formed in times of great fear, bewilderment, and uncertainty. There will be the *strength and purity* formed in us from walking in *God's ways* even when all the pressures and circumstances were arrayed against us to send us in another direction – our own way of self-preservation. The glory manifested in us will be glory which has not just been given us as a gift, but which has been *formed* in us in moments and seasons of great testing and pressure. This is the glory which will no longer be hidden by bodies of flesh, but will shine forth as we walk the streets of that city. *This* is *kingly character,* formed in the crucible of life in a fallen world as over and over again we reach upward for His life, His grace, His strength, His virtue, until finally that life, that grace, that strength and virtue *become* us. They are *formed* in us. Here we see that from the first to the last chapter of this book, *God's eyes are on this kingly people that have received Christ and share in His death as well as in His life.*

<u>How is it that the Lamb will win the victory when everything appears to be a defeat?</u> And how is it that the beast and ten kings LOSE when every appearance indicates their prevailing power? It is because *there's no foundation – no enduring, righteous foundation under these ten kings and the beast kingdom.* Jesus won, following His death, because He followed righteous obedience to the Father all the way through. Sin never got a hold on Him. In spite of His 'tree' being cut down, the stump and root remained healthy and strong, and *life* sprang forth, strong and undeniable, in His resurrection. In spite of Satan's tree appearing strong and great, it is corrupt and hollow within, and will *collapse* from its impact with the Stone cut out without hands! **The victory lies in our steadfast stand in the righteousness of the Father, even during the times of greatest darkness, pain, conflict, and loss. That is *the test* which will test all the earth; it is a test of *the roots, the foundation* of every individual, every entity on the earth. That which stands steadfastly in His righteousness, trusting Him, will WIN, despite every appearance to the contrary.**

---

1 Rev. 2:7, 2:11, 2:17, 2:29, 3:6,3:13, 3:22
2 Rev. 2:7, 2:11, 2:17, 2:26, 3:5, 3:12, 3:21
3 Luke 6:40

So, *here we are* in Revelation, participants – very important participants – as things reach a climax. Here we are, from beginning to end, presented in kingly and priestly roles, walking and working with the Lamb as He steps forth to take the earth back and complete His work of redemption. Those roles don't appear full of glory as we walk in them. They are servanthood roles and often entail humiliation, loss, suffering, and apparent defeat. But that *appearance* of defeat veils great steadfastness and faith – great adherence to the Lamb, and *great victory.*

Conclusion

We have been taking a close look at the role that we will play in all this. We stressed in the *preface* to this book that, given the vast body of knowledge regarding the end that is contained in Scriptures, it becomes a serious responsibility of God's people to grapple with that knowledge and to come to a place of understanding it. It is there for us *to understand, that we might be equipped and prepared for what is coming.* It's all been given for us to know and understand so that we have a lamp for our feet and a light for our path. Now, having concluded both *Part 1* and *Part 2,* we would add that in addition to being equipped and prepared for the coming season of the end, understanding it is necessary *so that we can take our place as participants* in God's purposes. During His earthly ministry, Jesus was careful to fulfill what He knew was written of Him. So we also will be careful to *fulfill all that is written of us* concerning the end of the age. We will walk with God and let Him lead, instruct, and empower us for the part each of us is to play! God's call is that we are *partakers* of Christ and partakers of 'the heavenly calling.' To do that, we will hold the foundation and the joyful declaration of our faith firm to the end![4] God gave Habakkuk a revelation of events at the end – tumultuous, cataclysmic, fearful events. As he concluded writing all of it, Habakkuk said:

> **17 Although the fig tree shall not blossom, neither shall fruit be in the vines; the labor of the olive shall fail, and the fields shall yield no meat; the flock shall be cut off from the fold, and there shall be no herd in the stalls:**
> **18 Yet I will rejoice in the Lord, I will joy in the God of my salvation.**
> **19 The Lord God is my strength, and he will make my feet like hinds' feet, and he will make me to walk upon mine high places. Habakkuk 3:17-19 KJV**

Even so, God is with us, making our feet like hinds' feet on our high places! Let us go forward joyfully, trusting in Him for great, ultimate victory!

---

4 Heb. 3:1,6,14

APPENDICES

APPENDIX 1
The Calendar Calculations
of Daniel's 69 Weeks

Chapter 2 - Daniel's Prophecy of the Seventy Weeks

When given by Gabriel, this 70-week time table was not connected to any calendar. It was a "floating" time-frame, so to speak. The calculations we speak of here have to do with *connecting* the key points of these 69 sevens with actual dates, beginning with the starting date. The final seven years is, of course, still future, so once the beginning point was established, the only issue remaining was identifying the ending point of the 69th week.

The mathematical and calendrical calculations involved in deciphering the 69 weeks are complex, and a debt of gratitude is owed Sir Robert Anderson, the head of Scotland Yard's Criminal Investigation Branch and a devout Christian. In his capacity with Scotland Yard, he had access to the Royal Astronomical Observatory and all of the equipment, information, and resources needed for this task. His research and labor, carried out around 1892, involved identifying the Jewish calendar (feasts, high days, etc.) back through the years and centuries according to the lunar phases, and then making the necessary calculations based on the information he gathered. His findings are all cited in his landmark book, *The Coming Prince*. We might not take them so seriously were it not that his key finding, that the end of the 69th week fell on Palm Sunday, is so consistent with the Scripture's own three-fold witness in Dan. 9:24-27, Zech. 9:9, and Luke 19:35-44.

The Starting Point of the 70 Weeks

Artaxerxes I ("Longimanus") ascended the throne of the Medo-Persian empire in 465 BC. According to the biblical account (Nehemiah 2), about twenty years later his Jewish cupbearer, Nehemiah, asked for favor to go back and rebuild the walls of Jerusalem. The temple itself was already rebuilt, but the walls and gates had never been repaired, and the city still lay waste and defenseless. On that day, the 1st of Nisan,[1] in the twentieth year of his reign, Artaxerxes authorized Nehemiah to return to Jerusalem to rebuild the city. Sir Robert established that date (the first of Nisan) as March 14, 445 BC in our Gregorian calendar. This then is the date on which the seventy weeks of Daniel began.

Finding the Ending Date of the 69th Week

With the beginning point established, there are calculations needed in order to figure out the ending date of the 69th week. We must begin with the biblical calendar and convert the time involved to the calendar in use at the end of the 69th week. As seen from the following examples, the biblical calendar is different than the one we use:

---

1 By Hebrew tradition when the day of the month is not specified (as in Neh. 2:1), it is given to be the first day of that month.

1. A look at Genesis 7:11 & 24, and 8:3-4, shows that five months exactly equaled 150 days. This tells us that a month in the Jewish calendar equaled thirty days. With twelve months in a year, one year equaled 360 days.

2. The duration of the reign of Antichrist is mentioned numerous times and in various ways in the Word, letting us know that *up to the end*, this same biblical calendar is still in effect:

    c. Time, times, and half a time (3½ years) - Dan. 7:25, Rev. 12:14

    d. 42 months - Rev. 11:2, 13:5

    e. 1260 days - Rev. 12:6

The only way for 3½ years to equal 42 months and equal 1260 days is to have a 360-day year with a 30-day month. We have 365 ¼ days in our year, and the number of days in our months varies from month to month, so our year is longer than a biblical year was.

Calculation of the days

To understand the dates in terms of our calendar, we begin by converting the 69 weeks into *days:*

    69 weeks x 7 (years/week) = 483 years total

    483 years x 360 days/year = the number of days in 69 biblical weeks of years

    483 years x 360 days per year = **173,880 days** -- the total scope of Daniel's 69 weeks in days

    From the total number of days, Sir Robert went on to calculate that 173,880 days after March 14, 445 BC. was

April 6, AD 32, the last day of the 69th week.

Determining the Date in our Modern Calendar

Because of the complexity of his work and the difficulty in duplicating it on paper, we will work *backward* from his conclusion and demonstrate how counting backward from April 6, AD 32 to March 14, 445 BC gives us *the exact number of days contained in the 69 weeks of Daniel.*

We begin by calculating how many of our *years* are involved from April 6, AD 32 to March 14, 445 BC, *using our calendar:*

Calculation of the years:

    445 BC
    <u>+ 32 AD</u>
    477 total
    <u>- 1</u> (From 1 BC to AD 1 is only 1 year)
    476 years

So the 69 weeks cover 476 years (from 445 BC to AD 32).

Now we calculate the number of days in that many years, as we are making the transfer from one calendar to the other *according to the days:*

    476 years x 365 days per year = 173,740 days in modern time

Since our calendar adds one day every four years for leap-years, we need to adjust for leap year days:

Calculation of the leap years

    476 years ÷ 4 = 119 leap year days

But not every fourth year is counted as a leap year, as *century* leap years are only counted every *400* years. Since there is only one century leap year in 476 years, we subtract 3 days from the 119 leap year days and we have 116 leap year days to add in.

Calculation of adding in the leap year days

     173,740 days

     <u>+ 116</u> leap year days

     173,856 Total days

Now we add in the days from March 14 to April 6 (inclusive, which is 24 more days.

     173,856

     <u>+ 24</u> days from March 14th to April 6th

     173,880 days total – the identical number of days we are looking for.

173,880 days, when calculated according to the calendar we use, brings us to **April 6, AD 32**. What in history occurred on April 6, AD 32?

Jesus' ministry began shortly after John the Baptist's, in the fifteenth year of Tiberius Caesar (Luke 3:1). Most historians agree that Tiberius Caesar's reign (as sole ruler) began in August, AD 14. That would place the beginning of Jesus' ministry as no earlier than August of AD 28. As it began at some period before Passover (John 2:13), it therefore began no later than April, AD 29. We understand the duration of Jesus' ministry to be three years, including, therefore, three Passovers (John 2:13; 6:4; 13:1), with the third being in AD 32, the one at which He was crucified. That year, the Sunday before Passover (Palm Sunday) fell on 10th Nisan, or April 6 in our calendar. This date, April 6, AD 32, occurred precisely 173,880 days from March 14, 445 BC., the exact number of days contained in the first 69 weeks of Daniel!

Sources

Anderson, Sir Robert. *The Coming Prince.*

McClain, Dr. Alva J. *Daniel's Prophecy of the 70 Weeks.*

APPENDIX 2
The Vision
of Tommy Hicks

Chapter 10 – The Antichrist – Going Forth to Conquer

As the vision appeared to me after I was asleep, I suddenly found myself in a great high distance. Where I was, I do not know. But I was looking down upon the earth. Suddenly the whole earth came into my view. Every nation, every kindred, every tongue came before my sight from the east and the west, the north and the south. I recognized every country and many cities that I had been in, and I was almost in fear and trembling as I beheld the great sight before me: and at that moment when the world came into view, it began to lightning and thunder. As the lightning flashed over the face of the earth, my eyes went downward and I was facing the north. Suddenly I beheld what looked like a great giant, and as I stared and looked at it, I was almost bewildered by the sight. It was so gigantic and so great. His feet seemed to reach to the north pole and his head to the south. Its arms were stretched from sea to sea. I could not even begin to understand whether this be a mountain or this be a giant, but as I watched, I suddenly beheld a great giant. I could see his head was struggling for life. He wanted to live, but his body was covered with debris from head to foot, and at times this great giant would move his body and act as though it would even raise up at times. And when it did, thousands of little creatures seemed to run away. Hideous creatures would run away from this giant, and when he would become calm, they would come back.

All of a sudden, this great giant lifted his hand towards heaven, and then it lifted its other hand, and when it did these creatures by the thousands seemed to flee away from this giant and go into the darkness of the night. Slowly this great giant began to rise and as he did, his head and hands went into the clouds. As he rose to his feet, he seemed to have cleansed himself from the debris and filth that was upon him, and he began to raise his hands into the heavens as though praising the Lord, and as he raised his hands, they went even unto the clouds. Suddenly, every cloud became silver, the most beautiful silver I have ever known. As I watched this phenomenon, it was so great I could not even begin to understand what it all meant. I was so stirred as I watched it, and I cried unto the Lord and I said, "Oh Lord, what is the meaning of this." I felt as if I was actually in the Spirit and I could feel the presence of the Lord even as I was asleep. And from those clouds suddenly there came great drops of liquid light raining down upon this mighty giant, and slowly, slowly, this giant began to melt, began to sink itself in the very earth itself, and as he melted, his whole form seemed to have melted upon the face of the earth, and this great rain began to come down.

Liquid drops of light began to flood the very earth itself and as I watched this giant that seemed to melt, suddenly it became millions of people over the face of the earth. As I beheld the sight before me, people stood up all over the world! They were lifting their hands and they were praising the Lord. At that very moment there came a great thunder that seemed to roar from the heavens. I turned my eyes toward the heavens and suddenly I saw a figure in white, in glistening white - the most glorious thing that I have ever seen in my entire life. I did not see the face, but somehow, I knew it was the Lord Jesus Christ; He stretched forth His hand, and as He did, He would stretch it forth to one, and to another, and to another. And as He stretched forth His hand upon the nations and the people of the world - men and women - as He pointed toward them, this liquid light seemed to flow from His hands into them, and a mighty anointing of God came upon them, and those people began to go forth in the name of the Lord. I do not know how long I watched it. It seemed it went into days and weeks and months.

And I beheld this Christ as He continued to stretch forth His hand; but there was a tragedy. There were many people as He stretched forth His hand that refused the anointing of God and the call of God. I saw men and women that I knew. People that I felt would certainly receive the call of God. But as He stretched forth His hand toward this one and toward that one, they simply bowed their head and began to back away. And each of those that seemed to bow down and back away, seemed to go into darkness. Blackness seemed to swallow them everywhere.

I was bewildered as I watched it, but these people that He had anointed, hundreds of thousands of people all over the world, in Africa, England, Russia, China, America, all over the world, the anointing of God was upon these people as they went forward in the name of the Lord. I saw these men and women as they went forth. They were ditch diggers, they were washerwomen, they were rich men, they were poor men. I saw people who were bound with paralysis and sickness and blindness and deafness. As the Lord stretched forth to give them this anointing, they became well, they became healed, and they went forth! And this is the miracle of it - this is the glorious miracle of it - those people would stretch forth their hands exactly as the Lord did, and it seemed as if there was this same liquid fire in their hands. As they stretched forth their hands they said, "According to my word, be thou made whole."

As these people continued in this mighty end-time ministry, I did not fully realize what it was, and I looked to the Lord and said, "What is the meaning of this?" And He said, "This is that which I will do in the last days. I will restore all that the cankerworm, the palmerworm, the caterpillar - I will restore all that they have destroyed. This, my people, in the end-times will go forth. As a mighty army shall they sweep over the face of the earth."

As I was at this great height, I could behold the whole world. I watched these people as they were going to and fro over the face of the earth. Suddenly there was a man in Africa and in a moment, he was transported by the Spirit of God; and perhaps he was in Russia, or China or America or some other place, and vice versa. All over the world these people went, and they came through fire, and through pestilence, and through famine. Neither fire nor persecution, nothing seemed to stop them. Angry mobs came to them with swords and with guns. And like Jesus, they passed through the multitudes and they could not find them; but they went forth in the name of the Lord, and everywhere they stretched forth their hands, the sick were healed, the blind eyes were opened. There was not a long prayer.

After I had reviewed the vision many times in my mind and thought about it many times, I realized that I never saw a church, and I never saw or heard a denomination, but these people were going in the name of the Lord of Hosts. Hallelujah! As they marched forth in everything they did as the ministry of Christ in the end-times, these people were ministering to the multitudes over the face of the earth. Tens of thousands, even millions seemed to come to the Lord Jesus Christ as these people stood forth and gave the message of the kingdom, of the coming kingdom, in this last hour.

It was so glorious, but it seems as though there were those that rebelled, and they would become angry and they tried to attack those workers that were giving the message. God is going to give the world a demonstration in this last hour as the world has never known. These men and women are of all walks of life, degrees will mean nothing. I saw these workers as they were going over the face of the earth. When one would stumble and fall, another would come and pick him up. There was no "big I" and "little you," but every mountain was brought low and every valley was exalted, and they seemed to have one thing in common -- there was a divine love, a divine love that seemed to flow forth from these people as they worked together and as they lived together. It was the most glorious sight that I have ever known. Jesus Christ was the theme of their life. They continued and it seemed the days went by as I stood and beheld this sight. I could only cry, and sometimes I laughed. It was so wonderful as these people went throughout the face of the whole earth, bringing forth in this last end-time.

As I watched from the very heaven itself, there were times when great deluges of this liquid light seemed to fall upon great congregations, and that congregation would lift up their hands and seemingly praise God for hours and even days as the Spirit of God came upon them. God said, "I will pour my Spirit upon all flesh," and that is exactly this thing. And to every man and every woman that received this power and the anointing of God -- the miracles of God -- there was no ending to it. I dropped to my knees and began to pray, and I said, "Lord, I know that this time is coming soon!"

And then again, as these people were going about the face of the earth, a great persecution seemed to come from every angle. Suddenly there was another great clap of thunder, that seemed to resound around the world, and I heard again the voice, the voice that seemed to speak, "Now this is my people. This is my beloved bride." And when the voice spoke, I looked upon the earth and I could see the lakes and the mountains. The graves were opened and people from all over the world, the saints of all ages, seemed to be rising. And as they rose from the grave, suddenly all these people came from every direction. From the east and the west, from the north and the south, and they seemed to be forming again this gigantic body. As the dead in Christ seemed to be rising first, I could hardly comprehend it. It was so marvelous. It was so far beyond anything I could ever dream or think of.

But as this body suddenly began to form, and take shape again, it took shape again in the form of this mighty giant, but this time it was different. It was arrayed in the most beautiful gorgeous white. Its garments were without spot or wrinkle as its body began to form, and the people of all ages seemed to be gathered into this body, and slowly, slowly, as it began to form up into the very heavens, suddenly from the heavens above, the Lord Jesus came, and became the head, and I heard another clap of thunder that said, "This is my beloved bride for whom I have waited. She will come forth even tried by fire. This is she that I have loved from the beginning of time."

As I watched, my eyes suddenly turned to the far north, and I saw seemingly destruction: men and women in anguish and crying out, and buildings in destruction. Then I heard again, the fourth voice that said, "Now is My wrath being poured out upon the face of the earth." From the ends of the whole world, the wrath of God seemed to be poured out and it seemed that there were great vials of God's wrath being poured out upon the face of the earth. I can remember it as though it happened a moment ago. I shook and trembled as I beheld the awful sight of seeing the cities, and whole nations going down into destruction. I could hear the weeping and wailing. I could hear people crying. They seemed to cry as they went into caves, but the caves in the mountains opened up. They leaped into water, but the water would not drown them. There was nothing that could destroy them. They were wanting to take their lives, but they could not. Then again, I turned my eyes to this glorious sight, this body arrayed in beautiful white, shining garments. Slowly, slowly, it began to lift from the earth, and as it did, I awoke. What a sight I had beheld! I had seen the end-time ministries - the last hour.

Again, on July 27, at 2:30 in the morning, the same revelation, the same vision came again exactly as it did before. My life has been changed as I realized that we are living in that end-time, for all over the world God is anointing men and women with this ministry. It will not be doctrine. It will not be churchianity. It is going to be Jesus Christ. They will give forth the word of the Lord and are going to say, "I heard it so many times in the vision and according to my word it shall be done."

APPENDIX 3
Souls Under
the Altar

Chapter 11 – The Fifth Seal – the Midpoint

It isn't surprising that in seeing martyrs of the Great Tribulation in heaven, John would see *souls*. After all, we do believe so that our *souls* might be saved. Our souls there look as our bodies do here, so are recognizable, but are not housed in a physical body as they will be when we receive our resurrection bodies.

But for John to see them *under the altar* is a bit perplexing. What could this mean? Anticipating his own martyrdom, Paul had spoken of it as a "sacrificial offering." He saw his own imminent death as part of and as a result of his sacrificial service to Christ.[1] Like Paul, these tribulation saints had offered their bodies as living sacrifices unto the Lord, giving their lives up for Him. This gives us a connection with 'the altar' – the place of sacrifice, but for them to be seen *under* the altar remains perplexing.

We consider the significance of the altar as we seek to understand this. Clearly, this is the altar present in the temple of heaven – the temple which had served as the prototype of Solomon's temple when it was built.[2] We know God had established His provision of the blood of animals to make atonement for the soul (Lev. 17:11). All the sacrifices, offered in a substitute death on behalf of the worshipper, were made at this earthly altar of burnt offering; furthermore, we see that the blood of the sacrificial animal was to be collected and held beneath the altar! In giving instructions for the sacrifices, the Lord had commanded the officiating priests to "pour all the blood of the bullock at the bottom of the altar of the burnt-offering."[3] We wouldn't really know what to do with this, except that Seiss, in connection with these souls seen under the altar, speaks of a visit he made to the interior of the temple site in Jerusalem:

> Under [the altar] there was a deep excavation in the solid rock into which the blood of the slain victims was poured… The ancient arrangement for the reception of this blood is still visible. I have myself stood in the opening, under the rock on which the altar had its place, and stamped my foot upon the marble slab which closes the mouth of the vast receptacle, and satisfied myself, from the detonations, that the excavated space is very deep and large. And as the life of the animal was in its blood, this vast subterranean cavity was, naturally enough, regarded as the receptacle of the lives of the victims which there were slain. The Muslims, to this day, as I was told on the spot, regard it as the place where spirits are detained until the day of judgment. They call it "The well of

---

1   Phil. 2:17
2   Heb. 8:1-5; 9:23-24
3   Lev. 4:7; 8:15

spirits." It is in the center of the Mosque of Omar, whose interior had, for ages, been most rigidly guarded from the visits or eyes of any but Muslims, but by firman from the government can now be seen. And as the deep cavern under the earthly altar was the appointed receptacle of the lives of the animal sacrifices, so the souls of God's witnesses, who fall in His service, are received into a corresponding receptacle beneath the heavenly altar.[4]

The blood held there corresponded to the repentant souls for whom the animal was offered and gave testimony of the atonement made for them. Blood has a voice -- it *speaks,* especially blood offered in *surrender* to *God's ways,* whether it's the blood of animals offered in faith, or the blood of believers shed as living sacrifices to Him. The blood of these martyrs is exceedingly precious to the Lord; it cries out to Him – from both heaven and earth -- for vengeance and judgment on the wicked. And as their prayer for God's vengeance is offered along with the sacrifice of their lives, it is *effectual* in releasing His mighty arm for the rescue of His suffering people and for His wrathful, just judgment on the wicked.

In the precious glimpse of this scene in heaven, we see the concern and anguish of these who've given their lives, we see their zeal for the rescue and vindication of the righteous, and we see God's response – both loving as well as firm in His assertion that His purposes will be completed and then the day of His vengeance, *now not far off,* will begin. In all this we are encouraged to *hold on firmly* and endure to the end!

---

4   J.A. Seiss, *The Apocalypse,* p.146. NOTE: This visit to Jerusalem would have been in the late 19th or early 20th Century, as Seiss passed away in 1904.

APPENDIX 4
My Wonderful Vision

Chapter 15 – The Rapture of the Church

This account of the vision of the Rapture of the Bride, as God gave it to Aimee Semple McPherson, was published in the October, 2006 issue of "The Revival Call," the official magazine of the End-time Handmaidens & Servants International. *It was taken from her life story,* This is That.

It had been a hot and wearisome day at camp meeting. My duties had been long and strenuous. Now the last sermon had been preached, the last seeking soul faithfully prayed for, but I still knelt on the altar. The hour was so late, and I was so tired and empty. I felt I must ask the Lord to touch and bless me before I retired.

"O, Jesus dear, precious Saviour, will you please lay Your hand upon my head and bless even me. Let me see Thy beautiful face, and hear Thy tender voice; strengthen, encourage and comfort me before I go."

Almost immediately my prayer was answered. A sweet tranquility descended upon my spirit like a mantle from the skies, wrapping me in a holy stillness. How calm, rested, and detached from my surroundings I felt. My body slipped to the floor before the altar, but I made no move to prevent it lest I disturb this "shut-in-ness" in the presence of the Lord. Then I saw a vision—

The whole world was wrapped in darkness. One could not see an arm's length through the blackness of the night.

But, hark! Out of the gloom there came a sound of voices sweetly singing:

"O Lord Jesus, how long, how long

'Ere we shout the glad song?

Christ returneth, Hallelujah!

Hallelujah! A-M-E-N.

At the sound of the great "Amen," a streak of lightning tore its way through the heavens, from the east unto the west, rending them in twain. As I looked, the skies began to roll apart as smoothly as folding doors upon their hinges. Shafts of heavenly light came streaming down through the opening, piercing the gloom of earth and illuminating it with wondrous radiance. Through the aperture I saw descending, first the pierced feet, then the garments white as snow, then the extended hands, then the beautiful face and head of Jesus Christ, my Lord. He was surrounded by an innumerable company of angels. In fact, quickly as a flash of lightning, the entire heavens were filled with seraphic heavenly hosts, cherubim and seraphim, angels and archangels—surrounding the Christ of God—they were coming down, down, down in a beauty that beggars description. I thought of those great skyrockets bursting in the air in multicolored glories and coming down in silent grandeur through the night. I know of nothing else with which to compare their wonderful descent.

Every angel carried a musical instrument. Many there were having harps of various shapes and sizes. They were different from any that I have ever seen upon earth and of marvelous workmanship. There were those who carried long silver trumpets and other musical instruments, the like of which I had never seen before. The first part of their glorious descent was made in silence. Then, suddenly, the Lord put His hand to His mouth and gave a shout, calling and awakening His people. At the sound of His voice, every angel struck his harp of gold and sounded upon the silver trumpets. (For years people have talked about the lost chord, but oh, surely there had never been a chord of such melodious, wondrous beauty as this.) As they struck their harps, it seemed that the very stars of the morning broke forth into singing, and trembled beneath its majesty. The earth began to vibrate, and the dead arose from their graves. They came from the East, from the West, from the North, and from the South, and ascended through the air in beautiful white garments that seemed to float about them; their faces were turned upward and their hands extended to the resplendent heavens.

They were rising higher and higher into the air to meet the central figure of the Lord as He came down with His host of angels. As the resurrected dead rose through the air, they seemed to gather in toward the center of the heavens, taking their places as though by prearrangement in a shape that began to resemble a body.

Then the Lord gave a second shout, and, at the sound of His voice, the angels again swept their golden harps and sounded upon their instruments—holding the chord until the very stars shook, the earth rocked and the mountains trembled. At that second shout, those who were living and remained upon the earth—whose garments were washed white and whose hearts were looking for the coming of the Lord—were caught up together with those resurrected from the graves to meet Him in the air. They came from every direction—from mountains, valleys, plains, and from the islands of the sea, to take their places in the Body. Some were in the head, some in the shoulders, some in the arms of the Body, some in the feet; for though there are many members, there is but one Body. (See I Corinthians 12.) What a picture! They were going up, and the Lord was coming down. Soon they would meet in the air, and what a meeting that would be! As I gazed upon this scene, I was overwhelmed, and my heart burst forth into the cry:

"Oh, dear Jesus, aren't you going to take me? Jesus, you know I love you. I have been waiting and looking for you so long. O Jesus, surely you are not going to forget me. O Lord, take me!"

Suddenly I found myself running up a steep and rugged hill as fast as my feet could take me. Once I stumbled and fell (that must have been the time I almost backslid, and got out of the Lord's work, running from Ninevah to Tarshish), but I arose and started to run again. Up and up I ran, and this time, praise the Lord, I did not stumble—up and up I went, until at last I had reached the top of the hill, but instead of going down the other side I went right on up, hallelujah!

The Bride was still rising to meet the Bridegroom, and I was rising too. What a wonderful sensation—sweeping through the air! All weights and fetters laid aside—rising to meet the Lord. As I went up, however, I began to weep again, crying:

"O Lord, is there no place for me in the Body? It looks as though 'twere completed without me?"

But as I drew near, I saw that there was a little place unfilled in the foot. I slipped in and just fitted there. Glory to Jesus! When the Lord gives us a vision, He does not tell us how high and important we will be, but shows us our place at His precious feet. It may be that the Lord will permit me to be a part of the foot of the glorious running, soul-winning Bride until He shall appear to take us to Himself forevermore.

With the Body completed, I seemed to be standing at a distance again. I saw the Bride and Bridegroom meet. Her arms were extended up to Him; His arms reached out and clasped her to His bosom. Oh, that embrace! Oh, that meeting in the air! How can I describe it? The angels were playing softly now upon their harps. How wonderful the music was! They talk about Mendelssohn's "Wedding March," but ah, you wait until you hear our wedding march at the meeting in the air. The Bride, however, seemed to be listening to nothing but the voice of the Bridegroom. I saw Him wiping the tears from her eyes and saying: *There shall be no more death, neither sorrow, nor crying, neither shall there be any more pain; for the former things are passed away.* Now they were going up together—higher and higher they rose, melting through the starry floor of Heaven, disappearing in the distance as the heavens rolled together again.

Upon the earth there descended a deep, thick darkness—a hundred times blacker than it had been before. 'Twas a famine for the Word of God. But in Heaven a light was shining brighter than the noonday sun. Oh, how bright and glorious it was—the mellow, golden light of a newborn sunrise seemed to rest upon everything, tinting each spire and dome with a border of gold and crimson. Here all was life, music and movement. The greatest day ever known in heaven or upon earth had dawned. The wedding day had come!

The angels had formed a great, long aisle leading from the heavenly gates to the throne of pearl, upon which sat One so wonderful, so dazzlingly glorious, that my eyes could not gaze upon Him. Line upon line, row upon row, tier upon tier—the angels stood or were suspended in midair at either side of the aisle thus formed. Above this aisle little cherubim formed an arch singing sweetly and playing upon tiny harps.

As they played the wedding march, down the aisle came the Bride and Bridegroom. She was leaning upon His arm and looking up into His face. Oh, the love, the joy, the hopes fulfilled that were written upon her fair and lovely countenance. 'Twas as though she were saying:

"Thou beautiful Bridegroom, Thou Prince of Peace, Thou Pearl of Great Price, Thou Rose of Sharon and Lily of the Valley—I love Thee, oh, I love Thee! How long I have been looking forward to this day, how I have yearned to see Thy face, to hear Thy voice. True, I have seen Thee through a glass darkly, but now, oh now, my Saviour, slain Lamb of Calvary, I see Thee face to face! Oh, Jesus, to think that I shall live with Thee forever and forever! I will never leave Thee more, but I shall lean upon Thine arm, rest upon Thy bosom, sit upon Thy Throne, and praise Thee while the endless ages roll."

As the Bride looked into His face, Jesus, the Bridegroom, was looking down and smiling upon her clad in her white robes with her misty veil floating about her. Oh, that look in His eyes, that tender expression upon His face. 'Twas as though He were saying:

"Oh, my love, my dove, my undefiled, thou art fair; there is no spot in thee. Before you loved Me, I loved you. Yea, I have loved you with an everlasting love. I loved you when you were deep in sin; I loved you when you were far away. I loved you enough to leave My Father's home to go forth to seek to save, to rescue, to draw you to Myself. I loved you so much that I died for you—I died to redeem you, and to fill you with My Spirit. Oh, my Bride, you have been faithful. Coming out of great tribulation you have washed your robes and made them white in the Blood of the Lamb. You have endured hardness as a good soldier, and now through Me you are more than conqueror. How long, how long, I have waited for this day when you should be caught up unto my side.

"Oft have your feet been pierced with thorns, but here the streets are paved with gold. Oft the way was rugged and steep and your tears have flowed unbidden; but now behold, the enemy--even death--is conquered. Nevermore shall a shadow fall across your pathway nor a tear-drop dim your eye. Forever and forever you shall dwell with Me in the presence of My Father and the holy angels—My Bride, My Wife forevermore."

As they made their way up the aisle and neared the Throne, the angels broke forth into soft, sweet singing:

Let us be glad and rejoice and give honor to Him; for the marriage of the Lamb is come, and His wife hath made herself ready. And to her was granted that she should be arrayed in fine linen, clean and white; for the linen is the righteous deeds of the saints.

As they walked into the brilliant light that sat upon the Throne, my eyes were blinded with the glory, and the vision faded from my sight, but it is indelibly stamped upon my mind.

Oh, I am looking forward to His coming, His glorious coming, and the day wherein the Bride shall be presented to the Bridegroom. Are you preparing for His coming? Would you be ready if the clouds roll apart and the heavens cleave in twain, and you should hear Him descending with a shout just now? If not, come to His feet today, fall upon your knees in contrition before Him, and cry:

"Oh, Lamb of God, I come. Help me to yield my life completely to Thee; make me all that Thou wouldst have me to be; cleanse my heart; fill me with Thy Spirit; fill my vessel with oil. Help me to bring others with me that, when Thou shalt appear, I shall see Thee and be as Thou art."

Then rising from your knees with heart made pure and garments clean, your voice will be added to the swelling chorus:

Even so, come quickly, Lord Jesus, come quickly! Thy Bride is waiting and longing for Thee."

APPENDIX 5
The Blessed Hope and the Glorious Appearing

Chapter 16 – Why Not a Pre-Tribulation Rapture?

> **. . . looking for the blessed hope and appearing[1] of the glory of our great God and Savior, Jesus Christ. . . Titus 2:13 WEB**

[1]*epiphaneia* - a conspicuous and bright appearance; a manifestation

Some pre-tribulationists separate "the blessed hope" and the "appearing of the glory" into two different events. They say the first refers to the "secret rapture" and the latter to the second coming of Christ at the end of the 70th week.

To begin with a *grammatical* perspective on this, the two phrases are joined with "and." In his *Word Studies*, Vincent says a more correct rendering of "and" would be "even" – that is, the conjunction indicates further clarification of the thing hoped for, causing it to read, "… the blessed hope, even the appearing…"[1]

For a *theological* perspective, we have taught – and continue to teach in these chapters on the rapture -- that as per Matthew 24, the *parousia* – the coming and remaining with – of the Lord Jesus Christ, will take place after a specified series of events occurs. At that *coming*, the saints will be gathered: **"And He shall send His angels with a great sound of a trumpet, and they shall gather together his elect. . . "** (Matt. 24:31). (Notice that He *gathers* them, He doesn't "bring them with Him" as He would if this took place at the end of the 70th week.) We have said that Jesus identified *the sign* of His coming as His visible presence in the sky, seen by all peoples of the earth as He gathers His saints. The Olivet Discourse describes this appearance, this manifestation, as one of power and *great glory*. This bright and glorious display will then disappear into the night sky; but that *manifestation – the epiphaneia –* of His presence was the *sign* given that He was now *present* and remaining near the earth, though not always visible.

We must emphasize again that although there are different phases to His coming, *there is only ONE coming.* Following the sealing of the 144,000 and the rapture of the church, the scroll is fully opened and the Day of the Lord begins. The dispensing of the scroll events is what unites the *parousia* into ONE COMING. That coming begins with the initial *epiphaneia* in Matt. 24, of which we have just spoken, and climaxes toward the conclusion of the scroll events with a second *epiphaneia* at the end of the 70th week, when Jesus actually comes down to the earth.

---

1   *Vincent's Word Studies in the New Testament,* (Electronic Database. Copyright © 2006 by Biblesoft, Inc.)

It will be the second manifestation, described in Rev. 19:11-16, that will destroy the Antichrist at the end of the 70th week:

And then the lawless one will be revealed, whom the Lord will consume with the breath of His mouth and destroy with the brightness[1] of His coming.[2] 2 Thessalonians 2:8

[1]*epiphaneia* – a shining forth, manifestation
[2]*parousia* - presence; to arrive and remain near, present with

Notice that this destruction occurs with the brilliant manifestation, again, of His Presence. The Presence has been near the earth since the Day of the Lord began. It just wasn't always manifest – that is, visible to the eye. So, there are *two* manifestations of Christ in His glory associated with the *one parousia.* In between them, as we said, are the events contained in the scroll.

The following verses refer to the initial manifestation:

. . . that you keep this commandment without spot, blameless until our Lord Jesus Christ's appearing,[1]. . . 1 Timothy 6:14

Finally, there is laid up for me the crown of righteousness, which the Lord, the righteous Judge, will give to me on that Day, and not to me only but also to all who have loved His appearing.[1] 2 Timothy 4:8

And now, little children, abide in him; that, when he shall appear,[2] we may have confidence, and not be ashamed before him at his coming.[3] 1 John 2:28 KJV

[1]*epiphaneia* -- a conspicuous and bright appearance; a manifestation
[2]*phaneroo* – to appear, become visible; become known (the verb form of *epiphaneia)*
[3]*parousia* – presence; to arrive and remain near, present with

Like the verses we looked at which showed the church being here until *the coming* of the Lord, and also until *the Day of the Lord,* these verses show the church also being here until the appearance - *the manifestation* - of the Lord. Obviously, this is not the manifestation that occurs at the end of the 70th week, but the one which occurs in Matthew 24:30-31, at the time of the *coming* and of the gathering of the saints. (The one for which Jesus gave *precursor events* so believers would have signals ahead of time.) Notice how the 1 John scripture clearly connects the *parousia* with the *epiphaneia* and with the rapture – that is, we will be here until Jesus' *appearance*, which will occur at the *parousia.*

There is not only *no need* Scripturally to separate the "blessed hope" from the "glorious appearing"; there is also *no basis* for doing so! To do so violates the clear passages we have quoted here and other places in the book. The saints are looking with the same expectation for both of these, because they are *one and the same event.* It is our tremendous hope and expectation that when He shall appear, then shall "we also appear with Him in glory" (Col. 3:4).

APPENDIX 6
My Dream of the Church

Chapter 17 – Readiness for the Return of Christ

Rebecca Berndt – December 8, 1993
I had a dream right before waking up:
We were at some kind of event – it seemed more social than anything, but connected with church – there were people from our church there, plus many people I didn't know. As the event wound down, I remembered there was a wedding in a church nearby on the grounds. My memory of *who* was getting married seemed to drift in and out. After hesitation and indecision, I decided to go. It was a traditional-type church. As I walked in (alone) the atmosphere seemed relaxed and casual – even sloppy. There was a murmur of conversation and people moving about.

As I walked up the aisle looking on the left for where to sit, I noticed that two of the pews were facing *backwards* (so the occupants either had to face backward or twist around awkwardly to see the front). I sat down and immediately became aware of a baby boy standing next to me (about a year old) with nothing on. I instinctively looked for a diaper to put on him, aware of how unfortunate an accident would be.

I was sitting very near the front—I think the front row. As I sat and waited for the wedding to begin, I became aware of a scratchy, muzzle-type thing over my mouth, and I realized I was wearing a green ski mask – the kind that goes over the face to keep the face warm.

My husband was sitting across the aisle and back a few rows from me. The Bridal March started playing. But it was kind of soft and tinny sounding – not full and rich and commanding attention. The murmur of movement and noise and conversation continued. A procession of people started up the aisle, but they seemed to be an odd assortment – not dressed properly at all, and not in any order as you'd expect. Some were children, some adults. Some walked in alone, others in groups of 2 or 3. I saw the bride at the back, all dressed as if ready to enter, but then she disappeared off to the side and didn't enter.

I was puzzled as to where she had gone, so I looked for her as I walked out to use the bathroom. In the bathroom, I checked myself and noticed my bra showing above the lowcut back of my dress. I saw some safety pins on the sink so I tried to pin the bra down. Then I looked at my eyes in the mirror and they were very round (like big marbles) and distended and were cloudy gray in color with little hard "grits" on them, almost like tiny grains of sand. I had to think hard as to whether this was their normal condition or not. After looking at them a couple of times, I became aware that something was wrong with them. Then I noticed that my vision seemed cloudy.

I left the bathroom and looked again for the bride. It appeared she was up in front, but had taken her gown off, had street clothes on, and was standing and playing the piano, as if performing for the people. Then it switched and it seemed like it was a young man who was standing in front of the piano trying to play a song with his left hand; he was carrying something over his right arm (I had originally thought it was the bridal gown). By this time, I was thinking maybe I should just go home because this was taking so long.

 I awoke and prayed, "Lord, what does that mean?" Immediately into my mind came, "That's how My people are concerning My return and upcoming marriage."

APPENDIX 7
The Last Trump

Chapter 18 – The Beginning of the Day of the Lord

Scripture is clear that the sound of a great trumpet will signal the gathering of the saints in the rapture:

> **And He will send His angels with a *great sound of a trumpet*, and they will gather together His elect … Matthew 24:30**

> **For the Lord Himself will descend from heaven with a shout, with the voice of an archangel, and with *the trumpet of God*. 1 Thessalonians 4:14**

> **We shall not all sleep, but we shall all be changed -- in a moment, in the twinkling of an eye, at *the last trumpet*. For *the trumpet will sound*, and the dead will be raised incorruptible, and we shall be changed. 1 Corinthians 15:51-52** (emphasis added)

It is "the *last* trumpet," in v. 52, that has caused confusion. Determining what 'the last trump' refers to has not been easy. There are those who look in Revelation to the trumpets and see the 'last one' as the seventh angel with a trumpet (Rev. 10:7; 11:15), thereby placing the rapture at this point in the chronology. It is, admittedly, the last reference to a trumpet found in the book of Revelation. If 'the last trump' *is* a reference to the sounding of the seventh angel, it would place the rapture in the middle of the wrath of God, which, as we have seen, begins with the sounding of the *first* trumpet. How then do we deal with this seeming perplexity?

The difficulty of making the 'last trump' the seventh angel with a trumpet is clear from what we have already established. First of all, this is a departure from the clear chronology that we have established which places the rapture *before the wrath*, at the 6th seal. Furthermore, it is impossible to find anything even close to a depiction of the rapture associated with the seventh trumpet (Rev. 10:7, 11:15). The seventh trumpet simply releases the bowl judgments – the remainder of the Lord's wrath. And there is nothing anywhere in the New Testament that comes close to depicting Jesus' return and the rapture as fully, as clearly, as powerfully, and as *obviously* as Matt. 24:30-31, and there is no hint of anything *like* the first six trumpet judgments in Matthew 24! So, the *contexts* of the seventh trumpet and of the rapture *do not bear out an association between the two.*

Second, we know that as God's people, we have *not been appointed to wrath*.[1] How then, without a clear vi-

---

1   1 Thess. 5:9

olation of that explicit statement, can we say the rapture occurs in the middle of God's wrath? We do not have permission to contradict the Word in this way! Rather than a rapture in the *middle of the wrath*, we see in Luke 17 that the rapture occurs right before the wrath begins – in fact, on the same day! This is not a difficult concept. It is established clearly in the Word: the wrath begins directly after the rapture. The time connection of these two is a loose point for many – they are all over the map on this issue, but it is a huge key as to the time placement of the rapture (whether they realize it or not). Furthermore, Scripture is not vague on when the wrath begins. If we will simply go by what it says (not bringing a personal, preconceived agenda to the table), it will help us establish when the rapture occurs.

As we pursue light regarding the 'last trump,' we begin, therefore, by establishing again that we do not have freedom to take a seemingly contradictory verse and use it to overturn an overwhelming body of passages that all indicate a 'pre-wrath rapture.' In determining what "the last trump" refers to, we may have to search for the answer, but as we do, we will honor the clear statements as well as the *chronology* laid out. *Every Scripture* must be taken into account and fit together into a whole harmonious picture! The seeming difficulty will have a resolution, as Scripture does not contradict itself.

The Feast of Trumpets

Seeing the great difficulty – impossibility, actually – of the rapture taking place in the middle of these wrath judgments, I have searched for an alternate understanding of "the last trump." As I researched, I began to consider the Jewish feasts. Each of the seven Jewish feasts represents a key aspect of the redemptive work of Christ. All the spring feasts were fulfilled in the key aspects of His atoning work at His *first coming*. The *summer*, lying between the spring and fall feasts, signifies the church age, while the fall feasts pertain to Jesus' second coming and the completing of His redemptive work. The *first* fall feast, which begins on the first day of the seventh month, Tishri, also became associated, many centuries later, with the beginning of the new civil year in Israel, and so also became known as Rosh Hashanah ("head of the new year"). (Tishri usually straddles our two months of September and October.)

The Fulfillment of this Feast

When God first instituted this feast, He called it "a memorial of blowing of trumpets" (Lev. 23:24). The memorial aspect is a key part of it, and we will look at that shortly. I have come to believe that in its fulfillment, this feast *signals the close of the summer season* and the beginning of the harvest of the earth, with the rapture and the Day of the Lord included. Let's consider and see if those events fit with the feast.

> **And in the seventh month, on the first day of the month, you shall have a holy convocation.**
> **You shall do no customary work. For you it is a day of blowing the trumpets. Numbers 29:1**

Notice that in this mention of the feast, it is characterized by *the blowing of trumpets,* plural. Jewish tradition teaches there are three blasts (perhaps there are even more), and these soundings are neither random nor whimsical, but done in a prescribed, purposeful manner. The first "blast" is a short, bass sound which ends abruptly; the second "trump" is a "long, resonant blast"; and the third, called "quavers," is a series of trills.[2] It's interesting to speculate how the three blasts might correlate with what will occur at the fulfillment of the feast; that is, that after getting the attention of the whole world – perhaps with the first blast? – the dead in Christ will rise first (perhaps following the second blast?), and then, perhaps, at "the last trump," those yet alive shall "all be changed." Although the term "last trump" refers to *the whole feast,* it's possible that when Paul associated it with the rapture, he was referring indeed to the *last* in whatever series of blasts will occur.[3]

Now notice the correlation of the trumpet here with the Day of the Lord:

---

2 Theodore Gaster, *Festivals of the Jewish Year* (William Morrow Company, 1953), p. 116.
3 We know that Paul (as well as the other apostles) was fully aware that the feasts pointed to and were fulfilled in Christ's redemptive work, and we can see places where he incorporated that awareness into his teaching. See 1 Cor. 5:7-8; 15:20, 50-51.

Blow the trumpet in Zion, and sound an alarm in My holy mountain! Let all the inhabitants of the land tremble; For the day of the Lord is coming, for it is at hand. Joel 2:1

Zephaniah also prophesies of the trumpet:

That day is a day of wrath, a day of trouble and distress, a day of devastation and desolation, a day of darkness and gloominess, a day of clouds and thick darkness, a day of *trumpet and alarm* against the fortified cities and against the high towers. Zephaniah 1:15-16 (emphasis added)

We have already seen the trumpet in use at the rapture; here we see it with *the Day of the Lord* – which, of course, immediately follows the rapture.

The Last Trump

Most significantly for the question we are dealing with, this feast is known among the Jews as **"the last trump,"** the term having a special significance that pertains indeed to its fulfillment at that time of the end. As Theodore Gaster explains, this feast was interpreted as "a symbol of the Last Trump and as the rallying call of Israel in its eternal battle for the Kingdom of God."[4] Being called this by the Jews does not necessarily indicate it is the last trump that will be blown before everything is wrapped up. Not only do the trumpet judgments of Revelation follow this "last trump," but the Day of Atonement, known to the Jews as *"the great trump,"* also occurs *after* "the last trump" of Rosh Hashanah.[5] The understanding of this solves our dilemma here and is another example of how these end time events are rooted in God's promises to the Jews.

The Three Books

The specific beliefs of the Jews regarding this "memorial of trumpets" link it strongly with what will actually take place at the rapture and the Day of the Lord. It is believed that Rosh Hashanah will be a time when all people will pass before the Creator for judgment. Three books will be opened, one for the righteous, who are immediately sealed for life; one for the wicked, who will be judged; and the third, for an intermediate group, which is given a 'respite' for ten days, during which time they are to prepare for the Day of Atonement.[6] For believers, it will be the final trump call to the great gathering unto Christ in the sky – their time of deliverance and reward. For the wicked, it will sound the alarm for final and inescapable judgment.

For Israel, the third group, the "last trump" is more complex. They are not wholly wicked or righteous, and for them 'the last trump' means the final and great call to turn back to God. It signifies a time of *choice,* and because of that, a time of remembrance – remembrance of their covenant with Him going back all the way to Moses and Abraham; remembrance of God's covenantal faithfulness in the past, as well as of His prophetic promises to them which are yet to be fulfilled; and remembrance of their own hardness of heart and waywardness. As they humble themselves, it also becomes a time to cry out to God for His intervention and salvation (see Joel 2:1,12-17). It's a deeply solemn time, a time of repentance in preparation for the high solemn feast of Yom Kippur 'ten days' later, which is, of course, God's designated time for *their national turning and atonement.* The complete failure of their covenant with the false messiah (preceding the Feast of Trumpets) has hopefully disillusioned them, humbled them, and softened their hearts. The Jews refer to these ten days as "Terrible Days" and "Days of Repentance." We again see testing in the number ten; as we know, these ten symbolic days are *fulfilled* in the wrath judgments that fall during the trumpet and bowl judgments, culminating in the great Battle of Armageddon, their final, *final* chance to turn to God. If they don't turn during these 'ten days,' they will not attain to the "great trump" of the Day of Atonement (Yom Kippur). So, though there will be other trumpet blasts to follow, there is a sense in which for

---

4 Ibid., p. 113.
5 Gaster says "a long blast is sounded on the ram's horn (shofar)" at the completion of Yom Kippur (Ibid., p. 181), and Victor Buksbazen agrees in his book, *The Gospel in the Feasts of Israel*, p. 43. Yom Kippur falls on the tenth day of Tishri each year, and, in its *fulfillment,* will take place at the end of the seven years when *all Israel repents* and undergoes national atonement and reconciliation with the Lord. Scripture doesn't seem to specify this blast except in the years when the Year of Jubilee occurs (and is then celebrated *on* the Day of Atonement, Lev. 25:9-10, see also Is. 27:12-13); which undoubtedly, in God's reckoning of years, will fall in that year when both the Day of Atonement and the Year of Jubilee are finally fulfilled for all of Israel, bringing about great joy, freedom, and national restoration.
6 Victor Buksbazen, *The Gospel in the Feasts of Israel* (Christian Literature Crusade, 1954), p. 26. David Baron, *Types, Psalms, and Prophecies* (Forgotten Books, 2012 – www.forgotten-books.org), p. 52. For related passages, see Ps. 50 and Is. 26:19-21.

all three groups, this is a *last* trump.

The Accuracy of the Dates

It is very interesting, as far as a timing issue, to think of the association of the Feast of Trumpets with the Day of the Lord. Each of the four feasts fulfilled at Jesus' first coming (Passover, Unleavened Bread, First fruits, and Pentecost) was fulfilled *on the very day* of the feast. Having no reason to think that the fall feasts will be fulfilled without the same accuracy date-wise, we would expect that the Day of the Lord (with the rapture immediately preceding it) would fall on the first day of Tishri – that is, on Rosh Hashanah of whatever year it comes. Since the ten "Terrible Days" which lie between Rosh Hashanah and Yom Kippur are insufficient to be the actual length of time for all the trumpet and bowl judgments to occur, we see them instead as symbolic in length. However, we would believe that the Feast of Yom Kippur (the Day of Atonement, the 10th of Tishri) would also be fulfilled *on the exact date*, just in a later year than the Feast of Trumpets. Furthermore, this places the making of the treaty at the same time of year – in the fall -- *seven years earlier*, and consequently, places *the midpoint in the spring* (perhaps correlating with Antichrist's imitation of Christ's resurrection.) **Understanding these actual days of fulfillment, particularly for the Feast of Trumpets, is part of watching for "the times and the seasons" of the end.**

APPENDIX 8
The Black Army

Chapter 24 – The Judgment of Babylon

May 7th, 1993

One night, while in Oregon, I dreamed the sky was getting dark. Then suddenly it turned pitch black! It was as if the whole world had gone dark at that moment! All the people were in a frenzy! They became disoriented, and some were even screaming. After some time, we heard the sound of an army approaching. Soon, we saw them coming out of the black mist. All were dressed in black, except one. That one seemed to be their leader. He was dressed in a red robe with a thick black belt over his waist. On his head, he had a sign. As I looked, I saw that in his hand he held the same kind of sharp spear as everyone else in his army.

"I am Lucifer!" he exclaimed. "I am the king of this world! I have come to make war against the Christians!" It looked as though all the Christians were huddled together in one big group. Some began to cry when they heard this. Others began to tremble, while some just stood without saying anything.

Lucifer continued to speak. "All of those that want to fight against my army and think they can be victorious; go to the right. Those that fear me; go to the left." Only about a quarter of the group stepped to the right. All the others went to the left.

Then Lucifer ordered his army, "Destroy those on the right!" The army began to advance and quickly surrounded the Christians on the right. As they began to close in on us, a powerful light appeared and encircled us.

Then an angel of the Lord spoke. "Take out your swords and fight. Defend yourselves and be victorious over the enemy."

"What swords?" A man in the group asked.

"The Word of the Lord is your sword," the angel answered. When we understood what the angel meant, we began to quote verses from the Bible. Then suddenly, as if we were one voice, we began to sing a song. Our voices thundered so loudly, that the Dark army began to retreat in fear. They did not have the courage to come against us anymore.

Lucifer, then filled with rage, turned to those on the left. "You, who all of your life have been trying to please two masters, because you could not stand against me; I have the power to destroy you." He then ordered his army to attack. It was a total massacre. The ones on the left could not defend themselves. One by one they all fell. This killing seemed to go on for a long time. After a while we could actually smell the stench of the dead.

"Why could they not be protected also?" someone asked.

The angel answered: "Because all their life they have been lukewarm. Because of their hypocrisy, the true church has been blasphemed. They have brought disrespect to the word of God. They were not clean."

As we continued to look, we saw the sun coming over the horizon. The black clouds began to break up. Then they disappeared. Only one was left - on which Lucifer and his army stood.

Lucifer looked at me shaking his fists and said, "I will destroy you even if I have to throw my spear at you from here!" Then that cloud disappeared too.

As I looked around, I began to see faces that I recognized among our group. I saw a pastor from Bellflower - another from Indiana - one from Michigan - as well as many of my American friends. This strengthened me greatly. Then I awoke. The first thought that came to my mind as I awoke was that this had been the last fight of the devil against the church. If we remain faithful, we will be victorious.

Excerpted from:
Dumitru Duduman
Dreams and Visions from God

APPENDIX 9
Vision of
Coming Deception

Chapter 35 -- The Vision of Margaret MacDonald

*The following is an excerpt from a prophecy given at the Elim Bible Institute Summer Camp meeting in 1965 by the late **Stanley Frodsham**. Brother Frodsham was a recognized prophet and teacher in the Body of Christ whose life and ministry spanned the Pentecostal Revival, the great Healing Revival, and the early days of the Charismatic Movement. He also authored the well-known book,* <u>Smith Wigglesworth: Apostle of Faith</u>.

When I visit My people in mighty revival power, it is to prepare them for the darkness ahead. With the glory shall come great darkness, for the glory is to prepare My people for the darkness. I will enable My people to go through because of the visitation of My Spirit. Take heed to yourselves lest you be puffed up and think that you have arrived. Many shall be puffed up as in the olden days, for many then received My message but they continued not in it. Did I not anoint Jehu? Yet the things I desired were not accomplished in his life. Listen to the messengers, but do not hold men's persons in admiration. For many whom I shall anoint mightily, with signs and miracles, shall be lifted up and shall fall away by the wayside. I do not do this willingly; I have made provision that they might stand. I call many into this ministry and equip them; but remember that many shall fall. They shall be like bright lights and people shall delight in them. But they shall be taken over by deceiving spirits and shall lead many of My people away.

Hearken diligently concerning these things, for in the last days will come seducing spirits that shall turn many of My anointed ones away. Many shall fall through various lusts and because of sin abounding. But if you will seek Me diligently, I will put My Spirit within you. When one shall turn to the right hand or to the left you shall not turn with them, but keep your eyes wholly on the Lord. The coming days are most dangerous, difficult, and dark, but there shall be a mighty outpouring of My Spirit upon many cities. My people must be diligently warned concerning the days that are ahead. Many shall turn after seducing spirits; many are already seducing My people. It is those who do righteousness that are righteous. Many cover their sins by theological words. But I warn you of seducing spirits who instruct My people in an evil way.

Many shall come with seducing spirits and hold out lustful enticements. You will find that after I have visited My people again, the way shall become more and more narrow, and fewer shall walk therein. But be not deceived, the ways of righteousness are My ways. For though Satan comes as an angel of light, hearken not to him; for those who perform miracles and speak not righteousness are not of Me. I warn you with great intensity that I am going to judge My house and have a church without spot or wrinkle when I come. I desire to open your eyes and give you spiritual understanding, that you may not be deceived but may walk in uprightness of heart before Me, loving righteousness and hating every evil way. Look unto Me, and I will make you to perceive with eyes of the Spirit the things that lurk in darkness that are not visible to the human eye. Let me lead you in this way that you may perceive the powers of darkness and battle against them. It is not a battle against flesh and blood; for if you battle in that way, you accomplish nothing. But if you let Me take over and battle against the powers of darkness, then they are defeated, and then liberation is brought to My people.

I warn you to search the Scriptures diligently concerning these last days. For the things that are written shall indeed be made manifest. There shall come deceivers among My people in increasing numbers who shall speak for the truth and shall gain the favor of the people. For the people shall examine the Scriptures and say, "What these men say is true." Then when they have gained the hearts of the people, then and only then shall Satan enter into My people. Watch for seducers. Do you think a seducer will brandish a new heresy and flaunt it before the people? He will speak the words of righteousness and truth, and will appear as a minister of light declaring the Word. The people's hearts shall be won. Then, when the hearts are won, they will bring out their doctrines, and the people shall be deceived. The people shall say, "Did he not speak thus and thus? And did we not examine it from the Word? Therefore, he is a minister of righteousness. This that he has spoken we do not see in the Word, but it must be right, for the other things he spoke were true."

Be not deceived. For the deceiver will first work to gain the hearts of many, and then shall bring forth his insidious doctrines. You cannot discern those that are of Me and those that are not of Me when they start to preach. But seek Me constantly, and then when these doctrines are brought out you shall have a witness in your heart that these are not of Me. Fear not, for I have warned you. Many will be deceived. But if you walk in holiness and uprightness before the Lord, your eyes shall be open and the Lord will protect you. If you will constantly look unto the Lord, you will know when the doctrine changes and will not be brought into it. If your heart is right, I will keep you; and if you will constantly look to Me, I will uphold you.

The minister of righteousness shall be on this wise: His life shall agree with the Word and his lips shall give forth that which is wholly true, and it will be *no mixture*. When the mixture appears, then you will know he is not a minister of righteousness. The deceivers speak first the truth then error, to cover their own sins which they love. Therefore, I exhort and command you to study the Scriptures relative to seducing spirits, for this is one of the great dangers of these last days.

I desire you to be established firmly in My Word and not in the personalities of men, that you will not be moved as so many shall be moved. Take heed to yourselves and follow not the seducing spirits that are already manifesting themselves. Diligently inquire of Me when you hear something that you have not seen in My Word, and do not hold people's persons in admiration – for it is by this very method Satan will destroy many of My people.

Bibliography

Anderson, Sir Robert. *The Coming Prince.* Grand Rapids, MI: Kregel Publications, 1984.

Barnes' Notes, Electronic Database Copyright © 1997, 2003, 2005, 2006 by Biblesoft, Inc.

Barnhouse, Donald Grey. *Revelation.* Grand Rapids, MI: Zondervan Publishing House, 1971.

Baron, David. *Types, Psalms, and Prophecies Being a Series of Old Testament Studies.* www.forgottenbooks.org: Forgotten Books, 2012 (1907).

Bercot, David W., Editor. *A Dictionary of Early Christian Beliefs.* Peabody, MA: Hendrickson Publishers, Inc., 2002.

Bonhoeffer, Dietrich. *Creation and Fall – Temptation.* New York, NY: Simon and Schuster, Inc., 1983.

Brandenburg, Hans. *The Meek and the Mighty.* New York: Oxford University Press, 1977

Branham, William Marrion. *An Exposition of the Seven Church Ages.* (No publisher or date is identified.)

Buksbazen, Victor. *The Gospel in the Feasts of Israel.* Fort Washington, PA: Christian Literature Crusade, 1954.

DeHaan, M.R., MD. *The Tabernacle.* Grand Rapids, MI: Zondervan Publishing House, 1955.

Elazar, Daniel J. *Government and Polity in Biblical Israel.* New Brunswick, NJ: Transaction Publishers, 1998.

Gaster, Theodor, H. *Festivals of the Jewish Year.* William Morrow Co., 1952.

Goodgame, Peter D. *The Second Coming of the Antichrist.* Crane, MO: Defense, 2012.

Hippolytus of Rome. *The Ante-Nicene Fathers.*

Hislop, Alexander. *The Two Babylons.* Neptune, NJ: Loizeaux Brothers, 1959.

Hunt, Dave. *A Woman Rides the Beast.* Eugene, Oregon: Harvest House Publishers, 1994

Josephus, Flavius. *The Works of Josephus, Complete and Unabridged.* Peabody, MA: Hendrickson Publishers, Inc., 1987.

Keil and Delitzsch Commentary on the Old Testament: New Updated Edition, Electronic Database. Hendrickson Publishers, Inc., 1996.

McClain, Alva J. *Daniel's Prophecy of the 70 Weeks.* Grand Rapids, MI: Zondervan Publishing House, 1980.

Missler, Chuck. *The Seven Letters to the Seven Churches.* Coeur d'Alene, Idaho: (Kindle Edition) © 2017 Koinonia House, Inc.

Nee, Watchman. *The Orthodoxy of the Church.* Anaheim, CA: Living Stream Ministry, 1991.

Rosenthal, Marvin. *The Pre-Wrath Rapture of the Church.* Nashville: Thomas Nelson, Inc., 1990.

Ryrie, Charles C. *The Basis of the Premillennial Faith.* Neptune, New Jersey, 1953.

Seiss, Joseph. *The Apocalypse: Lectures on the Book of Revelation.* Grand Rapids, MI: Zondervan Publishing House.

Unger, Merrill F. *Unger's Bible Handbook.* Chicago: Moody Press, 1966.

Vallowe, Ed F. *Riches of Revelation – An Exposition of the Book of Revelation, Vol. 1.* Taylors, SC: Faith Printing Company, 1973.

Van Kampen, Robert. *The Sign.* Wheaton, IL: Crossway Books, 1992.

Verduin, Leonard. *The Reformers and Their Stepchildren.* Grand Rapids, MI: William B. Eerdmans Publishing Company, 1964.

Viola, Frank; George Barna. *Pagan Christianity.* Barna Books, Tyndale House Publisher, Inc., 2002

Index

CPSIA information can be obtained
at www.ICGtesting.com
Printed in the USA
JSHW051656090423
39986JS00004B/17